HISTORICAL SPECTRUM

OF

VALUE THEORIES

Volume I

The German-Language Group

By

W. H. WERKMEISTER

FLORIDA STATE UNIVERSITY

JOHNSEN PUBLISHING COMPANY

LINCOLN, NEBRASKA

STANDARD BOOK NO. 910814-00-7

LIBRARY OF CONGRESS CARD NO. 72-136632

1970 © JOHNSEN PUBLISHING COMPANY

LINCOLN, NEBRASKA 68501

PRINTED IN THE UNITED STATES OF AMERICA

To the

Memory of

my Father and Mother

CONTENTS

PREFACE

In an age of analysis and of a transvaluation of all values, such as ours, it may be well to pause now and then and to re-examine the historical foundations and interpretations of the values men live by before we discard them altogether. The study here presented is intended as such an attempt. If, in the end, we are bewildered rather than enlightened by the complexities of the value problems and the multiplicity of approaches to their solution, this need not discourage us in our pursuit but may instead serve as a challenge to re-think all the issues and to find in our own way an understanding of values and value relations adequate as a guide for action in our own times.

The value theories here presented are the generally less accessible ones of the German-language group—of the German and the Austrian philosophers. In a subsequent volume I shall deal with the Anglo-American group.

Since my intention has been to present as clear and self-sustained an interpretation of each value theory under consideration, I have refrained as much as possible from including my own reactions to the various views. All I can say is that I have learned much from the philosophers here represented; and, in some respects, I have learned most from those with whom I radically disagree.

Because of space limitations, it has not been possible to discuss in greater detail some of the arguments or analyses of value issues. Enough has been given, however,—I hope—to give the reader a fair conception of each philosopher's point of view. If I have failed in this or that instance, I hope that a generous reader will forgive my inadequacies and will himself consult the primary sources.

I am deeply grateful to Florida State University for its generous support of my work on this book. More specifically, I wish to thank Robert O. Lawton, Dean of the College of Arts and Science, and the Department of Philosophy for granting me a part-time research leave so that I might have the leisure to write this book; and Robert M. Johnson, Dean of Graduate Studies and Research, for a grant that enabled me to obtain the needed source materials.

I also wish to thank Wallace Nethery, Librarian of the Hoose Library of Philosophy, University of Southern California, for making most of the source material available to me; and the libraries of Harvard University and Louisiana State University for giving me free access to their holdings.

Without such general support I could not have written this book.

W. H. W.

INTRODUCTION

Much has been written during the last seventy-five years about values and value problems. New insights and a better understanding of the basic issues involved in our valuations have been achieved. But it has also become evident that the crucial problems are much more complex and much more far-reaching in their ramifications than they appear to be at first sight. The multitude of conflicting value theories is in itself evidence of this fact. Confusion still persists with respect to fundamental issues, and much work must yet be done before we can rest satisfied that at least the foundations of a general value theory are secure.

Part of the difficulty arises from the fact that we are currently not in a position to view in historical perspective what has been achieved and what still remains unsettled. The time has come, therefore, to attempt to bring together the diverse points of view developed in the past, to evaluate them, and to set forth as far as possible what may be regarded as the present state of affairs in value theory. Such a survey can then serve as the basis from which to attack anew the problems that remain to be solved.

To write a complete history of value theory, omitting no details, is an almost impossible task; the literature in the field is immense. But it is also not the most rewarding task because a recital of minor differences and variations in the various approaches to value theory may add to the confusion rather than lead to a better understanding. A selection must therefore be made. And so, in the chapters which follow, I hope to present at least some of the high points in the development of value theory, emphasizing the work done since Hermann Lotze first projected the idea of a general value theory as distinguished from ethics, economics, aesthetics, religion, and the like, but foundational to them all. And I might as well confess to the belief that, so conceived, value theory is the very core of philosophy—if the latter is taken to be a search for a way of life. Whether or not current value theories are adequate in this sense is, of course, another question. It all depends on how successful we are in our efforts, if not to settle, then at least to clarify the crucial issues. May the survey here presented contribute to that clarification.

I

It is beyond dispute, I am sure, that the emergence and decay of cultural epochs in the course of human history are reflected in man's shifting valuations; that his responses to his social environment and to the cosmos as a whole are value oriented; that, in fact, his lived-in-world is essentially a world of values and value conflicts. Religious, moral, and aesthetic aspirations have at all times been value motivated—as has man's economic activity; and a breakdown of value standards has entailed periods of nihilism and cultural decay. It does make a difference in human existence whether the highest value is moral excellence or the possession of wealth; whether value standards are strictly applied or whether a general permissiveness is the order of the day; whether the stress is placed upon human beings as the supreme value, or upon profits and economic utility. What men regard as worthy of their best efforts, individually and collectively, determines the value pattern of their times and gives meaning and relevance to their general world-view. Every innovation rests upon a value judgment that "this is better" and, thus, is a challenge to old valuations. Anarchistic philosophies themselves have their ultimate ramifications in a commitment to values.

Even before the days of Greek philosophers, at least, men have looked toward the future and have projected an ideal to be realized in time. They have viewed history as progress toward some goal. To be sure, there has been a great diversity of opinions as to what that goal might be; but irrespective of this fact, the mere projection of a goal toward which history moves, i.e., the conception of history as progress, assumes specific valuations. The Stoics, as later the men of the Enlightenment, hoped for the ultimate triumph of Reason. Herder and Wilhelm von Humboldt envisioned an ever increasing realization of man's essential humanity, while Fichte and, more recently, Croce saw history as man's achievement of freedom. With the development of modern science and technology came an unshakable faith in a life of happiness to be attained through material progress. But whatever the interpretation of the goal, the basic assumption is that here are values worth fighting for; for the goals are conceived as values before they are projected as goals.

Just as history has been interpreted in terms of values and value-goals, so has reality as a whole been conceived in terms of values. In Plato's system, for example, the idea of the Good dominates all else. Not only is it the highest value for human beings to pursue, the standard for all valuations, it is correlative with true Being. Our empirical world derives its significance from it and, as a consequence, can be judged in terms of it.

Although Aristotle is more empirical in his orientation than is Plato, the problem of the Good is central even for him and has its ramifications in his metaphysics. The essential "forms" inherent in the world of things disclose to a greater or lesser degree the ultimately good. The levels of reality rise from that of dead things (mere matter) through the level of animal existence to the noblest embodiments of spirituality. An inner purpose moves all toward the highest degree of perfection attainable at each level and for the cosmos as a whole. It culminates in the realization of the highest Good (*Metaphysics,* I(A) 2,982b). Aristotle's ethics, making the development and perfection of our human potentialities the value standard, reflects that metaphysical orientation (*Nicomachean Ethics,* 1097a34; 1098a10f.).

Subjectivism, scepticism, and Stoic detachment, each in its own way, changed the value patterns radically. Epicurus, developing a materialistic metaphysics akin to that of Democritus, denied the existence of all values but bodily pleasures. Even so, however, it is obvious that value theory and metaphysics still go hand in hand. The Stoics achieved their detachment from the world and their indifference to human affairs because of their particular emphasis upon the value of Reason—a value orientation which left no room for feelings and sentiments. Since Reason is the same in all men, emperor and slave can show the same indifference to the vicissitudes of human existence. The slave can be as free as the emperor. That this Stoic world-view is value-centered is beyond all doubt.

In the philosophy of Plotinus, and in neo-Platonism in general, the highest Good and true Being are ultimately but the ONE from which all else emanates as levels of diminishing reality and value. Broadly speaking, the transition is from the ONE to the spiritual to the mental to the living to the material—to the very edge, that is, of non-being and the completely valueless. The whole system is thus a metaphysical rank-order of values as well as a theory of Being.

With the rise of Christianity, philosophy underwent a significant change. Its task was no longer the discovery of truth through reason and analysis, but the clarification and justification of the truth of religious faith. That the world-view of Christianity is essentially value-oriented cannot well be doubted; for God is taken to be not only the creator and sustainer of the world but the embodiment and fountainhead of all that is good as well. All levels of reality reflect, and testify to, the supreme goodness of God. They constitute a hierarchical order of values as well as of reality that is God-ordained and is directly encountered in the diverse stratifications of a Church-dominated society. The value-pattern is thus metaphysically grounded—culminating, as it does, in God as the *ens perfectissimum* as well as the *ens realissimum* (Thomas Aquinas). The cosmic drama of Fall and Redemption gives meaning not only to man's sojourn on earth and to historical events, but to the whole of reality. It is revelatory of God's limitless goodness. St. Augustin, therefore, could say that if you see the Good, you see God himself—not as a good among others but as *bonum omnis boni,* as the Good of all goods, the value of all values. The Kingdom of God thus encompasses the true, the good, and the beautiful no less than the real; and the degree to which the things of this world participate in those values determines the degree of their own reality. The world and all that is in it is here conceived as a hierarchy of values as well as of being.

When the writings of Aristotle were rediscovered in the beginning of the 13th century, the Platonic overtones of the Augustinian world-view lost their significance. In time, the moderate realism of Thomas Aquinas prevailed. But, of course, God was still conceived as the Absolute Ground of all there is and, therefore, as the cause of all that is good in the world. He is not only the Uncaused First Cause but the ultimate goal (the *causa finalis*) as well. All creatures strive to "imitate" His perfection. Even the smallest and most insignificant being has value because of its relation to God. Indeed, the very fact that there exists a world at all is already in itself good (*bonitas ontologica*). But values increase from level to level as we pass from the purely physical through the various forms of organismic existence to the spiritual and moral realm of human beings, to the cultural values, both profane and religious. The realization of this whole hierarchy of values is inherent in the divine plan of creation, and is inseparable from it.

The problem of evil—i.e., the problem of disvalues—is, of course, also inherent in the Christian tradition; and it, too, is understood as a metaphysical problem. What it amounts to is that the value dualism separating the spiritual and moral realm from the bodily and sensuous, the divine from the earthy, is ultimately unbridgeable and therefore disrupts the grand conception of the Thomistic world view. Thomas himself tried to cope with the problem; but his opponents were unrelenting. During the 14th and 15th centuries the Medieval synthesis fell apart. Renaissance thinkers, Humanists, and religious reformers increasingly stressed the value of the individual and of his freedom of choice and action. A newly developing science looked upon nature as essentially a value-free realm completely explainable in terms of quantitative laws only. A new world-view thus entailed a new standard of values, a new pattern of values. But who can doubt that this also meant a new metaphysics!

My point is that in the philosophical positions so far considered the conception of values and value patterns has been closely interwoven with the respective interpretations of reality; that value theory—if that term can be used here at all—is but a facet, an ingredient, of general metaphysics, not an independent branch of philosophy. My argument can, of course, be continued beyond the Renaissance. Leibniz, for example, speaking of ours as "the best of all possible worlds" introduced value considerations into his metaphyics; and Kant, attributing supreme worth to the self-legislative moral person, developed an ontology to which value considerations are central. He specifically states (*Kritik der Urteilskraft*, Kehrbach edition, p. 339): "Since we acknowledge only man, as a moral being, to be the purpose of creation, we now have a reason . . . for regarding the world . . . as a system of final causes" related to a "rational world cause." In this world of "interrelated purposes" every subordinate link is at the same time a means and an end. Only man is an end and not a means. The ontological stratification is thus paralleled by a stratification of values. The emphasis which Kant places on the primacy of practical reason but reflects this stratification.

One last example will suffice.

Karl Marx, giving Hegel's central concept of self-alienation a radically new meaning, projects its elimination and the restoration of man to his true humanity in a classless society. Authentic or total man will then create a new world of social relations and economic enterprise suitable to his own true being. I submit that despite its "dialectic materialism" this, too, is a value-centered view of the world. Authentic existence in a classless society is something to be hoped and worked for only if it is "better" than self-alienation.

II

Although the part which value considerations play in every comprehensive world-view is obvious to anyone examining the great systems of philosophy, it has been more customary to regard value problems as being essentially the same as moral problems. At times they have been completely identified. Thus, in enunciating the fundamental ideas of Stoicism, Cicero states that "once [we] pronounce anything to be desirable, once [we] reckon anything as good, other than moral worth, [we] have extinguished the very light of virtue, moral worth itself, and [have] overthrown virtue entirely" (*De Finibus,* Book III, 10). But even when such an extreme view is not maintained, the close relationship of value problems and moral problems is in evidence; and the problems themselves have given rise to diverse interpretations of the whole system of values.

When Protagoras proclaimed that "man is the measure of all things," did he mean to make the individual human being the "measure"? Or did he have in mind the species man? Plato, we know, maintained that the former was meant and that Protagoras was committed to a radical relativism. Aristippus took this to mean that the supreme good in life is pleasure of the moment, irrespective of its source. Antisthenes, on the other hand, though preserving the man-centeredness and admitting that all men seek to attain happiness, held that only a detached attitude towards pleasure—i.e., indulgence without becoming the slave of pleasure—characterizes the wise man. Only he can be truly happy who for his happiness depends on himself alone, not on external circumstances.

Socrates agreed that men always seek the good; but, he asked, do they know what good is? If values are made to depend upon desire, they change as desires shift and change, and the good itself is elusive. Concluding his long search, Socrates asserts that, in the end, "wisdom is the only good, and ignorance the only evil'" (*Euthydemus,* 281). Speaking for himself, Plato adds that reason, limiting pleasure, produces the happy life; that the "life of happiness and harmony" is a life "self-controlled and orderly, holding in subjugation that which causes evil in the soul and giving freedom to that which makes for virtue" (*Phaedus,* 256b). "An incorporeal order [measure and proportion] shall rule nobly a living body" (*Philebus,* 64b). And we know from the *Republic* that the key to this harmonious life under the guidance of reason is man's knowledge of the good—the good being at once the first principle of ontology as well as of ethics.

To be sure, Aristotle denied that anything is gained by making "the good" a basic category of ontology (*Nicomachean Ethics,* 1096a22; b2). Happiness, he maintained, is in itself "something final and self-sufficient" (*ibid.,* 1098a17). Still, in order to be happy, we must also be "sufficiently equipped with external goods, not for some chance period but throughout a complete life" (*ibid.,* 1101a15). But given these pre-conditions, "the refined and well-bred man will be . . . a law unto himself" (*ibid.,* 1128a32). His actions will be determined by his reason. Indeed, "the activity of reason, which is contemplative, seems both to be superior in serious worth and to aim at no end beyond itself, and to have its pleasure proper to itself" (*ibid.,* 1177b20). But be it noted in passing that the Greek term *hedone,* usually translated as "pleasure," also means "joy," "enjoyment," and "ecstacy."

For the Stoics, the highest good is moral worth; and moral worth is attained when we recognize "the harmony of nature" and live "in the light of that knowledge" (*De Finibus,* IV, 14). But only man is capable of recognizing that harmony, and only man, therefore, is capable of being guided by his own reason. In its Christian garb this theme recurs in Thomas Aquinas. The ultimate end of human activity, Thomas contends, is happiness. But he defines happiness as "the good or sum of goods which brings appetite to rest because there is nothing left to desire or seek." That is to say, happiness is the realization, the full perfection of human nature. There is, of course, a hierarchy of human appetites, for men seek life, health, pleasure, security, power prestige, knowledge, virtue, love—and all of these are good. But man's ultimate good must be appropriate to his nature—and this is the contemplative life of the intellect. It is a hunger for truth, for the good of the intellect for which, as the highest good, man's rational appetite reaches out. And the only object that can satisfy this desire is God. Indeed, "everything in seeking its good is unknowingly seeking God, for there is no good that is not a derivation of His goodness." God is thus the focal point in which all values find their culmination. He is the ultimate source and standard of them all.

With Hobbes we return to a point of view first encountered in Greek philosophy. As he sees it, nothing is ever good or evil in itself; for "whatever is the object of any man's appetite or desire . . . he for his part calleth *good:* and the object of his hate and aversion *evil* (*Leviathan,* 1, Chapter VI). Good and evil, therefore, are purely relative. They vary from person to person and, for the same person, from place to place and from time to time. There is one goal, however, which all men value and which all strive to reach: security. And from this fact follows, for Hobbes, his principle of "mutual abstinence" as a guide to conduct: Do not do to another that which he would not have done to himself.

To be sure, there was opposition to Hobbes' interpretation. Ralph Cudworth, for example, argued that the good life is the creative life; it is loving the good just because it is the good. And Richard Cumberland maintained that "the greatest benevolence of every rational agent towards all constitutes the happiest state of all"; that "therefore the common good of all is the supreme good" (*De Legibus,* Chapter I, Section 4). Shaftesbury, equally critical of Hobbes, developed an approval theory of value, defining "approval" as a liking, and "disapproval" as a disliking of our affective responses to the objects of experience (*Characteristicks,* II, pp. 28–33). And Hutcheson held, more specifically, that in the last analysis we approve or value what excites "admiration and love and study of imitation" (*Inquiry,* p. 120).

On the Continent, meanwhile, Spinoza had argued that, "since all things are produced by God in supreme perfection," it is but "a sham and an empty play" when we value what "most fortunately affects" or pleases us. Spinoza's ideal is that of the Stoics: self-sufficiency and self-mastery, and the joy "wherein the mind passes to greater perfection" (*Ethics,* III, xi, Scholium). Rational actions, Spinoza finds, are always good, and are good absolutely (*ibid.,* IV, App. iii). Evil is that which we know for certain to be thwarting us (*ibid.,* IV Df. 2). We call anything good because, as rational human beings, we "endeavour after, will, seek and desire it" (*ibid.,* III, ix, Scholium). In its way, this is a doctrine of self-realization, of self-fulfillment, although Spinoza himself does not use that term. It is a doctrine of self-fulfillment keyed to the rational nature of man and, in this sense, is part of the idealistic tradition that goes back to Aristotle and reaches its highest points in the philosophy of Hegel and T. H. Green. The self realizes itself, so Hegel argues, as it discovers that its own true interests are interrelated with the interests of family, community, the state and, ultimately, with art, religion, and philosophy; for it is in and through the latter that the finite self attains identification with Absolute Spirit (*Phenomenology,* pp. 457ff). No higher good than this can be conceived. To be sure, Green admits that "we cannot think of an object as good, i.e., such as will satisfy desire, without thinking of it as in consequence such as will yield pleasure." But he adds at once: "Its pleasantness depends on its goodness, not its goodness upon the pleasure it conveys" (*Prolegomena,* p. 194). The pleasure, in so far as it is a "necessary incident of any good," presupposes desire and results from its satisfaction, but desire does not presuppose "an imagination of pleasure" (*ibid.*), and the "moral good" is "that which satisfies the desire of a moral agent, or that in which a moral agent can find the satisfaction of himself which he necessarily seeks" (*ibid.,* p. 195). The basic circularity of this argument need not detain us; but it is evident that Green means to distinguish his own position from any form of hedonism.

A radically different conception of values was introduced into the discussion when Charles Darwin published his *Origin of Species* and *The Descent of Man.* The good was now identified with survival value. Herbert Spencer made the most of this theme; and the Pragmatists, combining selected aspects of Evolutionism and Utilitarianism, could now argue that the good is the resolution of conflicts which impede social progress, and that all valuations must constantly be submitted to the test of social usefulness. What is good or valuable must be so "in the long run" and for society as a whole. Ideals, embodying man's valuations, are but anticipations of possible solutions of particular social problems. In the process of social advancement we encounter, not values, but only valuations (Dewey); and these are our human valuations, rooted in human experience and projected as goals for human achievement. Man, therefore, is the source and the focal point of all that is thought valuable in the world; and his valuations determine his moral attitudes and actions.

III

Our brief survey is, of course, not intended to be complete or in every respect adequate. Its purpose has so far been merely to point up two facts: (1) that, in the venerable tradition of philosophy, values and valuations have always been at the center of metaphysical systems; and (2) that when value problems have been discussed more specifically, they have been closely related to, if not identified with, moral problems. General value theories in the modern sense, i.e., investigations of value problems *per se,* are not encountered until we come to the second half of the 19th century. There is one field, however, in which rather specific value theories were developed; and from the time of the Greeks on. This is the field of economics. These economic theories, however, also do not qualify as general theories of value, even though they may have served as a model in some instances.

Aristotle, we know, distinguished between intrinsic and use-values, between a real and an apparent good; and while he also discussed the exchange-value of goods, he related it specifically to human needs. An exchange of goods is just, so he argued, when equally strong needs of the exchange partners are satisfied. But Aristotle saw clearly that even this basic situation is inherently complex, for he pointed out (*Politics,* I, 9) that the usefulness of a thing is twofold. In one perspective the usefulness is a property of the thing itself; in another perspective it is not. Thus, if I wear a shoe, I make use of it; and when I exchange the shoe for something else, I also make use of it. But "making use of it" does not mean the same thing in the two cases. In the first case, Aristotle would say, the usefulness is a property of the shoe itself; in the second case it is not. But Aristotle also recognized the fact that a surplus of one kind of goods is of no benefit to the owner, and may even be of harm to him if he cannot exchange it for other goods of which he is in need. Need, therefore, is basic to all valuations and to the exchange of goods (*Politics,* VII, 1). Still, if goods are to be exchanged, they must in some respects be comparable (*Nicomachean Ethics,* V, 8), and this implies that there must be a value standard which has at least a measure of objective validity.

The Roman jurists attempted to provide such a standard by holding that it is not the specific situation in which a particular person experiences a need that determines the true value of things. It is rather the "normal" person under "normal" conditions whose needs provide the basis for all valuations and for every value standard (*Brentano,* pp. 10–11). Human needs were still considered crucial in value matters, but an attempt was at least made to distinguish on objective grounds between apparent (i.e., purely subjective) and real values. The Church Fathers gave substance to this Roman conception. Since, in their view, all men were created equal, they also have the same needs and, therefore, do value the same things in the same way. The conception of the "normal" person was now no longer an empty abstraction or a juristic fiction.

During the Middle Ages the Roman-Patristic conception of equality gave way to a new interpretation of man keyed to the newly emerging stratification of society. People living at different social levels could no longer be regarded as equal in their needs and their valuations (*Kaula,* pp. 58–59). Moreover, it was apparent that usefulness, the satisfaction of a need, alone could not be decisive in valuations, for many things are indispensable to human existence (e.g., water and air) but appear to have only little or no value. A new basis or standard for valuations was therefore required, and Albertus Magnus rose to the occasion. He was the first to maintain that the real value of a thing depends upon the amount of labor and cost that go into its production (*Opera,* p. 200), and that therefore an exchange of goods is a just one when the amount of labor and cost involved in the production of the goods to be exchange is the same. Thomas Aquinas held the same view but added that the element of risk in bringing the goods to the market (importing them from far away places) must also be considered. Duns Scotus gave full support to this view. Although human needs were still considered to be the ultimate reason why value is ascribed to things, the standard of valuation had now been shifted to the object side—to the cost of production and the risk involved—and had been completely tied up with the problem of the exchange of goods, with the market and its economy. This change created a trend of thought which is still essential to economic theory. But it also confined value theory to a narrowly limited area of human activities. Moral and metaphysical considerations were no longer basic.

Even so, however, the economic theory of value was by no means complete. William Petty (1623–87) regarded "land" as a major factor in economic matters. Said he: "Labor is the father and active principle of wealth, as lands are the mother" ("Treaty," p. 68). Goods, therefore, are worth a "measure of Land" combined with a "measure of Labour" (*ibid.,* p. 44)—the emerging theme of the Physiocrats. In 1755, Richard Cantillon added to this the idea that the value of labor itself is equivalent to the value of the produce of the land necessary for the maintenance of the laborer. And only two years later, Joseph Harris formulated what, in principle, is the "iron law of wages": "As the world goes," Harris wrote, "there is no likelihood that the lowest kind of labourers will be allowed more than a bare subsistence; if they will not be content with that, there will be others ready to step into their places; and less . . . cannot be given them" (*Essay,* p. 10).

To be sure, utility was still regarded as basic to all valuations, but it receded into the background as commercial and industrial interests became more and more prominent. As early as 1690, Nicholas Barbon argued that whatever supply exceeds need is without value—a theme taken up by the Mercantilists. The value of goods, so these economists argued, is determined, not by the needs of the "normal" person, but by the availability of the goods in the right places at the right time.

The second half of the 18th century witnessed the beginning of the Industrial Revolution. In 1776, Adam Smith set forth his influential interpretation and explanation of "the nature and causes of the wealth of nations," arguing that "wages, profits, and rent are the three original sources of all revenue as well as of all exchange value" (*Inquiry,* I, p. 63). He once more presupposed the conception of a "normal" person and argued that every human being is born with a desire to improve the conditions of his existence (*ibid.,* p. 415), and that this desire—essentially a "self-love"—is basic to all economic activities and all valuations. The word 'value,' Adam Smith maintained, has two different meanings. Sometimes it refers to the utility of some object or thing, and sometimes to "the power of purchasing other goods." That is to say, Adam Smith distinguishes, as others had not always done, between "value in use" and "value in exchange" (*ibid.,* pp. 34–35). And labor alone, he argued, is "the real measure of the exchangeable value of all commodities." "What every thing is really worth to the man who has acquired it, and who wants to dispose of it or exchange it for something else, is the toil and trouble which it can save to himself, and which it can impose upon other people" (*ibid.,* p. 35). Hence, "labor alone, never varying in its own value, is alone the ultimate and real standard by which the value of all commodities can at all times and places be estimated and compared. It is their real price" (*ibid.,* pp. 39–40). To this idea Ricardo added his own clarifying interpretations. Assuming the utility of a product, he argued that its "natural" value is determined by what it costs to satsify the demand under the most unfavorable conditions of the production of the goods demanded.

This "cost," according to Ricardo, includes capital and labor. But since capital is merely the result of past labor, all cost reduces in the end to labor—but not, as Adam Smith maintained, to the labor which one can buy as a result of the exchange; rather, to the labor spent in the production itself. And the "natural price" of this labor, Ricardo maintained, is "that price which is necessary to enable the laborers, one with another, to subsist and to perpetuate their race, without either increase or diminution" (*Master works,* p. 310). This means that the "natural price" of labor "depends on the price of food, necessaries, and conveniences required for the support of the laborer and his family" (*ibid.*).

This "labor-cost principle," first introduced by Cantillon and, as we have seen, formulated more precisely by Harris, Karl Marx made the basic axiom of his whole theory. To be sure, even for Marx it is "the utility of a thing [that] makes it a use-value" (*Capital,* p. 42); but "use-value," according to Marx, is not an attribute of the "commodities" themselves. The only value "contained in" the commodities as a property or attribute is their exchange-value (*ibid.,* p. 95). And when Marx speaks of "value," it is this exchange-value he has in mind. Value in this sense, however, is "realized human labour" (*ibid.,* p. 106). As Marx puts it: "As values, all commodities are only definite masses of congealed labour-time" (*ibid.,* p. 46). Commodities are values only because labor has been "objectified and materialized" in them. It is perfectly possible, therefore, for a thing to "be a use-value without having value." "This is the case whenever its utility to man is not due to labor" (*ibid.,* p. 47). Air, for example, is of use-value but has no value. It is labor and labor alone that determines the value of a thing; and the "expenditure of labour-power" is a measure of "the quantity of value of the products of labour" (*ibid.,* p. 82). Hence, "whenever, by an exchange, we equate as values our different products, by that very act we also equate, as human labour, the different kinds of labour expended upon them" (*ibid.,* p. 85). Money itself is a "measure of value only inasmuch as it is the socially recognized incarnation of human labour" (*ibid.,* p. 110); for "the magnitude of values . . . expresses the connection that necessarily exists between a certain article and the portion of the total labour time of society required to produce it" (*ibid.,* p. 114).

In brief, then, "the value of each commodity is determined by the quantity of labour expended on and materialized in it, by the working-time necessary, under social conditions, for its production" (*ibid.,* p. 208). This holds good also "in the case of the product that accrued to [the] capitalist, as the result of the labour-process carried on for him" (*ibid.*). But—shades of Joseph Harris —"the value of the labour-power [itself] is the value of the means of subsistence necessary for the maintenance of the labourer" (*ibid.,* p. 190), the minimum limit being determined by what is "physically indispensable" for the worker daily to "renew his vital energy" (*ibid.,* p. 192).

This "classical labor-cost theory" of value was forcefully challenged in 1853 by H. H. Gossen, who made the alleviation of needs and the satisfaction of desires (*Befriedigung von Bedürfnissen*) the basis of a system of economics and defined value—economic value—in terms of satisfactions. In order to realize the maximum satisfaction, so Gossen argued, we must strive to realize the greatest possible satisfaction of each desire. Beginning with the alleviation of our most urgent needs, we must pursue each desire to the maximum of its satisfaction. Whatever gives us that satisfaction is the greatest value in the perspective of that desire. But once the maximum satisfaction of some particular desire has been attained, further pursuit of that desire results in a "diminishing return" of the energy expended. And when the satisfaction of one desire sinks to the level of the highest possible satisfaction derivable from the pursuit of some other desire, the desires involved are in balance. A balance involving all our desires is the maximum satisfaction attainable. But in order to achieve it, we must have knowledge of all possible satisfactions and of the means necessary to their realization. Desire must thus be supplemented by rational considerations.

According to Gossen, then, the value of a thing—and this includes its economic value—is determined by the nature and the intensity of the need which it alleviates, or of the desire which it satisfies. If a thing satisfies various desires simultaneously, its value is enhanced correspondingly. But various things or "goods" may also be complementary in the sense that not one of them by itself provides real satisfaction; that they do so, however, in combination. When this is the case, the value of the last object needed to complete the combination may be greater than the value of all other objects already present. And it is also clear that objects which are not themselves consumer goods but are necessary for the production of consumer goods derive a value—an instrumental value—from that relationship. The magnitude of their value depends on their specific contribution to the process of production. In the last analysis, however, the value of all goods and of all means of production depends upon the intensity of the desire which the goods satisfy. It reduces to a minimum when the satisfaction attained or expected is zero. That in the determination of the degree of satisfaction the discomforts and efforts (labor) involved in obtaining the goods must be subtracted from the expected satisfaction is, of course, understood. It does not alter the basic conception—the conception, namely, that use-value or utility is the foundation of all value considerations and of economic values in particular; and that "marginal utility" determines the lower limit of values.

The great advantage of Gossen's theory over the classical labor-cost theory lies in the fact that it provides a standard equally applicable to the bounties of nature and the products of human enterprise. It explains the value of a diamond accidentally discovered as well as the lack of value of so-called "commodities" in the production of which much labor-cost is involved. But this is not the place to pursue the issue further. Enough has already been said to make it quite evident that in the development of economic theory the problem of value has taken various forms, has been seen in different perspectives, and has found diverse solutions. As early as 1872, Fr. J. Neumann called attention to these variations and to ambiguities thus entailed in value theory. Separating "subjective" interpretations from "objective" value conceptions—including among the latter such diverse matters as "wealth," "exchange-value," and "yield-value"—he pointed out that even these objective interpretations are not free from ambiguities; for underlying all value conceptions are the infinitely variable factors of human experience and their heterogeneous interpretations within diverse ideological frameworks.

IV

It would be a simple matter to show that value problems are also involved in our aesthetic experience and in the establishment and support of social institutions—the family, the state, the United Nations; that, in fact, all our decisions and rational acts presuppose value judgments and valuations. But all that this would prove is merely the need for a general value theory which, disregarding particular value areas, would yet be foundational to them all and would be concerned with the valuational aspects of human experience as a whole as science is concerned with the cognitive. In this broad and basic sense value theory has come into its own only toward the end of the 19th century. Its inception and development will be the topic of the chapters that follow.

BIBLIOGRAPHY

Abbott, L. D., editor, *Masterworks of Economics,* Garden City, New York, 1946.

Aristotle, *Works,* Oxford edition.

Brentano, Lujo, *Die wirtschaftlichen Lehren des christlichen Altertums,* Munich, 1902.

Cantillon, Richard, *Essai sur la Nature du Commerce en General,* 1st edition 1775, new edition, London, 1892.

Cicero, *De Finibus,* translation by H. Rackham, Loeb Classics, 1931.

Cumberland, Richard, *De Legibus Naturae,* translation by John Maxwell, London, 1727.

Gossen, H. H., *Entwicklung der Gesetze des menschlichen Verkehrs,* Braunschweig, 1853.

Green, T. H., *Prolegomena to Ethics,* edited by A. C. Bradley, 5th edition, Oxford, 1906.

Harris, Joseph, *An Essay upon Money and Coins,* London, 1757.

Hegel, G. W. F., *The Phenomenology of Mind,* Translation by J. B. Baillie, 2nd edition, London, 1931.

Hobbes, Thomas, *Leviathan,* 3rd edition, London, 1887.

Hobhouse, L. T., *Morals in Evolution,* 4th edition, New York, 1924.

Hutcheson, Francis, *An Inquiry into the Orginal of our Ideas of Beauty and Virtue,* 4th edition, London, 1738.

Kant, I., *Kritik der Urteilskraft,* Kehrbach edition.

Kaula, Rudolf, *Die Geschichtliche Entwicklung der Modernen Werttheorien,* Tübingen, 1906.

Kossell, Clifford G., "The Moral Views of Thomas Aquinas," *Encyclopedia of Morals,* edited by Vergilius Ferm, New York, 1956.

Kraus, O., *Die Werttheorien: Geschichte und Kritik,* Brünn, 1937.

Marx, Karl., *Capital: A Critique of Political Economy,* edited by Fredrich Engels, translation by Samuel Moore and Edward Aveling, New York, 1906.

Neumann, Fr. J., "Beiträge zur Revision der Grundbegriffe der Volkswirtschaftslehre," *Zeitschrift für die gesamte Staatswissenschaft,* Vol. 28, Tübingen, 1872.

Petty, Sir William, *Economic Writings,* Vol. I, "A Treatise of Taxes and Contributions," Cambridge, 1899.

Plato, *The Dialogues of Plato,* Jowett translation, Oxford.

Shaftesbury, The Earl of, *Characteristicks of Men, Manners, Opinions, Times,* London, 1711.

Sidgwick, Henry, *Outlines of the History of Ethics,* London, 1892.

Smith, Adam, *An Inquiry into the Nature and Causes of the Wealth of Nations,* London, 1776.

Spinoza, Benedict de, *Ethics,* edited by James Gutmann, 1966 reprint.

Stephen, Leslie, *The English Utilitarians,* London, 1900.

Untersteiner, M., *The Sophists,* translation by K. Freeman, New York, 1953.

von Rintelen, Fritz-Joachim, *Der Wertgedanke in der Europäischen Geistesentwicklung,* Halle, 1932.

Werkmeister, W. H., *Theories of Ethics,* Lincoln, Nebraska, 1961.

Wittmann, M., *Die Ethik des Heiligen Thomas von Aquin,* Munich, 1933.

CHAPTER I

THE BEGINNINGS OF MODERN
VALUE THEORY

It is clear from what has been said in the Introduction that the problem of value has many aspects—be they metaphysical, moral, economic, aesthetic, or whatever; and that all of them ought to be considered together within an all-embracing value theory. Can the term "value" be so defined as to become basic in all areas of human enterprise and decision making? And can a principle be found which will integrate the various areas and will, thus, give unity to our interpretations? Jeremy Bentham held that it can be done and developed his brand of Utilitarianism to prove it. In the end, however, he failed in his undertaking. Nietzsche, observing the nihilism of his time, was convinced that no viable value theory could be based upon the traditional foundations. He therefore demanded a "transvaluation of all values." Hermann Lotze, finally, suggested a new approach to the whole problem and, in doing so, took the initial steps in the development of modern value theory. Considering these facts, I believe that a brief discussion of the work of Bentham, Nietzsche, and Lotze will serve well as an introduction to the modern approaches to value theory, for such a discussion will suggest additional perspectives from which to view the problems with which value theory is concerned.

First, then, let us consider Bentham's effort.

I

It is significant that Jeremy Bentham (1748–1832) entitled his main work *The Principles of Morals and Legislation* (*Works*, I), thereby suggesting at once that he was not dealing with moral problems only but with problems in at least two interrelated fields. His theme was that "the greatest happiness of the greatest number is the foundation of morals and legislation" (*Works*, X, p. 561). That such a theme can easily be extended to include the

1

realm of the arts is obvious; that it can be the basis of economics as well, Bentham himself proved, even if he did not develop his ideas fully. Bentham's theory, therefore, is, in effect, a general value theory, encompassing the whole range of human activities.

The presuppositional assumption upon which this theory rests is stated well in that often-quoted passage: "Nature has placed mankind under the governance of two sovereign masters, pain and pleasure. It is for them alone to point out what we ought to do as well as to determine what we shall do." Lest there be any misunderstanding, Bentham adds: "On the one hand the standard of right and wrong, on the other the chain of causes and effects, are fastened to their throne" (*Works,* I, p. 1).

Supplementing the initial statement, Bentham then asserts that "pleasure is in itself a good; nay even . . . the only good: pain is in itself an evil, and indeed, without exception, the only evil; or else the words good and evil have no meaning" (*ibid.,* p. 48). In maintaining that pleasure is the only good and, therefore, the only positive motive for action, Bentham is quite willing to go to an extreme: "Let a man's motive be ill-will; call it even malice, envy, cruel; it is still a kind of pleasure, that is his motive: the pleasure he takes at the thought of the pain which he sees, or expects to see, his adversary undergo. Now even this wretched pleasure, taken by itself, is good: it may be faint; it may be short; it must at any rate be impure: yet while it lasts, and before any bad consequences arrive, it is as good as any other that is not more intense" (*ibid.*). It is obvious from this passage that, for Bentham, pleasure is pleasure, no matter what its source; that each person's own pleasure is the only positive value for him, and that his own pain is the only disvalue for him. Nothing can be desired or loved for its own sake but one's own pleasure; and nothing can be hated for its own sake but one's own pain. Bentham's fundamental position is thus, quite frankly, an ego-centric selfishness. The fact that Bentham also maintains that "individual pleasures, and exceptions from individual pains" are "the elements of happiness" (*Works,* IV, p. 540) does not alter the situation.

However, Bentham does hold that some pleasures are better than others. But this difference is not one of quality. Pleasure is pleasure and pain is pain, we are told; and there is an end to it.

That is to say, the pleasures and pains themselves are neither "ponderable" nor "measurable." "We have no measure" for them (*ibid.*). Still, a "calculus of pleasures" is necessary to guide us in our actions. It must be based, Bentham argues, not upon the qualitative characteristics of pleasure and pain, but upon their quantitative dimensions (*Works*, I, p. 3)—i.e., upon the intensity, the duration, the propinquity, and the certainty of pleasures and pains (*Works*, IV, p. 542). Of these, intensity and duration belong to pleasures and pains themselves, and do so irrespective of whether the pleasures and pains are "considered as past or as future." Taken together, intensity and duration constitute the "magnitude" of the pleasures and pains. To them must be added considerations of the nearness or remoteness of the pleasurable or the painful experience, and of its certainty or probability (*Works*, III, p. 287; I, p. 3; IV, p. 542). That is to say, an intensive pleasure of long duration that is certain to be realized immediately is better than one which is less intense, is of shorter duration, and whose realization at some future time is not certain at all. Similarly, an intensive pain of long duration that is immediate and certain is worse than a pain that is less intense, is of shorter duration, that lies yet in the future and whose occurrence is probable rather than certain. Variations in any one of these four dimensions, or in any combination thereof, correspondingly affect the magnitude of the pleasure or of the pain involved—increasing or diminishing it, as the case may be, and thus providing us with an infinitely variable scale of values.

Bentham himself illustrates how he thought the calculus might be used. Let us suppose, he said, that the intensity of an actual pleasure is "represented by a certain number of degrees." In order to obtain the true magnitude of this pleasure, we multiply that number by "the number expressive of the moments or atoms of time contained in its duration." If two pleasures have the same degree of intensity, and if the second lasts twice as long as the first, then "the second is twice as great as the first" (*Works*, IV, p. 540). Now suppose that the magnitude of a pleasure—its intensity times its duration—is given, then, if that pleasure is "not present"—i.e., if it is not actually experienced—its value is "diminished by whatever [the pleasure] falls short of being present." Lastly, "the value of [the pleasure] is subject to a further reduction by whatever it is deficient in, in respect to certainty." And "just so it is with pains" (*ibid.*).

The difficulties inherent in such quantitative interpretations are obvious but need not concern us here. We must take note of the fact, however, that Bentham adds considerations of "purity" and "fecundity" to the four dimensions of pleasure and pain just discussed. But neither purity nor fecundity "can be considered as belonging to the value of a pleasure or pain when considered by itself" (*Works,* III, p. 287). Purity, for example, refers to any given or anticipated experience as a whole in which pleasure and pain may occur together and may be "mixed" in various proportions. It is Bentham's contention that the pleasurable experience pure and simple is better than one in which pain, also being present, detracts from the "pure" pleasure. In marginal cases, pleasure and pain balance each other exactly. It may also be the case, however, that the pain outweighs the pleasure—in which case the experience as a whole is that of a disvalue.

The reference to fecundity is also to the experience as a whole rather than to the pleasure involved, for pleasure as such produces no consequences. What Bentham intends here is to assert that actions which are pleasurable now and lead to other pleasurable experiences are better than actions which have no such consequences or, worse yet, have consequences that are painful. Again one might ask how it can be known in advance and with certainty which actions have pleasurable, and which have painful, consequences. But, once more, the difficulties involved here do not concern us at present. And, in any case, Bentham might argue that past experience gives us at least a fair guide; and more than a certain degree of probability cannot be demanded.

So far Bentham's theory is concerned exclusively with the value experience of individuals. However, human beings live in communities; and this fact, also, must be taken into consideration. The question is, How do we get from the calculus of individual value experiences to the requirements of communal living? Bentham's solution of the problem is simple and straight forward; but we must go beyond the experience of pleasure and pain as such to the "sources" of these experiences—to the objects, conditions, and states of affairs which induce the pleasurable or the painful experience. When we do this, an additional factor is introduced into the calculus of pleasures. Bentham puts it this way: "Take any two sources of pleasure: the one productive of pleasure to one person and no more: the other productive of pleasure, the same in magnitude and value, to two other persons and no more. . . . The value of the second source of pleasure will be just twice as great as that of the first. . . . In a political community, the *extent* of a pleasure is as the number of the persons by whom it is experienced. Just so it is with pains" (*Works*, IV, p. 540).

What is significant in this passage is the emphasis placed upon the sources of pleasure (and pain), not upon pleasure (or pain) itself. And now Bentham's "utilitarianism" is quite understandable. It is the demand to create such conditions of human existence, to utilize the facts involved in that existence in such a way, as to make possible the greatest amount of pleasure in the experience of the greatest number of people. And since, according to Bentham (*ibid.*), happiness is but a summation of pleasurable experiences, the ultimate goal is to create happiness for the greatest number of people. Any action is good, therefore,—Bentham maintains—to the extent to which it tends to augment rather than to diminish the happiness of the community, and being good, such an action is right and ought therefore to be done (*Works*, I, pp. 3–4).

So understood, the "principle of utility" and the "greatest-happiness principle" are one and the same. The latter merely states "more expressively" the meaning of the former (*Works*, IV, p. 540). It explains its meaning more fully (p. 542). But once this principle has been accepted—call it the "principle of utility" or the "greatest-happiness principle" (it does not matter which)—certain consequences follow at once. To begin with, as Bentham puts it, "no otherwise than by reference to the greatest-happiness principle, can epithets such as *good* and *evil,* or *good* and *bad,* be expressive of any quality in the *act* . . . to which they are applied:—say an act of an individual: say an act of government: a *law,* a *measure* of government, a *system* of government, a *form* of government. But for this reference, all they designate is—the *state of mind* on the part of him in whose discourse they are employed" (p. 543). Only because of this reference to the "principle of utility" are those terms "indicative of qualities belonging to the objects they are applied to" (*ibid.*). Moreover, in "the warfare of tongues and pens" characteristic of the political arena, "justice and humanity," "economy and liberality," "liberty and licentiousness," and the like are but "trash" with which "the corruptionists feed their dupes" and "the holders of power pass for wise" (p. 542) until the "greatest-happiness principle" gives specific and concrete meaning to these terms. And lastly, "till the principle of utility, as explained by the phrase *the greatest happiness of the greatest number,* is, on each occasion, if not explicitly, implicitly referred to, as the source of all reasoning, . . . everything that, in the field of legislation, calls itself *reasoning* or *argument* will . . . be a compound of nonsense and falsehood" (*ibid.*).

In a letter to James Madison, President of the United States, Bentham wrote, in October 1811, that "the all-governing principle, viz., the principle of utility," will provide "a test, and the only test, by which, either the *absolute* fitness or unfitness of any one proposed body of laws taken by itself, or of the *comparative* fitness of each one of any number of bodies of law, standing in competition with each other" may be determined (*Works,* IV, p. 454). More specifically, Bentham maintains that, "in every political state, the greatest happiness of the greatest number [as end sought] requires that [the state] be provided with an all-comprehensive body of law" (*Works,* IV, p. 537); "that such body of law be throughout accompanied by its *rationale:* an indication of the *reason* on which the several arrangements contained in it are grounded" (p. 538); and "that those reasons be such, throughout, as shall show the conduciveness of the several arrangements to the all-comprehensive and only defensible end" (pp. 539–40): the greatest happiness of the greatest number. The "greatest-happiness principle" thus defines the end to be achieved through legislative acts and, at the same time, provides a criterion by which to judge the means employed, i.e., the legislative acts.

That Bentham's theory had, and was meant to have, broad implications is now clear. He himself applied it effectively in the fields of morals and legislation. However, the theory is relevant to economic matters also, even though Bentham did not press this point or develop his thoughts fully. Consider, to begin with, the following definitions of good and evil. "Good," Bentham maintains, "is pleasure or exemption from pain; or a cause or instrument of either, considered in so far as it is a cause or instrument of either. Evil is pain or loss of pleasure; or a cause or instrument of either, considered in so far as it is a cause or instrument of either" (p. 543). What Bentham is saying here is that the value of *things* depends upon whether or not they are causes of pleasurable experiences, i.e., whether or not they alleviate needs and satisfy desires. Utility is again the teststone. To remove any doubt as to his meaning, Bentham asks, more specifically, "on what account" is "an article of property, an estate in hand, for instance," valuable? And he answers: "On account of the pleasure of all kinds which it enables a man to produce, and, what comes to the same thing, the pains of all kinds which it enables him to avert" (*Works,* I, p. 17). But Bentham went a step farther and formulated an "economic law"—though he did not call it that—which, in all essentials, anticipated Gossen's law of diminishing utility. "The magnitude of pleasure" produced by any object, Bentham stated, "does not increase in so great a ratio as that in which the magnitude of the cause increases." To illustrate as well as to emphasize his point, Bentham continued: "Take . . . any individual: give him a certain quantity of money, you will produce in his mind a certain quantity of pleasure. Give him again the same quantity, you will make an addition to the quantity of his pleasure. But the magnitude of the pleasure produced by the second sum will not be twice the magnitude of the pleasure produced by the first. While the sums are small, the truth of this proposition may not be perceivable. But let the sums have risen to a certain magnitude, it will be altogether out of doubt" (*Works,* IV, p. 541). And, Bentham adds, "as it is with money, so it is with all other sources or causes of pleasure."

It is thus evident that, for Bentham, the greatest-happiness principle is foundational to his ethics, his theory of the state, and his interpretation of economic affairs. And since happiness is but the sum total of all the pleasures which the individual experiences when his actions are guided by the calculus of pleasures, the whole of Bentham's system reduces to a unified value theory for which pleasure and the absence of pain are the only value, and pain and the absence of pleasure the only disvalue. It is a grand conception and is in many respects a model of a value theory. Its deficiencies stem from the fact that Bentham recognizes no qualitative distinctions among man's pleasures; that for him the pleasure which a sadist derives from torturing his victim is as good—though perhaps not as long lasting—as is the satisfaction of the philanthropist who provides support and opportunities for the underprivileged. John Stuart Mill's statement that "Socrates dissatisfied is better than a pig satisfies" goes to the very heart of the matter. And is happiness really nothing but a summation of pleasures? The answer to this question may well be in the negative, for pleasures are essentially gratifications of our desires, whereas happiness may be found in the realization of rationally conceived goals that give meaning to our whole life. It may be found, in other words, in our self-fulfillment.

But Bentham's calculus of pleasures also entails difficulties. The quantifications which the calculus presupposes are largely impossible to obtain. How, for example, would one determine that the intensity of one pleasure is twice or three times as great as that of another pleasure—especially when, as is usually the case, the two pleasures are not yet experienced or are not experienced simultaneously? Also, we cannot anticipate with any degree of certainty the value of an action in terms of the indefinitely large number of persons affected. The manifold interrelations of causal dependencies make it impossible to foresee all the consequences of our actions.

Still, when all is said and done, we come back to the fact that Bentham did develop a general value theory, even if he did not call it by that name, and even if its inherent difficulties are insurmountable. The problem now is to find a better foundation for a theory that encompasses the whole range of our human valuations and preferences, our decisions and actions in whatever field, our hopes and aspirations—a theory which accomplishes at least as much, if not more than Bentham's theory ever did.

II

The man who called attention most forcefully to the problem of values was, of course, Nietzsche who, with his demand for a transvaluation of all values challenged every traditional value standard. Basic to this challenge was Nietzsche's firm conviction that it is man, and man alone, who creates values and who ascribes them to things. "Man as poet, as thinker, as God, as love, as power —: lament his royal largess with which he has enriched mere things in order to emproverish himself and to feel miserable! Thus far it has been his greatest unselfishness that he has admired and worshipped, and that he has concealed from himself the fact that it was he also who had created what he admired" (Motto: *The Will to Power*, II).[1] But all this is now to be different. "All the beauty and sublimity which we have bestowed upon real and imaginary things" Nietzsche will "demand back as the property and the product of man: as his most beautiful apology" (*ibid.*).

An interpretation of Nietzsche's philosophy is always difficult. His aphorismic style contributes to this fact. But, as the recent efforts of Heidegger and Jaspers have shown, there is also a question of the systematic unity of Nietzsche's thought. It is a fact, however, that the basic theme of the transvaluation of all values is reasonably clear; and that, despite its challenging and challengeable details, the development of the theme is consistent throughout (cf. Werkmeister, *Theories of Ethics,* Chpt. VI).

Nietzsche was dead set against hedonism in all its forms and against any religiously orientated value theory. He despised Darwinism and was, in general, against all traditional value standards. Above everything else he was trying to provide a new basis for our valuations and a new standard relative to which the height of all values might be determined. He regarded the philosopher as the "physician of culture" who must not only diagnose the ills of the times but must prescribe a cure as well.

---

[1] All quotations are my own translations from the German text of *Nietzsches Werke,* Taschen-Ausgabe, edited by Elisabeth Förster-Nietzsche, Leipzig, 1906. However, for the convenience of the reader who desires to check the context, all references (by volume and page) are to *The Complete Works of Friedrich Nietzsche,* edited by Dr. Oscar Levy.

Surveying his own Age, Nietzsche found much decadence. However, he was enough of a realist to be aware of the fact that "decadence belongs to all epochs of mankind" (VII, p. 272); that "every fruitful and powerful movement of mankind has always created also a nihilistic movement," that the destruction of the old standards might itself be "the sign of an incisive and most essential growth, of the transition into new conditions of existence" (XIV, p. 92). What is necessary, however, is "not to confuse the instincts of decadence with those of humanity; not to confuse the dissolving means of civilization . . . with culture" (XIV, p. 100).

Decadence, however, is not a symptom of cultural change only; it affects individuals as well as cultures. That is to say, the problem of a value standard is a personal problem no less than a problem involving the whole of mankind.

But decadence in any form culminates in nihilism—in a state of affairs, that is, in which "the highest values lose their value." "There is no answer to the question 'To what purpose?'" (XIV, p. 8). There is no goal that would give direction and meaning to human activity. In fact, "radical nihilism is the conviction that, as far as the highest values are concerned which one has acknowledged, existence is absolutely unjustifiable" (*ibid.*). Nietzsche's conception of nihilism has thus brought us face to face with the very crux of the problem of values. It has confronted us with a practical, not a merely theoretical, problem. It must be understood, however, that Nietzsche is not advocating nihilism; he is merely diagnosing the ills of our times.

As Nietzsche sees it, the very truthfulness which has given us our sciences now turns against morality itself and against all traditional valuations (XIV, p. 9). The conflict is real. It is the conflict "of not valuing when we know, and [for the sake of truth] not being allowed to value that with which we would like to deceive ourselves" (XIV, pp. 9–10). In the past, "the highest values in the service of which man was to live . . . were built up above man as if they were God's command, as if they were 'reality,' a 'true' world, a hope and a world to come. But now, when the lowly origin of these values becomes known, the whole universe seems to have lost its value, to have become 'meaningless'"

(XIV, p. 10). And with this development, man himself "has lost unbelievably much dignity" (XIV, p. 19).

Confronted with this collapse of his traditional values and value standards, man must find a new value-basis or despair in a universal nihilism. It is up to "the new philosophers" to initiate the transvalution of values and to discover a new basis for our valuations (XII, pp. 129–130). The task is not an easy one; for the "philosophers" will find themselves all the time in conflict wth all traditional valuations and value standards.

Their first question must be: "Under what conditions did man invent for himself the value judgments, good and evil?" More specifically, what value do those conditions themselves possess? "Are they a sign of distress, of impoverishment, of degeneration of life? Or . . . do they disclose the superabundance, the strength, the will of life, its courage, its self-reliance, its future?" (XIII, pp. 4–5). Whatever the answer, Nietzsche is sure of one thing: "It was man who assigned values to things in order to preserve himself; it was he who created the meaning of things—a human meaning!" And through his valuations alone is there value (XI, p. 67). Valuing, however, is also a creating; and all values and their modifications are "related to the growth of power of him who posits the values (XIV, p. 16). It makes a crucial difference, therefore, who is the creator of values. Is it the "aristocratic man," the "noble soul"? Or is it the "man of resentment," the "exhausted one," the "bodged" and the "misbegotten?"

In the past, so Nietzsche maintains, the creators of value have been the "exhausted people" (XIV, p. 46). "All that which weakens, teaches weakness, infects with weakness, [these] people have called God," and the "good man," as they conceived him, was but "a form of self-affirmation on the part of decadence" (*ibid.*). But Nietzsche means to change all of this. He wants to "teach the affirmation of all that which strengthens, which accumulates strength, which justifies the feeling of strength" (*ibid.*). Without such radical transvaluation, he holds, there is no hope for the future.

As long as religious conviction and a living faith is an omnipotent, all-wise and all-good God provided guidance for human actions, the idea of an absolute value standard found unchallengeable support in the metaphysics of such belief. But Nietzsche proclaimed that "God is dead" (XI, p. 6; p. 320); that he never was more than a "conjecture" (XI, p. 98), the creation of "exhausted people," of the "men of resentment." But "could you create a God?," Nietzsche asks and, assuming a negative answer, continues: "Then, I pray you, be silent about all Gods!" "I want that your conjectures reach no further than your creative will"; that it "be restricted to the conceivable" (XI, p. 99).

This repudiation of all traditional value standards necessitates, of course, the introduction of a new standard, for otherwise all would be chaos. "We must have a goal for the sake of which all love one another! All other goals are only worth annihilation" (XVI, p. 271). But our "will to truth" demands that "everything be transformed into the humanly conceivable, the humanly visible, the humanly sensible" (XI, p. 99). It is imperative, in other words, that we set our goal "not in a false world" but in "mankind's own continuation" (XVI, p. 269). We cannot create or even conceive God, but we can conceive and "create the Superman"—not we ourselves, perhaps, but the generations that are yet to come. This, then, is Nietzsche's callenge: "Transform yourselves into fathers and forefathers of the Superman; and let this be your best creating" (XI, p. 99).

The conception of Superman has often been misunderstood, and most radically so when it was conjoined with a misinterpretation of Nietzsche's conception of the Will to Power. The latter is, for Nietzsche, a metaphysical principle of creativity; the former is the projection of an ideal that is to give a new meaning—a profoundly human meaning—to the whole of reality. To be sure, Nietzsche does not give us a formal definition of Superman; but once he refers to him as a "Roman Caesar"—that is, a man of action—"with the soul of Christ" (XV, p. 380). Goethe—"that most beautiful manifestation of an integrated man" (XV, p. 318) —comes closest to the realization of the ideal which Nietzsche had in mind: "a strong and highly cultured man, . . . capable of self-discipline, having respect for himself; a man also who can permit himself the enjoyment of the whole fullness and richness of naturalness, who is strong enough for his freedom; a man of tolerance, not out of weakness but out of strength. . . . Such a spirit . . . stands in the midst of the whole universe with a feeling of joyous and confident fatalism, believing that only individual things are bad [but] that, taken as part of the whole, everything redeems and affirms itself. . . . [Faith in such a spirit] is the highest of all possible faiths" (XVI, pp. 109–110). It is the projection of a new and a meaningful value standard. But even Goethe, Nietzsche would agree, is only human, "all too human." He is not the realization of Superman but an indication of the direction in which the new ideal might be found (XI, p. 268). That ideal itself is "higher than the highest man."

The realization of this new ideal is, of course, not a matter of evolution (XVI, p. 129). "Darwinism" in all its forms must be repudiated (XVI, p. 71), for the struggle for existence does not lead to perfection (XV, p. 155), and the idea of adaptation— crucial to Darwin's theory—"misses the real essence of life." "It overlooks the fundamental pre-eminence of the spontaneous, aggressive, encroaching, re-interpreting, re-directing, and creative forces whose effectiveness alone entails adaptation" (XIII, p. 92; XV, pp. 153–154). The pursuit of the new ideal demands that man creatively mould himself into a new creature; and that, in doing so, he most effectively embodies the Will to Power. But the task is not an easy one, for it demands that much of what we are now be sacrificed for the sake of what might be. That is to say, there is much in us that must be "surpassed" (XI, p. 351; XV, p. 326), that must be suppressed without pity or must be sublimated and given a new meaninng. Our passions, though deeply rooted in our animal nature, must be "spiritualized." We must "enlist them in our service" (XIV, p. 95) as we create ourselves in conformity with our new ideal. And we must be ruthless with ourselves in this process. As Nietzsche puts it: "In man creature and creator are unified. In man there is matter, fragment, excess, clay, filth, folly, chaos; but in man there is also the creator, the sculptor, the hardness of a hammer, the divinity of a spectator, and the seventh day—do you understand this contrast? And [do you understand] that *your* compassion is concerned with the 'creature in man,' with what must be formed, broken, hammered, torn, burned, annealed, purified. . . . And *our* compassion—do you not comprehend with whom our *reversed* compassion is concerned? . . . There are problems higher than all the problems of pleasure and suffering and compassion; and every philosophy which culminates only in these is naïveté" (XII, p. 171).

"No one yet knows," Nietzsche maintains, "what good is or bad;—unless it be he who creates . . . man's goal and gives to the earth its meaning and its future" (XI, pp. 239–240). And viewed in this perspective, "good and evil, rich and poor, high and low, and all the names of values: weapons they shall be and sounding signs of the fact that life must again and again surpass itself!" (XI, p. 119). That such an orientation entails the repudiation of all valuations that are in conflict with it is obvious; and Nietzsche did his level best to demolish them. But this is not the place nor the proper context within which to evaluate his radicalism in the condemnation of traditional values. We are here concerned with his positive suggestions and with the values which, he believes, are entailed by a commitment to the Will to Power.

"In the foreground," so we are told, "is the feeling of fullness, of power, which wants to overflow, the happiness of high tension, the consciousness of a wealth which desires to give and share" (XII, p. 228). In particular, however, it is the transformation and sublimation of the passions which creates new values. One of the transformations is "the sublimation of sensuality" into love—into the "love of the remote," the love of the generations yet to come. Another is "the sublimation of enmity"—especially a sublimation of the conflicts within ourselves; for it is the sublimation of the "chaos within one" that "gives birth to a dancing star" (XI, p. 12). In the consuming flames of this inner chaos new values are crystallized, and the ideal which gives meaning and purpose to human living is purified. And "that your self be in your action . . . : let that be your formula for virtue" (XI, p. 112). Let your actions, that is, be the authentic manifestation of your own true self.

But this drive for self-realization is also a "yearning" to give and to bestow upon others out of the richness and the superabundance of one's own life. "Bestowing virtue" Zarathustra once called this virtue (XI, p. 231); and he added that "a bestowing virtue is the highest virtue" (XI, p. 86). Closely related to it is that "blessed selfishness" (XI, p. 233), that "healthy and holy selfishness" which enriches itself only in order to bestow the more abundantly—a selfishness whose very core is a "love which bestows" (XI, p. 86). And it is this love—this "bestowing-love"— which is to "give to the earth its meaning, a human meaning" (XI, p. 88). "Let your love to life be love to your highest hope; and let your highest hope be the loftiest thought of your life" (XI, p. 53).

Such an ideal, according to Nietzsche, includes "greatness"— the "greatness which is at the same time the superabundant life, perfection in the multiplicity of value-responses, depth and richness of life, and "the creative abundance of power" (XII, p. 154). In such greatness there is freedom: "the will to be responsible for oneself; [the will] to preserve the distance which separates us [from the rabble]; [the will] to become more indifferent toward hardships, severity, privation, and even life itself; to sacrifice men, oneself included, for one's cause" (XVI, p. 94–95). In all situations "let the future and the most remote [i.e., the ideal] be the motive of today" (XI, p. 70). Let the love of what is to come prevail over every concern for the moment, and "maintain holy your highest hope" (XI, p. 49). In the pursuit of that goal "we must overcome the past in ourselves"; we must "conquer" our instincts and must "consecrate" them anew (XVI, p. 261). Only thus can we realize our highest ideal.

The problem of a general standard of values and of the transvaluation of values which it entails had thus been clearly seen and had been brought forcefully to the attention of Nietzsche's contemporaries. This new "vision," however, anchored in an epistemology and a metaphysics which were generally unacceptable, demanded a re-examination of the presuppositions of all valuations and of the projection of value goals. To carry through this re-examination and to come up with positive suggestions became the task of the value theorists from the days of Lotze to our own days. And the problem has not yet been settled to everyone's satisfaction.

III

When next we turn to Lotze's philosophy, we discover at once that the problem of value appears in yet a different light. Concluding his *Metaphysik* of 1879, Lotze states: "When, several decades earlier, I dared to present a still more imperfect interpretation, I concluded with the statement that the true beginning of metaphysics is to be found in ethics.[1] I now withdraw whatever is not correct in that statement; but I am still convinced that I am right in seeking the ground for what *is* in what *ought to be*" (1879, p. 604). Here, in a capsule formula, is the theme which dominated Lotze's thinking for over thirty years and provided the background for his interpretation of values. The question is, What precisely does it mean? What are its ramifications and implications? The *Metaphysik* of 1841 gives us the answer.

Our qualitatively varied sense impressions, we are told, do not themselves belong to the realm of those "cosmological events" in which "matter and its mathematically determinable states of motion" exist. "There is neither light nor darkness without an eye; neither silence nor noise without an ear; neither something heavy nor something light without sensitive nerves. . . . All mechanical processes are merely stimuli. In themselves they are not qualitatively determined causes of that inner world of phenomena" (1841, p. 270). It would be presumptious, however, to maintain that in the colors and sounds and feelings of pleasure, which we encounter in our experience, the profound richness of reality has found perfect manifestation. The fact that the objects of experience and their interactions can be understood in terms of laws and in terms of "aggregates of matter" indicates that there must be more to reality than the shifting spectrum of fleeting sense qualities. Still, "all categories" of the understanding are "subjective phenomena" (p. 301), and it is therefore impossible to speak meaningfully of a reality which, in principle, lies beyond the very possibility of ever becoming an object of experience (p. 280). The question is, How can we surmount the difficulty which is clearly entailed by the nature of our experience itself?

[1] "The beginning of metaphysics is not in metaphysics itself, but in ethics" *Metaphysik*, 1841, p. 329.

If the real world is to be an orderly cosmos, so Lotze now argues, then all events and combinations of events encountered in our experience must be relatable to a "system of inner meanings" through which alone their "right to existence" is assured (p. 264). The laws discovered by science—i.e., the causal laws—cannot provide such meanings; for the ground for the validity of the causal laws cannot itself be a causal law. To assume that it is deprives the principle of explanation itself of validity. The problem can be solved, Lotze holds, if we interpret the facts in the case in terms of purpose. This need not surprise us, he points out, for it is always so: He who inquires into the why? of an event will have received a satisfactory answer only when it has been proven to him that the event was necessary in order that a certain purpose be fulfilled (p. 117). If we accept this "truth," then it follows that "everything that is to be regarded as real must find its place within a context of purposiveness" (p. 118).

When reference is made here to purposiveness and to purpose, it must be understood that no "subjective purpose" of this or that finite individual is meant (*ibid.*). What is meant is that "the ground of a determinate reality lies in that which emerges as the result of the [causal] efficacies, and that what happens to be the last and, therefore, the most dependent stage in the process of events is actually the driving force and the determining factor" behind the whole process (*ibid.*); it is that for the sake of which the process itself occurs. It is "what ought to be" (p. 119). Hence, as Lotze sees it, "nature necessarily brings forth sense impressions." "Only in them does the silent, the invisible world of cosmological entities attain the status of a genuine phenomenon. Sense qualities, and with them our feelings of pleasure and displeasure, thus constitute the foundation of those ideal events to which the dead and unexperienced context of cosmological reality arises" (p. 269), and that reality becomes subsumable under categories. Even now, of course, the qualitative predicates of sense-conditioned experience cannot be applied to reality as it is "in itself." Nor can it be assumed that the subject imposes its categories and concepts upon reality. On the contrary, reality "contains within itself the predestination" to become comprehensible to itself in terms of "determinate concepts" (p. 310).

That is, reality, ever in process, presses on until it culminates in a self-manifestation in experience and under the forms of experience.

To be sure, experience depends on the presence of a subject; but "subjectivity" is itself part of the same real event of which the emergence of the experienced object is another part. Subjective experience, in other words, is itself a real event. "The emergence of subjectivity in opposition to the object is part of what we encounter in the real world" (p. 313). This means that "what really happens" in experience is "the transition from an unknown reality to the phenomenon of cognition"; and "what appears" in experience "can appear only when it relinquishes its for-itself-ness and enters into the modifying light of appearance." "It is, therefore, in reality only what it will be as phenomenon" (p. 314). Although no predicate whatever can be ascribed to it, reality is "predestined" to find its fulfillment as "phenomenon" (*ibid.*). It is of the very nature of reality "to be, to appear, and to cognize." This much at least the actuality of cognition implies (*ibid.*).

But now the question arises, Is there any necessity, any meaning or "inner truth," in the fact that reality emerges as phenomenon? (p. 315). Making use of earlier considerations, and in close agreement with Hegel, Lotze argues that experience, being the last stage in the process of a developing reality, is also the ground and the very reason for that development. The metaphysical categories are the forms under which "things realize their destiny in so far as, in cognition, they become conceptualized" (pp. 318–19). But, while for Hegel "the logical idea is the absolutely valuable, the magnificent [goal] for the sake of which, in the last analysis, the whole unknown mechanism of Being exists" (p. 319), Lotze holds that to regard a merely logical idea as the ultimate goal, "the sum-total of all that ought to be," is to deprive reality of all value (p. 320). He still maintains, however, that "the genuine content of the world is that which ought to be." Such, he says, is "the metaphysical formal definition of the content of the world." But this "formal definition,"—"this relative form of ought . . . is, at the same time, the real form" of the world (p. 324); for "only in this form of the unfulfilled which

finds fulfillment in becoming [an experienced] phenomenon, is
the substance of all that happens what it is" (*ibid.*). However,
"only the good" can be the ultimate meaning of the ought (*ibid.*).
Only the good can be the absolute purpose for the sake of which
everything else exists, for the sake of which "the development of
the real is what it ought to be" (p. 328). And if this is so, then
"the value of subjectivity consists in bringing about the realization" of what ought to be (*ibid.*). All other things and events
have value only to the extent to which they contribute to that realization. In this teleological idealism Lotze's metaphysics finds
its culmination and his value theory its ultimate grounding (p.
329).

But now a specific difficulty arises; and Lotze himself was well
aware of it. The thesis that everything in the world has reality
and value only because it is a stage of transition in the self-manifestation, as phenomenon of experience, of that which, in an ultimate or absolute sense, ought to be, seems to entail a determinism from which there is no escape and which, therefore, robs even
the human being of his dignity as a responsible and creative person. "It would be unbearable," Lotze admits, if "everything that
finite beings do or suffer, hope for or fear, strive after or try to
avert, achieve or fail to achieve were only part of the machinery
or the embellishment which the Divine Spirit uses to present himself the drama of a conceptual unfolding of reality" (*Mikrokosmus*, III, p. 32). It is impossible to believe, Lotze adds, that the
ultimate meaning of our existence is merely to be "a point of
transition for the development of an impersonal Absolute" (*ibid.*).
If we were convinced that this is all that our existence amounts
to, we would refrain from any further effort to accomplish anything, for "we can discover in us no obligation to contribute on
our part to the support of a process which, for itself and for us, is
a matter of indifference" (p. 41). If, however, we could preserve
even under such conditions "the treasure of love, the sense of duty
and sacrifice," we would have to admit that, "in all its finitude
and perishableness, a human heart is an incomparably nobler, a
richer and more sublime being than is the Absolute and its inevitable self-development" (*ibid.*). Moreover, we cannot overlook
the fact that everything that happens in history is brought about

by "the thoughts, the feelings, the passions, and the efforts of individual human beings" (p. 32).

In view of these considerations it is not surprising that Lotze now decides to take a firm stand against all interpretations of reality that acknowledge only the unfolding of facts into new facts, of forms into new forms—interpretations that do not allow for the constant internalization of all these externalities into that which alone has value in the world, and is its truth: the blissfulness or despair, the admiration or contempt, the love and the hate, the joyous certainty and the despairing longing, the nameless suspense and the anxiety characteristic of all life that alone deserves to be called life. "Everything that is fact, thing, property, relation, or occurrence belongs to the realm of factuality which, without being itself good, prepares the ground for the good"— the good having its "sole and necessary place of existence in the vivid feeling of spiritual being " (pp. 43–44).

Thus, at the end of the first period in his philosophical development, Lotze still holds that, in transcending nature, spirit moves on to the realization of a realm of values; but the earlier metaphysical orientation is beginning to give way to what is essentially a psychological approach to values. And it is this approach which, initially at least, characterized the value theories whose authors derived their inspiration from Lotze.

The transition to this new position Lotze actually made in "Ueber den Begriff der Schönheit" (1845). The problem he faced here was to apprehend and to evaluate a specific object or event (the work of art) without viewing it in the perspective of a cosmic self-unfolding or reality. Lotze realized that, in order to be a work of art at all, an object (or an event, such as a symphony) must in itself—i.e., without reference to anything beyond itself— be aesthetically effective and valuable. This aesthetic "atomism," however, demanded at once an admission that we encounter here a multitude of individualized values rather than a system culminating in one highest or absolute value.

Lotze' argument now starts from the fact that any object under consideration—be it fact or value—must always be something which we ourselves can experience ("Schönheit," p. 292). But since experience is not limited to cognition, we may respond to any object with feelings of joy or feelings of grief, or with feelings that are variations of these. Our feelings engulf the objects that arouse them in us; and it is because of these feelings that we value what elicits them in us (*ibid.,* p. 295). An object, therefore, is called beautiful, not because beauty is one of its constitutive attributes, but because it has the capacity to elicit a specific kind of pleasure in a receptive subject (p. 293).

This aesthetic experience is perhaps best characterized as a form of empathy. That is to say, the experiencing subject feels its own affective-conative states as reflexively present in the object. Thus, if a person has once seen a loved one burdened with grief and bent with weariness, he may find that even a sketch, a mere outline, of such a figure awakens in him the same emotional response. He reads the grief and the weariness into the drawing (p. 300). And Lotze, going beyond the aesthetic experience, now argues that *any* object under consideration—be it fact or value— can never be anything other than what we ourselves can experience.

Inherent in this interpretation of experience—and in the interpretation of value experience in particular—is a subjectivism that was totally absent in Lotze's earlier position. However, dissatisfied with these implications of his new approach, Lotze himself now made various attempts to find a value standard that could still claim objective—i.e., universal—validity and thus would enable us to transcend at least a terminal subjectivism. His arguments in the pursuit of this goal are complex, depending in part upon a reconsideration of the subjective ground of value experience, and in part upon an analysis of the function of the objects involved. At times both lines of argument are intertwined; at other times they are kept separate. In the end, however, Lotze was not satisfied with what he had accomplished.

Let us consider, first, his approach to the problem from the side of the subject. After all, the relation of valuations to our various pleasures appears firmly established: We value what gives us pleasure (p. 295). Pleasure, on the other hand, is its own "self-affirmation" as a value. No further reason or justification is required. However, a standard of any kind must remain constant under varying conditions, and a value standard is no exception.

Pleasure, obviously, cannot serve as such a standard. It varies with the needs and the moods of particular individuals in particular situations.

Lotze is quite willing to concede that certain values—especially those of the agreeable and the useful—pertain primarily to the needs and particularities of empirical subjects. In the case of other values, however—of values in the intellectual and spiritual realm —Lotze makes no such concession. Here he demands that our valuations be objective and universally valid; and it is here, of course, that his difficulties arise.

A first suggestion of a possible solution is that we "postulate" a somewhat mystic "universal destiny of mind" (p. 305) which, revealing itself in human experience (and especially, of course, in our cultural achievements) determines the values which we encounter. But Lotze rejects this suggestion as irreconcilable with his empirical approach to all values.

A second suggestion is that we call valuable whatsoever is in harmony, not with just any of our experiences, but with the "patterned sequence" of our presentational experiences and our actions in so far as these are under "the complete dominance of our moral determinations" (p. 301). Such an interpretation, however, leads at once to the conception of a "normal consciousness" as the absolute standard of all valuations. All values of things and events still are values for us and are experienced in the feelings which the valued object elicits in us; but they are true and objectively valid values only when our experience is in harmony with the assumed experiences of the "normal consciousness," when they reflect "the universal and lasting" ideal which "our spiritual life ought to attain" (*Schriften,* III, p. 203).

The particularities of empirical subjects have thus been overcome. But even "universal subjectivity" still remains subjectivity; and the conception of a hypothetical "normal consciousness" as a value standard is inherently so fraught with difficulties—and Lotze himself points this out—that it can hardly be regarded as a solution of the problem for the sake of which it was introduced. Moreover, if "all enjoyment and value of the beautiful" is dependent upon the subject—and this pertains to all other values as well—then the question is: What is left of the valued object itself"? ("Schönheit," p. 304). All that is left, Lotze replies, is that in an encounter with a subject—an encounter which is purely incidental as far as the object is concerned—the object is the "innocent occasion" for the occurrence of a complex affective response of the part of the subject. It is still the subject, in other words, which, in the encounter, spreads "the warmth of its own feelings over the cold light of the object that elicits the experience" (p. 305). It is still the subject which ascribes value to the object."

This means, of course, that value is neither a "quality contitutive of the nature of the object" (p. 309), nor a self-existent ideal entity (p. 310). Values are encountered only in experience, and the reference to a subject cannot be eliminated. But they can perhaps be understood, so Lotze now suggests, when we interpret them as projected "ideals" which give context and meaning to the flux of experienced events. Values would then be anticipations within the cosmic process of "what ought to be" (p. 312). And in this sense, Lotze now holds, it is the "vocation" of beauty in particular to bring about a reconciliation of "stubborn matter" and a "prevailing idea," making the idea come to life in the material (p. 319). Every truly beautiful object—as also every other valued object—thus points beyond itself to that ultimate totality within which we find the focal point of all spiritual forces that indwell the events of the world and give them meaning and direction (pp. 328–29).

We thus find that, during this period of transition in Lotze's philosophical position and despite all arguments, our valuations, though definitely tied to our feelings and feeling-responses, are still seen within the framework of his metaphysics of 1841. As Lotze himself puts it, mind "knows itself as part of a valuable world" and can therefore demand, in the name of that world, that "whatever exists bow to its wishes and that there be revealed, as ultimate goal, the rich blessedness which stems from the harmony of a necessary world order with the eternally justified wishes and aspirations of mind" (p. 332). There is formed in the human mind the image of the prototype of a world in which "the eternal needs of our affections" are reconciled with, and find satisfaction in, what we can know of the whole process of reality's self-manifestation in its "sublime necessity." This vision of an ultimate fulfillment not merely illuminates our enjoyment of beautiful objects; it is also "the living source from which emanate all immortal works of creative art" (p. 333). It gives direction to the movement of the real, setting the goal to be achieved—the goal toward which reality itself presses on in its process of self-manifestation.

The difficulties inherent in this position forced Lotze to modify his views still further. Having introduced feeling-responses as essential to any value ascription, he had to accept the thesis that pleasure (in all its forms and refinements) decisively determines values and value differences (*Mikrokosmus,* II, p. 316). We encounter an object—a thing, a person—(so he now argues) and "take an attitude" toward it. This attitude is reflected in our value judgments: this is beautiful, this is ugly, this is good, this is bad, etc. But now the question is, On what grounds can such judgments be justified? And this question is crucial; for it is evident that value judgments differ in fundamental respects from cognitive judgments. For one thing, they cannot be verified in the same way; and for another, they do not describe objects or assert their existence or non-existence but state that a given object has the power to elicit in a receptive subject a particular kind of pleasure or displeasure.

As he develops his new position, Lotze again accepts as basic to his argument the principle that all values and in whatever sphere of human activity are first encountered in the pleasure we derive from certain objects, events, or situations. Pleasure, however, has frequently been decried as cheap and degrading and not worthy of man's highest aspirations. Although Lotze admits that such a verdict may be justifiable in the case of certain pleasures, he also insists that a reference simply to pleasure, without further qualification as to what is meant in particular situations, is essentially meaningless; for just as color is never actually seen—but only a red color, a yellow color, etc.—so pleasure as such is never experienced, but only pleasure of such or such a specific kind. And as a specific kind, pleasure is not merely subjective; it is object-determined. That is to say, in our subjective experience of a particular pleasure we encounter the objective basis which determines the quality of the experience. Our subjective experience thus points beyond itself and is revelatory of a transcendent realm of "the eternally essential" ("Bedingungen," pp. 205ff). That is to say, Lotze's contention is that, because of their object-determined qualities, our feelings give us knowledge of the very essence of reality. They play a role in our valuations that is strikingly similar to that which perceptions play in scientific cognition. Our valuations are rooted in them, and our value judgments find in them their terminal justification. In this perspective, value is but the conceptual apprehension of what our feelings reveal. It is a category in terms of which we truly apprehend reality and the very essence of individuality as well. The highest value, however, does not correspond to the maximum of pleasure quantitatively calculable as a summation of individual but qualitatively indistinguishable pleasures; it is, rather, the value disclosed to us in the qualitatively highest of all our feelings. And it is this value that is a "norm" for us and for the whole of reality as well.

Whether or not Lotze would have modified his position still further is a mute question. He meant to deal with value-theoretical problems in Part III of his comprehensive *System der Philosophie* but, unfortunately, did not live to carry out his intention. It remains true, however, that many of the ideas found in his earlier writings were taken up and developed extensively by others. Thus, for example, the close connection between value and our affective-conative experiences, which he emphasized, was taken up by Meinong (who, initially, made feelings alone basic) and by von Ehrenfels (who regarded desire as fundamental). Lotze, however, had maintained, not that feelings determine value, but that the object-determined qualitative differences of our feelings disclose "the independent value" of objects to us ("Bedingungen," p. 212)—an idea which Max Scheler was later to develop to the fullest. Lastly, Lotze had said that truths do not *exist* but are merely *valid,* and had argued that "validity" (*Geltung*) is a primitive—i.e., an unanalyzable—concept. Heinrich Rickert based his whole value theory upon this idea of validity—defining value as validity.

BIBLIOGRAPHY

Bamberger, Fritz, *Untersuchungen zur Entstehung des Wertproblems in der Philosophie des 19. Jahrhunderts,* Vol. I, Lotze, Halle, 1924.

Bentham, Jeremy, *The Works of Jeremy Bentham,* 22 volumes, edited by John Bowring, London, 1843; New York, 1962. Vol. I: *The Principles of Morals and Legislation;* Vol. II: "Codification Proposal, Addressed to all Nations Professing Liberal Opinion."

Kraus, Oskar, *Zur Theorie des Wertes: Eine Bentham-Studie,* Halle, 1901.

———*Die Werttheorien: Geschichte und Kritik,* Brünn, 1937.

Lotze, Hermann, *Metaphysik,* Leipzig, 1841.

———"Ueber den Begriff der Schönheit" (1845), in *Kleinere Schriften,* I, edited by David Peipers, Leipzig, 1885.

———"Ueber Bedingungen der Kunstschönheit" (1847), in *Kleinere Schriften,* II, Leipzig, 1886.

———*Mikrokosmus: Ideen zur Naturgeschichte und Geschichte der Menschheit,* 3 volumes, second edition, Leipzig, 1869.

———*Metaphysik,* Leipzig, 1879.

Nietzsche, Friedrich, *The Complete Works of Friedrich Nietzsche,* authorized translation edited by Oscar Levi, London, 1923–24 (reprint). Volume XI: *Thus Spake Zarathustra;* Vol. XII: *Beyond Good and Evil;* Vol. XIII: *The Geneology of Morals;* Vol. XIV/XV: *The Will to Power;* Vol. XVI: *The Twilight of the Idols* and *The Antichrist.*

Werkmeister, W. H., *Theories of Ethics,* Lincoln, Nebraska, 1961.

CHAPTER II

BRENTANO AND THE COGNITION
OF VALUES

Although Lotze envisioned the possibility of a general theory of value and is always given credit for having done so, it was Franz Brentano who actually developed one and whose students carried on the work. It is to Brentano, therefore, that we must turn next.

In his inaugural dissertation of 1866, Brentano maintained, with Thomas Aquinas and Kant, that we call something good because it is desirable; but we call it beautiful because its appearance is desirable. The difference of these two statements, though slight in the linguistic formulations, is crucial in implications; and this the more so since the question of how we know what is desirable was never raised. Brentano had not yet freed himself from the shackles of a philosophical tradition. However, in the years which followed, he became more and more interested in the problems of cognition in the field of values, and his views underwent notable changes.

His lectures at the University of Vienna during the winter semester 1875–76 disclosed for the first time outlines of a position which he formulated more precisely in a lecture delivered on January 23, 1889, before the Wiener Juristische Gesellschaft and subsequently published under the title *Vom Ursprung sittlicher Erkenntnis.* Of this slender volume (barely 40 pages) Oskar Kraus has said that "it has had the greatest influence upon modern value theory. It represents the most important progress in the history of value theory since the days of the Greeks." And when its English translation appeared in 1902, G. E. Moore said: "It would be difficult to exaggerate the importance of this work."

Brentano continued his university lectures on the subject until his retirement in 1894, expanding his arguments and preparing for publication a text which is now available to us in the posthumously published *Grundlegung und Aufbau der Ethik* (1952). Although the title again seems to restrict the discussions to prob-

27

lems of ethics, the book itself is proof that Brentano's intention was much broader; that he aimed at, and in effect developed, a theory which encompasses all our valuations and preferences, the highest as well as the lowest, the moral and the aesthetic as well as the economic and the political. We shall here consider his theory in this broad sense; but in doing so we must go back to 1874 and Brentano's *Psychologie vom empirischen Standpunkt.*

I

The key to Brentano's interpretation of values is his conception of experience as "presentational." There is no hearing without that which is heard; no believing without that which is being believed; no hoping without that which is hoped for; no joy without that which gives joy; and no striving without that which we strive for. Every experience we have involves an object that is being experienced. But the crux of the matter is that the relation of the subject to the object is always one of intentionality. The subject "intends" the object (*Psychologie,* I, pp. 124–25). The Object experienced may be part of an external world or it may be the creation of our imagination. It may be the content of a sense impression—the colors of a rainbow, for example; or it may be an object abstractly conceived in conceptual thinking, such as the idea of mankind. But whatever it is, if it is experienced at all, it is "present" to a subject, "given" in "inner perception" (*innere Wahrnehmung*). This "presentational experience," as we shall call it, is the primary fact basic to all our beliefs, to all our knowledge. It is the ground and warranty of rational inference as well as of all valuations. This is so because, in its very essence, presentational experience, as presentational and, therefore, as "inner," is "self-certifying." It is what it is. The color seen is *this* particular color. The object imagined is *this* object and no other. And the emotion felt is *this* emotion here and now.

However, as we reflect upon our inner experience, we must distinguish between the object experienced and the act of experiencing it: and this is important (pp. 177–79). We must realize, for example, that any reference to things, to an external world, assumes an inference made on the basis of directly experienced phenomena and that, in any particular instance, the inference may be wrong. Whether it is wrong rather than right depends on the warranty for our belief found in the immediacy of our presentational experience itself.

Experience is always the activity of one unitary self-consciousness (pp. 228–32). Analysis will reveal, however, that within the whole of experience three distinct, though interrelated, classes of intentional relations are discernible (*Psych.,* II, Chapter 6). There are, first, the "presentations" (*Vorstellungen*) themselves in the immediacy of their givenness, ranging from sense impressions to abstract ideas. There are, secondly, our judgments which involve an affirmation or denial, if not of the presentational objects themeslves, then at least of their having such and such attributes. And there are, in the third place, our affective and volitional responses to the objects in question, our being attracted or repulsed by them—responses which may vary from an immediate reaction to objects directly "given" in presentational experience to reactions that occur only after full consideration of the complex phenomena involving a choice of goals and of the means to their realization.

When we compare the three classes of intentional relations, we see at once that the second and third are analogous to one another in a very significant sense. The acts involved in both are two-dimensional: affirmation and denial in the one case, attraction and repulsion in the other. No such duality is found when presentational objects are simply "given." But where the dual nature of the experiential acts is encountered, there we also find that the subject's response to an object is either right or it is wrong, and that it must be one or the other. This fact, Brentano holds, is basic to value theory.

Let us consider briefly what is involved here in the case of cognitive judgments. The problem arises only when presentational objects are conceptualized—i.e., when we use concepts to denote them. Judgments based upon such conceptualization are either apodictic or they are assertoric. If they are apodictic, two types are distinguishable. The first is that of analytic judgments. They express (affirm or deny) the interrelation (i.e., the mutual inclusion or the mutual exclusion) of the meanings of the terms involved. If they express that relationship correctly, they are true, and are true beyond question or doubt and, therefore, are true universally. The warranty of their truth lies in themselves.

Apodictic judgments of the second type derive their warranty and therefore their truth from their relation to the "givens" of presentational experience. Thus, the judgment, "What I now see is a specific color pattern," is true, and is indubitably true, if the object I see at that moment is indeed a specific color pattern (the pattern of a rainbow, let us say). And similarly the judgment, "I hope that the war will end soon," is true, and is apodictically true, if it correctly expresses what I actually hope for. It is false if, as a matter of fact, I do not hope that the war will end soon. Judgments of this type, thus, are true not because they are analytic but because they are self-evidential in presentational experience. No argument can prove them to be true or false; only the actualities of immediate experience, being what they are as directly "given," can do it. When true, judgments of this type are also universal in significance—not, of course, in the sense that, when I see a specific color pattern, everybody else must also see it; but in the sense in which it is true that "At such and such a time, X saw a certain color pattern," when X indeed saw that pattern at the specified time. And in this form apodictic judgments of the second type play an important role in our empirical sciences. They are terminal to any process of inquiry.

The case of assertoric judgments is quite different, for these judgments depend on interpolations and logical inference. To establish their truth (or falsity) elaborate chains of proof are often required. And such proofs, in the end, depend upon terminal judgments of the apodictic kind.

Analogous conditions prevail, so Brentano maintains, with respect to our affective-conative responses to the objects of presentational experience. But before we go into this matter, several other facts must be considered.

To begin with, though Brentano clearly distinguishes between judgments and affective-conative responses to the objects of experience, he finds it impossible to separate completely feelings from acts of desire, volition and striving (*ibid.,* p. 84). As he himself puts it, "presentational experience reveals clearly the unity of the basic class of phenomena involving feelings and volitions" (p. 100). To be sure, differences do exist between despair, hope, longing, courage, etc.; but they do not disrupt the unifying texture of the affective-conative character of the experience involved; and the phenomena themselves are not cognitive acts. They do not reveal to us the value or the disvalue of things (p. 89). However, within the whole range of feelings and volitions there is no difference so evident, no pair of opposites so heterogeneous to any other pair as are approval and disapproval, love and hate, when contrasted with cognitive affirmation and negation (pp. 106–7).

Now, it so happens that volition and striving are the very essence of human action. They are not merely the wish or the desire that something be or that it come about; they are, instead, the "bringing about" of something as the consequence of an act. Yet, "volition is impossible [as an actual act] until the subject has attained the conviction or, at the very least, the expectation that certain phenomena of love [or approval] plus desire entail as their immediate or their mediated consequence the objects desired" (p. 115). But if such is the case, then it is necessary to examine more closely the role which approval and desire play in human decisions and actions; and such an inquiry leads us directly to Brentano's value theory.

Before we turn to that theory, however, let us remind ourselves that cognitive judgments as well as all acts of approval and disapproval presuppose and include the whole of our presentational experience. They are dependent upon, and conditioned by, the "givens" of that experience (p. 127). Next to the "presentations" (*Vorstellungen*) themselves, cognitive judgments constitute the class of the simplest experiential facts. They presuppose presentations but do not presuppose approval or disapproval. Approval and disapproval, however, presuppose not only presentations but in many cases judgments as well. Depending on whether a judgment pertaining to an object which we approve (or disapprove) assures us of that object's existence, denies its existence, or renders its existence only probable, our approval (or disapproval) engenders joy, sadness, hope or fear, or some other emotion; and our valuations depend upon this (p. 128).

II

With these preliminary matters out of the way, but retaining them as background for what is to follow, we now turn to Brentano's value theory proper. Basic to that theory is the assumption that, just as cognitive judgments find their terminal justification, their standard of validity, in the facts and conditions of presentational experience, so our value judgments find theirs in our affective-conative responses. Valuations not grounded in these experiences or not justified in terms of them are not true valuations at all.

As previously indicated, Brentano develops his value theory in greatest detail in the posthumously published *Grundlegung und Aufbau der Ethik;* and he does so in critical reaction to essentially the whole history of philosophical ethics, from Plato and Aristotle to John Stuart Mill and Herbart. Hume's view in particular looms large in these discussions (pp. 42–73, and elsewhere). What makes Hume so attractive for Brentano is the emphasis he places upon feelings and upon the role they play in ethics. What Brentano objects to is Hume's "imperfect psychological analysis" of the actual function of feelings in human experience (p. 57).

With Hume, Brentano holds that the ultimate goals of human actions are never determined by reason, and certainly not by reason alone. "They recommend themselves exclusively to our feelings and inclinations" (p. 50). If we ask someone why he takes physical exercises, he may reply that he does so in order to preserve his health. If we now ask why he wants to preserve his health, he may answer that illness is painful. But if we ask further why he dislikes pain, he can give no answer other than that he just does. Freedom from pain is for him an ultimate goal and not a means to something else. It is evident, therefore, that feelings play a crucial part in our knowledge of values. In fact, as perceptions are terminal conditions of cognition, so feelings are terminal in all valuations (pp. 53–4). We begin to understand the meaning of "good" when a "feeling of approval" has been awakened in us (p. 55).

What Hume did not see, according to Brentano, is that, just as we distinguish between perceptual experiences and our knowledge of them, so we must distinguish also between "feelings" *per se* and a "cognition of feelings." The distinction is obvious when today we speak of feelings which we actually experienced yesterday, or when we refer to the feelings of others. But it is equally real—and this is the normal condition—when our present feelings are involved; for we not only experience the feelings but are aware of them also. However,—and this is important for Brentano's value theory—in the immediacy of our experience, our awareness or cognition of the feelings is not a separate act but is part and parcel of the feeling-experience itself. Being aware of our feelings is thus an experience that is strictly analogous to our being aware of perceptions. And it is in this primary sense of an immediate experience that our feelings are the preconditions of value judgments and value principles just as perceptual experiences are the preconditions of cognitive judgments and scientific knowledge (p. 56). They are the empirical ground of all valuations just as perceptions are the empirical ground of all cognitions (pp. 79–87).

It is now necessary to take a closer look at what is involved in this basic situation. We have seen already that analytic judgments are "true" when they correctly affirm or deny the interrelation of the meanings of the terms employed. And we have seen also that empirical judgments are apodictically true or false when they pertain directly to our "inner perceptions"; that is, when they are judgments to the effect that "I exist," that "I see or hear or doubt or fear or hope for something," when at the time of making the judgment I actually do see or hear or doubt, etc. Such judgments are true because they are "correct." Truth means "correct" judgment (p. 141).

It is Brentano's thesis that "good" is to be understood analogously—but at the level of our affective-conative responses. "When we call certain objects good and others bad, we say nothing other than that he who loves [approves] the former and hates [disapproves] the latter takes a right attitude" towards the objects (p. 144). "Right loving" and "right hating" are, thus, the distinguishing marks of correct valuations. Both attitudes must find their terminal justification in the immediacy of our presentational experience.

The question now is: How do we know when a love (or a hate) is "right"? Are we to assume that whatever is being loved or whatever can be loved is by virtue of that fact alone lovable and good? Such an assumption is totally unacceptable; for, as Brentano points out (*Ursprung,* p. 18), one person may love what another person hates, and the same person may at one time hate what at another time he loves. Actually loving something no more proves the correctness of that love than the affirmation expressed in a judgment proves the truth of that judgment. The ground of correctness, as that of validity, must lie in something other than the acts of loving or judging themselves.

If we were to deny that there exists a distinction between correct and incorrect loving, between correct and incorrect approval, we would err in one or the other of two diametrically opposed ways; for we might hold (a) that *all* acts of approval are correct; or we might hold (b) that *no* act of approval is correct. In either case, the conception of the good as that which is "worthy of approval"—as distinguished from merely being approved—would be meaningless. The result would be a subjectivism comparable to that advocated by Protagoras with respect to truth and falsity. Man is the measure of all things, this subjectivism would hold, of the good that it is good, and of the bad that it is bad. According to such a view, something could be regarded as good and as bad at the same time. It would be good according to all who love it, and bad according to all who hate it; and "de gustibus non est disputandum." But such a view, Brentano maintains, is absurd and a falsification of the meaning of "good" in the same sense in which Protagoras' view was a falsification of the meaning of truth (p. 55). Aristotle had already pointed out this parallelism (*Metaphysics,* K6, 1062b13; 1063a5) and had distinguished between correct and incorrect desires, arguing that what actually is desired is not necessarily always the good (*De Anima,* III, 10), and not every pleasure is good; for finding pleasure in what is bad is itself bad (*Nicomachean Ethics,* X, 2). With these views Brentano is in complete agreement (*Ursprung,*

p. 58). They are essential to his thesis that *correct* loving and *correct* hating are basic to all our valuations.

At the lowest level of experience, to love joy rather than sadness, pleasure rather than pain, is a "right" love. If someone were to love sadness and pain rather than pleasure and joy, we would regard this as unnatural. The approval of joy (in all its variations) and the disapproval of sadness (and its variations) can therefore be characterized as "right"—as "right love" and "right hate," respectively (p. 21).

At a higher level of experience it is evident that to love or approve knowledge and to hate error is also the "right" attitude to take; and, surely, this is not simply a matter of taste. Indeed, to love error and to hate truth would be a perversion of our own rational nature (p. 20).

And, finally, an example of right loving is furnished also by our affective-conative responses themselves. Just as the correctness of a judgmental act is rightfully approved, so the rightness of an act of approval (or disapproval) is itself rightly loved. But a wrong love—a love of what is evil, for example—deserves our disapproval and is therefore hated with a hate that is right (p. 21). However, in order that an affective-conative act be entirely good, two conditions must be fulfilled: (1) The act must be right; and (2) it must be an act of approval, not of disapproval. Malicious joy, being a wrong love, violates the first condition and is therefore not entirely good—even though it is an experience of joy. Disapproval of injustice, though in itself right, fails to fulfill the second condition and, therefore, is also not entirely good. If an act fails to fulfill both conditions, it is, of course, that much the worse (*ibid.*, p. 60).

If all this is granted, then a first step has been taken toward an understanding of Brentano's theory of value. A further step is taken when we accept as crucial his distinction between a lower and a higher self (*Grundlegung,* p. 145). The former, he maintains, manifests itself in our animal needs and desires; whereas the latter finds expression in our intellectual and spiritual needs and aspirations. The testimony of philosophers from Plato and Aristotle to John Stuart Mill and beyond supports Brentano on this point. The distinction implies an approval of the higher forms of consciousness and human actions which, according to Brentano, is analogous to evidence in the case of cognitive judgments. If there should be human beings capable of rational judgments and valuations who yet hold the opposite view—regarding man's animal nature as being of greater value than are his specifically human characteristics—we should say, not that this is simply a matter of personal preference or taste, but that such preference is a perversion; that it indicates a wrong "love" and a wrong "hate." But when we find in us the "natural approval" of the characteristically human qualities of human existence, then "we apprehend the object not only as loved but as *worthy of love*" (p. 146)—i.e., as loved with a "right" love.

Still another problem arises; for there is much in our experience that we love with a right love and that we, therefore, acknowledge to be good. But the question is: What among all that is good—especially among the attainable good—is better? What is the highest attainable practical good so that we may make it the goal of our actions? The answer to this question depends, of course, on the meaning of "better." It is easy, Brentano believes, to go astray at this point; for a plausible misinterpretation is at once at hand. If "good" is what is being loved with a "right love," so it may seem, then the "better" is what is loved with a greater love. It is Brentano's argument, however, that "to love with a greater love" cannot possibly mean to love with a greater intensity; for if this were the meaning, then it would follow that in every concrete situation in which one enjoys something, only a certain measure of enjoyment is permitted, whereas it cannot possibly be reprehensible to enjoy wholeheartedly and with great intensity something that is truly good—even if it is not the highest good. Moreover, if the "better" were taken to mean "greater intensity of approval," one would have to survey in every instance of possible approval all that could possibly be approved in order to determine the proper degree of intensity of the actual approval; and such a survey and comparison are manifestly impossible. The degree of intensity, therefore, does not provide a criterion of the "greater love" (*Ursprung*, p. 22).

At this point the analogy with presentational and judgmental experiences breaks down; for truth has no degrees. What is true is true, and that is all there is to it. "Better," however, (and "worse") implies degrees of goodness (or badness) (*Grundlegung,* p. 147). As Brentano sees it, to recognize something as "better" than something else means to "prefer" it with a "right preference" (p. 148), the "worse" being but the reverse of the "better.'

But now again a crucial distinction must be made; for many of our "preferences" are purely instinctive and "blind." Others, however, are expressive of our intellectual activities; and it is these that are decisive for value theory. We not only love knowledge with a love that is "right," but we also prefer it to "mere faith" and to error with "a preference that can be characterized as being right"; and we "rightly prefer" "knowledge combined with joy" to "mere knowledge without joy." We know that "the whole" in this case is "better" than any of its parts (*ibid.*).

In summary form Brentano's basic position is this: He holds that (1) anyone who acknowledges something as cognitively evident and thus forms a "right judgment" acknowledges something as in some sense existent; (2) anyone who loves something with a "right love" and knows himself as loving it with a right love knows something as "good"; and (3) anyone who prefers something with a "right preference" and knows himself as preferring it with a right preference knows something to be "better" than something else (pp. 148–49).

If it should now be argued that in our human situation one person may love or prefer what another person hates or rejects; or that the same person may at one time love or prefer what at another time he himself hates or rejects; and that this fact entails a complete subjectivism; then Brentano replies that to argue so is to overlook the distinction (made above) between man's instinctive and blind responses and his intellectual and spiritual activities. While instincts and feelings *per se* may be purely subjective and may have no validity beyond the passing moment, the role which feelings play at the intellectual level is precisely the same that perceptions play in cognition; and no one would maintain that because empirical knowledge is terminally grounded in perception it must be completely subjective.

One further point is important. All right acts of loving and preferring are directed toward conceptualized objects. In so far, therefore, as a conceptualized idea of cognitive significance is foundational to our affective-conative responses, the latter are analogous not only to assertoric cognitions but to apodictic cognitions as well. That is to say, as we perceive in us an act of right love or right preference, we comprehend as with one stroke the goodness of the whole class of objects subsumable under one concept (p. 150).

III

So far we have considered only the barest outlines of Brentano's theory. We must now deal with it in greater depth. Methodologically our task will be simplified if we try to understand what Brentano meant by "the highest practical good." His interpretation of it is rooted in an analysis of the psychological aspects of human existence; and to this analysis we must therefore turn next.

As we have seen, Brentano distinguished between three fundamental classes of mental phenomena: presentational experiences (*Vorstellungen*), judgments, and affective-conative responses. In each of these classes some of the constituents are good or valuable, and some are preferred to others (p. 183). Knowledge, for example, which is a matter of judgment, is good; and love of knowledge is a right love. The more universal and penetrating our knowledge is—i.e., the more it leads to the discovery of new truths—the greater is its value. Also, basic insights and insights into laws—such as Newton's law of gravitation—are more valuable than is knowledge of, say, the characteristics of a certain species of plants. And just as knowledge is good, so error is bad (p. 184); and the love of error is a wrong love.

Since knowledge is good, the search for knowledge is also good; but it is good primarily as a means, and "the goal is of greater value than are the means" (p. 185).

Pleasure also is "something good in itself," and is loved with a right love. Its opposite, pain, is hated with a right hate and in itself is an evil. But as long as pleasure and pain are merely bodily responses, they are essentially instinctive and blind, and are therefore less valuable than is the joy which we experience at the intellectual or the spiritual level. Who would compare, Brentano asks, the pleasure of smoking a good cigar with the enjoyment of a Beethoven symphony?

But let us consider the basic class, the class of presentational experiences, in greater detail.

It goes without saying that we love many of these experiences, and that we love some of them to a high degree. Even a child may find hearing and seeing something rather enjoyable; although, of course, the reverse is also true. We read the works of poets and novelists, listen to music, look at paintings—and we do all this because we take pleasure in presentational experiences. It is immaterial whether the objects of such experiences actually exist or are the creations of our imagination. We are satisfied simply having the experience, and we enjoy having it. To be sure, if we have several presentational experiences at the same time, our enjoyment may be lessened—not because the experiences, when considered individually, are not good, but because, when taken together, they may clash and thus interfere with one another. Nevertheless, if confronted with a choice between unconscious existence or having presentational experiences of some kind, Brentano maintains, we would no doubt choose the latter, knowing that as a manifestation or an enrichment of life presentational experiences of any kind have a value (p. 189).

If it now be argued that, even so, not all presentational experiences are good; that, in fact, some of them are repugnant to us, Brentano's reply is that, in their direct immediacy, presentational experiences simply are what they are. They are no more actual valuations than perceptions *per se* are knowledge. Only right love and right hate determine their value or disvalue, as the case may be.

Among our presentational experiences we encounter "the agreeable," "the beautiful," and their respective counterparts: "the disagreeable," and "the ugly." All of them are determined by right love and right hate. This means that "the ugly" is what is hated with a right hate. But since "the ugly" is an object of presentational experience, this means that at least some presentational experiences are bad—a conclusion which obviously contradicts the thesis that all presentational experiences are good. In order to avoid this contradiction Brentano examines at length what is meant by "beautiful" and what by "ugly." The discussion is somewhat simplified, however, by the fact that "the beautiful" is taken to be a form of "the agreeable," "the pleasing." Their difference is that "the pleasing" simply pleases, whereas "the beautiful" is acknowledge to elicit a pleasure that is right.

People in general, so Brentano points out, call that beautiful whose appearance can, for its own sake, be preferred to ordinary appearances and can be so preferred with a right love—i.e., with a love expressive of good taste; and they regard it to be the mission of the artist not only to create for us the occasion for presentational experiences but to "awaken in us to a high degree a pleasure characterized as right" (p. 194). In order to achieve all this, the artist seeks to avoid as far as possible that which displeases and detracts from our enjoyment. He uses discordant elements only so that through their suspension or resolution he can heighten our pleasure. In art, therefore,—and especially in music, the drama, and the novel—a sequence of agreeable and disagreeable or displeasing moments has its proper place. Only if the tensions are not resolved in the end do they become torture and, therefore, a disvalue. What the artist should aim at is the perfection of a presentational experience and the highest possible degree of a "right pleasure." Even our instinctive and blind affective responses called forth by the experience should be made to serve that pleasure. But when art is made the servant of sensuality, "it ceases to be a fine art and sinks to the level of a culinary art that aims in the most cunning way to please the palate" (p. 198). And when, through his work, the artist calls attention to his skill rather than to the beauty of the presentation, he may create pleasure for us—even a legitimate pleasure—but it is not the pleasure of the beautiful. The true artist, avoiding such mannerisms, achieves his highest triumphs when the person beholding the art work forgets the artist as well as himself in his enjoyment of the beautiful.

Despite these excursions into the realm of aesthetics, Brentano's real purpose at this time was to justify his thesis that all presentational experiences are good because they can be loved with a right love. What he has accomplished is to point up the fact that, as far as he is concerned and within the range of what is pleasing, presentational objects are beautiful when they elicit and justify a particularly high degree of pleasure. In this perspective, the displeasing and the ugly are but deficiencies of what might otherwise be beautiful; they do not contradict the thesis that all presentational experiences, simply as presentational, are good; that an increase in the range of our presentational experiences is, therefore, an increase of what is valuable and good. But since presentational experiences are basic to all other mental activities, it follows that every mental activity is in itself valuable or good (p. 201); and this fact opens up broader perspectives of value theory.

IV

To begin with, if presentational experiences can be loved with a right love, there is no reason whatever why we cannot love (i.e., approve of) the experiences of other persons as well as our own. The facts in the case surely support the thesis that, in our love, we are not confined to our own limited sphere. Nobody would regard the statement "X takes an interest in the happiness of Y" as self-contradictory; and all might agree that to prefer a much greater good of others, and especially of many others, to one's own smaller good is a right preference. Indeed, people have sacrificed themselves for others—"a friend for a friend, a mother for her child, a patriot for his country, a fanatic for an idea" (p. 203)—and they have done so because they have valued more what they died for than they valued their own life. Even Bentham admits that people take pleasure in the happiness of others, and that their pleasure is good.

But it is not only the happiness of others in which we can take an interest and which we can love with a right love. Other aspects of human experience—be it our own or that of others—may equally well find our approval or disapproval.

To be sure, we have so far spoken only of presentational experiences, of pleasure, of happiness, and of knowledge—our own and that of others. We have said that they are good. All of them, however, are forms of mental states or mental activities; and the question now is, Is something other than mental states or activities good in itself or is everything we call good good only because of its relation to some specific human experience? Are plants, for example, simply as plants and in themselves, good? Is their organismic structure in itself valuable? Is a thing—not seen in the perspective of utility but simply as thing—good? A metaphysician may find these questions challenging. From Brentano's point of view—i.e., from the point of view of a general value theory which is empirically grounded and which is to serve as a guide for human actions—the answer is quite simple. Since the basic thesis is that valuable or good is only that which is or that which can be loved with a right love, and since neither plants nor things are capable of such love, their value depends entirely on their relation to human experience. This means that only mental states and activities—our own and those of other persons—are in themselves valuable and good. Only they can be loved with a love whose rightness is evident because terminally grounded in the immediacies of presentational experience—just as the truth of cognitive judgments finds terminal verification only in perception. But if this is so, then only presentational experiences, cognitions, and affective-conative responses are good or valuable in themselves. It is not necessary that all human beings accept for themselves and as their goal the same good. It is necessary, however, that all acknowledge as good what is worthy of a right love (pp. 209–210)—just as all must acknowledge as true what is stated in a true judgment.

Further analysis of "right preference" will now bring us closer to an understanding of what Brentano means by "the highest practical good."

The "better," so he has argued, is whatever is preferred with a right preference. We must now note that different experiential situations may involve different types of preference. There is, first, the situation in which we prefer something that is good, and known to be good, to something that is bad, and known to be bad. We thus prefer joy to suffering, and knowledge to error; and such preferences are right. There are, secondly, situations in which we prefer the existence of something good to its non-existence, or the non-existence of something bad to its existence. Related to these situations are our preferences for something entirely good as against the same good with an admixture of what is bad, or for something only partly bad as against the same thing when it is entirely bad. Related to these situations are also those in which we prefer the whole of the good to any part of it, but a part of the bad to the whole of it. We thus prefer with a right preference the happiness of a lifetime to the pleasures of a passing moment, and the pains of that moment to the unhappiness of the days and years yet to follow.

Our preference is right also in situations in which, of two anticipated events that are equally good, we prefer the one most likely to be realized. And situations arise in which right preference pertains, not to "greater sums" of the good, but to qualitative distinctions between what is valued. Under otherwise equal circumstances, positive knowledge is thus to be preferred to negative knowledge. Although, in themselves, right loving and right hating are always good, the experience of right loving is preferable to that of right hating because the latter involves always something that is bad, whereas the former does not. Similarly, though pleasure is always good, pleasure taken in what is good is "better" than pleasure taken in what is bad; it is preferred with a right preference. Finally, a process which leads from what is bad to waht is good, or from a lesser to a greater good, is "better" than one moving in the opposite direction. It, too, is preferred with a preference that is right (pp. 211–214).

A special problem arises when preferences pertain to different classes of goods; when we must choose between goods of essentially different types. For instance, is pleasure more valuable than knowledge? Is knowledge better than right love? How can we determine the rank-order of such diverse goods? More specifically, how can we determine whether or not a specific item of knowledge is better than a pleasure which we are now experiencing; or whether or not some other person's virtue is better than our own knowledge? The historical controversies that have centered around these questions are sufficient proof that no reliable criterion for the solution of the problem can be found. But this fact, Brentano points out, proves nothing against all those situations in which we are capable of preferences that are right. And *"right is in all situations to love and to prefer in accordance with the degree of the value"* (p. 216. Italics in the original), to prefer the higher to the lesser good.

V

Up to this point we have discussed right loving and right preferring as such. We must now augment this discussion in a very important respect.

We may, of course, and often do love and prefer something that is "given" and, being "given," is beyond our control. Right loving and right preferring may in that case be said to have theoretical significance only. But we may also love and prefer something that is not simply "given" but is in our control, something that we can alter or even create. Right loving and right preferring have in this case a practical significance as well—the significance, namely, of serving as guides for our actions. The problems which here arise are the concern of our "practical disciplines," of which ethics is the highest. Whatever solution it provides for the problems in question will be valid for the other disciplines also.

Now, as a practical discipline, ethics is concerned not only with right loving and right preferring but with choice and volition as well. In fact, choice and volition are its primary concern. But to understand what is involved here, we must first clarify Brentano's distinction between preference and choice.

Preference, he argues, is the broader of the two concepts; for every choice is a preference, but not every preference is a choice. We may, for example, prefer a cool summer evening to a stormy winter day; but we have no choice in the matter. In order for a preference to become a choice, two conditions must be fulfilled: the preferenec must be directed toward something which we ourselves can control or bring about; and there must be a decision to act (p. 218). It is perfectly possible for us to love (or approve of) two "things" which are incompatible when brought together. We may love to solve mathematical puzzles and to write poetry. Our love for the one does not preclude our love for the other. In specific situations, however, we may have to decide in favor of one or the other; and the decisions are incompatible. But a decision in this sense alone is not sufficient for action and is therefore not really a choice. We must also be able to bring about what we have decided upon. Volition and choice are therefore essentially the same.

But now the question is, When is a decision the right one? Brentano's answer is obvious. The decision is right when we choose "the best possible of whatever is attainable" (p. 221). The problem, however, is not as simple as it appears to be at first glance; for in order to ascertain what that "best possible" is, we must take into consideration not only the immediate results of the action contemplated, but its far-reaching consequences as well; and we have no *a priori* knowledge of those consequences. Only past experience, and perhaps only the experience of a lifetime can give our conjectures a certain degree of probability. The situation is still further complicated by the fact that we must make appropriate conjectures for all alternative courses of action that are possible in the given situation, and must compare the anticipated results as to the values involved. Only when this has been done can we determine with some degree of probability what in that situation the highest practical good really is. And only the choice of that good is the right choice.

From these general considerations it is evident that the realm of the highest practical good encompasses everything that might be affected or controlled by our actions. This includes not only our own self, our family, our nation, all of mankind, but the whole range of the living world (for animals also experience pleasure and pain), and the distant future no less than the present. To further as far as possible what is good or valuable in this great realm is "the right purpose of life"—a purpose that gives meaning and significance to all our actions. It is "the one, the highest commandment which human understanding can discover; all others depend upon it" (p. 222).

But Brentano is a realist who is well aware of the limitations of human insights and human capabilities. He therefore guards against the "enthusiasts" who, in a spurious love of "all there is," forget the actualities of their own existence and "reach for the impossible." They forget that the part we play in the realization of the "noblest goals" depends on many conditions, and that our influence is to a large extent indirect rather than immediate. Our practical concern must therefore be primarily with the means rather than the goal; and our duties lie, first of all, in the area of the "useful" and the "harmful."

To be sure, what is useful or harmful in a given situation is in part beyond our control; but some of it at least we can alter or even create. And of the latter we can realize some with certainty and some with probability only. Also, something is useful (or harmful) to a particular person or to a group of persons, and not to others; and usefulness and harm may themselves be specific or they may be ill defined. In making our choices we must allow for all this.

Among the pre-eminently "useful" Brentano counts (on the "personal side") life, health, vigor, beauty, and intellectual and emotional dispositions that make possible a rational and stable life, a good memory, the power to observe, to think abstractly, knowledge, good taste, moral virtues. These goods, however, are augmented by the necessities of life, by what provides pleasure and serves as a means toward the realization of valued ends, and by social conditions which enhance our chances of realizing what is good: a high cultural level of the society into which we were born or in which we find ourselves, a high moral and intellectual climate, flourishing arts and sciences, but especially social justice and equitable laws, protection of the fruits of our labor, peace, and the peaceful cooperation of the diverse social classes. Does the society in which we live have a need for the values which we, because of our specific endowments, can contribute to its progress? What is the artist, the scientist, the philosopher if nobody values his greatest achievements? Human beings are often blind as to who are the true benefactors of mankind and condemn them to a life of martyrdom. At times nothing would be more necessary than to destroy the evil of hating other nations. But this necessity does not prevent people from celebrating the instigators of such hatred as patroits while decrying the advocates of reason and justice as traitors (pp. 225–28).

Underlying Brentano's argument throughout is the assumption that we may expect more good than evil from the continuation of

the life of individuals and of mankind as a whole. But this assumption cannot be justified on empirical grounds. At this point,
therefore, Brentano must make an appeal to metaphysics; but
he makes it only in passing. His own position, however, is theistic;
for as a theist he can view human existence as rooted in an eternal order of law. He knows that, in pursuing at all times the best
that is possible for him, he "stands in the service of a development
for which there can never come an end" (p. 231)—an ever continuing pursuit of the highest practical good.

VI

The brief reference to his own theistic orientation does not seriously affect Brentano's empirical approach to value theory. As
a matter of fact, that approach again dominates his discussions
of what are pre-eminently problems in the field of ethics. His
analysis of the free-will problem (pp. 235–299), for example, is
throughout empirical in orientation. Arguing effectively against
both, indeterminism and a mechanistic determinism, he points out
that we are free in the morally relevant sense only when, and
to the extent to which, our knowledge of the good and the better
becomes the determining ground or motive for our actions. We
are free, that is, when our love of the good determines what
we do.

Even so, however, it would be helpful if rules specifying the
best possible order of preferences were available. The general
maxim, "always choose the best possible of what is attainable,"
though basic, is not sufficiently specific to be of great help; and
the appeal to "the highest practical good" is but another form
of that same maxim. Moreover, as we make our every-day decisions, it is not always possible to keep "the highest practical
good" in mind. What is possible, however, is that we act the
way one reasonably would in order to reach a certain goal. That
is to say, one plans one's actions and then proceeds according
to the plan. More specifically, in order to realize one's intension
of pursuing "the highest possible good," one projects a life-plan
and, since a lifetime consists of successive days, one plans each day
in conformity with the life-plan and resolutely adheres to it.

"Only thus does one's life attain a noble unity" (p. 309). Foundational to such a life-plan are, of course, right loving and right preferring, and a knowledge of one's own possibilities and powers. And since no individuals are alike and all find themselves in different circumstances, no one life-plan can possibly suit all. In principle, therefore, each and every one of us must determine for himself what in his particular situation the highest attainable practical good may be (p. 333).

In actuality, however, this radical indiviualism is modified by the fact that, in a less rigorous sense, human situations generally have important features in common, and that it is therefore possible to classify them and to formulate rules of conduct for the members of the respective classes. Such rules define the "duties" of the members (p. 336).

Every human being, examining his own concrete situation and that of others, and being reasonable about it, could come to the conclusion that someone else is better qualified than he is to act in a certain "sphere of influence," while he himself is better in some other sphere. Such insight could lead to a natural division of spheres of effectiveness and entail, in effect, the state of "natural law" in a given society. Unfortunately, this ideal situation does not exist. Not all human beings are guided in their actions by the conception of "the highest practical good"; and even if they were, not all have sufficient insight and understanding to define or assign the spheres of action in the interest of the highest good. Even the best of intentions would not compensate for this fact. Dissentions and conflicts would be unavoidable. It is for this reason that agreements must be reached among individuals for a co-operative pursuit of the highest good. Such agreements entail the formulation of rules and regulations, and "positive law" thus supplements and codifies "natural law" (p. 350).

Actually, three levels of law are discernible: that of natural law, that of positive law sanctioned exclusively by moral considerations, and that of positive law sanctioned by external authority. These levels, however, must not be taken as successive stages in a historical development. Moral considerations as sanctions for positive law are far from prevalent even today; but laws, even when imposed by external authority, are better than no law at all.

There is, nevertheless, a limit beyond which a deviation of positive law from natural law cannot be tolerated—a limit beyond which revolt is morally justified (p. 352). Brentano himself, however, advocates not so much "the violent resistance of the revolutionary" as "the passive but unbending resistance of the martyr."

The fact remains that in the communal effort to attain the highest possible practical good, law—be it natural or positive law—is indispensable; but so, according to Brentano, is personal property. Only if every member of the community—especially, however, every responsible member—has exclusive control over a given sphere is communal living a blessing (p. 261). The question, of course, is: What is meant by "property"?

There can be no doubt, Brentano maintains, that every member of a community should "own" his own person, his own "body and soul." But what about material goods? Here the opinions have varied greatly in the course of time. There are the extremists who defend rigid and limitless property rights; and there are those who, like Beccaria, maintain that "property is a horrible and by no means necessary right"; or who assert with Proudhon that "property is theft." However, neither the historical debate nor the actual practice entailed by some of the theories is here under consideration. Brentano's contention is that personal freedom and a division of labor—both of which are necessary for the pursuit of the highest practical good and are therefore morally justified—are impossible unless the individual human being has exclusive control over certain things as his property. He is in need of them not only for his bodily existence but for the acquisition of intellectual and spiritual goods as well. This does not mean that personal property is an absolute right; for what belongs to us is but entrusted to us "in the service of the good." "Duties of love," if not "duties of law,"—i.e., considerations of the highest possible practical good—impose upon us the obligation to make the best possible use of what belongs to us in the pursuit of the highest good. But this means that, at least in a limited range, we control our state of affairs. If the state alone were the owner of property, it alone would be the master, and its subjects would be slaves—a situation irreconcilable with the principles of a liberal state.

It is perfectly true, Brentano admits, that today the distribution of goods is not equitable; that we have a surplus of riches on the one hand, and dire poverty on the other. "How often has not wealth been purchased with the misery and the tears of others, and how often is it not used wrongly!" (p. 366). But perhaps the time will come when society will demand of the wealthy an accounting of their stewardship; and public opinion will demand a greater concern for the highest possible practical good. The state itself may play an important role in this connection; for, as Aristotle already maintained, the state came into being and continues to exist only for the purpose of sustaining and enhancing the good life (p. 401). Among its concerns, therefore, is the security of its citizens and the protection of their rights and their property.

But the state is not simply an "insurance institute"—Brentano's reaction to Hobbes!—which provides "security for its citizens in return for their obedience" (*ibid.*). And neither is it a police state. It is concerned also with the enactment of laws equitable to all, and with the distribution of wealth most conducive to the welfare of all. "An unjust distribution is a curse for the very rich no less than for the very poor; for it is the source of immorality in the one case as in the other" (p. 402). But Brentano does not advocate a "brutal interference with historically developed ownership relations," for to do so might entail disastrous consequences. He believes, however, that "experience seems to show that, under certain circumstances, economically well-considered laws can have a beneficial influence or can even be the only means of preventing great evils" (p. 402), the goal and the basis for judgment being always the realization of the highest possible practical good.

VII

And so it is evident that Brentano's value theory has, in effect, covert the whole range of value problems; that it is indeed a general theory of value. Subsequent investigations revealed, however, that the problems involved in the whole field of values are much more complex than Brentano suspected. In making acts of right love, of right hate, and of right preference the basis for his interpretation of the good, Brentano apparently freed value theory from metaphysical entanglements, and this in itself was a great achievement; for it was the inception of value theory as an independent branch of philosophy. However, Brentano himself had to assume the essential rationality of human nature and to interpret the course of human history as a progressive and unending unfolding of that rationality; and these are matters which lead us right back into problems of metaphysics. Moreover, Brentano assumed that there are only three distinct levels of experience—the merely presentational, the judgmental, and the affective-conative. The last of these includes the acts of right loving, right hating, and right preferring—the acts, that is, which determine what is good, what is bad, and what is better. However, the fusion of the affective and the conative aspects of experience which Brentano here assumed was rejected by Meinong and von Ehrenfels, who insisted that a distinction must be made between feeling and desire. But when this distinction is made, then Brentano's definition of the good is no longer acceptable; for the question now is: Should the good be defined in terms of feelings or in terms of desire? And to this question Meinong and von Ehrenfels gave diametrically opposed answers, one accepting feeling as basic, the other making desire foundational. We shall deal with both views in the chapters which follow.

BIBLIOGRAPHY

Brentano, Franz, *Psychologie vom empirischen Standpunkt,* Vol. I, Leipzig, 1874, Vol. II, Leipzig, 1911. Second edition, edited by Oskar Kraus, Vols. I and II, Leipzig, 1924.

———*Vom Ursprung sittlicher Erkenntnis,* Leipzig, 1889. Second edition, edited by Oskar Kraus, Leipzig, 1921. Translated by Cecil Hague as *The Origin of the Knowledge of Right and Wrong,* Westminster, 1902.

———*Grundlegung und Aufbau der Ethik,* edited by Franziska Mayer-Hillebrand, and posthumously published, Bern, 1952.

Eaton, Howard O., *The Austrian Philosophy of Value,* Norman, Oklahoma, 1930.

Kastil, A., *Die Philosophie Franz Brentanos,* Bern, 1950.

Kraus, Oskar, *Franz Brentano: Zur Kenntnis seines Lebens und seiner Lehre,* München, 1919.

———*Die Werttheorien: Geschichte und Kritik,* Brünn, 1937.

CHAPTER III

MEINONG'S APPROACH AND ITS MODIFICATIONS

Brentano's thesis that values and valuations are a matter of "right loving" and "right hating" assumed that our value experience is at once affective and conative; that it involves feelings no less than our attitudes toward them. But the question soon arose as to which should be regarded as basic—the feelings or the attitudes? It was Meinong's contention that our feelings are decisive; and he set out to prove it. However, in the course of more than twenty years of work in the field of value theory, Meinong's views underwent significant changes—changes which can be fully understood only when we consider them in their historical sequence. We shall therefore begin our interpretation of Meinong's theory with a discussion of his views as presented in Part I of *Psychologisch-Ethische Untersuchungen zur Werth-Theorie* (1894) and in "Ueber Werthaltung und Wert" (1895). We shall then examine the works of the transition period: *Ueber Annahmen* (1902), "Ueber Urteilsgefühle" (1906), and "Ueber emotionale Präsentation" (1917). And finally, we shall concentrate on *Zur Grundlegung der Allgemeinen Werttheorie*, which, posthumously published in 1923, gives us a systematic formulation of his final position.

I

Although Meinong was one of Brentano's students, he never in any way referred to his teacher's work in value theory. Strained personal relations (referred to by Oskar Kraus in *Franz Brentano*) may have had something to do with this fact. Nevertheless, for Meinong, as for Brentano, an initial psychological orientation served as the starting-point for his value theory. Strictly speaking, so both maintained, there are no problems which do not have their psychological aspects. Not only a question but also that with which the question is concerned is, first of all, something an

52

individual encounters in his own experience. The value phenomena, in particular, are no exception. They occur exclusively in our affective-conative responses and can be described only with reference to those responses (*Untersuchungen,* p. 4); and this fact is of special significance to the value theorist. Since all of our experiences (no matter what is involved) actually do, or potentially may, affect our emotions, a value theory keyed to our emotional responses is capable of encompassing the whole range of human experience. It is limited neither to problems of ethics nor problems of economics but, in principle, involves all aspects and areas of our interests and actions, and in this sense is indeed a general theory of value.

In the past, economic theories rather than any others have been concerned with the broad aspects of value problems and have been technically the most precisely formulated interpretations. Some of the key ideas of economic value theory may therefore still play an important role in general value-theoretical considerations. One of these ideas (apparently also supported by common sense) is that a thing has value for us only in so far as it satisfies our needs (p. 6). The thesis seems simple and straightforward. Yet, the question inevitably arises, Just what is meant here by "needs"? And once this question is being asked, it is evident that the answer, whatever it may be, must in one way or another refer to our affective experience. We thus have a need for something when we feel a deficiency or experience a displeasure because of the absence or non-existence of whatever is involved. But if this is our meaning, then what about the value of things that does not depend upon a prior experience of a need? Instances of this kind are by no means rare. In all such cases it seems preferable to interpret value in terms of utility rather than in terms of need. Economic theory and common sense appear to favor such a view. Actually, however, this thesis also does not solve all problems. The much-debated question now is, What is the relation of utility to value, and vice versa? Common sense may take for granted that what is of no use for anything also has no value. But such a simplicistic belief leads to various paradoxes. Thus, if value is to be equated with usefulness, how does it happen that, under ordinary circumstances, such useful things as air and water have no value? In order to account for facts such as this, the economists developed the idea of marginal utility. But is this idea universally applicable? Meinong maintains that it is not. Moreover, if we wish to make utility the key idea in value theory, we must first specify what we mean by "useful." We may say, for example, that a thing is "useful to me" when—directly or indirectly—it gives me a feeling of satisfaction, a feeling of pleasure, or when it sustains such a feeling that was previously aroused. In brief, we may say that anything is useful if it causes pleasure and, in an extended sense, if it prevents or dissolves displeasure.

But, again, the interpretation is too simple; for cases occur in which utility is not identical with "causing pleasure." One such case, for example, is that of a child who is being taught how to write. We would all admit that being able to write is useful even if, at the beginning of the learning process, the child has nothing to write about and derives no pleasure from acquiring the ability to write. Where, in this case, is the cause of pleasure? If we mean that the ability to write will be useful in the future (even though it is not useful now), we have already separated utility from an actual pleasure-causing. And even if the ability to write causes pleasure at some future time, we cannot overlook the fact that to cause pleasure is something quite different from causing (or bringing about) a cause of pleasure. But consider another example. Let us suppose that we are enjoying a beautiful sunset. Here we have a direct causation of pleasure. But is the sunset useful? As the term "useful" is ordinarily understood, it is not. It does not seem reasonable, therefore, simply to identify utility with pleasure-causation.

Suppose now that we modify our definition slightly and maintain that something is useful, not when it causes pleasure, but when it produces, or helps to produce, something of value. This, however, is also an untenable position; for, as Meinong points out, value cannot now be identified with utility, nor can it be defined in terms of utility; for the meaning of "usefulness" is now made to depend on the reality or the occurrence of a value. When all is said and done, therefore, we have no approach to value except via an analysis of experience itself. The crucial question is, What is the specific aspect or characteristic of experience that is revelatory of, and foundational to, our values?

As Meinong sees it, the objects of experience are in themselves not decisive; our attitude toward the objects is. When we say of a thing that it is of value to us or that we value it, we have an experience of a particular nature such that the object attains a characteristic significance for us. We take a specific attitude toward it. This attitude-taking, this "valuing," is basic to all value considerations. It accounts equally well for the fact that value is antecedent to desire and the fact that we value many things which we already possess.

The attitude towards objects that is involved here is one of affection or feeling—as distinguished from cognition and volition. But not every feeling is a value-feeling. Thus, the value we place on a stove, though obviously based on the comfort of the warm room which the stove helps to bring about, is not itself a sensuous feeling—such as warmth is. And even a feeling of pleasure is, as such, not a value-feeling. The value experience, as Meinong sees it, is more complex than this. His thesis is that we can value something only (a) because we believe that it exists, or (b) because its non-existence is of value to us. In other words, "it is of the essence of our value-feelings that they are existence-feelings (*Existenz-Gefühle*)" (p. 16).

It must not be presumed, however, that the connection between value-feelings and the objects valued is some form of causality. The very fact that the non-existence of an object may be the occasion for a value experience disproves any causal interpretation. But even in those cases in which causal connections could or do exist, they are not decisive for the value experience. If they were, we could value an object only so long as it actually caused a value-feeling in us. Our valuations, however, transcend such passing moments.

What is basic in value experience is not a causal connection between an object and our feelings, but a judgment that such and such an object does or does not exist. It is an existential judgment, in other words, that sets up the relation between value-feeling and value-object (pp. 21; 23–4).

But even this interpretation is still too simple; for value is not the same as value-feeling, and the value of an object does not consist in our valuing the object. After all, we may value something which really has no value—superstitions old and new prove it; and, conversely, many things which are of real value never have been and are not even now valued. We may say, therefore, that value is not dependent upon an actual valuation but upon a possible valuation; and even then we must assume favorable circumstances—such as adequate knowledge and a normal mental and emotional life. In brief, value consists not in something being valued, but in the possibility of its being valued under the necessary favorable conditions. This means, however, that the properties of an object do not in themselves constitute its value. Value remains relative to a subject who values. That is, when we ascribe value to an object, we assert at the same time the existence of a subject for whom the existence of the object involved can become the occasion for a value experience. Or, to put it differently, an object has value when it is so constituted that if someone knows of its existence, he will be favorably or unfavorably affected by that knowledge. The capacity of the object thus to affect a subject is basic to the value we ascribe to it (p. 29).

II

So far Meinong's thesis has been that value-feelings and, therefore, our valuations depend upon existential judgments; that values cannot be defined without reference to both, feelings and judgments. But to argue that values are composites in this sense does not solve the basic problem, for the specific relation of feelings to judgments must yet be clarified.

To establish his point, Meinong makes a sharp distinction between presentational experience (*Vorstellung*) involving no judgment, and experience involving acts of judgment (p. 32). In presentational experience the content of the experience is simply "given." It is "there." We see it. We hear it. We perceive it in some other way. And that is all there is to it. However, a feeling may become attached to the content of any presentational experience and may have that content as its psychological presupposition. A feeling thus grounded Meinong calls a "presentation-feeling" (*Vorstellungsgefühl*).

To be sure, we may also have feelings which have other feelings as their presupposition—the *Gefühlsgefühle;* and still others which presuppose desires—*Begehrungsgefühle.* There is hardly a content of our experience to which a feeling may not be attached. And neither is there, nor can there be, a feeling which does not have some content of experience as its psychological presupposition.

But when judgments are also involved, the content of an experience is not simply "given." It is either affirmed or denied. And if now a feeling is attached to the content, then the judgment, too, is part of the psychological presupposition (*Mitvoraussetzung*) of that feeling. Feelings so grounded Meinong calls *Urteilsgefühle*— "judgment-feelings" (p. 35). They alone are basic to his value theory. In fact, at this time in his development he regards judgment-feelings as being the same as value-feelings.

III

If we now consider the objects of our experience, we find that there is hardly anything which cannot become the object of a value-feeling—either directly and in itself or because of its relation to something else. Closer examination shows, however, that, by and large, all objects fall into one or the other of two classes. They are either physical or they are mental. If they are physical, their values are essentially the concern of the economists, and Meinong disregards them in his analyses. His concern is the value of the mental objects; and here, he finds, further distinctions must be made.

There is, first of all, that which is actual as distinguished from what is dispositional. There is, secondly, the distinction between self and other self. There are, in the third place, four groups of "elementary mental facts" which cut across the first two divisions. They are: presentations (*Vorstellungen*), judgments, feelings, and desires. And there is, in the fourth place the distinction between what is present now in our experience, what belongs to the past, and what is yet to come (p. 40). Value problems arise in connection with all of these aspects of experience. But we must never lose sight of the fact that, in their very essence, value experiences are judgment-feelings. Meinong specifically affirms, for example, that a sensory feeling—such as a feeling of pleasure, or pain—is in itself not a value-feeling. It may become the content of one when it is also the content of an existential judgment. And "dispositional elements" are available for value considerations only when they manifest themselves in the actual.

In principle, there is no difficulty here so long as we are concerned exclusively with our own experience; for, in its direct immediacy, our own experience is itself the warranty for our value judgments. But what about the validity of value judgments which pertain to the experience of "others"? This problem, Meinong points out, must be seen in broad perspective, for it involves also the problem of our knowledge of an external world. It is not necessary, however, to consider at this time all the problems of epistemology, for we all believe that we know such a world; that our sciences are concerned with it; and that our value-feelings have direct reference to objects of that world. We can let it go at that, taking the existence of an external world for granted. And we also take for granted that "the other person" is part of that self-same world. That my feelings can be concerned with "the other" is therefore no more a mystery than that I can know the rest of reality and can respond to it with value-feelings. However, it is true just the same that, with respect to "the other," the value problem takes on a new dimension. It is no longer simply a question of what value "the other" is to me, but is: Can I value the good of another as a good for him? That is to say, the problem now is the age-old issue of egoism versus altruism.

Since "the other" is a human being, our feeling-responses to him are responses primarily, not to his physical, but to his psychic reality. That reality, however, is so rich and diversified in details that it will be advantageous at this time to consider only a few broadly grouped aspects. There are, first, the beliefs which "the other" holds and which quite frequently are not a matter of indifference to us—beliefs to which we respond with value-feelings. Our feeling-response is perhaps especially intense when "the other's" beliefs pertain directly to us. We all know, for example, the satisfaction we feel when we are understood by "the other," or when he shares our beliefs. We respond negatively in the reverse situations.

But the beliefs which "the other" holds are rarely free from affective overtones; and we react to his feelings as well as to his beliefs. We respond to them with feelings of sympathy or feelings of antipathy; i.e., we respond to them with positive or negative value-feelings. More specifically, when we respond to the pleasures which "the other" experiences with a feeling of pleasure on our part, ours is the experience of a shared happiness. When we respond with a feeling of displeasure to the pain or the displeasure which he experiences, ours is a feeling of compassion. Similarly, when we respond to his pleasure with a feeling of displeasure, ours is an experience of envy. And when we take pleasure in "the other's" displeasure, in his suffering, we experience malicious joy and, dispositionally, a basic cruelty (pp. 46–47). That our feeling-responses may vary in intensity is, of course, obvious. And it is equally obvious which of them are to be called altruistic and which not.

Finally, we may respond with a specific value-feeling to the desires of "the other" no less than to his beliefs or his feelings. A positive feeling-response to his desires may then be an expression of our "good will." This is especially so when our response is the manifestation of our dispositional attitude. Responses of this type are of particular significance in the realm of ethics but need not concern us further at this time since we are dealing now only with problems of a general value theory. However, we must consider—even if only briefly—the time element involved in value reponses.

IV

Underlying the discussions up to this point has been the unacknowledged assumption that our value-feelings are concerned with what is actually present in our experience; that our value-responses are to the here and now. The question is, Can our value-feelings transcend the present and be concerned with what has been or with what is yet to be? That is to say, Can they be a response to something which does not actually exist? That, as a matter of fact, we are concerned with what is not now an actuality is evident whenever we hope for, or fear, some future event and take action to bring it about or to prevent it from happening.

One might argue that a future state or event has value for us in so far as it would have value for us if it existed or occurred right now. But such an interpretation is untenable. A simple example will make this clear. Let us suppose that you are about to fly to London; and let us suppose also that you are taking out a "flight insurance policy" in order to provide for your loved ones— just in case! In what sense can it be said that this insurance is of value? If the present state of affairs were decisive, then, as long as your plane has not actually crashed, there is no need for the insurance. If it be argued that the insurance would have value if the crash were now a reality, then the present has been falsified to suit such a theory, for it has now been assumed that the crash has occurred when in reality it has not. "Who would fear the tiger now securely locked in a sturdy cage just because he would be extremely dangerous if he were at liberty?" (pp. 49–50).

If it be maintained that some future state or event has value now because it will have a value at the anticipated future date, then it follows that something which, as far as we can foresee, could never be present to us—an event, for example, that will occur after our death—can also have no value for us. If one were to argue that it would have value for us if we could experience it, then the actualities have again been falsified in the interest of a theory which, without such falsification, would be untenable. Applied to past events the theory is, of course, subject to the same criticism.

But when we now consider Meinong's thesis that judgment-feelings are basic to all our value experiences—that value-feelings are responses to existential judgments, not to objects and events directly—, then the difficulties disappear. After all, if in our cognitive experience we can transcend the present and can reach out into the future (or into the past)—i.e., if in our judgments we can legitimately affirm or deny future (or past) events—and if our value-feelings have judgments as their immediate presuppositions, then there is no reason whatsoever why valuations of future (or past) events are not just as immediate and just as valid as are our value-responses to what is present here and now. In either case, our value-response is to the content affirmed or denied in the cognitive judgment (p. 51).

But now we must also realize that not all judgments that constitute a presupposition for a value-response stand in precisely the same relation to our feelings. For instance, if we value a key because it opens the door to a room which we wish to enter, then, strictly speaking, two judgments are basic to our value response. One is the judgment that the key actually exists. The other informs us that the key is suitable for the intended purpose. Although in this case the second judgment is indispensable, judgments of its kind are not necessary presuppositions in every value experience. Judgments of the first kind are. Meinong calls them "principal judgments" (*Haupturteile*)—in contradistinction to "subordinate judgments" (*Nebenurteile*). It is the function of the principal judgments to affirm or to deny the "reality" to which we respond with a value-feeling, and thus to provide the content for our valuations. In other words, principal judgments are the immediate presuppositions of our value-responses (pp. 59–60).

It is evident, however, that in some cases our valuations are mediated—usually via secondary or subordinate judgments which relate an object or an event to something which is directly valued. Still, something which at first is valued only because of its relation to something else—because of its usefulness, let us say, or because of a memory association—may in time come to be valued without regard to anything else and strictly for its own sake. Such transfer of feelings, though little understood, is a well-known fact of human experience. It is obvious, however, that, if many things are of value to us because of their relation to other things, there must finally be an end to this reference to other things, and then we have the case of valuing something for its own sake only. We have what in more modern terminology is called a terminating value experience.

V

We now return to a problem mentioned earlier—the problem,

namely, of the objective significance of our value experiences. After all, value-feelings are simply psychological facts and, therefore, purely subjective events. They are not the values themselves; for, as Meinong tells us, "value is a property of something real" (p. 67). The question is, To what extent are valuations (manifest in our value-feelings) and values tied together? To what extent does the one depend upon, or coincide with, the other? And if one is basic, which is it—the value-feeling or the value?

It is Meinong's thesis that value does not depend upon valuation—at least not in the sense that it comes into existence when valuation begins, or ceases to be when valuation ceases. "The value which a thing has for me is a lasting property [of it] which is completely independent of how often or how seldom I think of the thing. In this respect at least value stands in analogy to all other properties of the thing" (*ibid.*). On the other hand, however, it can not be said that valuation occurs only in conjunction with a value. If I rejoice over an event which has never actually occurred, then there obviously is no value—i.e., nothing of value exists—despite my valuational experience. And if someone regards an innocent stick as a magic wand and values it accordingly, his attitude is but further proof that valuations may occur without a value being present.

However, the examples just given also make obvious the solution to our problem. As Meinong puts it: Every valuation which concerns something that is presumed to be real indicates a value. It indicates a purely subjective value when the cognitive judgments that are its presupposition are false. It indicates an objective value when those judgments are true. The valuation itself is merely symptomatic, not constitutive, of the presence of a value. And so we have obtained the important conclusion that "every objective value is also a true value, and every true value is objective" (p. 81). Failure in value ascription does not necessarily mean the absence of a value; it may mean merely a cognitive failure—a failure, that is, in the interpretation and full understanding of the nature of the object with which we are concerned at the time.

VI

The essential elements of Meinong's initial position in value-theoretical matters have now been indicated. The rest of *Psychologisch-Ethische Untersuchungen zur Werttheorie* deals with problems of ethics only and adds nothing new in principle to the general theory outlined above. However, this initial position Meinong modified almost at once. In a conversation with Meinong, von Ehrenfels had raised certain objections and Meinong, conceding that his theory was "incomplete and inadequate in one of its basic contentions" ("Werthaltung," p. 327), tried to meet the objections by augmenting his theory.

According to Meinong himself, the principal aspects of his initial position can be summarized thus: (1) Value can be traced back to a valuation (*Werthaltung*)—to a feeling, that is, which is associated with our (actual or presumed) knowledge of the existence or non-existence of an object, the "value object" (*Wertobjekt*). (2) The value of an object can therefore be defined as the capacity of the object to be valued by an "intellectually and emotionally normal subject" (p. 328). (3) But this must not be taken to mean that valuation itself is the value. (4) Still, in order to determine the magnitude of a value, we apparently have nothing to go by except "the intensity of the value-feeling" of the "normal subject." It is this implication of his theory, Meinong now admits, that does not square with the facts of experience (pp. 328–332). He believes, however, that this indicates, not that his theory is wrong, but only that it is incomplete.

Taking his cue from economic value theory—more specifically from the "law of marginal utility" (pp. 335–36)—Meinong now argues that "the magnitude of a value depends not only on the intensity with which the existence of an object is valued, but also upon the intensity with which its non-existence is experienced as a disvalue" (p. 337). Only the balance of the opposed feelings is the true measure of a value. And the value of an object is that object's capacity to elicit in us a value-feeling by virtue of its non-existence as well as by virtue of its existence.

At this point, however, Meinong finds it necessary to modify his theory still further by pointing up the significance of our desires in matters pertaining to values. "Of two attainable objects I choose the one which I desire with greater intensity, the one for which I have a stronger desire" (p. 339). Stated differently, I desire most strongly that object (or that state of affairs) which, when realized, elicits in me the strongest value-feeling; and I do so, Meinong adds, "irrespective of whether the desire is rooted in the value-feeling or the value-feeling is rooted in the desire" (*ibid.*). Correspondingly, we can regard value as "the capacity of an object to maintain itself in the struggle of motives as an object of desire" (p. 340).

A long step has thus been taken toward a desire theory of value. At the very least an ambiguity has been introduced into Meinong's original thesis. Meinong himself, however, still feels that "what characterizes value directly" are the feelings an object elicits in us (p. 341); and "even if we can not really feel a value," we value an object when, on the basis of our feelings, we ascribe a value to it (p. 343).

VII

Meinong, of course, could not rest at this half-way point. In his next publication, *Ueber Annahmen* (1902), he again responded to criticisms advanced by von Ehrenfels (*ibid.*, p. vi) and devoted the major part of his book to a re-statement of his own position.

In the first four chapters of *Ueber Annahmen* he advanced the thesis that a distinction must be made between a judgment and a proposition; that every judgment is the affirmation or the denial of something; and that what is being affirmed or denied is the proposition, the "*that* part" of the statement: "I affirm that *the earth is round*," "I deny that *the sun is inhabited*." Actually, however, three elements must be distinguished in a judgmental situation: the object as an actually existing entity (when there is such an object present), the act of judging, and the "objective" (*das Objektiv*) or that with which the judgment is directly concerned and which may or may not denote an actually existing object. It is because judgments are concerned only with "objectives" that they can pertain to non-existing as well as to existing "entities"—to "the present king of France," for example, as well as to the book in which you are now reading.

"Objectives," however, are essential also to all "presumptions" (*Annahmen*) and all presentational experiences (*Vorstellungen*) (p. 134). They therefore play an important role in our affective-conative responses as well; for it is to the "objectives" that we respond. To be sure, no "objectives" are involved in sensory feelings pure and simple. But value-feelings—"I like . . . ," "I regret . . . ," "I fear . . . ," "I hope . . . ," etc.—and valuations are of necessity responses to "objectives," i.e., they are responses to objects *as understood* or *as imagined;* and so are all desires (pp. 162–164).

Since both, feelings and desires, are responses to "objectives," Meinong now sets out to determine to what extent feelings may be involved in desires. "Nothing seems more natural," he points out, "than that I desire what pleases me and because it pleases me" (p. 289). It is tempting, therefore, to regard pleasure as the only true object of desire, and to maintain that we desire objects only because we expect that they will give us pleasure. A "law of the relative enhancement of pleasure" may then be taken to be basic to all valuations—a view fully developed by von Ehrenfels (see Chapter IV). Meinong, however, does not accept this interpretation because, as he shows, it is in conflict with certain facts of experience (pp. 290–98). Nevertheless, some of von Ehrenfels' arguments were sufficiently forceful to compel Meinong to revise his own theory in important respects.

The crux of the matter is that not all desires conform with the "law of the relative enhancement of pleasure." Strictly speaking, so Meinong maintains, only those desires conform which aim at an absolute enhancement of pleasure. Many desires, however, aim at relative pleasures only; and a "crushing mass" of them are accompanied even by displeasure (p. 301). Is he who takes up the struggle against forces he cannot possibly hope to conquer any happier than he who resignedly accepts the inevitable? And does not a desire for the unattainable add more suffering than pleasure to our human lot? The difficulties thus pointed up Meinong hopes to overcome through recourse to his theory of presumptions.

In developing his argument, Meinong considers once more the interrelation of desires and feelings. At first glance we may get the impression that we desire something simply because it gives us pleasure—assuming that the "it" refers not to desire but to the object desired. But it is precisely here that the difficulty arises; for that which is desired cannot itself give us pleasure because it has as yet not been attained; and a "pleasure of expectation" cannot be the determinant of desire because desire precedes expectation. As Meinong sees it, he who desires accepts what he desires as the "objective" of a presumption (p. 307). A presumption, however, that the object of a desire exists (or does not exist), that it has (or has not) such and such qualities is not in itself sufficient. What is needed also is the further presumption that the object in question will elicit such and such feelings in the subject involved. The motivation of a desire thus seems to be the contemplation of what the feelings might be which the subject would experience if what is desired were ultimately attained. Experience shows, however, that in most cases at least the feelings themselves, not the contemplation of them, are decisive. This means that, despite Meinong's recourse to presumptions, the initial difficulties have not been overcome.

Meinong's next step is to point out that certain experiences occupy a middle ground between presentations (*Vorstellungen*) and feelings. What, for example, are the "fear" and the "compassion" awakened in us by a tragedy enacted on stage? They certainly are not real fear or real compassion. The spectator, nevertheless, experiences something which, though it is "neither pleasure nor sadness, neither fear nor hope in the ordinary sense," is yet "something similar to all of this" (p. 313). Moreover, what the spectator thus experiences is not itself an "aesthetic pleasure" or an "aesthetic feeling of any kind," but is, nevertheless related to an aesthetic experience. For want of a better name Meinong calls the feelings referred to "fantasy-feelings" (*Phantasiegefühle*), feelings of the imagination (p. 314).

Having thus identified "fantasy-feelings" as a special class of experiences elicited by "presumptive objectives," Meinong now argues that these feelings play a hitherto overlooked role in the motivation of desires; that, in fact, it is they that "awaken" desire (p. 321). "Fantasy-feelings" can play this role because they are genuine feelings but are elicited by "presumptive objectives." We thus no longer face the difficulty, previously noted, that a non-existent object can arouse a desire. Not only does recourse to "fantasy-feelings" account for the fact that a pleasing feeling elicits a positive desire whereas a displeasing feeling calls forth a negative desire or repulsion, but it also makes intelligible what is involved in the "competition" of objects of desire which as yet do not actually exist.

The shift in Meinong's position is now clear. Initially he had maintained that all valuations and value-determined attitudes are based on feeling-responses to real objects. In fact, he had identified "value-feelings" with "reality-feelings" and had defined value as the power of the existing object to elicit in us a "value-feeling." The introduction into his theory of the idea of "presumptions" and "fantasy-feelings," and the roles assigned to them, has changed all that. It is evident, however, that even now Meinong regards feeling rather than desire as basic to all valuations. "Reality-feelings" and "fantasy-feelings"—the former as responses to reality-judgments, the latter as responses to presumptions—dominate and determine all desires (p. 337).

VIII

Meinong felt, however, that not all difficulties had been overcome; that the value experience is much more complex than he himself had realized. In "Ueber Urteilsgefühle" (1906), he tried to remedy this situation.

When we speak of joy, he now points out, we do not, as a rule, refer to an elementary feeling but to a very complex response to a "total situation" in which the nature and quality of our feeling is but one ingredient, and not necessarily the decisive one (p. 586). As he put it some six years later: "The value of an O subsists in the fact that an S takes an interest in O, could take an interest in O, or, quite reasonably, should take an interest in O" ("Psychologie," 1912, p. 9)—a thesis that was fully developed by Ralph Barton Perry in 1926.

Meinong's original interpretation of values in terms of feelings had now been supplemented by an interest theory according to which an object has value not merely because a subject actually takes or could take an interest in it, but also, and most importantly, because the object "deserves" or is "worthy of" this interest. As thus amended the basic theory is hardly recognizable; and while some problems had been solved, new ones appeared and the difficulties were multiplied. Meinong himself felt that a new approach was called for. In "Ueber emotionale Präsentation" (1917), he attempted to develop one.

He started with a consideration of the fact that whenever we experience an "object," no matter what its nature might be or in what manner it is being experienced—i.e., whether it is being perceived, thought, imagined, or remembered—the experience is "presentational." Something is being "presented" to a subject (p. 5). This is obvious, of course, in the case of all cognitive experiences: If no object is encountered or "given," then there can be no knowledge of one. It is Meinong's contention, however, that our emotional experiences are likewise "presentational" (p. 27). But there is a difference. Whereas the objects of cognition are the content of the cognitive acts themselves, the object of an emotional presentation is not the content of the emotion but of the experience which is the "psychological presupposition" of the emotion. It is what Meinong calls a "presuppositional object" (p. 30) and must not be confused with the content of the emotion as such. It must not be confused, in other words, with the joy, the happiness, or the despair for which it is the presupposition.

Although we encounter objects always in a penumbra of emotional significance—they strike us as being "wonderful," "pitiful," "awe-inspiring," "ridiculous," "delightful," "painful," and so on—we are not aware of any causal dependencies. If an object impresses us as being beautiful or awe-inspiring, or whatever, it is directly experienced as itself possessing those qualities, not as producing in us "aesthetic feelings." The emotional experience is much like seeing an object immediately as red or as blue, and not as causing red-like or blue-like sensations in us. When we see a rose as red and also as beautiful, we attribute to it two properties, one of which is disclosed to us in a sense impression, the other in a presentational feeling (p. 33). This fact, however,—so Meinong maintains—does not contradict his original thesis that the psychological presupposition of a value-response is an explicit or implicit existential judgment (pp. 84–85), for the ascription of any attribute to an object presupposes the "existence," in one form or another, of the object concerned (p. 89). The facts, nevertheless, indicate that there is an aspect of our value experience which, so far, Meinong had neglected. He now discusses it at length.

Basic to the new interpretation is Meinong's thesis that "acts" and "contents" of experience go together; that there are no acts without reference to a content toward which they are directed, and that there is no content which does not have an act as its indispensable presupposition. Still, it seems reasonable to believe, so Meinong continues, that values or valuations are logically prior to desire. It seems reasonable, in other words, that men desire something because they value it, and that it would be a distortion of this "natural" relationship to maintain that they value something because they desire it. But if this is so—that is, if it is true that an act of desire (volition) is determined by the "end" or goal sought because that end is valued—then it is crucial that the valuation of the end be cognitively defensible; and this means, Meinong maintains, that our valuations must themselves be cognitive acts, and that, like all other cognitive acts, they must find their justification in our own experience (p. 120), not with reference to "something out there."

Let us assume that we value a certain O; and let us assume, furthermore, that we believe some C to be a necessary condition for the occurrence of O; then, as a matter of actual fact, we may, but (for various reasons) need not necessarily, value C. However, if the relationship of C to O is as assumed, and if our valuing of O is justified, then our valuing of C is also justified, and our indifference to it, or our negative valuation of it, is not justified (p. 125). The situation is clear as far as our valuation of C is concerned. But what about our valuation of O?

In the case of O, certain facts are also at once evident. For instance, if we take pleasure in, or value, the existence (or the nonexistence) of O, then we cannot at the same time and in the same respect be displeased by, or value negatively, that very existence (or non-existence) of O. And it is equally obvious that, if the existence of an O pleases (displeases) us, then the non-existence of that very same O cannot also, and in the same respect, please (displease) us. Whether our initial valuation of O is itself justified or not is immaterial to the *a priori* relationships just indicated (p. 126).

When we consider valuations in relation to desires, still further facts must be noted. As Meinong puts it: "To desire what has value and because it has value; to desire the more valuable rather than the less valuable; to prefer, in case of conflict, the greater value to the lesser one; to desire the means because one desires the end to which it is a means—all this is self-evident in the sense of being 'reasonable'" (p. 128); it is *a priori* knowledge. But even now we do not know in what sense or under what conditions our valuation of O is justified.

It is clear, however, that value-feelings (and desires) are always responses to some object with which we are concerned and whose existence or non-existence is the indispensable precondition of our value experience. More specifically, if Q is the quality of O which elicits a feeling-response (or a desire) q, then that feeling-response (or that desire) is justified with respect to O if, and only if, Q is indeed a property of O. That is to say, our feeling-response (or our desire) is justified if, and only if, the judgment "O is Q" is justified (pp. 130–31; 140)—i.e., it is justified only if O does in fact possess the quality attributed to it in a cognitive judgment.

The qualities of O, however, are only part of the conditions basic to all valuations; for, surely, if there is no feeling-response to O, there is also no valuation of it. In an ultimate sense, therefore, it is the existence of a responsive subject that is foundational to all valuations and all values.

But now a new problem arises. Cognitive experience is undeniably dual in character, embracing as it does the object experienced and the act of experiencing it. And since Meinong holds that all valuations are cognitive, he must also hold that they, too, are inherently dual, involving a value and the act of experiencing it. This duality, however, seems to imply that values are objective "entities" of some sort; that they exist in and for themselves in a manner analogous to the existence of the things of the "external world." In Meinong's words: "I cannot deny that it seems to me that the relation-free concept of value, hitherto neglected by value theorists, deserves preference" over any relational concept of values (p. 152). Max Scheler was to develop this idea to the fullest. Meinong himself, however, still believed the relational concept of value to be of utmost significance. As he saw it, the facts of value experience cannot be accounted for in terms of relation-free values alone. This is especially evident in situations, common in daily life, in which several persons respond valuationally to "the same conditions" but respond differently. Thus, if A is sick, the value-responses to his condition as experienced by members of his family, by his physician, by his enemies, and by his insurance agent may differ widely; but we cannot say that any of the responses are "wrong" merely because they are different. What this case shows, however, is that any value theory is inadequate if it is centered exclusively on relation-free value concepts; for it is evident that the different perspectives under which various persons respond valuationally to "the same situation" have a decisive bearing on their valuations. Generalizing this fact, Meinong now asserts that in all value experience a relative value is encountered—a value, that is, which is relative to the conditions and the perspective of the experiencing subject (p. 153).

This relativity, however,—so Meinong continues—does not preclude the possibility of speaking of "relation-free values" if the term "relation-free" is properly understood. What Meinong means by it is, not that the values exist in themselves and detached from all experience, but that they are encountered in a valuational experience for which a justified judgment "O is Q" provides the occasion. Values are in that case as objective, and as objectively compelling, as are the judgments on which they depend. Meinong can therefore still maintain that the value experience and what is immediately accessible to us in that experience is and remains basic. All valuations start with and remain anchored to that experience. But in valuations based upon justified cognitive judgments we rise above mere relativity to an acknowledgement of "objective values"—just as in cognition we rise above mere sense impressions to the idea of an "external world" (p. 159).

IX

Considering the many changes in Meinong's position, we need not be surprised to find that, toward the end of his career, he tried to bring together his new insights and tentative solutions in one all-encompassing theory. The result of this effort is contained in the posthumously published book, *Zur Grundlegung der allgemeinen Werttheorie* (1923), the first part of which (pp. 1–123) is devoted to a description of value experience, and the second part of which (pp. 123–176) deals with value *per se.* But only the whole gives us an adequate account of Meinong's definitive position.

In the opening pages of *Grundlegung* Meinong points out the bewildering complexity of value problems, and the different meanings of the German term *'Wert.'* At least six distinct areas can be distinguished in which the term 'value' may legitimately be employed: (1) There is the area of "quantitative values," of which mathematics is representative. Here 'value' means a specific magnitude. (2) There is the radically different realm of morals, where 'value' means worthiness. (3) There is an area of human activities where it makes sense to speak of achievement values. (4) And there is a related area in which the primary concern is "use value" or utility. (5) Quite different, again, is the broad field of the arts where "aesthetic values" are the center of interest. And (6) there are the "truth-values" which we encounter when we are engaged in attaining knowledge. That some of these areas overlap is immaterial. The question is, What have the six areas in common that warrants the use of the term 'value' in all of them?

A first answer to this question might be that in all cases whatever is valued is somehow related to a person; that "nothing has value if it does not satisfy a need" (p. 12). But is this an acceptable answer? As commonly understood, any reference to need means essentially a reference to bodily needs—to needs, that is, which animals, too, experience. But can we stop there? Plants also "need" light and air and moisture if they are to grow. Throughout the whole of organic nature the connection between need and survival is evident. But the problem of survival arises only in cases of exceptionally great needs, whereas ordinary needs—ordinary hunger, for example, or ordinary thirst—do not endanger an individual's existence. Though related to survival, needs cannot be defined in terms of survival. And what about a vain person's need for flattery? This need is neither a threat to his survival nor is it a bodily need. Furthermore, a need satisfied is, strictly speaking, no longer a need. And if value were defined in terms of need, would this mean that an object which satisfies, and thus eliminates a need, has no longer any value? We must at least broaden the relation of value to needs so as to include the many cases of needs satisfied. This can be done, Meinong believes, if we acknowlege that there are "latent" as well as "effective" needs. We might then say that we have a need for anything which we would miss if we did not have it (p. 16). In the end, however, even this broadened interpretation does not provide an adequate basis for all values; for the realm of values transcends all needs. We may, for example, value highly an original painting by Böcklin even though we feel no need to possess it. And if it now be argued that the painting satisfies an aesthetic need, then Meinong replies that any reference to "aesthetic needs" plays fast and loose with the term 'need' (p. 18). But if we take the term 'need' in so broad a sense as to include in it every case or form of value, then need is at best but "another side" of what we call value and has no distinctive meaning of its own. It would then be much better, and more natural, to speak of interest rather than need when we attempt to define value (p. 19).

If value cannot be adequately defined in terms of need, is it possible to define it in terms of utility? At first glance it seems to be almost self-evident that something has value because it is useful. Closer examination soon reveals, however, that value and usefulness are by no means one and the same. A work of art, for example, may have great value but, in itself, may be of very little use. Iron is in many respects more useful than gold; but gold is of greater value. And can it ever be said that the value of a flawless diamond is proportional to its usefulness? The fact of the matter is that in every case of an evaluation the over-all situation must be taken into consideration—be it existentially personal, economic, political, or whatever.

It is true, of course, that in the context of economic concerns value and utility are interrelated. But even here they must not be identified or confused with one another. To be sure, whatsoever is useful is also valuable to the extent of its usefulness; but not everything that is valuable is also useful. A work of art, for example, can be counted among the useful things only in so far as a profit may be realized from its sale or in so far as it covers a hole in the wall, etc. But this means that its utility value is by no means the same as its aesthetic value. And who would identify the value of friendship or of love with utility? That under certain circumstances a friend may be of great help to us need not be denied. But such "usefulness" is hardly the essence of friendship, nor is it the same as the value of friendship itself.

Even when we define 'useful' in the broadest sense possible and maintain that anything is useful that does or can serve as a cause or condition of a pleasing experience, or that is or can be a means toward the realization of that which is pleasing, it still is impossible to identify value and utility. What is crucial here is that the useful is always a means, either directly or indirectly, to some value end—to a pleasing experience, for instance, and that it derives its value from this relationship. That is to say, usefulness neither constitutes nor defines value but always presupposes it (p. 23).

If it now be argued—as it may well be in the realm of economics—that the value of an object consists in the sacrifices made for its sake and on its behalf, then it can readily be shown that this also will not do as a definition of value; for as Meinong points out quite rightly, sacrifices as such do not constitute a value; they presuppose one. In fact, sacrifices cannot even be referred to as sacrifices unless they already have at least a negative value. This does not mean, however, that sacrifices may not be indicative of the magnitude of the positive value which we attribute to an object; for they do. But this implies that sacrifices presuppose both, positive and negative values.

Value, furthermore, is not the same as price. This is evident even in the simple purchase of a loaf of bread for a stipulated price—a transaction which, under normal circumstances, is typical of all business deals. The buyer values the bread more than he does the money he has to pay for it; whereas the seller values the money more than he does the bread. Without such difference in valuation there would be no buying or selling (p. 30). The price agreed upon is but an index of the respective valuations and presupposes them.

Finally, a "labor-cost" theory of value is also inadequate because it can never account for the value of such intangibles as friendship, love, or honor. In fact, this theory cannot even account for the value of economic goods; for no matter how much labor and cost of production have gone into the manufacture of some particular article, if that article is of no use to anyone, it also has no value. And if the article is of use, then its usefulness rather than its labor-cost determines its value; and that usefulness, in turn, depends upon the existence of an end to the realization of which it is useful. We are forced back, therefore, to a consideration of that which may be a valued end in itself. As far as Meinong is concerned, this means that we must examine value experience itself in order to discover what constitutes a value (p. 31).

This much, however, seems evident: the idea of usefulness stresses the relation of an object to a subject, whereas the idea of need emphasizes the relation of a subject to an object. The value experience, therefore, involves both, an object and a subject; and what is characteristic of values depends on the subject-object relationship (p. 33). The question is, What is it that transforms this relationship into a value experience?

In "Präsentation," Meinong had argued that a value experience is essentially an emotional experience—taking 'emotional' in its broadest meaning. This thesis he now re-affirms. "That which is sufficiently closely coordinated with value to be called a value experience must be essentially of an emotional nature" (*Grundlegung,* p. 35). Even desire assumes that we are not indifferent emotionally to the object desired. It is inconceivable, Meinong holds, that we would ever desire an object or a situation if its attainment did not please us, or if failure to attain it did not displease us. Hence, if forced to make a choice between feeling and desire as basic to a value experience, Meinong would decide in favor of feeling. "But," he asks, "are we actually confronted with such a choice?" And his answer now is—as against his earlier position—that we are not; that feelings and desires both play a fundamental role in value experience (p. 45).

Even now, however, Meinong admits that there is a certain disparity between feelings and desires in value experience; for, while desires do not occur without feelings being involved, feelings may still be a part of a value experience even in the absence of desire. Feelings must therefore be regarded as primary, desires as secondary (p. 46). The question is, Is this all that there is to it?

Let us consider first the matter of feelings. It is Meinong's contention that, although all value experiences have feelings as a component, not all experienced feelings are value experiences. We cannot simply identify experiencing a feeling with having a value experience. Sensory feelings in particular are not in themselves a value experience—even if, under certain conditions, they may serve as the basis for one. For example, I may value a stove because it warms my room. But when I feel warm, I by no means feel a value; I feel warmth. Only when my feelings pertain to or are directed toward an object do they constitute a value experience.

When we consider desire as a component of a value experience, it is at once evident that nobody can desire without desiring something; that all desires are directed towards "objects." More specifically, Meinong maintains, desire is always directed toward the existence (or non-existence) of the "object" in question, or, in special cases, toward the existence (or non-existence) of some particular characteristic or feature of the "object" (p. 53). This very fact, however, casts new light upon the feelings involved in value experience; for the feelings also pertain to the existence (or non-existence) of the "object" valued. That is to say, value feelings are not feelings in general but "existence-feelings" (*Existenzgefühle*). It must be understood, however, that these feelings encompass not only objects which actually exist, but also objects which "exist" in imagination or in memory only. "The realm of values transcends the realm of [actual] existence" (p. 55).

If it now be asked how value-feelings are connected with "existence" (in the broad sense here intended), then we know already from Meinong's earlier work that the relation is not one of causality; for the value experience is in all essentials an intellectual experience. That is to say, in every situation in which a value experience is involved, the existence or the nature of the object is first asserted (or denied) in a cognitive judgment; and the value-feeling is a response to that judgment. "Value-feelings," therefore, are "judgment-feelings." It is immaterial, however, whether the judgments involved are true or false. What is crucial is that they are accepted as descriptive of the objects valued—and are accepted irrespective of their truth or falsity. That this is so is especially evident in the case of our value responses to imaginary objects. It is also worth noting that, although all value-feelings are keyed to judgments, not all judgments need arouse value-feelings or elicit a value response.

Closer analysis now reveals that our value-feelings may depend either on the act of judging (affirming or denying) or on the content of the judgment. If the former is the case, Meinong speaks of "feelings of presentational acts" (*Vorstellungsaktgefühle*). They play a particularly important part in value experience. Indeed, they encompass the whole range of objects, from real to imaginary, from dream objects to the world around us, and are, in effect, the presuppositions of all judgments pertaining to "presentational content" (p. 64).

Since every value-feeling is a response to a presentational judgment of some kind, it is evident that it is not the object as such which elicits the value response in us, but the "theme" of the judgment—that which Meinong calls the *"Objektiv"* (p. 66). For example, if my watch keeps time well and I value this fact, it is not the watch as such nor the time-keeping that I value, but the judgmental "theme": "my-time-keeping-watch." Such a "theme," referring to a specific object or quasi-object, is the indispensable presupposition of every value-feeling. If in a particular case the "theme" is not at once evident, a simple analysis of the experience in question will reveal it.

Having thus clarified—at least to his own satisfaction—what is involved in value-feelings, Meinong now redefines what he means by valuation (*Werthaltung*). In his earlier writings he had identified valuation and value-feelings. He now wishes to identify valuation only with those feelings which, through the intermediacy of the "theme" of the existential (in the broad sense) judgment, are directed toward an object or a quasi-object. That other feelings may also be value-feelings need not be denied; but they are such only if they are at least also "implicit valuations" (p. 68).

It is necessary for valuations, as thus understood, that the judgments which are foundational to them are certain rather than conjectural—certain at least in the practical sense of expressing a firm belief, even if that belief should prove to be false, and irrespective of the reality or quasi-reality of the objects involved. A firm belief concerning imaginary objects is as effective as a precondition of a value experience as is a belief concerning real objects. Things hoped for and things remembered could not otherwise become objects of an evaluation. It is evident, however, that value experiences are inherently complex, involving not only feelings but presentational experiences (*Vorstellungserlebnisse*) and judgments concerning the "presentational objects" as well. What elicits a value feeling is the presentational content, the "theme" or *"Objektiv,"* of a judgment.

It is, of course, a well known fact that all our feelings vary in intensity and duration. Meinong, however, points out that they differ in quality also, and that this difference depends on the nature of the objects which elicit them. An aesthetic experience, for example, has a "feeling-tone" that differs in quality from the sensory pleasures of a gourmet—just as the beautiful differs from the agreeable; and the "feeling-tone" elicited by economic facts and conditions differs from that of a moral situation.

It is also a fact (as Meinong had already pointed out in "Präsentation") that, in any given situation, some characteristics of an object may please us, whereas others displease us. That is to say, one and the same object may arouse "opposed" feelings in us; and this fact, quite obviously, adds to the complexity of the value experience. In valuing an object, a subject ought to take all feelings into consideration; and the valuation ought to reflect the synthesis (as it were) of the opposed feelings. Whether or not a particular subject actually achieves such a synthesis or limits himself to one or the other of the opposed feelings is a purely empirical matter and depends in each case on the disposition of the subject in a given situation (p. 90).

A further aspect of our value experience—also discussed in "Präsentation"—involves the "transfer" or extension (*Uebertragung*) of our valuations to objects which are related—either as means to an end or in some other significant way—to objects which we value. We thus value the key because it opens the door to a room which we wish to enter; and we value a "part" because of its relation to a "whole." In each case, extending the valuation from O to P is justified because of the relation of P to O. But the transfer is actually made only when we know that the relation exists. Knowledge of the interrelations of things is thus basic to the transfer or extension of valuations. That it may also entail a transfer or extension of desire is obvious.

It is Meinong's contention that all the relations which justify the transfer of a value can be interpreted as variants of an "implication." He thus sets "emotional implication" in parallel to "intellectual implication" (pp. 109–111). If this idea is accepted, then a general principle summing up the function of transfer can be formulated. It is this: If the existence of P implies the existence of an O which we value and which, therefore, is a good, then P also is a good. But if the existence of P implies the non-existence of O and if this non-existence is a disvalue, then P is an evil. On the other hand, if the non-existence of P entails the existence of an O which we value, then P is an evil; but if the non-existence of P entails the non-existence of O and thus results in a disvalue, then P is a good (p. 113).

All of this is clear and convincing; but the principle of the transfer of value fails to solve one crucial problem. When we consider the character of a value experience, it is obvious that there are no valuations unless there is a subject who values; just as there are no desires, no judgments, no presumptions, no presentations when there exists no subject that has the experience in question. The value experience in its actuality is, in effect, that "O has value for me." There is, however, a difference between "O has value for me" and "O has value"; for the latter means "value for any appropriate subject," not just "for me." The problem, therefore, is, How to transcend the essential subjectivism of "value for me" and to justify the thesis that "O has value for X, Y, Z, or any other subject"—or, simply, that "O has value." The principle of transfer does not help us here. And in this fact Meinong sees the limitations of any psychological approach to values.

X

It remains true, nevertheless, that we have no access to values except through experience; and the question is, In what way can that experience be circumscribed more precisely so as to lead to a clarification of what is meant by value?

The first fact to be noted is that value and value experience are by no means one and the same. Many things have value—and have value for me—even when I do not think of them at the moment or, if I think of them, when I do not know which of the attributes are foundational for their value to me. Moreover, our actual value experience is not only imprecise, it is also in flux. We may today experience as valuable what we did not so experience yesterday; or we may now feel as a disvalue what tomorrow we value. The notion of value, however, implies a "tendency toward constancy" and a precision which stand in marked contrast to the fluidity of our experience and our valuations.

One obvious step beyond our actual value experience is, of course, a reference to a possible value experience; and this is a step justified by experience itself—in our memory, namely, of experiences of the past as well as in our anticipations of experiences yet to come. We may therefore say that "an object has value in so far as it is the object of a possible value experience" (p. 124). Value has in that case been liberated from the flux and the changes of actual value experience. But even this is not sufficient to characterize the true nature of value. This is so because we have failed to take into consideration the role which the subject plays in the value experience.

As Meinong sees it, the possibility that an object can be valued depends "exclusively on the characteristics of the object in question"; the fact that it actually is valued depends, however, also upon the existence of a subject (p. 128). That is to say, every value experience involves an object of a given nature with which the experience is concerned, and it involves a subject which concerns itself with the object. In addition, however, the actual occurrence and intensity of the value experience depends also on various circumstances—circumstances that may include the presence and quality of other objects of the same type, or of objects which elicit value responses of a related and, therefore, of a competitive nature. And such circumstances include of necessity the characteristics and peculiarities of the subject—such as predispositions, past experiences, interests, and understanding (p. 130). The "dispositional character" of the subject—not only the subject's existence—is as important for value experience as are the characteristics of the object. From this it follows that when all circumstances determinative of the experiential situation remain constant, then it is, in effect, irrelevant and immaterial as to which particular subject has the experience. The very same object can continue to be a "value object" for any *qualified* subject and, therefore, for *any number* of qualified subjects. This means, however, that the value experience does not depend upon the existence of some particular subject. It depends only upon the existence of "a" subject capable of reacting to the "value object" in an appropriate manner (p. 130).

The radical subjectivism inherent in Meinong's psychological approach to the problem of values has thus been overcome. Reference to a subject, broadly understood, is, however, still essential; for "values come into being and cease to be as do the subjects for which they are values" (p. 135).

XI

Having thus clarified further the nature of a value experience and its presuppositions, Meinong now analyzes more specifically various aspects of value itself. It may seem reasonable, he tells us, to suppose that the "higher" value is correlated with the "stronger" value-feelings. Actually, however, no such correlation exists. Even in the simplest of our value experiences the value is related to both, a feeling which assumes the existence of the valued object and a feeling which assumes its non-existence; and both feelings contribute to the value. But since an object cannot exist and not-exist at the same time, the two feelings, though belonging together as components of the total value, can never be experienced together. And his means, as far as Meinong is concerned, that the total value—or the value as such—of an object is never directly experienced. It can only be thought.

So far, however, we have considered value only in relation to a subject—i.e., we have considered value as "person-dependent" (p. 143). In doing so, we have found that, given a subject and its specific aptitudes and desires, the value of an object consists in "the fitness of that object (by virtue of its characteristics and its position) to be an object in whose existence or non-existence the subject takes an interest" (p. 144)—a theme first introduced in "Für die Psychologie und gegen den Psychologismus in der allgemeinen Werttheorie" (1912). But Meinong does not rest his case here. He now points out—as he did earlier, in "Ueber emotionale Präsentation" (1917)—that the idea of "person-dependent" values (as just defined) does not really express what is ordinarily meant by value. Errors in valuation, in particular, are revelatory in this respect. Thus, if value consists simply in the fitness of an object to elicit the interest of a subject, and in nothing else, then what right do we have to say that a "charm" or amulet has no value or that its value is purely imaginary? After all, people do take an "interest" in such things and believe in them. What emerges here is the problem of an objective standard of values and, therefore, of the objectivity of the values themselves. Are not truth, the morally good, loyalty, and love, for example, values that have objective significance and that do not depend on the particularities of a subject?

If value cannot be freed from its close connection with feeling-responses, then it cannot be separated from the emotional idiosyncracies of the various subjects and loses all objective significance. However, in "Präsentation" Meinong had already maintained that value-feelings are essentially presentational experiences and have a cognitive function comparable to that of perceptions. He now makes the most of this thesis.

As experience a value-feeling is always subject-related—as is also every perceptual experience. But just as the dependence of sense impressions upon a subject does not compel us to regard what we experience as purely subjective, so the fact that we encounter values only in a value experience does not compel us to regard all values as purely subjective. In both cases we face the problem of conceptualizing what we experience; and, Meinong believes, the conditions for a definitional clarification of what is meant by "impersonal" or objective values are especially favorable because presentational value experiences allow a more definite characterization than does, for example, the difference between perceived color and perceived sound. This is so because, as Meinong has argued repeatedly, value-feelings are judgment-feelings. Their presuppositions clearly separate them from all other feelings, and their presentational content, their "dignitative," occupies a place and serves a function in our experience that is similar to the place and the function of "objective" in cognition. Moreover, even person-dependent valuations, so we have seen, involve, in principle and at the same time, both an "existence-feeling" and a "non-existence-feeling"—feelings, that is, which are direct opposites; and this is true also in the case of "impersonal" or objective values. In neither case is the value simply identical with one or the other of the two value-feelings. In the case of person-dependent values, however, it is the function of the subject to fuse the opposed value-feelings into a unified conception of the value—and this is precisely what makes the value person-dependent (p. 160). The question is, Can the idea of person-dependent values and the idea of "impersonal" or objective values be fused into one conception "value" that will encompass all relevant phenomena?

On the face of it, such a fusion seems to be impossible; for what is characteristic of a person-dependent value—namely, its dependence upon a subject—is precisely what would destroy the idea of an "impersonal" or objective value. If it now be suggested that it is of the essence of person-dependent values, not that they depend upon this or that particular subject, but upon a "subject in general," and that therefore the person-dependent values attain themselves the status of objectivity, then Meinong points out that not much is gained by such an argument, for what has value for a particular subject does not necessarily have value for every subject, and we have no assurance that what is common to the nature of all subjects is a sufficient basis for a value experience (p. 162). The so-called "normal" subject is but a speculative abstraction. It is significant, however, that it makes sense to say of some value-feelings—but not of all—that they are "justified"; for "being justified" does not depend on the nature of the subject having the experience; it depends on objective criteria. The parallel to perceptual experiences that are basic to scientific knowledge is quite clear. Meinong himself had referred to it in "Präsentation." It must be noted, however, that even the values disclosed in a "justified" value feeling—i.e., the "impersonal" or objective values—are only relative. To regard them as absolute would mean to take them entirely out of the context of human experience and thus to make the concept "value" empty and meaningless.

As Meinong now sees it, "personal" and objective values can all be brought together in one encompassing interpretation. To be sure, not every objective value is also a "personal" value for every subject but, "justifiably," it ought to be one; for "whatever has objective value has value for every valuing subject; what has objective value, therefore, has at all times also personal value. But not everything that has personal value has objective value as well" (p. 165). It would be demanding too much if we were to insist that, in order to be acknowledged a value at all, a value must be demonstrably "impersonal" or objective. After all, every value-feeling directly "legitimatizes" the value of that which is valued, and it "legitimatizes" it for the person who actually experiences the feeling. That is to say, the value-feeling directly legitimatizes the value as a "personal" value; and in this respect it can be no more in error than is a sense impression in its immediacy. The situation is quite different, however, when "impersonal" or objective values are involved. In this case error is possible; and it is possible because the value-feeling is but the experiential basis for a judgmental apprehension of a "universally prevalent" or objective value. In making the judgment we go beyond our presentational feelings and, in doing so, we may go astray (p. 167).

BIBLIOGRAPHY

Eaton, Howard O., *The Austrian Philosophy of Values,* Norman Oklahoma, 1930.
Findlay, J. N., *Meinong's Theory of Objects and Values,* Oxford, second edition, 1963.

Meinong, Alexius, *Psychologisch-Ethische Untersuchungen zur Werttheorie,* Graz, 1894.

————"Ueber Werthaltung und Wert," *Archiv für systematische Philosophie,* Vol. I, 1895, pp. 327–346.

————*Ueber Annahmen,* Leipzig, 1902. Second edition 1910.

————"Ueber Urteilsgefühle, Was sie sind und was sie nicht sind," *Archiv für die gesamte Psychologie,* Vol. IV, 1906, pp. 21–58.

————"Für die Psychologie und gegen den Psychologismus in der allgemeinen Werttheorie," *Logos,* Vol. III, 1912, pp. 1–14.

————"Ueber emotionale Präsentation," *Sitzungsberichte der kaiserlichen Akademie der Wissenschaften* (Philosophisch-Historische Klasse), Vol. 183, Vienna, 1917, pp. 1–181.

————*Zur Grundlegung der allgemeinen Werttheorie* (posthumous) Ernst Malley, editor, Graz, 1923.

Kraus, Oskar, *Die Werttheorien: Geschichte und Kritik,* Brünn, 1937.

CHAPTER IV

VON EHRENFELS AND DESIRE AS THE BASIS OF VALUES

Christian von Ehrenfels had studied under both, Brentano and Meinong, and was strongly influenced by both. His interest in value-theoretical problems had been aroused by them. Nevertheless, even his first publications—"Ueber Fühlen und Wollen" (1887) and the more extensive "Werttheorie und Ethik" (1893) —reflect his conviction that Brentano was mistaken in his effort to make "right love" and "right hate" the key concepts in value theory, and that Meinong had failed to establish the thesis that feeling is the sole basis of all valuations. His own belief was that desire was decisive.

In 1895, in an essay entitled "Ueber Werthaltung und Wert," Meinong had responded to von Ehrenfels' criticisms by modifying his initial position (as stated in *Psychologisch-Ethische Untersuchungen zur Werttheorie,"* 1894). At the same time, however, he also advanced impressive arguments against von Ehrenfels' thesis. And to these arguments von Ehrenfels replied in 1896, in the *Archiv für systematische Philosophie:* "Von der Wertdefinition zum Motivationsgesetze," admitting that, in order to meet Meinong's criticisms, he had to modify his position in certain respects but placing renewed emphasis on the close connection between value, on the one hand, and the causal relation between desire and feeling, on the other.

Because of the role which desires and feelings play in value experience, two distinct definitions of value are apparently possible—one making desire the crucial factor, the other making feeling decisive. Meinong had acknowledged both possibilities but had regarded feeling as basic. Von Ehrenfels, also recognizing both possibilities, accepted desire as foundational (p. 104). His first definition was: "Value is the relation—erroneously objectified by the language we use—of a thing to a human desire that is directed toward it" ("Werttheorie," p. 89). "Desire" is here intended to include all possible as well as all actual desires and, therefore, refers to a desire-disposition (*Begehrungsdisposition*) rather than to any specific desire (p. 209).

Meinong objected to this definition of value, arguing that we can desire only what we know or believe to be non-existent, and that therefore (on von Ehrenfels' definition) everything that exists must be without value. Accepting this objection as justified, von Ehrenfels modified his original definition. "Value," he now states, "is the relation—erroneously objectified by the language we use—of a thing O to the desire-disposition of a subject S in consequence of which O could be desired by S insofar or as soon as S is not convinced of the existence of O." And he adds: "This correction is the only modification I consider necessary in view of Meinong's arguments" ("Wertdefinition," p. 104). The real point, however, is that value is here taken to be a relation and as existing only as a relation; that it does not exist in the way things and their attributes exist.

Meinong, it will be remembered, had identified value-feelings with judgment-feelings, and had argued that the certainty or "firmness" of a belief rather than its truth is the indispensable precondition of a value-response. Von Ehrenfels does not deny that exitsential judgments may in some of our value experiences be the psychological factor that determines the quality of the value-feelings; he maintains, however, that "the ultimate and necessary causal link" is not a judgment concerning the existence or non-existence of an object but "the concrete and vivid [anticipatory] presentation (*Vorstellung*) of the realization and non-realization of that object" (p. 113). That is to say, "we ascribe value (or disvalue) to a real or to a merely imagined object insofar as the appropriate concrete and vivid presentation of its realization causes an enhancement (or a dimunition) of happiness as compared with the presentation of its non-realization" (p. 116).

If we now ask, where does desire enter into the value experience as just described, von Ehrenfels replies that "desire is not a new primary mental phemonenon but merely a special case of our presentational experience as this conforms with the law of a relative enhancement of happiness (p. 121). This law, as formulated by von Ehrenfels, states that "the presentations which enhance happiness, and just because they enhance happiness, have a tendency to maintain and strengthen one another in the struggle for attention" (*ibid.*); and it is this tendency that von Ehrenfels calls desire. But the term 'desire' has a rather broad meaning. So long as the presentations in question remain isolated, desire is merely a *wish*. When presentations of means for the attainment of what is wished for are added and an effort is actually made to attain it, desire becomes a *striving*. And when the subject is convinced that the wished-for goal can be attained through his own activity, desire becomes *volition*. "The strength of a desire, moreover, is not the intensity of a specific mental quality—such as pleasure or displeasure—but the degree of resistance with which the presentational experience that is constitutive of the desire opposes any other experience in the struggle for attention" (p. 121).

Enough has now been said about von Ehrenfels' initial position to give us a basis for a more detailed consideration of his definitive views in the field of value theory—views which he set forth in Volume I of his *System der Werttheorie* (1897), which, incidentally, bears the subtitle "Allgemeine Werttheorie, Psychologie des Begehrens," thus indicating the scope as well as the basic orientation of the work. Volume II of the *System,* published in 1898, and subtitled "Grundzüge einer Ethik" is an application to the special field of ethics of the broad principles developed in Volume I. Volume III was to have been devoted to an application of those same principles to the field of economics; but it was never published. Since our interests here center on the problems of a general value theory, we shall concentrate on Volume I, and shall touch upon problems of ethics only incidentally. It would have been of special significance, however, if Volume III had been completed; for von Ehrenfels, who was exceptionally responsive to the socio-cultural conditions and developments of his time, was convinced that, under the influence of Jevons and Gossen, the Austrian economists (notably Menger and von Wieser) had "completely disproven" the Marxist theory of value (*System,* I, p. vii); that, nevertheless, economic values are but "a special category of the value-facts of human experience in general" and should therefore be considered within a context which also includes the problem of moral values. Unless they are so considered, the socio-political struggles and the requests for social reforms will remain without proper guidance. The problem seemed all the more urgent because of Nietzsche's demand for a transvaluation of all values and because of the implications of Darwin's theory of evolution. "There can be on doubt," von Ehrenfels wrote, "the conviction grows ever more that what is needed urgently is a scientifically based theory which encompasses all areas of human valuing" (*ibid.,* p. ix). And he intended to develop just such a theory, making full use of his own (essentially introspective) researches into the nature of desire.

I

It is a prejudice of long standing, so von Ehrenfels begins his study, to speak of values as if they were properties or constitutive parts of external things whose presence makes the things themselves desirable. But our author intends to do away with this prejudice by basing his interpretation upon an analysis of our value experience. As he puts it, "we do not desire things because we recognize in them that mystic and incomprehensible essence 'value,' but we attribtue 'value' to things because we desire them" (p. 2). The situation is complicated, however, by the fact that not all things which we desire are also valuable; that, in fact, only things worthy of being desired are truly valuable.

If we could assume that values inhere in things, it would be easy to deal with the problems here involved; for if values inhere in the things themselves, then we can readily show that only those objects worthy of being desired should actually be desired. But this path is not open to von Ehrenfels. His initial commitment to an experiental approach to values forestalls it. The question, therefore, is: Can von Ehrenfels determine on his own grounds whether or not a thing is worthy of being desired? That it can be desired or is being desired is easily ascertained. But is an object that is being desired also worthy of being an object of desire? Von Ehrenfels maintains that this, too, can be demonstrated on empirical grounds—provided we analyze correctly the role which desires and feelings play in our value experience.

"Feelings," in von Ehrenfels' terminology, are all "those mental states which are characterized by pleasure or suffering" (p. 5) —irrespective of whether such states are more specifically defined as joy, agreeableness, well-being, or as pain, disagreeableness, and suffering, respectively. The varying degrees of intensity of pleasure and suffering, moreover, can be arranged in a one-dimensional continuum, ranging from the highest ecstasy to the deepest despair.

The term 'desire' (so we have already seen) refers to all forms of wishing, striving, and willing. That is, it refers to all mental acts which have in common that they are directed toward the realization of some goal or purpose, or toward the avoidance of some event. We thus experience positive and negative acts of desiring. All desires, however, are motivated; and concerning the nature of their motivation two views are commonly held. According to one, feelings are the causative factor: I desire this or that because it pleases me. According to the other view, feelings or inclinations may by causative in a good many, if not in all, cases of desire; but human beings have the capacity to subordinate such desires to the imperatives of reason. This second view, von Ehrenfels maintains, entails difficulties and contradictions which cannot be resolved. This is so, he points out, because reason itself can become effective in practical affairs only through the intermediacy of feelings. In every concrete situation, thought discloses to us a certain number of possibilities or directions of action. Of these we actually adopt only one; and we adopt it because of its emotional appeal (p. 9). The second view, therefore, reduces to the first; and von Ehrenfels now accepts that view as his own. That is to say, he accepts the view that the occurrence or non-occurrence of any desire whatever, and the strength and persistence of the desire, depend upon the feelings which the existence or non-existence of specific objects and projected alternatives of action arouse in us.

But further analysis is necessary; for the relation that exists between feelings and desires can be interpreted in various ways. For example, it may be maintained that feeling and desiring are one and the same mental phenomenon; or it may be argued that feeling depends upon desire rather than desire upon feeling. But these views von Ehrenfels explicitly repudiates. As to the first of them, he points out that we can and do experience pleasure or pain without experiencing desire, just as we can and do desire without experiencing pleasure or pain. Von Ehrenfels here takes a position comparable to that of Meinong who meticulously distinguished loving and hating from feelings of pleasure and pain as well as from desiring. Moreover,—as did Meinong before him —von Ehrenfels maintains that a fundamental difference exists between feeling and desiring which is comparable to the difference between presentational experiences and judgments. In view of this difference one might be inclined to regard pleasure and pain as simple and undefinable "acts" and might then interpret desire as a complex mental phenomenon in which feelings of pleasure and/or of pain are component elements. This, it may be remembered, was Meinong's original thesis. Von Ehrenfels, however, does not accept it. His thesis is that we can and do desire without at the same time experiencing a feeling. It is perfectly possible, for example, to will something even if the intensity of the accompanying feeling has sunk so low that, despite serious efforts and attention, we can no longer discern it. Moreover, our volitions can be accompanied by fluctuating feelings and yet remain steady and resolute, not undergoing comparable fluctuations. And there is no *a priori* reason why the accompanying feelings might not at times vanish altogether without affecting our volition (p. 16).

If all this seems to contradict von Ehrenfels' thesis of the causative role of feelings referred to earlier, he now re-asserts that the origin as well as the strength of the desire is determined solely by the feeling which the individual is capable of experiencing in view of the existence or non-existence of the object desired. The influence of the faculty of thought upon desire is restricted to giving us an idea of which objects are desirable, of the means by which they may be attained, and the judgments that these means do indeed lead to the objects. But he now adds that "the inner core of desire is not to be found in feeling"; that it lies in "the realm of the possible"—a realm which has nothing in common with the simple feelings of pleasure and displeasure (p. 23). But neither is feeling a product of desire.

If we now attempt to formulate more precisely the interrelations of feelings and desires, three possibilities of interpretation suggest themselves: (1) Every desire may be assumed to have as its ultimate aim the realization of one's own pleasure or the prevention of one's own suffering. (2) In every case, that object or situation is desired the idea of which arouses a feeling of pleasure in us, and that is avoided the idea of which produces a feeling of suffering. (3) Our emotional dispositions, either alone or in conjunction with imagined or actual feelings, determine our desires.

The first of these alternatives, identified as "absolute psychological egoism" (p. 24), von Ehrenfels repudiates. He admits that, occasionally, the feelings expected as the result of alternative courses of action may be decisive in our selection of the alternative actually to be pursued; but he points out that in many situations of choice and desire no reference to our own future pleasure or future suffering can be discerned. This is especially true in the affairs of our ordinary daily routine. Still more important, however, is the fact that we may, and do, desire goals which entail emotional experiences the like we have never had before and of which we can therefore have no clear idea, or we may desire goals which lie so far in the future that we cannot possibly hope to attain them and experience the emotion which they might cause. It thus does not make much sense to maintain that every desire has as its ultimate aim the realization of one's own pleasure or the prevention of one's own suffering. And it is also a fact that in at least some of our actions we completely neglect our own future feelings and desire goals which transcend our self-interest; for we may and we do directly desire the happiness of others (p. 29).

When we now turn to the second possible interpretation mentioned above, then we must admit, so von Ehrenfels maintains, that when, after some hesitation and indecision, we decide upon a specific course of action, reflection will reveal that we have chosen that course which, initially at least, gives us more pleasure than does any alternative action. This does not mean that, as our action proceeds, it must continue to enhance our pleasure or diminish our suffering. The psychological fact that we experience an initial feeling of pleasure at the moment when we decide upon a course of action is perfectly reconcilable even with the fact that we may actually desire our own destruction and not our happiness (p. 31). The preponderance of pleasure need occur only at the moment of choice. At that moment, however, it must occur if the choice is to be made at all in the direction indicated. Von Ehrenfels sums this up in the following "basic law": "At the moment of its initiation every act of striving or willing [i.e., every act of desire] enhances the state of happiness as compared with that state which would be experienced if the act in question were omitted" (p. 32). This does not mean that every act of desire brings about an absolute increase in happiness; for it is possible to strive to prevent an evil which, nevertheless, steadily increases, thus making us ever more wretched. But it does mean that an enhancement of pleasure must occur at the moment of our initial decision. The view under consideration, however,—the second possible interpretation of the interrelations of feelings and desire—goes beyond this simple fact; for it entails the thesis that the enhancement of pleasure is actually the motive for our choice. And this thesis, von Ehrenfels holds, is a distortion of what is actually experienced. We simply do not desire objects or distant goals for the sake of the pleasure which we experience at the moment of determining our course of action (p. 34).

According to the third interpretation mentioned above, the controlling factors in determining the direction and strength of our desires are our feeling-dispositions (*Gefühlsdispositionen*), not the feelings themselves. The acts are "an immediate manifestation (*Ausfluss*) of the feelings-dispositions" (p. 36). Only thus, von Ehrenfels believes, can we account for the "law of the relative enhancement of happiness" (p. 37). If it should be argued (as Carl Stumpf proposed) that the feeling of pleasure which accompanies a desire is sufficient to account for the enhancement of happiness, then the facts of experience contradict the argument; for, in the first place, feelings of pleasure do by no means accompany all our acts of striving but only those where we are confident that we will attain our objective. And, in the second place, even if pleasure would, without exception, accompany all our acts of striving, it remains a fact that, compared with the phenomena of our anticipatory conception of the desired object—our hope of gaining possession of it, or our fear of losing it—our striving and willing themselves are rather weak sources of emotions. If the more potent sources of our feelings do not determine desire, then it might well be the case that the pleasure derived directly from the acts of willing and striving is more than compensated for by the displeasure arising from other sources. The result would be that our actual striving and willing represent a more unpleasant feeling-state than does our inaction. But this never happens; for if it did, we would not act. We may conclude, therefore, that acts of desire (including all striving and willing) are determined by the more potent sources of pleasure just referred to.

One other fact must be considered. The maximum sacrifice (i.e., giving up pleasure and/or accepting suffering) that one is willing to make for the sake of a desired goal is the measure of the strength of the desire; and the degree of suffering or displeasure sufficient to lead to the suspension of the pursuit of a goal is an (approximate) measure of the relative increase in the total happiness that was hoped for when the course of action was decided upon. This is so, von Ehrenfels argues, because an act of volition or striving will not be carried through when it is no longer expected to bring about a state of greater happiness than would its omission.

Since what is true of striving and willing as forms of desire is true also of wishing (though perhaps to a lesser degree), von Ehrenfels now formulates the following "universal law": "All acts of desire are determined in their goals as well as in their strength by the relative enhancement of happiness which they entail in view of the feeling-dispositions of the individual concerned— both, when they first enter his consciousness and, thereafter, for the time of their duration" (p. 41).

This law is the culmination of von Ehrenfels' "psychological excursus" which is foundational to his value theory. But if, in any given situation, desire always tends to realize the best possible feeling-state conceivable by the subject; and if the strength of the desire is always proportional to the difference between two feeling-states which the subject cannot realize or even conceive together at the same time; does not this suggest that there must be a deeper lying, genetic connection between feeling and desiring which will account for the facts of experience? This problem von Ehrenfels discusses when he resumes his psychological analyses. In the meantime, however, the value problems proper require attention.

II

It follows from the discussions so far that von Ehrenfels cannot accept the notion of absolute values. He himself recognizes this and is keenly aware of the fact that, on this point at least, his value theory contradicts, and must contradict, the "stubborn tradition of common sense." This consequence von Ehrenfels is willing to accept; for if value theory is to achieve the status of genuine knowledge, it can contain nothing which is not directly "given" in experience, or which cannot be justified on the basis of that experience. Nothing more is here claimed for value theory than what is generally conceded in the case of the natural sciences.

Von Ehrenfels begins his argument in a somewhat pragmatic vein. If someone were to deny absolute values, he points out, and were then to desire error and hate knowledge, his position (though unusual) would not in itself be an absurdity; for it is not self-contradictory. But if this same person were to act in accordance with his preferences, he would soon encounter undesirable and contradictory consequences. Experience would speedily reveal to him the "utility value" of knowledge and the disvalue of error in relation to any goal whose realization depends on the employment of appropriate means (p. 47). If we now assume, for the sake of argument, that someone might prefer pain to pleasure (as some ascetics actually do), then analysis will soon show that the pleasures rejected and the pains preferred are essentially "bodily" pleasures and pains, and that beyond them looms large the hope for a state of bliss as the driving motive; that every successful denial of the pleasures of this world and every realization of pain contribute in themselves to an ultimate happiness. The rejection of pleasure and the desire for pain thus turn out to be only facets of a much more profound desire. And if this should

not be the case, we would regard the preference of pain over pleasure as indicative of a perversion of human nature.

Brentano, it will be remembered, had stressed what he regarded as a value-theoretical analogue to cognitive experience,
and had argued that just as analytic and perceptual judgments are
in themselves evident, so "right loving" and "right hating" find
their justification in the immediacy of our affective-conative responses. He had left undecided, however, the question as to which
is basic in that experience, feeling or desire. What von Ehrenfels
finds acceptable in Brentano's philosophy is the empirical approach which makes an "act of valuing" (*Werthaltung*)—i.e., of
ascribing value to things and situations—and not the uncritical
assumption of some absolute value the basis for value considerations. He regards it as essential, however, to make the commitment which Brentano did not make; and so he states bluntly:
"We ascribe value to things because we desire them" (p. 51). Desire rather than feeling has thus been made basic; and upon this
premise von Ehrenfels' theory now rests.

If it be argued that this foundation is inadequate because we
ascribe value to things even though we do not desire them because
we already possess them, it will be remembered that Meinong already raised this objection and that von Ehrenfels responded by
modifying his initial statement slightly. He now restates that
modified form: "We ascribe value to those things which we either
actually desire or which we would desire if we were not already
convinced of their existence"; but this is merely another way of
saying that *"the value of a thing is its desirability"* (p. 53). "Even
the magnitude of the value is proportional to desirability—i.e., it
is proportional to the strength of the actual desire that corresponds to the desirability: the stronger the desire with which we
desire (or would desire) an object, the higher is the value which
that object possesses for us" (*ibid.*).

It must be noted, furthermore, that von Ehrenfels specifically
acknowledges that we can and do desire not only things but
"events" and "states of affairs" as well, and "even relationships
and possibilities." In every case, however, so he points out, our
desire is directed, not toward these "so-called objects" as such,
"but always toward their existence or non-existence" (p. 54).

Moreover, if we desire the existence of an "object"—taking that term in the broad sense just indicated—we may also desire that it be available to us; and if we desire its non-existence, this may mean merely that we desire being spared its presence. Every desire which is directed toward the existence or availability of an "object" is the basis for a *positive value* or, simply, for a *value*. Every desire which is directed toward the non-existence of an "object" is the ground for a *negative value* or a *disvalue*. However, by a process of conversion—i.e., by an interchange of the references to existence and non-existence—every disvalue can be transformed into a value, and every value into a disvalue. The non-existence of pain, for example, has as much value as the existence of that pain has disvalue.

Since desire is determined in its direction as well as in its strength by "'feeling-dispositions," it seems possible to define value also "through a recourse to feelings"—as Meinong had proposed. Meinong's thesis, it will be remembered, had been that "value-feelings" are "existence-feelings"—feelings of pleasure and displeasure pertaining to particular "presentational content" (*Vorstellungsinhalt*) of an experience insofar as that content is at the same time also the content of an affirmative or a negative existential judgment. According to Meinong, therefore, the value (or disvalue) of an "object," O, is proportional to the sum of the intensities of the feelings of pleasure and displeasure elicited separately by the two judgments, "O exists," and "O does not exist." This interpretation von Ehrenfels regards as unacceptable. Even a refinement and reformulation of the interrelation of the feelings involved—a refinement that would bring Meinong's thesis into closer harmony with experience—remains deficient so long as the role which cognitive judgments play in value experience is completely neglected. After all, cognitive judgments are in large measure basic to, and determinative of, the meaning and specificity of our presentational experiences and, therefore, of our feeling-responses. That is to say, quite similar concrete and vivid presentational experiencs (*Vorstellungen*) elicit different feelings, depending on the cognitive judgments which interpret them. The pain in our chest, for example, may be as severe as ever, but the judgment that it is the result of indigestion rather than of a heart attack alters materially our feeling-response. Or, to use another example, we may experience intense positive feelings when we witness a well-constructed, well-written, and well-acted tragedy in the theater. But if the events taking place on stage were judged to be actual and not "theater," we would be horrified. Judgment thus completely transmutes our feelings. What might have been experienced as a disvalue now is a positive value.

The function of cognitive judgments in value experience is actually twofold. They tend to make presentational experiences more specific and concrete, thus increasing their vividness; and they raise into consciousness presentational complexities which, without the judgments, would remain unnoticed. But since these are their only functions, it is possible to eliminate all explicit references to cognitive judgments from further consideration by stipulating, as von Ehrenfels does, that "by existence-feelings we mean a feeling which arises as the result of *the most concrete, the most vivid, and the most complete presentational experience possible* of the existence or non-existence of an object" (p. 62).

To be sure, cognitive judgments still function as before; but they are now considered as merely a part of the presentational experience; and their inclusion in that experience makes possible von Ehrenfels' definition of value as that relation between an object and a subject in which the most concrete, the most vivid, and the most complete representation possible of the existence of the object elicits in the subject a feeling higher on the pleasure-displeasure scale than does the feeling aroused by an equally concrete, vivid, and complete representation of the object's non-existence, the magnitude of the value being proportional to the strength of the desire and the distance between the two feelings in the pleasure-displeasure scale (p. 65).

If this definition is accepted, then—so von Ehrenfels maintains—we may, *in a transposed sense*, also call value all those attributes of an object by virtue of which the relationship characteristic of any value experience exists between a subject and an object; and, in an extension of this transposed sense, we may even call the object itself a value. The context within which the term 'value' is being used thus determines in each case just what is meant.

In a strict sense, every value—be it interpreted as relation, as attribute, or as the object itself—is "given" only in relation to some particular subject at some particular time. This is so because the dispositions basic to the feelings that determine our desires may vary in countless ways—not only from individual to individual, but for the same individual in the course of his life-time; and these variations are reflected in differences in valuations. Even so, however, it remains true that every definition of a value aims at a more or less comprehensive generality and, for this reason, assumes a generalized (and even fictitious) "normal state" of feeling-dispositions, "either for a number of individuals or for whole classes of them" (p. 67). We can thus speak of the valuations of "different age-classes," of different professions, of social classes and cultural groups and, finally, even of mankind as a whole. Such generalized valuations may then be contrasted with, and superimposed upon, the individualized valuations of our immediate and unreflective experience and may thus serve as standards for our valuations. They may serve as "norms" which the individual "ought to" adopt (p. 69).

A very important differentiation of values derives from the fact that many objects come into a valuational relation to a subject only through the intermediacy of a judgment to the effect that they are means necessary to the realization of some valued end. What von Ehrenfels points up here is (in C. I. Lewis' terminology) the distinction between "intrinsic" and "instrumental" values. But once this distinction is recognized, a further distinction— that between "real" and "merely presumed" values—must be made. This distinction depends on the truth or falsity, respectively, of the factual judgment asserting the means-end relationship.

Summarizing the distinctions just made, we find that von Ehrenfels recognizes the following variations in our references to value. We may mean: (1) *Value proper,* defined as a characteristic relation between subject and object; (2) *value in a transposed sense,* meaning attributes of objects or the objects themselves; (3) *individual* as distinguished from *general* values; (4) *momentary* as distinguished from *normal* values; (5) *actual* as distinguished from *normative* or "imperatival" values; and (6) *real* as distinguished from merely *presumed* values. That these groupings are not mutually exclusive is obvious; and that various characterizations of values can be combined is also evident. An individual value, for example, may also be actual and normative, and a general value may be normal as well as general.

Corresponding distinctions may, of course, be made when we deal with disvalues.

When we turn next to a consideration of the subjective acts that are characteristic of value experience, we find that von Ehrenfels again recognizes various distinctions. Thus he speaks of *werten, werthalten, Wertung, bewerten, wertgeben, wertschätzen,* and *Werturteil.* In its transitive sense, *werten,* "to value," means the same as *werthalten,* namely, "to regard as valuable" or "to be conscious of the value which a particular object has for one." *Wertung* or "valuation" refers more specifically to that consciousness itself and to the feeling- and desire-dispositions underlying it. The term may be used, however, to refer to the dispositions alone; and it is in this sense that von Ehrenfels usually uses it. *Bewerten* means "to evaluate," i.e., to determine the magnitude of the value of an object, either absolutely or relative to other values—but especially in terms of the sacrifices one is willing to make for its sake. *Wertgeben* means "to ascribe a value to an object," either as experiential relation or, in the transposed sense, as an attribute. *Wertschätzen* is used ambiguously by von Ehrenfels. At times he takes it to mean the same as (positive) *valuing;* but at other times he uses it as a synonym for *evaluation. Werturteil* or "value judgment" is simply the judgmental acknowledgment of the existence of some particular value relation, the object of a positive value relation being a good, that of a negative value relation being an evil.

The acts of valuing and evaluating are, of course, of special significance, the former being the very essence of a value experience; the latter being the indispensable pre-condition for all preferences. But as von Ehrenfels sees it, the most frequent as well as the most natural occasion for evaluating an object is the real or presumed knowledge that one is able to exert some influence upon the existence or non-existence of the object concerned. If such knowledge is absent, the act of evaluating is simply a "squandering of energy." And this fact reveals most convincingly the close connection between the ascription of value and desire; for the latter is but the mental phenomenon through which man consciously exerts his influence upon the existence or non-existence of internal as well as external objects. Experience does not show, however, so von Ehrenfels continues, that every act of desire, and every decision in the case of a conflict of desires, is preceded by an act of valuing or evaluating. What does take place is this: The expected course of events as it would occur without the intervention of the subject is first imagined (*vorgestellt*). Then, if the case does not involve a conflict of desires, the existence of the "object" that will emerge in the end, and all foreseeable consequences, will also be imagined. If this second act indicates that the course of events would lead to an enhancement of happiness, then "in this very act desire is also given" (p. 72). If, however, there is a conflict, then the anticipatory presentation (*Vorstellung*) of the existence of that "object" which entails the expectation of the greatest enhancement of happiness will prevail in the end and will determine the subject's action. In the struggle of competing anticipations, the subject may become aware of those feelings and their differences which are essential to valuing and evaluating; but for the occurrence of the desire such awareness is by no means necessary. The reason for a value ascription (*Wertgebung*) is the fact that, at times and because of an inadequate or a faulty understanding of the anticipated course of events or its alternatives, an "object" is being desired which, when actually attained or realized, turns out to be the less pleasant. The feeling of remorse experienced after a misdirected desire has come to fruition is sufficient inducement to consider henceforth more carefully the "affective consequences" (*Gefühlswirkungen*) of alternative courses of action. The precise determinations of these consequences, obtained for the purpose of avoiding remorse, are our valuations and evaluations of objects and events. However, the human mind is so constituted that, once our interest in valuations and value ascriptions has been aroused, we value and evaluate objects even though we know that we can have no more influence upon their existence or non-existence than we have upon the stars in heaven. But these valuations always strike us as mere "theorizing" and even as playful.

III

Just as we desire many objects because they are a means to a
valued end, so we value others because they stand in a causal
and/or constitutive relation to objects which we value for themselves (p. 75). Such "mediated valuations," however, depend
upon the known or assumed connection of their objects with the
object of an unmediated or direct valuation. But if this is so, then
three different cases of mediated values are possible: Either the
connection is constitutive only, or it is causal only, or it is a mix-
ture of the causal and the constitutive—as it is, for example, in
the case of some ore which is valued because of the iron it contains when the iron itself is valued only because of its usefulness.
Of these three types of "mediated valuations" the first-mentioned
is of special significance, for we can easily combine it with the
class of "unmediated values" into a major class which includes
all values pertaining to "objects" because the "objects" are valued either because of what they themselves are, or because of
one or more of their constituent parts. This class von Ehrenfels
speaks of as the class of "intrinsic values" (*Eigenwerte*). The
remaining two classes he regards as derivative; but since causal relations most frequently mediate the value relation, he suggests
that we combine the two classes and speak here of "efficacy-val-
ues" (*Wirkungswerte*). The following schema represents the relationships just indicated:

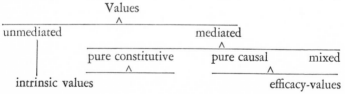

A similar schema can be constructed for the corresponding
types of disvalues. It must be understood, however, that the distinctions here indicated do not preclude the possibility that one
and the same "object" may be the "bearer of several value-relations" (*Wertbeziehungen*). It may, for example, be an intrinsic
value in one context and an efficacy-value in another; or, because
of some of its properties, it may have a positive value when, because of other properties, it also has a disvalue (p. 78).

IV

When we now turn to the problem of determining the "magnitude" of a value or the "value-height," von Ehrenfels suggests that we begin our investigation with mediated or "derivative" values; for, if we do so, we can make use of certain principles developed by the economists—notably by Menger, von Wieser, and Böhm-Bawerk of the "Austrian School." The most obvious of these principles is "the law of marginal utility" according to which the derivative value of any object arbitrarily selected from a given supply of interchangeable "goods" is determined, not by the foreseeable actual usefulness of the object, but by its marginal utility (p. 84). This law assumes, however, that, in the pursuit of his economic goals, man is on the whole a reasonable creature. It is an assumption that must be made for value theory in general.

The economist's concern is essentially with the "object" rather than with the subject in the value relation; and this "object-approach" falls short of giving us a satisfactory solution of the basic value problems. There are two reasons for this: (1) Even the law of marginal utility assumes the existence of a subject interested in the realization of certain ends. If that subject is taken out of the picture, any reference to values is meaningless. (2) A solution of the problem of derivative values is not in itself also a solution for the problem of unmediated or intrinsic values. Also, several subjects may value the same object, and may value it differently. How can we compare and correlate such valuations when we approach the problem from the side of the object? The answer, of course, is that we can not. But when we take the subject to be the key to the whole value problem, then a solution can readily be found.

Earlier in his discussions von Ehrenfels had suggested that we might attempt to compare all positive values in terms of the disvalues one is willing to accept—i.e., in terms of the sacrifices one is willing to make—in their realization. While this procedure is quite useful when we deal with economic matters, it does not help much when we try to understand the nature of value itself, for it merely "measures" one value in terms of another. Von Ehrenfels, however, believes that it may also serve well when we try to compare the valuations of different individuals; for we can then say that A ascribes to O a greater value than does B if, given the same circumstances, A is willing to sacrifice more for the sake of O than is B (p. 94). The whole meaning of value-height is thus keyed to the relative power of motivation with respect to O. And if this is granted, so von Ehrenfels argues, then "the magnitude of a collective value is equal to the sum of the individual relative value magnitudes as determined by the various subjects involved" (p. 101).

It may readily be admitted that "collective values" are of special importance—both, in theoretical as well as in practical respects—in economics and ethics; but it is doubtful that von Ehrenfels has succeeded so far in formulating adequate criteria for determining the magnitude or the height of values. A reference to our willingness to make sacrifices—either individually or collectively—is no more illuminating as far as a scale of values is concerned than is a direct appeal to the relative strengths of our motives. A well-grounded value theory must have a more secure basis than this.

The problem is complicated further by the fact that our value experience is not free from error. Actually, errors occur in our valuations as readily as in our value ascriptions and, therefore, in our evaluations; and errors of various types occur. Thus, since some valuations and value ascriptions presuppose factual judgments concerning the nature of the objects involved, they are right or wrong depending on whether the judgments are true or false. Errors of this type may pertain to intrinsic as well as to derivative values. Related to this first type of error is the situation in which an object or event A is mistakenly taken to be the cause of some other object or event B which we value (either positively or negatively). Because of the mistake in fact, we may ascribe to A a value corresponding to our valuation of B when A does not deserve such valuation. Errors of this type pertain essentially to derivative values only. Both types of errors, however, are errors in valuation or value ascription in a transposed sense only; for, given the false judgment, the valuation or value ascription itself may be right. But there also occur situations in which our valuations or value ascriptions themselves are wrong, even though the factual judgments upon which they rest are true. Thus, we may value as a means what is actually the valued end "for the sake of which. . . .". A mountain climber, for example, may deceive himself into believing that he chose the most dangerous ascent to the top "for the sake of the view" when, as a matter of fact, he undertook the climb "for the sake of the climb itself" (p. 105).

More prevalent than the types of errors just referred to are errors in evaluation—i.e., errors pertaining to the determination of the "measure" or magnitude of values, be it the "measure" (the "value-height") of relative values with respect to one another, or the "measure" of some absolute value. Errors of this type are especially significant when they pertain to absolute values, for they suggest, if they do not entail, the relativity or subjectivity of all values. This is so because error concerning an "ultimate" value jeopardizes the whole value scale.

Von Ehrenfels tries to overcome this difficulty by arguing that the value of an object for any particular subject is not established when that object is actually evaluated, but only when conditions prevail which make its proper evaluation possible. But this leaves the problem unresolved; for the question now is: What are the conditions requisite for a "proper" evaluation? Von Ehrenfels' earlier discussion of this matter remained unsatisfactory. If we were to grant that he did solve the problem of the requisite conditions for any particular level of experience—such as the economic or the aesthetic level—there would still remain the crucial problem of a dependable standard for the interrelations of the various levels and, thus, the problem of an ultimate standard of values. And with this problem von Ehrenfels does not deal at all.

V

As von Ehrenfels sees it, more important than the problem of error and of an ultimate standard in value experience is the fact that our valuations may and do undergo various changes (p. 116). There occur, for example, temporary transformations in our value ascriptions—as when we value food more when we are hungry than we do in the state of satiety. Such changes, however, are rather superficial and do not affect our basic conception of values. Their explanation, moreover, is obvious. But there occur also profound changes in our valuations—changes which are caused by modifications of the dispositions that are basic to our feelings and desires. Such changes are permanent and irreversible, and are therefore of utmost importance.

One type of these profound changes is fairly obvious. Dispositions, though inborn, vary in strength and prevalence within the life-cycle of each and every individual. Dispositions characteristically in evidence during infancy do not as such prevail during maturity and old age. As we grow up, new dispositions manifest themselves while old ones change in strength and pervasiveness. The awakening and subsequent slackening of the sex drive exemplifies the changes that may occur. Such transformations of dispositions are quite normal as part of the process of growing up; but they do entail profound changes in our valuations.

In addition to the organically determined changes, there also occur transformations which are psychologically or socially induced and conditioned. They are the results of acquired habits—of our association with other human beings, of our training and conditioning in a human society. Social pressure, example, suggestion—these are some of the psychological factors that bring about the changes. But creative imagination, a new vision, or the transfer of feelings from effects to causes believed to be responsible for the effects may also alter our dispositions. And as our dispositions change so also change the feelings and desires to which they are foundational, and with them change our value responses, our valuations and evaluations.

The transformations of our value experience may move in any one of three directions: downwards, upwards, and "sideways." Von Ehrenfels means by a change downwards a shift in our valuation from the "end" pursued to the "means" necessary to its realization. By a change upwards he means a shift from the "end" pursued to the consequences which that end entails. The shift "sideways" or "inwards" requires special consideration. However, basic to all of these shifts is the fact that (a) one and the same object may be valued for its own sake *and* as a means to some valued end; and that (b) the means-end relation ordinarily involves a chain of successive events such that each event is the cause (or part of the cause) of the next following event (p. 134).

A shift downwards would be exemplified by the person who, planning an extended vacation, is saving his money toward that end and for whom saving money gradually becomes an end in itself. The shift upwards involves more complex circumstances but is just as real. The simplest case is one in which the shift entails advantages for the individual. Thus, a small child is motivated in some of his actions by the hunger drive, the consumption of food being itself the valued end. A mature person, however, besides being motivated by the hunger drive, will value not only food but the preservation of his health as well. He may therefore curb his hunger drive in order to reduce his weight in the interest of his continued well-being. In his case the satisfaction of the hunger drive, though still valued, is no longer decisive. The emphasis in valuation has shifted from a satisfaction here and now to the entailed consequences. In von Ehrenfels' sense it has moved upwards.

There is one aspect of the shift upwards in our valuations which deserves further consideration. It involves the fact that the preservation of a valuation can itself be valued—a fact which is of special significance for the cultural environment in which an individual finds himself, and for the valuations which prevail in that environment. Thus, once an individual's valuation of knowledge, of art, or of law is itself valued and, therefore, respected by others, his valuations become part of the ground-pattern of the prevailing culture and in that way contribute to the progress (or the lack of it) of mankind. Also, within this pattern of socially preserved valuations of valuations the individual finds his own value fulfillment as an effective member of the group (pp. 142–44).

In principle, valuations may vary in unlimited ways, both in quality and in degree of intensity; but no human being can experience them all. Man's capacity for value responses is limited. The result is that any given valuation tends to prevent or to displace all competitive valuations. In this fact is grounded the essentially tragic character of man's existence: the conflict of values is unavoidable and cannot be resolved without the violation or suppression of some valuations. The only hopeful aspect is that, if our intellectual power does not slacken and if the evolutionary development of mankind continues in its present direction, then we can at least recognize ever more clearly our crucially important valuations and can determine ever more deliberately the values which shape our destiny. They are the values to which we are committed in an ultimate sense and which concern generations yet to come no less than they do our own existence here and now.

It must be observed in passing that, initially, von Ehrenfels spoke of pleasure as the positive value *par excellance* and looked upon suffering as the corresponding disvalue. He now speaks of the "preservation of the species" in a culturally significant sense as desirable. There is no proof, however, that the pursuit of pleasure and the avoidance of pain in themselves are a guarantee of that preservation. Nor is it necessarily true that we value the preservation of the species simply because we desire pleasure or try to avoid pain. Values of a different order or dimension are obviously involved.

A closer examination of the interrelation of feelings and desire is therefore in order .

VI

According to von Ehrenfels, the relation in question is deeply rooted in the laws which govern the course of our presentational experiences, be the experiences induced by sense impressions or be they imaginary (p. 177). Whichever the case may be, only objects which elicit in us the expectation of a relative increase in pleasure or happiness become objects of desire; the intensity of the desire being proportional to the expected increase in happiness. This means, however, that it is the differential in the expected feeling-states—not our positive feelings *per se,* or even a steady increase in happiness—that prompts us to action and that determines the expenditure of energy in the pursuit of a given course of action. Von Ehrenfels calls this the "law of the relative enhancement of happiness" (p. 192).

If it now be argued that some people seem to prefer a course of action which leads to what for most people would be a state of unpleasantness or unhappiness, von Ehrenfels replies that for such "morbid" persons the presentation of what they aim at is indeed the more pleasant. Far from contradicting the "law of the relative enhancement of happiness," their case actually confirms that law.

Von Ehrenfels tries to obtain further support for his law by underpinning it with a physiological theory of mental events that is keyed to the physical law of the conservation of energy (pp. 195–200). But, in the end, he insists that the validity of his law—"empirically established as it is"—is not contingent upon the acceptance of any physiological interpretation.

However, the "law of the relative enhancement of happiness" is not the sole determinant of our actions. Reference has already been made (see p. 100) to the role which existential judgments play in our valuational responses. The presentation of an "object" which we regard as real or as realizable elicits in us a response that is more lasting and more effective in the pursuit of a goal than is the response to the idea of an unreal or unrealizable "object." It is therefore the function of the existential judgments to assert the inclusion of really existing objects in the causal nexus of our experience and to exclude purely fictitious objects from that nexus (p. 206). Through them, also, we transcend any given moment of experience and reach out into the past or the future. When we turn to the past, desire remains essentially only a wishing; for the past cannot again be actualized. But even in this case the idea of the object wished for is woven into the causal nexus of our valuational experience and may contribute to, or detract from, our happiness. When we turn to the future, desire may turn into volition. Such is the case when we become convinced that the goal can be reached, and that it can be reached by the means employed or the course of action chosen. We now pursue our goal with deliberation. It is a fact, however, that every desire includes an element of wishing, and that every volition includes an element of desire (p. 223). And it is a fact, furthermore, that all desires and all volitions are subordinate to the "law of the relative enhancement of happiness," and that their various interrelations make possible diverse shifts "sideways" in our valuations.

Moreover, the interrelations of wish, desire, and volition inevitably make us wonder what the discernible attitudes have in common. Von Ehrenfels insists that there is no special elementary psychological factor 'desire' (wishing, striving, willing) (p. 248). *"What we call desire is nothing other than the idea (Vorstellung)*—*productive of a relative enhancement of happiness—of an object's inclusion in, or exclusion from, the causal nexus [of experience] centering in the actual and concrete ego-presentation"* (p. 249. Italics in the original).

The implication of this assertion is, of course, a complete determinism. However, von Ehrenfels maintains that only a metaphysical indeterminism would be detrimental to any attempt to pursue value goals. "In the practical affairs of life, even the most consistent advocate of a mechanistic world-view cannot avoid expecting what he wills to be the effect of his volition" (p. 261). That such an interpretation faces difficult and as yet unsolved problems von Ehrenfels readily admits; but he feels sure that, in time, psychology will find appropriate solutions (p. 265).

VII

However, Meinong at once objected to an interpretation which denies the existence of a basic psychological element "desire" and reduces desire to nothing but the inclusion in, or the exclusion from, the causal nexus of experience the idea of an object productive of a relative enhancement of happiness (Meinong, *Ueber Annahmen,* p. 293). Like von Ehrenfels, Meinong also bases his arguments upon introspective evidence; but he sees the "facts in the case" in an entirely different light. To be sure, he agrees that introspection does not, and cannot, prove that "desire" is simple or irreducible; but he finds "astonishingly little" evidence of the "happiness-enhancing inclusion and exclusion" of "objects" which von Ehrenfels made the capstone of his whole interpretation. Still, by his very efforts at an interpretation, even von Ehrenfels implies (so Meinong maintains) that, "normally," we find in our inner experience evidence of "the presence of desires"; and this could not be the case if von Ehrenfels' interpretation were correct—i.e., if the "relative enhancement of happiness" were constitutive of desire. Von Ehrenfels himself regards that "enhancement" as "the difference between a real and a possible." Meinong points out, however, that "concerning that which is not real but only possible—more accurately, concerning that which would have to occur under circumstances which, in fact, are not realized —our inner experience (*innere Wahrenhmung*) can give us no information" (p. 295). If we are to speak meaningfully about a "relative enhancement of happiness" at all, then rather complicated considerations of circumstances and not the direct evidence of introspection are required. That is to say, if von Ehrenfels were right in his interpretation of "desire," then anyone who would like to know whether he actually desired something or not would have to compare his present with his former state of pleasure. Normally, however, we are not aware of making a comparison of this kind even though we may be fully aware of the fact that we have a desire. And this evidence of our inner experience alone, so Meinong maintains, decisively disproves von Ehrenfels' thesis (p. 296).

But Meinong does not rest his case here. He points out that von Ehrenfels holds that "the more agreeable—or the less disagreeable—objects of the imagination last longer than one might expect them to merely from the point of view of habit and fatigue," and that these "objects" also "maintain themselves longer and more vividly than do under otherwise equal circumstances the indifferent and disagreeable ones—and they do so even without an inner act of will being directed toward them." But when we now ask von Ehrenfels to elucidate this rather complex thesis, we are told that it would be superfluous to give any examples of this law of the most encompassing significance; for he who, on the basis of a psychological survey, feels compelled to accept it will find examples in great numbers, whereas he who denies it will not be persuaded by examples. The individual case shows nothing but that this or that relatively agreeable idea remains so or so long in consciousness. That it could not remain thus long if it were not agreeable—this conviction "can be obtained only on the basis of that far-sighted induction based upon psychological imagination which everyone must carry out for himself" (von Ehrenfels, *System,* I, p. 190). To which Meinong replies: "All honor to 'psychological imagination'; but the summary appeal to it . . . is, after all, too summary" (*Ueber Annahmen,* p. 297).

And now Meinong returns to the more specific question concerning "the essence of value," of the nature of the psychological events that are foundational to all values. It will be remembered that Meinong had argued that our emotional responses to reality are basic to all value conceptions; that he had identified "value-feelings" and "reality-feelings," and had defined value as the capacity of any "existent" to elicit such "value-feelings" or "valuations" under sufficiently favorable conditions. Von Ehrenfels, on the other hand, had made desire basic and had identified "valuable" (*Wert-haben*) with "being desired" (*Begehrt-werden*) or, at least, with "capable of being desired" (*Begehrt-werden-können*) (in "Werttheorie und Ethik"). Meinong had responded (in "Ueber Werthaltung und Wert") by recognizing the fact that in our valuations the non-existence of the value-object plays as important a role as does its existence. Von Ehrenfels had thereupon attributed to Meinong a definition of value in terms of "desirability" much like his own (*System,* I, p. 53, Note 2), but had admitted also the role which feelings play in our value experience. It now seemed that two irreconcilable definitions of value—one in terms of feeling-responses, the other in terms of desire—were warranted by the facts of experience and that a choice would have to be made on more or less arbitrary grounds. (See, for example, W. M. Urban, "Recent Tendencies in the Psychological Theory of Value," *Psychological Bulletin,* IV, 1907, No. 4). Meinong, however, argued that von Ehrenfels was mistaken in believing that he (Meinong) had made "concessions" to a definition of value in terms of desire. He thus puts himself once more squarely in opposition to von Ehrenfels.

But if there are two definitions of the same concept, is not one of them superfluous? One is tempted to say at once, Yes. But when one considers the various purposes which a definition might serve and also how many ways there might be of finding the "right" definition, then the answer is not so simple. He who wants to ascertain what value is must, first of all, be clear in his own mind as to what he actually means when he attributes a value to things. If the term 'value' is not ambiguous and its employment not uncertain, then there can be only one correct use of it—a fact which does not preclude, however, the possibility of subsequent definitional modifications which make the term still more precise. It is necessary, therefore, at the beginning of an investigation to be clear about the general characteristics of the facts to be examined, to determine what is and what is not relevant. If this initial clarification has been achieved in the case of our value experiences, then—so Meinong maintains—our subsequent analysis will lead either to desire or to feelings as ultimate, but not to both (*Ueber Annahmen,* p. 326).

Now the question is, Is von Ehrenfel's definition of value as "desirability (*Begehrbarkeit*) acceptable? That "desirability" rather than "being desired" (*Begehrtheit*) should be the key concept he justifies by pointing out that we cannot make that an object of desire which either now is the case or already is part of the past; but we can value it. Such "objects," in other words, have value without being "objects" of a desire. But are they "desirable" objects? If they are not, then the substitution of "desirability" for "being desired" is of no help in our search for a definition of value. If they are "desirable" objects, then the question is, On what grounds can their "desirability" be defended?

At this point, von Ehrenfels attempted to clarify his position by stating: "We ascribe value to those things which we either actually desire or which we would desire if we were not already convinced of their existence" (*System,* I, p. 26). But Meinong now raises this question: "Can I still call desirable that which is desirable only under a condition which, under the given circumstances, cannot be fulfilled? Is not the attribution of desirability to what no longer exists equivalent to calling a rhombus a square because it would undoubtedly have the properties of a square if its angles were right rather than oblique angles?" Meinong himself, however, no longer regards this essentially *a priori* argument as decisive against von Ehrenfels, for "desirability" (he now admits) is a "capacity for being desired" and as "capacity," it can be ascribed to "objects" as a "kind of property"—even though it is a special kind of "property" (*Ueber Annahmen,* p. 327).

The situation is different, so Meinong holds, when we consider the empirical evidence. This evidence, he insists, clearly shows that our feeling-responses are primary and should therefore be accepted as the basis for our definition of value. Meinong's detailed argument we have considered in Chapter III. It is not necessary to repeat it here.

VIII

Volume II of *System der Wertlehre* sets forth von Ehrenfels' application of his value theory in the field of ethics. Since the application does not modify the basic theory I shall deal with it only briefly.

It is characteristic of von Ehrenfels' approach in general that he regards "ethics as the psychology of moral value-facts" (*System* II, pp. 4–5), and that it is also "a branch of a general value theory." As he sees it, "the basic facts of all ethical manifestions of life—the *high esteem* in which we hold the good, and our *disrespect* for evil—are but themselves value phenomena"; and so are "the *objects* of our moral valuations, namely, the *good* and the *evil*." The key concept in all ethically relevant phenomena is that of *"moral approval and disapproval."* It is "moral valuation as such" and pertains to the "moral value-objects" no less than to the "value-subjects," including the disinterested observer as well as the actively engaged person and "everything that affects the latter in consequence of his good or evil deed" (p. 14).

The question is, Do the psychological facts of moral valuing have any strictly universal characteristics in common which set them off from other facts? And if they have, what are those characteristics? As von Ehrenfels sees it, the best approach to the problem is via an analysis of the ethico-cultural environment in which we live and, being active, are forced to apply certain ethical concepts.

Such an approach reveals that our actions are basic in moral matters. Every action, however, is "a kind of striving or willing through which an intended effect is produced" (p. 16), "intended" being the key concept. This allows for the fact that not all "intended effects" are actually realized. For one reason or another we may be frustrated in our actions. Still, in the case of every action (be it frustrated or not) we must distinguish between the purpose or goal, the intention, and the desire and feeling-disposition basic to it all. But more or less closely related to any action are also "the effects which, though expected, were not intended, and the actual effects (whether intended, merely expected, or not even foreseen)" (pp. 17–18). Only those effects, however, which were or should have been foreseen are relevant to a moral valuation of any action—and they are so even if they did not actually occur. But this means as far as von Ehrenfels is concerned that only desire and the expected effects are crucial for the moral evaluation of an action.

We know, however, from earlier discussions that desire is determined by our feeling-dispositions—a determination which implies that, "in the last analysis, the moral evaluation of an action pertains to the *presence or absence of feeling-dispositions of a specific kind*—a presence or absence revealed through the actions themselves" (p. 22. Italics in the original). And so, while actions are, and remain, the initial class of moral value-objects, the dispositions which they reveal and, therefore,—by virtue of his dispositional character—the person himself are objects to be valued (positively or negatively) in a moral sense.

The question now is, What are the common characteristics for the sake of which some of these dispositions deserve our "moral esteem" whereas other dispositions, either through their presence or through their absence, call forth our moral disapproval, and still others leave our moral valuation neutral? Foremost among the characteristics that deserve our "highest esteem," so von Ehrenfels maintains, is what Christian morality expresses in the commandments: "Thou shalt love the Lord thy God with all thy heart . . . [and] thy neighbor as thyself." But in an age of dwindling faith, von Ehrenfels continues, it might be well to interpret this challenge as meaning essentially a demand for a "universal love of mankind." The feeling-disposition underlying this love would rank highest in our moral valuation but it is by no means the only one that is morally relevant. Others are "justice, loyalty, honesty, sense of duty, truthfulness, self-respect, sense of shame, purity, moderation, diligence and love of work" (p. 29).

Among the "immoral feeling-dispositions" von Ehrenfels ranks first an "indifferentism" with respect to all morally valuable objects. He ranks second all dispositions leading to perverted responses—to the disapproval of values (such as those just mentioned) and the approval of their opposites. As opposites of a universal love of mankind, maliciousness, vindictiveness, and cruelty deserve special condemnation.

When next we ask what is common to all the actions and dispositions that justifies their moral valuation in either a positive or a negative sense, von Ehrenfels replies that it is the relation to mankind's "common welfare." All feeling-dispositions which we value positively contribute in their effects to that welfare and, in this sense, are useful. All feeling-dispositions which we value negatively have the opposite effect, being harmful to the common welfare. But this does not mean that we are committed to a utilitarian ethics; for, while it is true that all ethical values embody an element of utility, the converse is not necessarily true. Some useful actions have no moral significance.

In order to clarify this distinction it is necessary to explain more precisely what is meant by "common welfare." What von Ehrenfels means by it is "the greatest possible excess of pleasure over displeasure" or (at least) "the smallest possible excess of displeasure over pleasure" (p. 41). Such a state of affairs can be realized only when we attain "the greatest possible physical and mental health of the whole" (p. 48)—a conception rooted in the idea of the *preservation* not only of the present generation but of all generations yet to come. This means, however, that we rank the *enhancement* of the general welfare above mere utility (p. 50). Moral actions are those which contribute to that enhancement—in the individual as well as in the social whole; and in this sense all moral values are "survival values," determined by man's place in the universe and conditioning his destiny.

At this point we have left the psychological approach to value theory far behind and are entering the realm of metaphysics. Von Ehrenfels did not pursue the specific value problems any farther—at least not in his *System der Wertlehre;* and we shall break off our exposition of his views at this point.

BIBLIOGRAPHY

von Ehrenfels, Christian, "Ueber Fühlen und Wollen," *Sitzungsberichte der kaiserlichen Akademie der Wissenschaften* (Philosophisch-historische Klasse), Vol. 114, Vienna, 1887, pp. 523–636.

———"Werttheorie und Ethik," *Vierteljahrschrift für wissenschaftliche Philosophie*, Leipzig, Vol. 17, 1893, pp. 76–110; 200–266; 321–363; 413–475, Vol. 18, 1894, pp. 77–97.

———"Von der Wertdefinition zum Motivationsgesetz," *Archiv für systematische Philosophie*, Vol. 2, Berlin, 1896, pp. 103–122.

———"The Ethical Theory of Value," *International Journal of Ethics*, Vol. 6, 1896, pp. 371–384.

———*System der Wertlehre*, 2 vols., Leipzig, 1897, 1898.

Eaton, Howard O., *The Austrian Philosophy of Values*, Norman, Oklahoma, 1930.

CHAPTER V

KREIBIG AND A NEW APPROACH

The psychological approach to the problems of value theory, initiated by Brentano and developed along different lines by Meinong and von Ehrenfels, found its culmination in Josef Clemens Kreibig's much neglected work, *Psychologische Grundlegung eines Systems der Wert-Theorie* (1902). The task which Kreibig set for himself was to determine the psychological characteristics of the interrelations of values, and then to base a philosophical value theory upon this descriptive foundation.

Two ideas were crucial to this undertaking: the thesis that the basic psychological fact in all valuing is feeling, and the thesis that the criterion of positive values is the enhancement of man's spiritual and bodily achievements. Kreibig's goal was to prove that the interpretation of values here attempted leads neither to hedonism nor to a psychological eudaemonism but culminates in a new appraisal of man's whole life.

I

Analysis, so Kreibig points out, reveals four irreducible aspects of man's mental life: sense impressions, thinking, feeling, and volition. Of these, feeling is "the ultimate and decisive factor" in all value experience (p. 4). But "feeling," as Kreibig uses the term, refers not only to the actually experienced hedonic or algedonic feeling-tone here and now, but also to "the dispositional feeling-mood whose existence and quality manifest themselves in their influence upon our volitions." Corresponding to the two forms of feeling—the actual and the dispositional—we can distinguish also two forms of valuings—the actual and the dispositional; and both must be investigated.

As far as actual valuations are concerned, the crucial fact is that, in the value experience, the subject "emotionally prefers" some objects to others. That is to say, the subject ranks some objects "higher" and others "lower" on a scale of valuations—on a scale, that is, which includes the whole range of disvalues as well as of positive values. The preference itself may be induced directly by the object involved, or it may have been "mediated" by various "associations." In either case, however, it may vary with the maturity of the subject having the experience.

The subject directly involved in the value experience is, of course, the individual human being. However, in consequence of man's communal living, quasi-subjects of a "higher order"—such as the family, the clan, the nation and, ultimately, the whole of mankind—are also formed. They function as "bearers of traditions, of mores, and of law." Through education and social pressures they condition in manifold ways the valuations of the individuals that are members of the "group." To the extent, therefore, to which a person participates in the life of his community his primary and his socially induced valuations tend to fuse—a fact that is reflected in his value scale and in his actions.

However, irrespective of the nature of the subject involved, there is no value experience unless there is also an object that is being valued. The term "object" must here be understood in a very broad sense. As Kreibig uses the term, the reference is not only to anything that may be a part of the external world, but to all phenomena of our "inner world" as well—to sense impressions, to "objects of thought" and of the imagination, including even the idea of "the non-existence of a pleasure-inducing object" (p. 6). But no matter what the nature of the valued object, the all-important fact is that its value is never one of its inherent qualities or characteristics but is of a "purely subjective nature." Kreibig explicitly repudiates the idea that values have an objective existence.

Value experience is in still another respect complex rather than simple. Even though value is a "felt significance" (*Gefühlsbedeutung*), the felt value experience is in itself not yet a value judgment. Such a judgment is needed, however, if we are to ascribe value to an object or if, indeed, any reference to values is to be meaningful at all. And the question is how value judgments are related to the feelings that are basic to all value experiences. As Kreibig sees it, the situation is this: Whenever in connection with our experience of some particular "content" (*Inhalt*)—such as the taste of an orange—we also experience a value-feeling (a feeling of pleasantness, for example), then there corresponds to this feeling, but on the intellectual side of the experience, a correlative value judgment—a positive valuing, let us say—which expresses that feeling. In fact, the value judgment merely expresses the directly felt approval (or disapproval) in much the same way in which cognitive judgments express the immediacies of sense impressions. If the experience in question is one of pleasure, the judgment correlated with it ascribes to the object involved a "positive significance." If the experience is one of displeasure, the judgment ascribes a "negative significance" or a disvalue to the object. But whichever is the case, the judgment as such is a "primary value judgment." It is "certain and true," and is "terminal" (p. 9).

Value judgments which are not correlative to the immediately felt value experience but depend upon a mediating cognitive judgment or upon a process of association are "secondary value judgments" and do not carry with them the same sense of certainty or truth which primary judgments do. That is to say, the secondary value judgments may be false.

It remains a fact, however, that the basic feeling of pleasure (or displeasure), being what it is, is in itself neither true nor false. The primary value judgment is true when it expresses the value-feeling adequately. But when the secondary judgment is also true, "we may speak of the true value of the valued object." And if we were now to define "objective value" as any value which corresponds to a true value judgment, then, "obviously, objective values exist." Kreibig doubts, however, that such a definition can be allowed, for subjective values cannot be identified with values that correspond to false judgments, and even true judgments may pertain to merely subjective values.

When Kreibig speaks of "objective values" he means the values ascribed to objects in accordance with the true judgments of an "ideal person" who, having full knowledge of all the characteristics of the objects involved, knows also all empirically possible emotional responses to those objects and who judges accordingly. Whether or not such an "ideal person" ever exists is a mute question. One may well reject the whole idea as an empty abstraction. Kreibig does not press the point.

A moment ago it was pointed out that some objects directly elicit a feeling-response in us, whereas others do so only through the intermediacy of various kinds of associations. If the former is the case, Kreibig speaks of "values proper" (*Eigenwerte*); if the latter is the case, he speaks of "effect-producing values" (*Wirkungswerte*): the objects produce "effects" which elicit a feeling-response in some subject. Among the "effect-producing values" Kreibig lists "tools and machines, books and the laws governing a society"; but these are only samples. The range of this type of values is extraordinarily large.

If the associative connection between effect-producing values and values proper lies below the threshold of consciousness, a value transference may take place such that the effect-producing value is actually taken to be a valve proper. This fact, however, need not obscure the distinction between the two types of values. Kreibig preserves that distinction when he now states the following definition of "value in general": Value is the significance which an object of perception or of judgment has for a subject by virtue of the actual or dispositional feeling immediately or associeively connected with it. Positive value corresponds to an experienced pleasure; negative value or disvalue corresponds to an experienced displeasure (p. 12).

Kreibig speaks of "valuing" or "valuation" when he refers to the act of "ascribing a positive or negative significance" to some "object." Seen in the perspective of cognition, valuation is thus an act of (value) judgment; but seen in the perspective of a man's actions, it is an act of the will.

This definitional basis of his theory, Kreibig believes, makes it possible to deal satisfactorily with all value problems and with the whole range of values. That range he views as essentially three-dimensional, including (1) the values related to the valuing subject itself—i.e., the "realm of the autopathic"; (2) the values related to "the other person"—the "realm of the heteropathic," notably, of course, the field of ethics; and (3) values not related to either oneself or "the other"—the "realm of the ergopathic" (p. 16). The most important of these divisions are the autopathic (values for me) and the heteropathic (values for others). Their separation is at times difficult and conflicts arise frequently.

It is significant also that every valuational situation may be interpreted from two distinct points of view, each having its own particular significance. Thus, seen in one perspective,—as directly experienced by a subject—"the good" is pleasure: pleasure in all its forms. Seen in another perspective, "the good" is any source of pleasure; and "sources of pleasure are value-objects." Correspondingly, "evil" is (subjectively) any experienced displeasure and (objectively) any "source of displeasure." In either case, however, the experiental aspect is primary. Unless some subject experiences either a pleasure or a displeasure elicited by some object, no value-object exists.

Analysis will show also, so Kreibig maintains, that the experience of pleasure is "always connected with an awakening or an enhancement of the mental or the bodily activity of the subject," whereas the experience of displeasure results from a hindrance in that activity, or from frustration. Viewed from the perspective of the objects, this means that "goods" are the causes of the experienced enhancement, and "evils" the causes of frustration. And if such is the case, then—so Kreibig continues—"the empirically highest, i.e., the most valuable good, is the richest possible unfolding and activity of the mental and the bodily powers of man. It encompasses the maximum realization of values" (p. 18). The highest conceivable good, however, involving the entire range of values, lies beyond man's actual achievements and must therefore remain the "highest ideal"—unrealizable but inspiring. This theory, Kreibig holds, is in harmony with the basic idea of biological evolution no less than with the facts of man's personal development from infancy to maturity, and with his cultural history. The whole development is a pursuit of goals which are not realizable at any level that has actually been achieved; they are projections beyond the actual. In this perspective of biologico-cultural development the highest good attainable by man is the historical unfolding and activation of all of his spiritual capacities in a community in which there is ample room for the particular interests and abilities of each individual.

In the course of their normal development the individual and his social group, acting as primary and secondary value-subject, respectively, reflect upon future goals and possibilities of action and, taking experiences of the past into consideration, establish norms for future valuations and for value-objects. The result may well be the formulations of rules and "maxims" for future action. When such maxims become part of an habitual behavior pattern —i.e., when they become "dispositional"—they take on the character of "inner norms." The subject now feels an "inner compulsion" to act in conformity with the maxims even in situations in which external circumstances elicit an inclination to deviate from the norm. Insofar as the norms are embodied in the mores and laws of a society, they assure the conforming individual of respect within that society and may even grant him rewards for socially beneficent actions. Violations of the norms, on the other hand, entail condemnation and punishment. In any case, however, the valuations embedded in tradition and social environment either re-enforce or weaken the valuations which the individual accepts on the basis of his own experience. They provide a standard against which he can measure his own valuations. But there is one limitation. According to Kreibig, "norms" which contradict the "universally human" character of man "cannot prevail for any length of time," for they entail the "rapid decay" of the social group (p. 26).

II

Let us now consider in greater detail Kreibig's position and his arguments in support of it.

His thesis, as we know, is that feeling is foundational to all values: "Everything that is valued is felt; everything that is felt is valued" (p. 27). The presupposition of this thesis is that feeling is a specific and irreducible aspect of all mental phenomena.

Characteristic of the nature of feelings is the experiential contrast between felt pleasure and felt displeasure—a contrast encountered wherever value experiences are found. A second contrast is that of actual and dispositional feelings; and this, too, is encountered at all levels of value experience. Actually, it is against the background of the dispositional feelings or "moods" that we experience the immediately felt values.

The value-feelings themselves are characterized by quality (be it pleasure or displeasure), intensity, and duration—characteristics which play an important part in the interpretation and evaluation of our value experiences. Of equal significance, however, is the fact that value-feelings may be experienced in connection with sense impressions as well as with objects of thought; that, as valuations, they find expression in value judgments; and that they are related to volitions—to our "wanting to be or to have" and our "not wanting to be or to have" (p. 32).

As far as quality is concerned, the distinction between feelings of pleasure and feelings of displeasure is exhaustive of all possibilities. No other quality is characteristic of value-feelings. However, as far as the intensity of the feelings is concerned, Kreibig distinguishes (on the positive side) between the agreeable, the pleasant in a narrow sense, and the delightful, and (on the negative side) between the disagreeable, the unpleasant in a narrow sense, and the painful. But what about the distinction which has frequently been made between "higher" and "lower" feelings? In the popular tradition, bodily feelings are, as a rule, regarded as "lower," the "so-called spiritual feelings" as "higher." The question as to whether or not such a distinction is justified is crucial to value theory, for upon the answer to it depends not only an order of rank of values but the possibility of formulating principles of valuation as well.

It is Kreibig's contention that, from a purely psychological point of view, there is no basis for making a distinction between "spiritual" and "bodily" pleasures. As experienced, all pleasures are mental events, differing only in intensity and duration; and this difference depends entirely on the objects which elicit the feelings and on the conditions under which the objects are encountered. Still, so Kreibig maintains, "the purely quantitative aspects assure the primacy of the so-called spiritual pleasures"— provided we take into account not only the "intensity of a passing moment" but also our dispositional attitudes. Referring to Bentham's thesis that "intensity, duration, certainty, nearness, fecundity and purity" are criteria for the differentiation of pleasures, Kreibig admits that in most of these respects spiritual pleasures are indeed superior to bodily pleasures. He points out, however, that all but the quantitative aspects are secondary considerations which transcend the psychological approach to values.

III

We have seen earlier that, according to Kreibig, every value-feeling is experienced in connection with some sense impression, some memory content, some object of thought, or in situations involving them all. In some instances, however, the feelings may be so faint that we are barely aware of them. Still, the basic principle of Kreibig's theory is: "No value-feeling without sensory impression or an object of thought; no sensory impression or object of thought without a value-feeling" (p. 44). And it is understood that, in addition to our actual feelings, our "dispositional feeling-moods" (*dispositionelle Gefühlsstimmungen*) are of "far-reaching significance for our whole mental life" (p. 41).

In addition, as a rule, pleasure is associated with objects which sustain and enhance our spiritual and/or our bodily existence. Displeasure is associated with objects having the opposite effect. Exceptions to this rule indicate imperfect adjustments to the realities of our existence. The question is, What is meant by the "enhancement" or the "hindrance" of our existence, be it our bodily or our spiritual existence? As Kreibig sees it, "physiological furtherance of life occurs when our responses to external and internal stimuli consume no more, but also no less, energy than can be supplied to the affected parts of the body through nourishment and circulation" (p. 45). Any surplus or deficiency in energy will be experienced as unpleasant. This means, in effect, that the normal functioning of a healthy body, and all that sustains or enhances that functioning, is experienced as pleasant. But beyond this, and for the intellectually mature person, there is nothing more enjoyable than the unfolding and employment of his intellectual abilities "within the limits of the replenishment of his energy." Enforced inactivity of the mind entails an intense displeasure.

In view of these facts Kreibig finds that the following generalization is empirically justified: "A life-furthering content of experience is one which enhances the unfolding and activity of our mental and physical powers in their totality, i.e., within the limits of the replenishment of our energy. Experiences which weaken or suppress that activity are life-hindering" (p. 46).

An essentially introspective analysis now leads Kreibig to the formulation of a number of "laws" governing the relation of value-feelings to the intensity of the valued experiential content. The following are but a sample; they are, however, indicative of the psychological orientation of Kreibig's theory: (1) Only experiences of sufficient intensity to be noted at all elicit overt value-feelings. Subliminal experiences, however, may affect our dispositional moods. (2) In general, the strength of a value-feeling increases with the increase in intensity of the valued content of experience; but it does so only up to a point. Beyond that degree of intensity, pleasure is replaced by a rapidly increasing displeasure. (3) Only experiences of sufficient duration to be noted at all elicit actual value-feelings, although imperceptibly brief experiences may affect our moods. (4) Value-feelings and experiential content enter consciousness simultaneously. (5) If in a case of prolonged and constant awareness of a valued content the actual value-feeling is one of displeasure, it does not change in quality but, beyond a certain point of endurance, it loses its intensity. However, if the feeling is one of pleasure, then, beyond a certain point, it is replaced by a feeling of displeasure. (6) Value-feelings can be experienced repeatedly if the experiential contents which induced them initially are also experienced again. (7) A value-feeling is stronger than it might be if it follows one of an opposite quality. (8) When we act in order to reach a valued goal, unintended side-effects may occur, and these also elicit value-feelings. Their effect in our experience is cumulative and may augment or enhance the value of the goal or they may detract from that value and may do so to a point at which they replace the value of the goal altogether. Kreibig calls this the "law of the heterogony of values" (pp. 47–66).

IV

Convinced that the psychology of volition is basic to value theory, Kreibig discusses at some length what he believes to be the well established and pertinent results of that psychology. He finds, for example, that three characteristics are "constitutive" of all volitions, namely, (1) quality ("the will to have or to be, and not to will to have or to be"), (2) intensity ("strength or vivacity"), and (3) temporal determinateness ("duration"). In addition, however, "will in the narrower sense" is characterized also by three elementary relationships: (1) "being bound to a sense impression or to an object of thought"; (2) "being dependent upon a positive or a negative value judgment"; and (3) being related to "a feeling of like quality that is basic to the value judgment in question." As far as reflex actions, instincts and drives are concerned (all of which are aspects of volition in the broader sense), the characteristics just mentioned are vague or are not present at all (pp. 67–70). But every act of will has a "direction" which is determined by a given sensory content or by an object of thought, such as an anticipated goal, and it has a "quality" which depends upon an actual or a dispositional value-feeling. "The intensity and duration of the volition correspond directly to the intensity and duration of the feeling which elicits it" (p. 71). The goal which gives direction to an action and imbues it with a purpose may be a terminal goal or an intermediate one—a link in a series of subordinate goals which leads to a last or ultimate goal. In either case, however, the conception of the goal must include the idea that the goal can be realized. If it does not include this idea, we deal with a wish rather than with an act of volition. The motive for an action is "the pleasure (displeasure) accentuated idea (*Vorstellung*) which, because of this value quality, determines the direction of every act of volition" (p. 72). But motives are associated with the intermediate goals no less than with the terminal goal and may form a whole series of interrelated motives which, in accordance with the "principle of the heterogony of values," may be disrupted or modified by other value considerations so that the original goal will be abandoned and will be replaced by another. And in this connection the valuation of the means necessary for the realization of a goal is of special significance, for the employment of the means is justified only if their disvalue does not outweigh the value of the goal itself.

It is evident that in all of these considerations the relation of value-feelings to the acts of volition is of special significance. Kreibig puts it succinctly: "The will is motivated by value-feelings" (p. 80). But he realizes that futher analysis is necessary.

When in a given situation we are aware of and respond to several possible goals, we cannot act until some particular goal has been decided upon. This means that, initially, we experience a conflict of motives—a conflict, that is, of feeling-determined valuations—which is resolved only when one goal, because of the greater intensity and duration (the greater strength) of the value-feeling associated with it, wins out over all others. That this interpretation is essentially deterministic Kreibig readily admits. "It is our conviction," he tells us, "that, from the psychological point of view, the will is completely (*durchgängig*) determined by the value-feelings which are bound up with the motives" (p. 83). And it is Kreibig's further conviction that "with the acceptance or the rejection of psychological determinism every value theory stands or falls" (p. 85). In fact, Kreibig accepts not only psychological determinism but metaphysical determinism as well, viewing the individual human will as part of the causally determined world-system which encompasses both, the physical and the mental.

V

Within the framework of this perspective Kreibig now formulates additional "laws" that govern our value experience.

He first turns to the realm of autopathic valuations. This realm, it will be remembered, includes all valuations directly concerned with the subject who does the valuing. "The foundation of the autopathic value realm is the positive value-feeling connected with experiences which elicit pleasure or displeasure pertaining to ourselves" (p. 89). 'Good' here means "to cause pleasure for the subject who does the valuing"; and 'bad' means "to cause displeasure" for that subject. A scale expressing "degrees of more or less" pleasure or displeasure connects the two extremes of "greatest pleasure" and "greatest displeasure."

As Kreibig sees it, three "laws" govern the value experiences that are here involved:

1. "The greater the intensity and the longer the duration of the pleasure elicited by some experiential content, the higher will that content be valued autopathically relative to the subject who does the valuing. Intensity and duration of displeasure determine the measure of the autopathic disvalue" (p. 90).

2. "The degree of an autopathic valuation is inversely proportional to the temporal distance of the anticipated occurrence of a feeling-accentuated content of experience" (p. 91).

3. "The degree of an autopathic valuation depends, furthermore, upon the frequency of the repetition of the same experiential content, upon the rhythm of the sequence of experiences, upon the effect of contrasts, upon the arrangement of subordinate feelings (if such occur), and upon the influence of the interrelations of various experiences" (p. 92).

To the subjective value-feelings there correspond "autopathic goods"—the "sources," namely, of the experienced pleasures. These goods may be "real things, social situations, and personal circumstances." In this sense, goods of a high order are "good health, keen senses, maturity of the intellect, emotional sensitivity and richness, a strong and disciplined will," and above all the harmonious integration of all mental faculties (p. 93). The highest autopathic good for the valuing subject is "the richest possible development and employment of his own mental and physical powers." The greatest autopathic evil is the impossibility of such development and employment, an impossibility frequently caused by severe mental or physical illness (p. 94).

In all value experiences the individual human being, valuing autopathically his own experiences, is the primary subject. However, because of the laws of social interrelations, secondary subjects—social groups—emerge whose valuations approximate the average autopathic valuations of the individuals concerned. Value judgments of this kind pertain to the preservation and welfare of the social group "as an individual of a higher order," or to the preservation and the welfare of the individual members of the group. Value judgments of both kinds, originating as valuations

common to the individuals comprising the group, are being preserved in the form of traditions. Every member of the group exerts
in his own valuations an (often little noticed) influence upon the
value judgments of the group and, in turn, receives from that
group a powerful suggestive response to his valuations. That some
persons—"lawgivers, men of science and of the arts, and powerful clergymen"—influence the social whole more than do others
is, of course, obvious.

It must be noted also that, although the intellectually less
gifted person is inclined to ascribe the relative highest value to
objects which satisfy sensuous desires ("food, housing, women,
ornaments, weapons"), an increase in intellectual activity emphasizes ever more the autopathic value of the so-called "cultural
goods" (*Kulturgüter*) and, notably, of "the spiritual sources of
pleasure." Hand in hand with this shift in emphasis goes an increasing concern for the future, and the intricate adjustments in
the sphere of social living may lead to the development of "autopathic norms." The principle underlying such development is that
of "the realization of the least possible displeasure and of the
greatest possible pleasure for the person who does the valuing"
(p. 96).

The particular segment of autopathic values that can be viewed
under aspects of "production, exchange, distribution, and consumption" belongs, of course, to the field of economics and is
dealt with effectively in "modern economic theory." Kreibig regards the interpretations of the "Austrian economists" of his
time—i.e., Karl Menger, Heinrich Gossen, von Wieser, Böhm-
Bawerk *et al*—as in essential agreement with his own value theory, and suggests that their theories should be incorporated in
his own.

VI

When next we turn to the "heteropathic valuations," we encounter problems of a somewhat different sort, for we deal
here with valuations pertaining to the pleasure or the displeasure of other persons.

The major part of all heteropathic valuations belongs, of course, to the realm of ethics. Valuations are ethical, Kreibig holds, when the valued contents are "dispositions" (in the sense of "lasting and firm directions of the will") and when the value-contrasts, "heteropathically good" and "heteropathically evil," are predicates characterizing those dispositions. "A disposition is ethically good when its aim is to cause (awaken, increase) pleasure for someone else, or to repress (decrease, eliminate) displeasure for someone else. A disposition is ethically evil when its aim is to cause (awaken, increase) displeasure for someone else, or to repress (decrease, eliminate) pleasure for someone else" (p. 108). These two characteristics together constitute "the elementary criterion of ethics."

Basic to "good will" as a "volitional disposition" is the feeling-disposition of sympathy and compassion. Basic to an "evil will" is the feeling-disposition of cruelty and envy. It must be remembered, however, that both, good will and evil will, are concerned with the pleasures and displeasures, the joys and sufferings of other persons—good will taking pleasure in the pleasures and the joys of others, and displeasure in their displeasures and their sufferings; evil will taking pleasure in the displeasures and the suffering of others, and displeasure in their pleasures and their joys. Ethically significant is the fact that in each case the volitional disposition, not the success or failure of an act manifesting it, is decisive. The good (or evil) intention is what counts. A "good action" is, thus,—and irrespective of its success or failure—one that is initiated by a good will. An "evil action" is, correspondingly, one initiated by an evil will (p. 111). But since both, good will and evil will, are rooted in (opposed) feeling-dispositions, feelings—especially feelings of sympathy and compassion—are the "foundation of ethics" (p. 114).

This interpretation, Kreibig points out, leaves open the possibility of determining more specifically the "sources of pleasure and of suffering" in accordance with "the place, the time, and the maturity of both, the valuing subject and the other person." And because of this fact, he insists, it is not warranted to repudiate without further analysis an ethical theory as "hedonistic or as a low and degrading view of noble things" simply because it is based upon the pleasure-displeasure dichotomy. Moreover, the thesis—advanced by Helvetius and Holbach—that an action involving sympathy and compassion always "springs from an egoistic and shrewd calculation" is contradicted by our every-day experience which shows that men do act out of sympathy and with compassion, and without other considerations (p. 117).

Kreibig's theory thus entails a repudiation of hedonism and eudaemonism as well as of "pan-egoism." He finds that all three positions are irreconcilable with the established facts of human experience. These facts show that the goal of human existence is "the richest possible development and employment of man's mental and physical powers." Admittedly, such a goal is related to the thesis that man's ultimate aim is to realize "the greatest possible pleasure." However, it is not the idea of pleasure but that of maximum self-realization which guides us and is the motive in "the realization of the goal of our human existence." We cannot even conceive of pleasure in the abstract or as unrelated to some goal other than pleasure itself (p. 127).

VII

In view of Kreibig's over-all position, the primary moral value judgments are (1) judgments ascribing praiseworthiness to a good disposition, and (2) judgments ascribing blameworthiness to an evil disposition (p. 128). In a secondary sense, both types of judgments may refer also to persons (as having the dispositions) and to actions (as manifesting the dispositions). In any case, however, they express a "preference-worthiness" (or unworthiness) relative to some other disposition, person, or action.

Still, "all moral valuations [although judgmental in character] are merely the expression in thought of a feeling-process (Gefühlsprocess)." That is to say, "if the feeling of preference for the value of the good over the disvalue of evil were absent, the value judgment would have no significance for the person making the judgment, except that of its purely verbal meaning (pp. 128–129).

Meaningful moral judgments, however, may be of three kinds: (1) those of the person who is morally qualified to act; (2) those of the person whose welfare is affected by the action; and

(3) those of an "impartial witness"—i.e., those of a person who, without autopathic or ergopathic considerations, values from a purely moral or heteropathic point of view.

If the morally qualified person evaluates his own actions, he may approach the point of view of the "impartial witness." In this possibility Kreibig sees the psychological precondition of conscience—conscience being the disposition that makes evident "whether or not a contemplated or a completed action is in conflict or in harmony with our own moral disposition" (p. 129). If there is a conflict, we experience displeasure—and often an intensive one—which, when we still contemplate acting in a certain way, may provide the motive that determines our decision and which, after an action has been completed, is identifiable as remorse and self-condemnation. If the action is in harmony with our moral disposition, we experience satisfaction and/or relief. Conscience, however, presupposes a fairly high level of the morally good disposition. It would be futile to ask a cruel or envious person to listen to the voice of his conscience.

Any valuation of a man's disposition implies a scale of higher-lower, characterized by the following "laws":

1. In general, a disposition is higher the stronger the compassion that is of its essence, and the more emphatic the repudiation of evil. The disposition is valued higher also in proportion to the number of persons affected and the extension of benefits into the future. Its value depends, furthermore, on the value of the goods which the other persons try to realize, on the degree to which sympathy and compassion have become dispositional, and on the maturity of the moral agent (p. 132).

2. In the case of a conflict between compassion and self-love, the value of a good disposition is rated higher the smaller the benefit to the other person is in proportion to one's own sacrifices. However, since the highest heteropathic or moral good is "the richest possible development and employment of the mental and physical powers of the other person," any individual is pursuing the highest moral good if his goal is "the realization of the highest autopathic good to the other person" (pp. 136–37).

The primary moral agent is, of course, the individual human being. Social groups, however,—so we have seen earlier—function as secondary value-subjects. Their valuations are reflected in the mores and laws which prevail in any given society and which, as part of his social environment, influence and may even determine the valuations of the individual. Education and the enforcement of laws play here their part. The morally mature person, however, is motivated in his pursuit of the good not by social pressures but by the "inner motive" of sympathy and compassion. For him, "the morally good actions are at the same time the source of the strongest, the purest, and the most lasting own pleasure" (p. 142). On the other hand, "he who does not take pleasure in doing good but finds satisfaction in the tormenting of his fellowmen lacks the inner basis of morality, and no chain of logical reasoning, no imperative of some ethical system can directly instill it in him" (p. 143). What is required is a change in his dispositional attitudes, in his feeling-dispositions.

The morally mature person, as a rule, has reached a level of development higher than that of the average of his social group. If he also possesses greater intellectual maturity and a deeper insight into the realities of the situation in which he finds himself, he is burdened with the responsibility of helping his group as a whole reach a higher level of moral existence—and ultimately one at which sympathy and compassion are extended to the whole of mankind, indeed, to all sentient creatures.

Summing up his views on ethics, Kreibig formulates two "basic norms":

1. Every individual is duty-bound to do everything possible on his part to increase rather than decerase the happiness of his fellowmen, now and in the future, and to reduce rather than increase their unhappiness. "This demand is fulfilled only when the realization of the highest autopathic good of all sentient beings has become the moral agent's permanent goal" (p. 144).

2. Every person is duty-bound to do everything possible on his part to develop the moral disposition within himself and in others.

Both norms are actually but different aspects of one and the same moral imperative, for the second norm can be derived from the first. Their separation, however, has certain pedagogical advantages. Together they are the basis for all moral "maxims" and commandments.

VIII

Kreibig deals at some length with the ergopathic value-feelings—i.e., with the feelings of pleasure and displeasure resulting from a contemplation of objects simply as of objects and without relation to any particular subject. The value contrast here is that of "beautiful" and "ugly"—taking both terms in a very broad and loose sense. In this broad sense, any content of experience— "a boring lecture" no less than a work of art or the fragrance of a rose—can become the object of an ergopathic valuation, provided only that it lends itself to "a purely contemplative attitude on the part of the [valuing] subject" (p. 155). That ergopathic valuations include the whole field of aesthetics is thus evident; that they extend beyond the realm of the arts is equally clear.

An object is beautiful if, by virtue of its form (*Gestaltqualität*), it induces pleasure in the subject contemplating it. It is ugly in the contrary case. The *raison d'être* of all art is the enhancement of the ergopathic pleasure. Aesthetic judgments merely express the feeling-response to an object. If the feeling is absent, then the aesthetic judgments—as also the moral judgments—have no significance beyond their verbal meanings. They may still play a role in aesthetic theory—for instance, in the purely theoretical comparison of objects, or in the subsumption of aesthetic objects under a preconceived conceptual framework of valuations—but they are no longer value judgments in the true sense of that term. It must be noted, however, that "the sublime, the heroic, the sentimental, the tragic, the comic" are terms which refer not to various "species of value-feelings" but to "different sources" of such feelings and of "mixtures of feelings" (*Gefühlsmischungen*) (pp. 158–59).

Precondition for the occurrence of an ergopathic value experience is, "above all else," the nature of the object involved. Decisive qualities center around spatial configurations ("figure, proportion, symmetry"), temporal relations—simultaneity (e.g., harmony), succession (e.g., melody)—and movement (e.g., rhythm). Beyond such qualities, however, associations frequently determine the character of the ergopathic experience. This is true in particular when the object that elicits the feeling-response is a painting or a work of literature. "Without this influence [of the significant associations] Leonardo's 'Last Supper' or Goethe's *Faust* would remain unintelligible" (p. 162), and the ergopathic experience would be diminished as a result. Kreibig here quotes with approval Fechner's statement that, "if all associations were eliminated, nothing would remain of the Sistine Madonna but a gaudy (*kunterbunte*) tableau of colors which the pattern of every carpet would surpass in pleasantness."

It is an experiential fact that the feeling of pleasure increases if it follows an experience of displeasure. This, according to Kreibig, is simply the "law of an increasing intensity as the result of a sequential contrast in quality" (p. 163). This law, however, is supplemented by the "law of summation" which states that the pleasing character of an experience as a whole increases when the constituent elements of that experience are so arranged that the order of their qualities and intensities enhances the contrasts and produces an end-effect that is especially impressive. Dramatic works and musical compositions illustrate the point.

Perfect works of art always lead to an "inner liberation and enrichment of the beholder"; but the artist achieves such an effect only when, in creating his work, he is guided by the highest aesthetic value, not by a desire to satisfy the shifting demands of the masses.

IX

It is not customary to speak of aesthetic "virtues"; yet, the term may be acceptable if it is interpreted as meaning (with respect to the "observer") "dependability of taste, sensitivity to hidden beauty, ability to respond to diverse forms, etc.," and (with respect to the creative artist) "technical skill, boldness in conception, clarity in execution, etc." (p. 169). That there has been progress in aesthetic valuations, Kreibig maintains, is a demonstrable fact of cultural history. When the struggle for physical survival was man's primary concern, he valued aesthetically those objects which were (or seemed to be) also advantageous to him: weapons, war dances, and the like. But, "with increasing material security and intellectual maturity, the more refined sensory and intellectual value objects came into the foreground of his attention: the dwelling places of the gods, public buildings, vestments, ornaments, festive songs, pageantry. The highest level in this development is the cultivation of literature, of dramatic and symphonic music, of the graphic and sculptural representation of spiritual events. The object most intensively valued by observer and creative artist alike approaches ever closer the highest aesthetic good" (p. 171). Kreibig does not mean, of course, that the aesthetic development here indicated is uninterrupted progress. As he puts it: "The development of art shows a relatively rapid change from flowering to decay, and a permanent retrogression . . . is precluded only insofar as the available treasures of ideal models have become lasting points of orientation" (*ibid.*). Knowing these "norms" of the past, the creative artist must find "new ways of representing beauty." It is thus that he becomes a "master" who "raises his art to a higher level of development."

The suggestion that utility is basic to aesthetic values Kreibig repudiates. Listening to a symphony by Beethoven or viewing a lithograph by Dürer has in itself nothing to do with considerations of utility. Moreover, the aesthetic experience does not depend upon autopathic nor upon heteropathic presuppositions. It is complete and sufficient within itself. To be sure, cathedrals and other buildings that can be classified as aesthetic objects have also a utilitarian value; and it is true that their structure and form must be in harmony with the purpose they serve. A cathedral, for example, must "express symbolically man's relation to God" (p. 176). But this "inner purposiveness" is a purely technical matter for the architect's consideration. Structure and ornamentation must enhance the associative meaning. Their "inner harmony" is aesthetically important. But the external purposiveness or utility is not a constitutive characteristic of beauty.

Another problem arises because "confluences of aesthetic and moral values are among the most common value phenomena."

Thus, valuable works of art, notably literary works, make manifest distinct moral valuations. This does not mean, however, that aesthetic and moral values are the same, or that one type can be reduced to the other. However, when aesthetic and moral values are in harmony, they re-enforce one another; when there is a conflict between them with respect to a particular work of art, then (so Kreibig maintains) "even the least moral disvalue is sufficient" to affect negatively the aesthetic value of that work. He adds, however, that "this decision in favor of the primacy of moral values" is not to lead to "a gloomy attitude toward life—an attitude that is opposed to all beauty"; for "in the enjoyment and the creation of the beautiful is found the source of pleasure" which, when it becomes part of our heteropathic pursuits may even become "a moral duty" (p. 179).

Kreibig's lengthy discussion of "value formulae" which, suggesting a mathematical exactiude that is obviously spurious, adds nothing to the essentials of his theory. He does maintain, however, that "only value theory, through its determination of what the highest goal is," can indicate the direction which education ought to take.

BIBLIOGRAPHY

Kreibig, Josef Clemens, *Psychologische Grundlegung eines Systems der Wert-Theorie,* Vienna, 1902.

CHAPTER VI

HEYDE AND THE FOUNDATIONS
OF VALUE THEORY

In 1916, Erich Heyde published his critical survey, *Grundlegung der Wertlehre*—an expanded version of his doctoral dissertation, *Ueber den Wertbegriff*. Ten years later he followed this up with a statement of his own value theoretical position, *Wert: Eine Philosophische Grundlegung*. Taken together, these books represent a significant point of view—one that deserves more attention than it has so far received.

I

Confusion prevails, Dr. Heyde points out at the outset, as to what is meant by 'value.' That something *is* meant is beyond question, for otherwise the term 'value' would never have been introduced or would never have been accepted so widely. In some way we evidently know something that can appropriately be called "value." In this general and vague sense "value is given in consciousness" (*Grundlegung,* p. 3). It is the primary task of value theory to determine what this "given" is and what it is not. The first question, therefore, must be, When do we speak of value? We say, for example, that an automobile *has* "value"; that virtue *has* "value." But we also say that health *is* a "value"; that a commodity *is* a "value." We thus use the term 'value' in two different senses: something *has* "value," and something *is* a "value." Heyde calls the former "value₁" and the latter "value₂." Although both meanings must be clearly distinguished, they are, nevertheless, closely related, for "value₁" is basic and "value₂" is derivative. When we assert that something *is* a value, we actually mean that something exists which *has* value₁ or is "valuable" (p. 5). "Value₂", in other words, reduces in this sense to a derivative of "value₁." An analysis of value problems must therefore concern itself first of all with "value₁"; and it must be noted at the outset that "value₁" is encountered only in connection with something that *has* "value₁"; it is never "given" by itself alone. Nor is it ever encountered as a particular individual—either physical or mental; for it is a *universal* which can be shared by any number of individual "things" (pp. 7–12).

The question now is, What, specifically, characterizes this universal called "value"? Is it a universal like "magnitude" and "shape"? Or is it a universal like "perception" and "feeling"? If the former were the case, then "value" would be a property of "things"—a property, that is, which things possess in and by themselves. The facts, however, are otherwise; for when we say that something *has* "value" we mean that it has "value" in this or that respect, i.e., in relation to something else. "Value," therefore, is neither an individual thing nor a property of an individual thing. *It is a relation.* But it is not just any relation between two particulars. It would be nonsense to say for example that a pen has value relative to Westminster Abbey. To be sure, that which *has* value may be almost anything: "trees, books, money, character, self-restraint." But that relative to which all these "givens" *have* value is always one and the same, namely, consciousness. "He who speaks of 'value' always expresses a special relation of the given which has value to a consciousness—and he does so irrespective of whether he says 'something has value for me' or merely 'something has value' without mentioning the person for whom it has value, for what he means to say in particular when he uses the latter phrase is: it has value not only for me but for all minds" (p. 18). But when we eliminate any actual or implied relation to consciousness, there is nothing left but the "object" itself and value is not one of its properties. If someone were now to argue that even in the absence of any consciousness whatsoever sunlight is still of value in the formation of chlorophyll, Heyde replies that a more careful analysis will reveal that even in this argument a consciousness has been postulated—be it human, divine, or plant-like—that is interested in the existence of chlorophyll. Similarly, it would be meaningless to say that a painting retains its value even though at some time in the future there no longer exists a consciousness (human or otherwise) to which it might be related.

But if it now be admitted that value is indeed a relation, only part of the problem has been solved, for properties may also involve relations. "Causal efficacy," for example, manifests itself only in a relation of one "thing" to another; and a property (such as "sweet" or "red") may depend upon the causal relation between specific particulars. It must be noted, however, that in cases such as these the property itself is grounded in the (causal) relation. Value, on the other hand (so Heyde maintains), is *not grounded* in a relation; "it *is itself* a special kind of relation" (p. 19). And "if we destroy that which has value as well as that relative to which it has value, then nothing remains and, especially, no 'relation'" (p. 20). In this respect "value" is similar to "similarity"; it is nothing in itself. Any reference to a self-existent realm of values is therefore a falsification of the facts in the case.

It follows, furthermore, that "it is imprecise to speak of *values,* i.e., of a plurality of special values," so long as we mean by value "value$_1$"; although, of course, many "values$_2$" do exist, namely, all the given particulars which have "value$_1$." Just as there are no "different volitions" but only one volition aiming at different objects or the volition of different subjects (e.g., of a child, a mature person, etc.); and just as there are not various relations called "similarity" but only various properties and fewer or more properties in which given "objects" are similar; just so there is only one relation "value" and not several kinds. The presumed difference of values—the logical, the aesthetic, the moral, the religious, etc.—has its ground in the differences of the "givens" that have value and in that through which they have value. "Beauty" and "goodness" are thus not different "values$_1$". Their difference lies in the nature of that which *has* value. When we say that something is beautiful, we refer to one kind of objects, and when we say that something is good, we refer to another kind.

Lastly, if value is indeed a relation between that which has value and a consciousness for which it has value, then both focal points of the relation must be real. If, for example, value is ascribed to a painting (be it an aesthetic or an economic value), then the painting itself no less than the consciousness for which is has value is real. And if, inadvertently, value is ascribed to something that is not real, then closer analysis will show that the "object" was, nevertheless, thought of as real. According to

Heyde, therefore, it is characteristic of "value relations" (*Wertbeziehungen*) that the relata are always real. But if this is the case, then it follows that the "value relations" are also real; that value itself is a real relation; that it is "something real."

Against this interpretation it may now be argued that relations—even when they are relations between realities—are not themselves real, and that it is consciousness, and consciousness only, which relates the individual "givens" to one another. Heyde maintains, however, that such an interpretation is erroneous; that consciousness does not create the relations between "things" but discerns them. For example, when two things are "similar" in some respects, their similarity is something which we discover rather than something which we bring about. But if we encounter relations among real things, the relations themselves are unquestionably real. Thus, when we find that two children are similar in some respects, it makes no sense to say that, although the children are real, their similarity is not real. Similarly, if value is a relation which exists only between a real object and a real consciousness, then this relation, too, is encountered in reality, i.e., it is something real.

To be sure, the view that value is not something real is deeply rooted in philosophical tradition; and if values are understood as "particulars" (*Einzelwesen*), then that tradition is right. There exist no entities "value." And neither are values real properties of real things. The relation to a subject for whom something has value is indispensable for all values. Underlying the philosophical tradition which Heyde here repudiates is the assumption that only "particulars" and their "properties" can be real; and if this assumption is accepted, then value (not being a "particular" nor a "property") cannot be real. What is at issue, therefore, is the validity of the basic assumption concerning the nature of reality.

If only that is to be called real which produces effects ("*Wirklich ist was wirkt.*"), then the traditional interpretation is fully justified and values cannot be regarded as real, for in themselves they do not produce effects. But if it is true (as Heyde has argued) that we encounter or discover, rather than create, relations among particular entities—i.e., if it is true that relations are themselves an essential part of what is real—then we can disregard tradition and can include value with what is real. The crucial decision must be made at this point.

II

Whenever value is regarded as "not real" (because it is not a "real entity" nor a "property" of such an entity) but is yet acknowledged to be something "given," the tendency is to regard it as something mental and to take a psychological approach to all value problems. It may be remembered that, reflecting this fact, von Ehrenfels bluntly stated: "It is certain that the definition of value must be a purely psychological one" (*System,* I, p. 87). The result is what Heyde has called "psychologism" in matters of value theory; and to this he opposes his own view that value is nothing "mental" but is a relation of an "object" to a mind (*Grundlegung,* p. 35). The "object" may be "real" or "not real." In neither case, however, is it "in" the mind (in the sense of being a constituent part of it). Essential to the mind are only its "determinations" (*Bestimmtheiten*): perceiving, thinking, feeling, etc.; and only in the sense that we are aware of, perceive, or think an object—i.e., only as something "given" in a particular mode of experiencing—can that object be said to "belong" to a mind. Taken by itself, the "given" (e.g., a stone) cannot be regarded as mental, and as "given"—i.e., as related to a consciousness—it retains its own nature. It is not transformed into something mental merely by being experienced by someone. What is true when the "given" is a particular thing (such as a stone) is true also when the "given" is a relation (such as the "value relation"). That is to say, as something "given," the "value relation" is neither a "thing" nor something "mental"; and not being "mental," it is also not a proper subject-matter for psychology.

As we have seen in the preceding chapters, interpretations of values and value problems have been attempted from a psychological point of view. Feelings and desires have been regarded as foundational to all values; and since they are unquestionably something mental, the inference has been drawn—albeit erroneously—that, as "givens," both the object and its relation to the subject experiencing it are mental and therefore the legitimate concern of psychology; that, in other words, psychology provides the foundation for value theory. This line of reasoning, however, overlooks the fact that, as something "given," the relation between the "mental" (be it feeling or desire) and the "object" is not, and cannot be, mental in the sense in which feeling (for example) is in itself mental. But if, as "given," the "value relation" is not mental, then value theory can no more be conceived as a psychological discipline than can physics—even though value is a relation between an "object" and a "mind." The so-called "value-feelings" are at best but indications of the presence of a value (p. 38).

However, as Heyde sees it, psychologism is not satisfied with merely intepreting value as "mental" but, in a completely misleading sense, regards consciousness as the foundation of values. It is true, of course, that unless there is consciousness, there can be no relation between an object and consciousness. But this does not mean that consciousness alone establishes the value of anything. It does not mean, in other words, that consciousness—i.e., the mental activity of valuing—is the causal condition of values. In making valuing (*Werten*) basic, the psychologists distort the facts in the case; for value cannot be understood as the effect of an activity. An "effect" must be a change of some kind in the "object" toward which an activity is directed; but no change whatever is induced in an "object" merely because it is experienced as having value.

The psychologistic approach may also take a somewhat different form. Instead of viewing the act of valuing as producing an effect in an "object," we may interpret it to mean "to posit" or "to create" a value. Heyde, however, (taking his cue, as on other occasions, from Johannes Rehmke, *Philosophie als Grundwissenschaft*) argues that, strictly speaking, a "creation of values" does not, and cannot, occur because "creation" is impossible. "The scientific mind is taken aback by the idea of 'creation'." We know that everything without exception that comes into being is an effect; but we know also that in order for there to be an effect at least two, and not only one, entity must exist, for "effect" means "change in something." "Creation," therefore, cannot be productive of an "effect," and to regard it as "the sole condition of something real" is, in a strict sense, meaningless. We may still speak of "artistic creation"; but it is obvious that creation in this sense is not the "sole condition" of the art work. It is a change brought about in something that already exists.

Furthermore, "valuing" also does not mean that he who "values" brings it about that "something becomes a value." Phrases such as "ascribing or attributing a value" to something distort the facts in the case, for they imply that value depends on the whims of human beings and, demonstrably, this is not so. If someone were to take the phrase "ascribing a value to something" literally, we could ask him, for example, why he does not ascribe a positive value to a severe illness. He cannot now answer "because it has no value," for such an answer would imply that he ascribes value only to those "objects" which, as a matter of fact, have value, admitting thereby indirectly that value does not depend on the "arbitrary decisions" (*Willkür*) of the subject.

It may now be argued that "valuing" (*Werten, Werthalten*) is not a purely subjective act but a "context" involving a determinate "object" and a determinate "mood"; that in its very essence "valuing" is the same as "having a value-feeling" with respect to an "object." But if this is what is meant, then "valuing" (i.e., "having a value-feeling") is indeed something mental, but it cannot be the "causal condition" of value since no feeling can be a "value-feeling" without being a response to an "object" which already "has" value. Far from implying that the feeling creates the value, the "value-feeling" merely discloses the presence of a value. It is a form of knowing. In this sense, therefore, to "value" something means to know or to discover that something has value; that it has value at least for the subject who experiences the "value-feeling."

To be sure, all "valuing" has its mental aspects—such as feeling and representation (*Vorstellung*); but this fact does not imply that it is "nothing but" a mental phenomenon. If "valuing" means (as just indicated) "to encounter," "to discover," or "to come to know" something as "having" value—i.e., if "valuing" is a form of knowledge—then to this extent it lies outside the field of psychology and, rightfully, is subject-matter of an epistemology (*Wissenslehre*) (p. 50).

This interpretation is re-enforced by the fact that "valuing" is of the nature of "value judgments" rather than of the nature of "feelings." In all "valuing" we form a judgment that such and such an "object" *has* value. And judging that something "has" value or is "valuable" does not bring about a change in the "object" thus judged; it merely means that we experience something as a "determinate given" insofar as it is determinate *as possessing value*—just as the cognitive judgment, This tree is green, has validity only if the tree actually is green.

III

The problem is somewhat different when we examine a position brought into prominence by Heinrich Rickert (see Chapter IX), who asserted that he himself had abandoned a "psychologistic" approach to values, but who, in Heyde's opinion, still shared with "psychologism" the prejudice that only particulars and their properties are real. But if value is not to be regarded as "mental" (in the "psychologistic" sense) nor as real but, nevertheless, as in some sense "given," then what is it? To this question Rickert had replied that "the values themselves . . . form a realm of their own which lies beyond subject and object" ("Vom Begriff der Philosophie," *Logos,* I, p. 12); but this interpretation Heyde also repudiates (*Grundlegung,* p. 57).

True, value is neither a particular "thing" nor a particular "mental entity" or "mind," nor is it a particular property of either. It is, however, a real relation between a "thing" and a "consciousness," and, together with them, it belongs to the realm of reality, not to some transcendent realm of its own—and especially not to a realm that antedates or is logically prior to actual being. It is real as a relation between a real "object" and a real "subject" and, therefore, is at least co-real with them (p. 59).

If, for the sake of argument, we were to grant that value "lies beyond all reality," the consequences of this thesis would make the thesis itself unacceptable. In the first place, so Heyde points out, when values are said to transcend the real and to constitute a realm of their own, they must be conceived as particulars *(Einzelwesen),* as something akin to Platonic ideas: unchanging and eternal. Thus, when Rickert says that value is "attached to" or "connected with" "real particulars" *(Wirklichkeiten),* he speaks of the values themselves as particulars since only a particular can be "attached" to another particular. Value, however,—so we have seen earlier—is a relation and, as such, it is not and cannot be "attached to" or "connected with" a particular.

If it be said now that the value intended when it is asserted that "value is a particular" is not "value₁" but "value₂" (a particular which has "value₁"), then a new difficulty arises because "value₂", being a "good" among "goods," does not lie "beyond what is real."

A further difficulty arises from the assertion of the "non-reality" of value; for how can the "non-real" be "attached to" the real? If it makes no difference to the real whether or not a "non-real" is "attached" to it, then any reference to the "non-real" —i.e., to value—is of no significance. But if it does make a difference, then the "non-real" produces an effect upon the real and, therefore, must itself be real (for "real is what produces an effect"). And if "being attached to" real particulars were taken to mean merely that, somehow, values "belong" to the real, then even this assertion would imply that the values themselves are real, for only what is itself real can be a property or an essential part of the real.

When the transcendentalist in value theory asserts that value itself is a particular, the question is, What kind of a particular is it? Since value is assumed to lie "beyond" particular things as well as "beyond" particular minds, it cannot be of the nature of a thing nor of the nature of mind; it must be something *sui generis.* If we now ask, And what, specifically, is its nature?, Rickert replies that "the essence of a value is its validity *(Geltung)"* ("Vom Begriff," *op. cit.,* p. 17). This answer, however, entails insurmountable difficulties.

In the first place, it is not at all clear what "vality" here means, and Rickert, following Lotze in accepting the term as primitive, has given us no precise definition. This much, however, seems evident: "validity" is a relational term and therefore cannot also identify the very essence of the "presumed particular" (*angebliches Eigenwesen*) called "value." If, confronted with this fact, the "transcendentalist" abandons the idea that value is a "particular" and interprets it as a relation, then to say that "the essence of value is its validity" would mean: the essence of the *relation* "value" is validity. "To have value is to have validity." But even this modification of the original thesis is unacceptable; for, if "to have value" means "to have validity," then everything that has value ought also to have validity; but the facts are otherwise. We can all agree that brakes on a car have value, that vitamins have value, and that good health has value; but is it meaningful to say that they are valid? Moreover, in those cases in which something has both, value and validity, it can be shown that validity is the *ground* of its value. A ticket to a theater, for example, has value *because* it is valid; but its value and its validity are clearly two distinct aspects (*Grundlegung,* p. 66).

A closer inspection of the various meanings of "validity" reveals that, in one way or another, all entail a reference to an "is to be." Thus, "the ticket is valid" means the ticket "is to be" accepted as admitting one to the theater, to a dance, to a trip to Europe, or whatever the ticket may specify; "the law is valid" means the law "is to be" obeyed; and "the argument is valid" means the argument "is to be" accepted as sound. It must be noted, furthermore, that wherever an "is to be" is involved, there is also a consciousness to whom the "is to be" is directed, and one who thus directs it. "The plane ticket is valid" thus means that the person issuing the ticket directs another person to admit the holder of the ticket to the specified flight. Validity, therefore, is not a property of the "valid object" *per se* but a relation between one consciousness and another (p. 70); and as relation it cannot be the essential nature of value when the latter is taken to be a "particular." But neither can validity be regarded as the essence of value when the latter is taken to be a relation because, as we have seen already, not all values are instances of validity.

IV

Having dealt critically with both, the "psychologistic" and the "transcendentalist" approaches to value problems, Heyde now develops more fully his own thesis that "value is a real relation between a real object and a real consciousness." His first question is, What is the nature of this relation? More specifically, Why does something have value for someone? We speak of the value of a typewriter, of an electric lamp, of an airplane; but we also speak of the value of a painting, of a symphony, of an ornament; and, on the face of it, it seems that these examples resuppose two distinct types of values. Heyde designates them respectively, "value$_a$" and "value$_b$."

When we examine instances of value$_a$, we discover that in all such cases a "third factor"—change—is involved, in addition to "object" and "consciousness." Thus, using a typewriter means to produce desired marks on a piece of paper, and turning on an electric lamp illuminates a dark room. When change is not possible, we also do not encounter value$_a$. A traffic light at the North Pole has no value$_a$ because there is no traffic there in the flow of which its operation could make a difference.

However, it is not always the case that value$_a$ is present when object, consciousness, and change are "given." A storm, for example, may destroy houses and trees, but we do not say that because it brings about this change it has value$_a$. What must be noted is that in all instances in which we speak of value$_a$ the change (whatever it may be) is intended—i.e., it is desired or willed. *"Value$_a$ of an object thus means its usefulness (Zweck-dienlichkeit). The valuable object is related to a purpose—i.e., it is related to what is willed by the consciousness in question"* (pp. 79-80. Italics in the original).

Heyde's position here becomes quite clear when we examine more closely what he means by "usefulness."

His basic argument is that "to will" always means "to want to produce an effect," "to want to bring about a change." The effect or change is the "purpose" of a volition and is always "pleasure-accentuated" *(steht im Lichte der Lust)*. That is to say, the idea of the intended effect or change is always associated with an idea of pleasure. Hence, when we say that something has "value$_a$" or that it is "useful," we mean that it is a condition for the realization of an intended pleasure-accentuated change. This does not preclude, however, that "pleasure-accentuated" may mean merely a reduction in displeasure (p. 82).

We can now summarize these findings: In every situation in which value is present, there are also present: (a) a "particular" which produces an effect or brings about a change, (b) a "particular" in which the change (effect) is produced, and (c) a "particular" that intends or wills the effect because it is pleasure-accentuated. But it is the "particular" referred to under (a) that *has* "value_a" in the sense of "being useful" for any "particular" referred to under (c). "Value_a," therefore, is the efficaciousness of (a) as (c) employs (a) to bring about a change in (b).

If it now be argued that an object has "value_a" even though, at the moment, it is not employed to bring about an effect, and that therefore producing an effect is not necessary for "value_a," Heyde replies that "value_a" is to be understood as "capable of producing an effect *(Wirkenkönnen),*" not necessarily as actually doing so. And in this sense efficaciousness is indispensable to "value_a." But proof that we are justified in regarding anything as having "value_a" only reality itself can furnish. And the assertion that "something has 'value_a' for me" does not mean that I must always will the change which it can bring about, but only that *if* I want to bring it about, then the object in question is useful. "Value_a" presupposes merely that the change which an object *can* bring about is a willed or intended one (p. 86).

One other point must be noted, however. We must not confuse a "pleasure-accentuated change" *(im Lichte der Lust stehende Veränderung)* with "change producing pleasure" *(Lust bringende Veränderung).* That is to say, we are concerned here with changes the idea of which is associated with an idea of pleasure, not with changes which in themselves produce pleasure as a state of mind *(Lust als Zuständliches).* The crucial point is that *the change must be intended or willed.*

V

However, the identification of value with usefulness is not the only meaning of 'value.' Thus, when we speak of the value of a work of art—of a painting or a poem—it is evident that we do not mean usefulness but something else. What remains true even here, however, is the fact that the objects involved have "value"—we shall call it "value$_b$"—for some consciousness; and the question is, In what respects does "value$_b$" differ from "value$_a$"? It is Heyde's contention that in all cases of "value$_b$" pleasure is involved. But "pleasure" must be understood in a broad sense and must not be limited to sensory pleasures. "He who speaks of the 'value' of a poem or a sonata takes pleasure in these objects; . . . this is beyond disput" (p. 92).

However, so Heyde now argues, it is not always the case that, when we experience pleasure, "value$_b$" is present. An agreeable sense impression is, as such, not yet a "value$_b$." In order that a pleasurable experience may be a "value$_b$," it must be supplemented by "specific inner experiences" (*besondere Innenempfindungen*). The valued object effects in me (us) a change, and it has "value$_b$" because it is "the effective condition" of these changes. In an abbreviated manner of speaking we can say that an object has "value$_b$" when it is a "pleasure-giving" object. This formulation makes it evident that, just as in the case of "value$_a$," so the object which has "value$_b$" is an effect-producing object. The "particular" undergoing the change is a consciousness. And the effect is pleasure and "specific inner experiences" (p. 94). But, also as before, it is not necessary that the object having "value$_b$" actually be "pleasure-producing" at any given time. It is sufficient that it be known to be capable of producing pleasure. However, it is possible that one might be in error here. One might believe that a certain object is capable of producing pleasure when, as a matter of fact, it is not capable of doing so. Nevertheless, the capacity for producing pleasure and those "specific inner experiences" is the sole basis that justifies us in saying that something has "value$_b$."

It may now be argued that, so understood, "value$_b$" is but a special form of "value$_a$"; that the object having "value$_b$" is "useful" in realizing an intended pleasure. Heyde counters by saying that "value$_a$" completely depends on the fact that the change produced is intended or willed; but that in the case of "value$_b$" the change which the object effects need not be intended. A beautiful painting, for example, produces pleasure, and on this basis *"alone," "without"* the pleasure *"being intended,"* we regard it as "valuable" (p. 97. Italics in the original).

We need not deny that one can "intend" or "will" pleasure; that pleasure is the purpose of an act; and that therefore that which serves this purpose or produces the pleasure may be called valuable in the sense of being "useful." It is evident, however, that in all such cases the pleasure itself, though "valuable," does not have "value$_a$"—i.e., it does not have value in the sense of usefulness. "Value$_b$," therefore, cannot be reduced to "value$_a$." And since "value$_a$" (usefulness) cannot be reduced to "value$_b$" (pleasure), at least two distinct types of "values" must be acknowledged. That is to say, whenever we encounter "value" (in the sense of "value$_1$," of something "having" value), we encounter "value$_a$" or "value$_b$." That is, the object which "has" value is either useful (in the sense of effecting an intended change) or it causes pleasure and those "special inner experiences" referred to earlier. There is no third alternative, although the same object may fulfill both functions at the same time (p. 101).

An object has disvalue when it effects a change that was not intended or when it causes displeasure. It may, of course, do both at the same time.

VI

It will be remembered that, from the very beginning, Heyde understood value to be a real relation between real things and a real consciousness. The nature of that relation has now been shown to consist in the fact that the object which "has" value—be that "value$_a$" or "value$_b$"—brings about "special results" *(Besonderes)* which affect a mind (consciousness). If no consciousness is involved, if there is no experience of pleasure or displeasure, then there is also no value. "It is nonsense to talk about a realm of values for which it is not necessary that they (the values) exist for a consciousness" (p. 103). But, also, no value is ever "given" if no "effect-producing object" *(wirkender Gegenstand)* is involved. This means that all values are "values of efficacy" *(Wirkungswerte)*.

Opposed to such a thesis is, of course, von Ehrenfels' contention that the relation which is basic to all values is that of desire rather than that of efficacy. As von Ehrenfels puts it: "Value is a relation between an object and a subject such that the subject either actually desires the object or would desire it if it were not convinced that the object already exists" *(System der Werttheorie,* p. 65). That is to say, "the value of a thing is its desirability." Heyde must now come to terms with this contention.

His argument is, in effect, that if value were the same as desirability, then (a) everything valuable would have to be such that it could be desired *(dass es begehrt werden könnte);* and (b) everything that could be desired would have to be valuable. But neither (a) nor (b) is the case *(Grundlegung,* p. 108). Many things have value although we do not desire them and cannot desire them because we already possess them. A painting in my living room, for example, has value for me but I cannot desire it since I already possess it. To say that the painting has value *because I would desire it if I did not already own it* does not get us around the difficulty which Heyde here points out: The value which the actual painting in my living room has for me— and this is the point in question—does not and cannot depend upon my desire. Conversely, not everything that can be desired is valuable. Thus, we may desire pleasure—and may desire it for its own sake. But we have already seen that to experience pleasure is not the same as "to value," for "valuing" means "to know something as pleasure-producing"; it does not mean to experience pleasure.

But even if we were to grant that everything that has value can be desired and, conversely, that everything that can be desired has value, it would still be impossible to identify value with "desirability *(Begehrbarkeit).*[1] The fact that, in a given situation, one and the same object is valuable and can also be desired does not in itself justify an identification of "valuable" and "being desired" (p. 109). When we encounter an object which is valuable and which also can be desired, then the ground or reason for our desiring the object is its value. And this is a thesis

---

[1] It must be noted that Heyde always uses "desirability" as meaning "capable of being desired" *(begehrt werden können),* not as meaning "worthy of being desired."

which von Ehrenfels, who identifies value and "desirability," denies. If value is the same as "desirability," then it cannot also be its ground. Heyde, however, can maintain that we desire an object *because* we find it to be valuable—i.e., because it is useful or pleasure-inducing. And he can also maintain that value and purpose must be similarly distinguished. That something is or becomes our purpose or goal means that (for us) it has value. "Having value" is the condition for anything becoming a purpose for us (p. 115).

A related problem arises when value is defined as "need-satisfaction" *(Bedürfnisbefriedigung)*—a definition that has been carried over into general value theory from the field of economics. But what is meant here by "need"?

No need exists, so Heyde points out, if there exists no one who "experiences the need" of "something." "Experiencing a need" is possible, however, only for beings having consciousness. Hence, to say for example that plants have "needs" is but a figurative way of speaking or it presupposes a panpsychism which finds little support in known facts. But when a "need" is experienced, it is experienced as a feeling and, more specifically, as a feeling of displeasure. The "object-aspects" of the experience are "distinct inner sensations." Thus, he who feels the need for some water experiences certain "inner sensations" combined with a feeling of displeasure. Actually, the displeasure derives from and pertains to those "inner sensations." And it is this fact which specifically characterizes all "felt needs." If the displeasure is not related to some "inner sensations" but derives from other "objects" or from "external situations," we do not legitimately speak of "needs." However, to the "inner sensations" as the ground of the displeasure we must add "inner urges" and "drives," and the "objectives" (in the form of anticipatory ideas) as that for which a need is felt.

In the case of volition, there is encountered (in addition to the above) the intention to bring about a pleasure-accentuated change in the experiential situation. The contrast of the felt displeasure and the anticipated pleasure is indispensable if the subject is to relate itself *causally* to the objective—i.e., if the subject *wills* something. But it is precisely this "causal relatedness" that is lacking when we deal with needs only. To *need* something and to *will* something are, thus, quite different experiences, and the satisfaction of a need is understood better as "elimination of a displeasure" (*Unlustentwirklichung*) and of "inner urges" than as "realization of pleasure" (*Lustverwirklichung*) (p. 120).

If it now be asked whether or not satisfaction of a need is the same as value, then Heyde replies that, although at first glance they appear to be the same, careful analysis shows that, actually, they are not; for whenever value is equated with the satisfaction of a need, that satisfaction is intended or willed and the object (or situation) which satisfies the need thus has "value in the sense of utility" (*Wert im Sinne der Zweckdienlichkeit*) (p. 121). Here, as in other cases, the value actually lies in the realization of a purpose, not in the satisfaction of a need merely as satisfaction; and the "object" satisfying the need (i.e., the object which is useful in the realization of a purpose) has "value$_a$"—as have all objects that serve a purpose. And if it be argued that it is "value$_b$" (pleasure-causing) rather than "value$_a$" (usefulness) that is involved in the satisfaction of a need, we need remind ourselves only of the fact that many objects—a painting or a poem, for example—have "value$_b$" without being objects that satisfy a need ("need" understood in the strict sense in which Heyde has defined the term). But if not every satisfaction of a need is a value nor every value the satisfaction of a need, then value cannot be the same as satisfaction of a need.

VII

A special problem arises when we consider the "magnitude" or "degree" of value. To be sure, we experience pleasure in varying degrees—i.e., we experience "greater or more intensive pleasure" and "less or less intensive pleasure"; and it is therefore reasonable to maintain that an object has a greater "value$_b$" (= pleasure-giving) than has some other object if it gives us greater pleasure than does the latter. But such an interpretation appears not to be adequate for "value$_a$" (= usefulness); and yet, since volition always aims at a "pleasure-accentuated" goal, it is the anticipated intensity of the pleasure that is to be realized which determines the magnitude of the value of the object useful in the realization of the goal. In one way or another, therefore, "the magnitude of pleasure is the measure of all values" (p. 125); and the values of two objects having "value$_a$" and "value$_b$," respectively,—say, "a pocketknife and a painting by Rubens"—can be compared in terms of the pleasures that are ultimately involved. It may, of course, be argued that, even so, the value of a pocketknife and the value of a painting remain incomparable because, in a situation in which the pocketknife would be most useful and would therefore have great "value$_a$," the painting would have little or no value at all; whereas, in its proper place, the painting has great "value$_b$" when in that same place (on display in a museum, let us say) the knife has very little or no value. Heyde suggests, however, that we consider the problem in this way: Suppose that someone—let us call him John—is to be given a present and that he has a choice between a pocketknife and a painting by Rubens. Unless the values of the respective objects can in some way be compared, no choice between them is possible. But John actually makes a choice and selects the painting. If we now ask him why he did so, he will answer that the painting has a "greater value for him" than has the pocketknife. The comparison, however, that is basic to this decision cannot rest upon a direct confrontation of "value$_a$" (which the pocketknife has but which the painting does not have) and "value$_b$" (which the painting has but the knife does not have); it can rest only upon the (actual and/or anticipated) pleasures which John associates with the two objects. The preference is given to the object which yields (or promises to yield) the greater pleasure. It is this object that has the "greater value" for John.

But other distinctions must also be made. Thus it has become traditional to distinguish between aesthetic, moral, and logical values. They are spoken of as Beauty, Goodness, and Truth, respectively, and Value is then regarded as the universal under which the three types are subsumable. It is Heyde's contention, however, that this tradition finds no justification in the facts of experience.

To be sure, an object which is "aesthetically valuable" is "pleasure-giving" and therefore has "value$_b$"; but a special aesthetic pleasure is not discernible. What distinguishes the aesthetic object from other objects having "value$_b$" is not the pleasure it causes but the special type of "inner sensations" (Innenempfindungen) it produces. The pleasure is just that—pleasure; and as pleasure it determines the value-essence of any "value$_b$." The differentiation is rooted in the specific "inner sensations" which, as such, are not the determinants of any value-essence (p. 128).

When next we turn to "moral value," we are, of course, concerned with values pertaining to actions and volitions, to "the intentional realization of goals." But not all actions have moral value. Only those have it which are "manifestations of a moral will," of a "consciousness," that is, which in its actions, "knows itself as being at one with other consciousness" (p. 129). What is decisive here is not the action as action nor the effect of an action simply as effect. Rescuing someone who is drowning, for example, is certainly an action and it produces effects. But the action may have been prompted, not by a desire to help the person who is in danger, but by vainglorious self-esteem and, thus, may lack true moral value. This means, however, that, according to Heyde, an action has moral value, not because it gives us pleasure, but because its intended effect is a moral one—i.e., it is one which is concerned with "the other consciousness," "the other person" (p. 130).

Just as we identify "beautiful" with "being aesthetically valuable," and "good" with "being morally valuable," so we usually identify "true" with "being logically valuable" and regard "truth" as a special form of value$_1$. Heyde finds, however, that such an interpretation is untenable. One of his arguments centers on the fact that, in aesthetics, it makes sense to say that one object is more beautiful (aesthetically more valuable) than another, and, in ethics, it makes sense to say that one action is better (morally more valuable) than another; but it makes no sense to speak of degrees of truth. A given proposition is either true or it is false; there is no third possibility, although one true proposition may be more valuable than another true proposition. Truth, therefore, cannot be identified with (logically) valuable. But a still different difficulty is also involved here; for truth is neither a "particular existent" (Einzelwesen) nor a property of such an "existent." It is, rather, a relation between a proposition and the "real" which that proposition describes or expresses. Relations, however, produce no effects; and since, according to Heyde, only that which produces effects can have value, it is meaningless to speak of the "value" of truth. Still, the phrase "value of truth" is being used; but when it is, its real meaning is either "to speak the truth has value₁," or "knowledge of the truth is value₂." And "logically valuable" can mean only that a true proposition serves the purpose of "a clear understanding of the real"; and, of course, different propositions may serve that purpose in different degrees.

It follows from these discussions, according to Heyde, that we do not encounter "different values" anywhere, and that the distinction between aesthetic, moral, and logical "values" is justified only in terms of the specific character of that which has value and of the properties through which it has value. It is not justified in terms of value as such—although, to be sure, as one and the same universal, value can be encountered in numerous and diverse instances.

VIII

One final problem remains: Are all values relative or are some at least absolute? The answer to this question depends on what is meant by "relative." Thus, if "relative"—let us call it "relative₁"—means that value itself is a relation (which, as we have seen, is Heyde's thesis), then a value would be "absolute" if it were not a relation. But "relative"—i.e., "relative₂"—may mean that value "stands in relation" to something else—either to an object or to a subject. In this case, a value would be "absolute" if it did not stand in such a relation. A third meaning of "relative"—"relative₃"—would be that the value of an object is determined by the particular nature of the subject for which it is an object. A value would then be "absolute" if it were not so dependent but were "universally valid" (*allgemeingültig*).

If a value is "relative₁," then no absolute value can ever be encountered, for the very idea of it is self-contradictory. Similarly, if value were "relative₂," no absolute value could occur, for value is not a self-existent particular. As far as "relative₃" is concerned, it must be admitted at once that some objects have value, or have an especially high value, only for certain subjects but not for all, and the reason for this lies in the peculiarities of the various subjects. A threshing machine, to use Heyde's own example, has value$_1$ for a farmer but not for a professor of philosophy. It is debatable, however, even in this case whether or not an absolute value is ever encountered. Persons who deny absolute value in this sense—"absolute$_3$"—argue that only one value can be "the highest absolute value," and since different people regard different values as "the highest," it is meaningless to speak of an absolute value. Heyde challenges this line of reasoning. To be sure, if value is taken in the sense of value$_1$—i.e., as meaning that somthing *has* value—, then it is true that there can be only one highest value. The universal "highest absolute value$_1$" can be exemplified any number of times but, being a universal, it cannot itself be multiple. Yet, only if it were multiple could we speak of several "highest absolute values$_1$."

However, when it is said that several highest absolute values are possible, what is meant by value is not value$_1$ but value$_2$—i.e., value in the sense of "something *is* a value" or is "a valuable something." And if this is the meaning, then to acknowledge that several "highest absolute values$_2$" are possible does not entail a contradiction and therefore not a repudiation of the very idea of "absolute value" (p. 149). Whether or not several "highest absolute values$_2$" are also actually encountered is at this point in the argument quite irrelevant.

Heyde's final conclusions are these: (1) Value is always relative and never absolute insofar as value itself is a relation—i.e., insofar as it is "relative$_1$." (2) Value is never absolute insofar as the relation "value" can never exist by itself; and value is never relative insofar as the relation "value" stands neither in relation to an object nor in relation to a subject—i.e., to a consciousness. (3) Value is absolute as well as relative insofar as we can say of a number of objects that they must have value for all subjects, whereas other objects have value only for some subjects. This means that the value of some objects is determined by characteristics which all subjects have in common, whereas the value of other objects depends on the peculiarities of the valuing subjects.

IX

When next we turn to Heyde's second book, *Wert: Eine Philosophische Grundlegung* (published ten years after the first), we find, in effect, a restatement of his position as presented above. However, his arguments have now been clarified and take into consideration opposing views not referred to in the earlier work. It may therefore be well to conclude our discussion of Heyde's point of view by taking at least a cursory look at his new formulations.

At the very outset, Heyde agrees with the phenomenologists (and especially with Max Scheler) in holding that, "as phenomenon," value is not simply a "psychological datum" but a "given fact" encountered "by consciousness in consciousness." A psychologistic approach merely obscures the specific "object-character" *(Gegenständlichkeit)* of the "given" (p. 12). What, then, is meant by "value"?

Consider the following statements: (1) "The (beautiful) vase *has* value"; (2) "The (beautiful) vase *is* a value"; and (3) "The beauty (of the vase) is a value." Of these three formulations Heyde regards the first as basic, and here speaks of "$value_1$" ($=$ something *has* value). The second statement he regards as derivative, interpretating it as meaning that the vase is something which has $value_1$. This derivative meaning he calls "$value_2$." If clarity in value matters is to be achieved, then "$value_1$" ($=$ the value which an object has) and "$value_2$" (the object which has the value and is therefore a valuable object) must always be distinguished. It is even more important, however, to be clear on the meaning of statement (3) above: "The beauty (of the vase) is a value." The phrase "is a value" suggests that "beauty" is a "$value_2$"—i.e., that it is something which has "$value_1$." But another interpretation is also possible—namely, that in itself and in its own right "beauty" is a particular kind of value. Although Scheler and other phenomenologists take this to mean that "beauty" (along with other values) is "$value_3$," Heyde finds that this is not so; that the reference to value in statement (3) is either to "$value_1$" or to "$value_2$" (pp. 21–29). It follows, therefore, that to the extent to which we understand the meaning of "$value_1$" to that extent we also understand all other values.

Now, "value₁," according to Heyde, is a universal. It does not exist as a particular in the world of particular things. Its very nature is such, however, that it must belong to a particular. Value is, thus, always a "value for." But since it may be a "value for" *any* subject—i.e., for any conscious being whatever—, Heyde's position is not subjectivistic. His view is that value is "objective" because it is independent of the peculiarities of any particular subject. Nevertheless, value is a relation involving an object and a subject. But the question is, What kind of a relation is it?

As Heyde sees it, value it not the result of a relating—i.e., it is not the result of a conscious activity called valuing. Expressions such as "positing a value," "forming a value," or "creating a value" all miss the point. The value which an object has for me is "not created by me but is encountered; it is not invented by me but is found" (p. 63). "I can value only what actually *has* value" (p. 62). But value is neither something physical nor something mental; and if by "being real" we mean "producing or suffering an effect," producing or undergoing a change, then value is not even real (p. 65). But neither can it be identified with validity—as Rickert would have us believe. On the contrary, value is a special kind of relation in which an object stands to a subject. As this relation it is irreducible and non-derivative; and the concept "value" is therefore a "primitive or fundamental concept (*ein Grundbegriff*) (p. 78).

The thesis that value itself is a special kind of relation in which an object stands to a subject was explicitly repudiated by Max Scheler who, admitting that "values may provide the foundation of a relation," insisted that "value is not a relation" (*Der Formalismus in der Ethik und die materiale Wertethik*, p. 248). What had persuaded Scheler to take the position he did was the (presumably insurmountable) difficulty he found in distinguishing between "value in itself" and "value for me" if value were taken to be a relation.

It is Heyde's contention, however, that the idea of a "value in itself" is self-contradictory when it is taken to mean "value for no one." It is an acceptable idea only when it is taken to mean "value for every consciousness, not just for me" (*Wert*, p. 83). Without (explicit or implicit) reference to a "value subject"—

be that subject identified or not—there is neither an "object value" nor a "value object."

Scheler's thesis that value is not a relation but a quality also is unacceptable to Heyde because it is not clear whether value is to be taken in the sense of a primary quality (like size or shape) or in the sense of a secondary quality (like color). If the former is meant, then the thesis is manifestly false, for no quality "value" is ever encountered among the primary qualities of an object. But if the latter is meant, then the thesis amounts to an admission that value, if it is not itself a relation, at least involves a relation to a subject. But Heyde goes a step further by pointing out that, in the case of the traditionally acknowledged secondary qualities (such as color), the object actually possesses identifiable physical characteristics that are causally associated with our experience of the secondary qualities. Thus, corresponding to specific color perceptions, we find in the object the physical conditions for the absorption of certain rays of light and the reflection of others. But no such physical conditions are correlated with values. Moreover, not all valued objects are physical in nature. Not all, therefore, can have physical correlates to our value experience—a fact which sets values apart from secondary qualities. And, lastly, the so-called "secondary qualities" are all qualities of sense impressions; value experience, however, is essentially a concern of the emotions (pp. 87–91).

Since any reference to value is meaningless if it does not (implicitly or explicitly) involve a subject as well as an object, and since, furthermore, value experience is essentially a concern of the emotions, a clarification of the role of the "value subject" is of utmost importance. Simply to assert that "value is a relation to a feeling-experience" will not do, for value involves always, and at once, an object as well as a subject. As Heyde puts it: "Value is the relation of an object to a (feeling) state of a subject and can be found neither on the side of the subject alone nor on the side of the object alone" (p. 106). But what manner of a relation is it?

Although "pleasure may be an indispensable characteristic of a value experience," this does not mean that the value of an object can be identified with the object's "actually causing pleasure," for pleasure is but a passing experience whereas the value of an object transcends any given moment. This contrast between the "constancy of the value" and the "inconstant pleasure caused by the object" is crucial (p. 115). The difficulty cannot be overcome by arguing that value is the potentiality of the object to cause pleasure, for if it were, then the basis for valuing objects which do not actually cause pleasure would consist of non-real or merely imagined pleasure. The facts of experience show, however, that our valuation of objects which, at the moment, do not cause us pleasure depends, nevertheless, on "real pleasure." And it is also possible that value is present even though no object-induced pleasure is being experienced. Thus, "the health-value of honey," to use Heyde's example, does not consist in the honey's causing a passing pleasure but in its "health-furthering effects"—though, admittedly, "the idea of good health can be connected with pleasure—a fact which does not prove, however, that good health and pleasure are one and the same" (p. 116).

Moreover, the presence of pleasure is not in itself sufficient to transform an experience into a value experience. A further ingredient is needed—to wit: those "inner physiological processes" that are "most intimately related to the vital functions of the organism, to the life-preserving and life-furthering activities of the human body" (p. 124)—processes which constitute "a very special group of inner feelings" and which "occur only when we experience something as valuable" (p. 125). A value experience thus involves both, a feeling of pleasure and, as its objective basis, those special "inner feelings" associated with "life-furthering" activities.

A value is "higher" than another in proportion as the object which elicits the value experience intensifies our feeling of "life-enhancement" and therefore of pleasure. This fact, however, should not mislead us into assuming that value is simply a causal relation in the sense that "the value of an object consists in its particular capacity to enhance our feeling of vitality" (p. 140). To be sure, we ascribe value to an object because it possesses the capacity just mentioned; but, as Heyde points out, to *ascribe* a value to an object *because* of this capacity is not the same as to hold that the value *is* the capacity. In order to understand the special kind of relation which value is, it is necessary to understand that "value consists in the mutual coordination of (value-)object and (value-)feeling." What is significant here is that the "mutual coordination" be acknowledged, not that a specific instance of it be actually given. In other words, "he who makes a value statement simply expresses the fact that he has found the coordination of an object and a feeling-state of some subject; whether or not the value subject is conscious or may become conscious of the value-feeling—i.e., whether or not the subject is actually aware of the coordination of its own value-feeling and the value-object —affects in no way the fact that there is value and that it can be found. Confusion arises only when we insist that the feeling-state to which a value-object is coordinated must be actual or real, for in that case we either slide into complete subjectivism or, in order to preserve a value objectivism, we must postulate an independent "realm" of values (as Max Scheler did). But when we distinguish between "belonging to" and "reality of" a subject, then we can regard value as the relation of an object to a value-feeling (i.e., as "belonging to") without having to acknowledge at the same time that the value-feeling in question must always be real, or that it must be my own value-feeling. Valuing can then be interpreted as the "disclosure" (*das Sich-offenbaren*) of a relation to a value-feeling" (pp. 155–56).

The interpretation of value as a specific kind of relation is further clarified by the following considerations: a house (for example) is valuable because it is a "dwelling"; it "provides protection against the inclemencies of the weather" and thus "effects" or actualizes a human purpose. That is to say, the reason why the house has value is its usefulness. This does not mean, however, that "usefulness" and value are the same thing. Value does not consist in usefulness; in the case of the house it presupposes and rests upon it. *Because* the value-object is useful it is valuable as well (p. 164). However, not all value "rests upon" or depends on usefulness. The fragrance of a flower, for example, has value not because it is useful but because it is pleasant. The "actualization of pleasure" (*Lustverwirklichung*) is thus a second "ground" for value (p. 166).

But even this does not tell the whole story. What, for instance, is the ground of "the value of a moral person"? It can be neither usefulness nor pleasure-giving. As Heyde sees it, the reason why we value a moral person is exclusively (*einzig und allein*) that person's own moral character (p. 169)—which is but another way of saying that in some cases the value of an object is rooted exclusively in the object itself. This fact deserves special attention, for it seems to support a value objectivism such as Scheler's. It is Heyde's contention, however, that the advocates of this value objectivism confuse the "*ground* of value" and the "grounded *value.*" What is correct is that, in certain cases, value does not depend upon "producing an effect" (utility) or upon causing pleasure, but has its ground in the object itself, in its structure and quality, and, in this sense, is independent of the subject. But this does not affect in the least the nature of the value itself, for even now value is and remains a relation of an object to a value-feeling—i.e., it is and remains a coordination of subject and object. It is still a value for a subject.

BIBLIOGRAPHY

Heyde, Erich, *Grundlegung der Wertlehre,* Quelle & Meyer, Leipzig, 1916.
——— *Wert: Eine philosophische Grundlegung,* Kurt Stegner, Erfurt, 1926.

CHAPTER VII

MINOR APPROACHES TO
VALUE PROBLEMS

.

As far as I have been able to ascertain, the first Ph.D. dissertation in the field of value theory was submitted to the Philosophical Faculty of the University of Heidelberg in the year 1893. Its author, Moriz Naumann, argued in effect that a theory of value is basic to economics, and that the concept of value is relevant to all problems with which the science of economics is concerned. The second dissertation in the field of value theory—at least to my knowledge no other was published prior to this date—was submitted in 1909 to the Philosophical Faculty of the University of Leipzig. Its author, Walter Strich, made "the feeling for language" (*das Sprachgefühl*) basic to his approach to value theory, thus adding another facet to the complex problem. During the interval between 1893 and 1909, still other interpretations were developed by Ritschl (1893), Krueger (1898), Eisler (1902), and Grotenfelt (1905). They were minor efforts, and we shall consider them only briefly.

I

The point of departure for Naumann's theory is the principle of marginal utility. His contention is that a close analysis of our experiences of pleasure and displeasure will yield an adequate basis for the validity of that principle.

Pleasure and displeasure, Naumann argues, are "the movers of the will." They call forth our desire to attain the one and to avoid the other. Desire, once aroused, sharpens our powers of observation and analysis, for we must learn to distinguish between objects and situations that give us pleasure and those which cause displeasure. As soon as this "practical knowledge" has been acquired, desires are no longer directed toward pleasure *per se,* or toward a particular kind of pleasure, but toward the objects and situations which we have come to know as possible causes of

166

pleasure. Our desires can now be spoken of as "needs," and the desired causes of pleasure as "objects of a need" (p. 13).

Needs may be present or actually felt needs, or they may be future or anticipated needs. The former are basic. The latter are derivative and are the result of a better understanding of what gives us pleasure. How far we can anticipate future needs depends upon native ability, education, and existing conditions. The range of the needs is determined primarily by the requirements of our "physico-organismic nature." But as knowledge and cultural achievements increase, that range is broadened and our desires are modified in various ways.

Present or actually felt needs are satisfied through the use and the consumption of things (food, clothing, housing, etc.), and through the services others render us (as when physicians contribute to our well-being). Anticipated needs, reflected in our concern or worry about the future, can be dealt with now (i.e., in the present) by creating conditions which assure the availability, *when needed,* of what will satisfy our needs when they become actual. Assurance of such an availability is the actual possession of the needed goods, and the protection of that possession through law. We should aim, therefore, at establishing the necessary legal order, and at acquiring the needed goods. The acquisition may be accomplished in two ways: through production and through exchange. Production involves work (either one's own or that of someone else). Exchange presupposes the possession of goods that can be exchanged. But whether we deal with production or with exchange, the aim is to maximize pleasure and to minimize displeasure. This fact is basic to all economic activity—be it that of consumption, of possession, or of acquisition.

Having made the distinctions just indicated, Naumann concentrates on the economics of acquisition. His detailed discussions, however, reveal little that is not common knowledge in the field of economics. Still, it is of interest that, in the end, Naumann's arguments carry him beyond the field of economics—which is the only reason for including reference to his work in a book dealing with general theories of value.

The realization of pleasure and the avoidance of displeasure, so we have seen, Naumann took to be basic to all (economic) valuations. But he now is forced to admit that the pleasure-displeasure scale is not necessarily the only basis for valuations; for objects and events may be said to have value in proportion to what they contribute to the realization of a specified purpose. We may thus speak of the value which a particular drug has in combating a specific disease, or of the value which a strategic move has in winning a battle. The values so ascribed to objects and events Naumann calls *Zweckwerte*—purpose-determined values. And "a *Zweckwert* is no longer an economic value."

As we relinquish the reference to pleasure and displeasure, the term "value" can be transposed to other than purely economic fields. But even in the economic field itself pleasure and displeasure are not the exclusive determinants of value. An evaluation in terms of what is "truly useful," for example, is not reducible to a pleasure-displeasure estimate although in a good many cases of our every-day valuations—in our valuations of food, clothing, housing, and the like—"pleasure-value" and "true use-value" may be intertwined. But that they are not identical is obvious. The nourishing quality of food is by no means proportional to its pleasing taste.

And it is also the case that the use-value which an object has for a particular person and which is therefore relative to the needs and desires of that person in particular situations, is quite different from the general economic value of that same object. Thus, the value which a factory has for its owner who enjoys the pleasures he can afford because of the income derived from the factory, is quite different from the value which that same factory has as a factor in the national economy. This latter value cannot be defined in terms of the owner's pleasure or in terms of the pleasure of anyone else. It must be defined in terms of the goods produced, the employment offered, and, thus, in terms of its contribution to the national economy. Not only are the valuations in terms of pleasure and in terms of the interests of the national economy not identical, "they are not even commensurable" (p. 73).

II

In *Ueber Werthurtheile* (1895), Otto Ritschl developed a religious approach to value problems. His starting-point is Kant's famous distinction between *price* and *dignity*. "In the realm of ends," Kant argued, "everything has either a price or a dignity. If it has a price, something else can be put in its place as an equivalent; but if it is exalted above all price and therefore admits of no equivalent, then it has a dignity." And Kant added: "What is related to the universal human inclinations and needs, has a market price; that which, even without presupposing a need, accords with a certain taste—i.e., with satisfaction in the mere purposeless play of our mental powers—has an affective price (*Affektionspreis*); but that which contributes the condition under which alone anything can be an end in itself has not merely a relative value—i.e., a price—but has an intrinsic value—i.e., dignity" (*Grundlegung zur Metaphysik der Sitten,* Hartenstein edition, IV, pp. 282–283). In his *Anthropologie* Kant elaborated this idea by pointing out that talent has a market price, temperament an affective price; character alone has "an intrinsic value and is exalted above all price" (Hartenstein, VII, p. 214).

Man achieves this "dignity beyond all price" when, as self-legislative agent, he accepts "the formal practical principle of pure reason" as the sole determinant of his will. It is respect for the moral law which elevates man above all else and establishes him, as Kant puts it in the third *Critique* (§ 83), "as the ultimate purpose of nature relative to which everything else in nature constitutes a system of purposes." And Kant adds (§ 86) that "the value which man alone can give himself and which consists in what he does and how and in accordance with what principle he acts—not as a part of nature but in freedom, i.e., as a good will—this alone bestows absolute value upon existence and relative to it alone can the existence of the world have an ultimate purpose." As moral being man has absolute value, and as absolute value he is "the ultimate purpose of creation."

Ritschl is here in basic agreement with Kant, although he disavows the latter's formalism which disregards the role of the "value-sensitive subject" in moral decisions (p. 5). Lotze, so Ritschl tells us, has seen more clearly what is involved—as have others: de Wette, A. Ritschl (the well known theologian), W. Herrmann, Kaftan, and Scheide. The last-named came to the conclusion that "the judgments of religious cognition are post-ulates based upon value judgments" (p. 12). It is this conclusion which led O. Ritschl (the author here under discussion) to his analysis of value judgments *per se.*

In line with the general intellectual orientation of his time, Ritschl approached his problem from a psychological point of view. His basic assumption is that "in every moment in which one or the other of its functions is effective, the soul (which must be thought of as unitary) is involved also with the rest of its capacities (p. 13). To be sure, in some situations the cognitive faculty may predominate. In other situations feelings may be most prominent. And in still other situations, desires and volitions may be especially in evidence. In all situations, however, all of these aspects are involved in varying degrees. This fact is especially clear when we consider situations in which desire is dominant; for when we pursue a goal, we must have some idea of what that goal is, but that we actually desire it is determined by the feeling which the thought of it evokes in us. Moreover, it is a well known fact that, when children experience something new in the world around them, their response is colored by feelings of pleasure or displeasure, and by desire or aversion. Their responses, in other words, involve what in effect are value judgments. To put it differently: From its first conception on, our idea of what is real depends upon valuational as well as upon existential judg-ments (p. 22). That in our sciences we tend to disregard the valuational aspects of our experience is no proof to the contrary.

As far as Ritschl is concerned, the question now is: How and in what sense can religious cognition be related to value judg-ments? First, however, we must know what is meant here by religion. It will not do to identify it with Christianity or with any other historically established "religion." What is needed is an all-comprehensive concept that covers all forms of religion, from the most primitive to the most advanced. Ritschl finds it in Luther's classical formulation according to which trust and faith alone make the difference between God and idols. We call God that from which we expect everything that is good and to which we turn for help in our need, and if faith and trust are right, then God also is right; for faith and God are correlative terms.

But whether a particular religion holds out the promise of sensuous pleasures or of spiritual goods, whether it involves the worship of one God or of several, whether its service consists of empty ceremonies or demands moral effort and a pure heart— nothing of all this is of the essence of religion as here understood. Whether an individual is religious in his own way or whether we are concerned with some of the great religions of the world—this also is not germane to the issue (p. 19).

It is important, however, that, to begin with, the correlation of "right faith" and "right God" is an equation with two unknowns. To make it meaningful, at least one of the terms must be identified with something known that lies outside the equation. Luther accepted revelation as justification of "faith"; but this is unacceptable to Ritschl, who must now look for another basis for religion.

Ritschl begins his search with the elementary fact of experience that no one would knowingly place his trust in anything if he did not believe this act to be justified. This means, however, that trust in something is rooted in value judgments. That it is rooted in existential judgments as well is not surprising; for both types of judgment, as we have seen, are basic to our conception of what is real. That with the advancement of science our understanding of reality has undergone manifold changes is a historical fact; that it will undergo even more changes in the future is a reasonable expectation. But do these changes necessitate a radical revision or even an abandonment of our value judgments?

It is evident that value judgments cannot be abandoned, for normal human beings never cease to trust or have faith in something and to hope. If they no longer have faith in one thing, they have faith in, and trust, something else in its stead. The process is the same whether the shift is from a trust in a loving and just God to a trust in economic forces, or whether it is from a faith in magic to a trust in a divine or moral order of things. What ever the shift may be, it involves value judgments and, as Ritschl points out, it fully conforms to the broad definition of religion that is basic to his argument.

It is true, however, that the geocentric view of the universe, assumed in the Bible as self-evident, can no longer be defended;

and the question is, Does this fact affect the value judgments that are essential to Christian faith? Ritschl's contention is that it does not; for science, he holds, is not competent to deal with the spiritual or valuational aspects of that faith. The Christian conception of God and of His self-revelation in the person and the work of Christ, the conception of a Community of Saints, of sin, of justification, rebirth, and eternal life—all of these are inaccessible to science. They are, however, knowable through faith and, as realities believed in and valued, they elicit our trust in them. The world of values implicit in Christianity has thus its own order, its own laws, whose validity or non-validity is not determined by the achievements of science (p. 25). Religious cognition is autonomous.

But even if science can have no voice in determining what are and what are not religious verities, this does not mean that the Christian's faith reveals those verities more adequately than does some other religion.

In order to deal effectively with this new problem, we must keep in mind the role which, according to Ritschl, value judgments play in our knowledge of reality, for the religious verities are essentially valuational realities. However, a subjectivistic approach to values, so Ritschl maintains, can never establish the objective validity of values that is requisite to religious faith.

It is a fact, of course, that material things have a reality prior to their satisfying the needs of any particular person, and prior, therefore, to their being valuable in this respect. It is Ritschl's contention, however, that the "ideal values" in the world are also realities, and that they are realities not only because they are apprehended in and through some person's feelings but because prior to such apprehension they are "given." Humanity has always acknowledged such values even before any particular individual has been in a position to acknowledge them and to choose among them. Moreover, the individual's choice is free only in a limited sense because only those values are available to him which have already been accepted in the environmental situation into which he was born. That is to say, apart from the valuations of any particular individual, there is given an evaluation that finds expression in the mores, the public opinion, the "spirit of the times"

(*Zeitgist*), good and bad taste, etc. All of this is the precipitate of the historically conditioned valuations of countless generations. It is true, nevertheless, that the individuals here and now also affect this inheritance of valuations; that individual and tradition affect one another. Every value which an individual fully accepts is, without doubt, his inner and personal possession; but every value acknowledged by a group of individuals has a validity of its own. To be sure, the values accepted by the individual and by the group may be the same; but they may also be different. And when they are different, the individual may find himself forced to question or challenge one, some, or all of the prevailing values. He may try to modify those values or their place in the value scale, or may attempt to replace them by better ones. In doing this, individuals bring about the great valuational transformations in the spiritual life of mankind. The history of religions is proof of this fact.

But the question now is, Which of all religions and of all world-views in general will triumph over the rest? As Christians we may anticipate or hope that it will be Christianity; but there is no possibility of proving that such will actually be the case. Only a "practical proof'" is possible; for faith alone can give us the necessary assurance and can inspire us to accept those duties and tasks in the world which will make the object of our hope a reality.

The goals set by religion are determined exclusively on the basis of value judgments whose validity can be anticipated only as the ultimate result of the struggle for a universally valid world-view. In this struggle the achievements of science are but means for the realization of goals set by religion (p. 35).

III

In *Der Begriff des Absolut Wertvollen* (1898), Felix Krueger is concerned primarily with the foundations of moral philosophy. But he does raise the question, What is it that has absolute value for man?

As Krueger sees it, we face an alternative: "Either morality, moral value, is a prejudice, a word without meaning,—or something exists that has absolute value"; and he maintains that "the criterion of the moral value can be found only in the person himself"—as "a specific quality of the human will" pp. 27–28).

On all of these points Krueger is in essential agreement with Kant. He is convinced, however, that Kant's formalistic rationalism and consequent neglect of empirical data as irrelevant to the moral law is no longer tenable; and that "he who denies *a priori* the applicability of the methods of psychology to the problem of morality actually denies in advance the possibility of a scientific ethics" (p. 29). Krueger's own approach to the problem of an absolute value will therefore be psychologically oriented.

Value judgments, he tells us, are not combinations of meaningless words but are genuine judgments having determinable content. They presuppose specific psychological facts in the experience of the person who asserts them—i.e., they presuppose a relation between his volitions and feelings and the value-object, a relation that is best described as valuing. And it is this relation which Krueger wishes to analyze.

At the time when Krueger wrote his book, the valuable was generally identified with what is agreeable or pleasing, or with what is desired. Meinong, it will be remembered, had spoken of "value-feelings" and had defined them as feelings of pleasure which are at the same time "judgment-feelings." That is to say, they are feelings of pleasure elicited by our knowledge of the existence or the non-existence of that to which they are related, of that which is valued. Meinong modified his earlier view, however, and pointed out that we may also value an object (in the sense of asserting a value judgment concerning it) at a time when there is no opportunity for our valuation of it (in the sense of an "existence or non-existence feeling") because we do not yet know whether or not the object will ever exist; and we may value something that is but abstractly conceived, and may do so without being concerned about its existence or non-existence.

For Krueger this means that there are psychological states involving values that are independent of value-feelings as defined by Meinong; that value phenomena involve more than actual feelings of pleasure. If it now be maintained that basic to every value judgment is an expectation (rather than an actuality) of pleasure, this also is not adequate, for the expected pleasure may never become actual—a fact which, nevertheless, does not affect the value judgment. Meinong, who was well aware of this fact, tried to cope with it by arguing that an object has value, not because it is actually experienced as valuable, but because "it has the capacity for becoming the actual basis of a value-feeling for someone who is normal and is sufficiently well informed about the object." But this interpretation is an evasion rather than a solution of the basic problem (p. 32).

According to von Ehrenfels, a value judgment expresses the fact that a certain object is desired by me; that it is an object of my desire. Krueger is willing to accept this thesis as "undoubtedly correct within certain limits"; but the limits are there, and von Ehrenfels did not indicate them. Keeping those limits in mind, Krueger now asserts: "Valuable for me is only that which I desire with relative constancy, that toward which, under certain psychological conditions, I regularly direct my desire" (p. 33). What this means becomes clear when we consider the following: "When, unexpectedly, I perceive a fragrance or hear a full and pure musical tone, I may say that these sensations are agreeable, pleasurable, etc., but not that they are valuable. . . . The actual pleasure-accent of an experience is not sufficient for us to ascribe to it the predicate value. And neither do we regard as valuable the object of a momentary mood or of a sudden and passionate impulse or desire merely because of that mood or that desire" (*ibid.*). On the other hand, "valuable for me are my books, my musical instrument, my knowledge, my relation to a friend, and countless other matters which, at this moment, are neither experienced as pleasurable nor desired but belong to a context of objects and conceptions (*Vorstellungszusammenhang*) that stands in a constant relation to my desire" (p. 34). Actual desires which, under certain circumstances, are indispensable to valuations may not arise for a long time, and their absence will not affect in the least a particular valuation. This is so, Krueger maintains, because a valuation differs from an actual desire by virtue of its (relative) constancy. To put it differently: Valuations are constant volitional states in the sense that, under certain psychological conditions, the valued object will always be desired—no matter what the other conditions may be under which the experience occurs. It is therefore possible, so Krueger goes on, to regard the valuations as "dispositions to particular acts of desiring" (*Dispositionen zu bestimmten Begehrungen*) (p. 39).

As here understood, valuations are by no means the same as value judgments. The vast majority of our valuations never find expression in the form of judgments. We may not even know about them—although their effects are actually experienced in our volitions; and we may deceive ourselves about them. It is a well-known fact, for example, that people frequently do not admit making certain valuations when actually they do, or that they imagine making some which, in fact, they do not make. But this means that our value judgments can be true or false, whereas a valuation as such simply is what it is, and is as little true or false as is a feeling or a pure sense impression. But value judgments presuppose valuations in the same sense in which cognitive judgments presuppose perceptual or other non-judgmental experiences. The crucial point is that the absolutely valid value judgment must be the expression of the specific orderliness (*Gesetzmässigkeit*) of our volitional experience as given in the facts of valuation. The content of such an unconditionally valid value judgment is an absolute value (p. 51).

But what is unconditionally or absolutely valuable must have value for every valuing subject, and must maintain its value under any and all possible conditions. As far as Kruger is concerned, only one possible value-object fulfills these requirements. As he puts it: "Absolutely valuable can be nothing but the indispensable subjective condition of all possible values; and this is the functional property of human personality." That is to say, "the psychological ability or function of valuing is the object of an absolutely valid value judgment or the unconditionally valuable" (p. 61). Everything in the world would lose its value for me at the very moment at which I lost the ability of relatively constant desire. The ability to value anything is the *a priori* presupposition of every value judgment and of every empirically possible systematic order of values. Being the necessary condition for all values, it cannot be replaced by anything else and therefore has an absolute value for all persons who actually value something. But this implies that "the absolute or moral value of a person is directly dependent upon the degree to which that person participates in the absolutely valuable," i.e., in the ability to value (p. 63).

Now, the human being, the person, is essentially a unity, an existential whole. This means that our desires are interrelated; that they do not exist in isolation and merely side by side. But this in turn means that, in the long run, valuations can occur only in systematic order—an order determined by the integrative pattern of the drives; and "the energy of valuing can enhance itself lastingly only in the sense of an organic growth" which increases the unity of the person (p. 76).

Besides the unconditional or absolute value of valuing there is no other value that is beyond the possibility of a conflict with other values, or beyond the possibility of being corrected through new experiences and their after-effects. The richer and the more differentiated a value system is, the more numerous are the possibilities of conflict. On the other hand, however, every real resolution of a conflict is at the same time an enrichment of our valuing existence; and the gain is the greater in proportion to the success or the adequacy of the resolution. But, then, life is always richer and more varied than is theory.

The ethical ideal which, according to Krueger, emerges from all this is that one be, to the highest possible degree, a valuing human being. The moral task is to combine into a valuational unity an ever increasing multiplicity of possibilities of desire; for it is characteristic of moral development that unlimited progress in the direction indicated is possible.

In the end, Krueger thus agrees with Kant that the human being, the person, is the only absolute value. But whereas Kant believed this to be so because man is the only being capable of legislating for himself, Krueger holds that man is an absolute value because he is the indispensable presupposition of all valuing.

IV

Eisler's publication, *Studien zur Werttheorie* (1902), actually consists of five essays that were written during the years 1899 to

1901. Their theme is that values can be defined without reference to psychological presuppositions.

Eisler's starting-point is a philosophical concern with historical facts; for, he points out, it is when we attempt to explain those facts that we encounter the problem of values. What, then, is explanation in history?

In our personal history—i.e., in our development as a person—the "historical phenomena"—i.e., the objects and events of our experience—are encountered in close correlation with feelings, especially with value-feelings which serve as motives for our actions. When we transpose these facts of experience onto the plane of history it seems possible to give an explanation of the historical phenomena in terms of the following interrelations: (a) historical phenomena are the result of actions; (b) actions are expressions of a will; (c) the will is motivated by feelings; (d) feelings arise in response to our environment. But at least two assumptions must be made with respect to these interrelated aspects involved in historical explanation: (1) There must be a necessary connection between parts of the environment and feelings—such that, because of their connection, the former turn out to be values. (2) There must also be a necessary connection between feelings and the will—such that it is of the nature of pleasure to be desired, and of the nature of displeasure to be avoided. The combination of (1) and (2) entails the thesis that "it is of the nature of values to be desired" (p. 14).

The value concept which has thus been introduced is, to begin with, both ontological and objective, for values (and disvalues) have been directly ascribed to parts of the environment. Such "objectification" of the value-feelings is, however, indefensible. It assumes that value-feelings are the necessary effects of the values themselves; but, as von Ehrenfels has shown, no criterion other than the value-feelings can be found for the values. The explanation of value-feelings in terms of values is, therefore, a vicious circle.

But does this now mean that pleasure and displeasure are in themselves ontological values? They are evidently regarded as such as long as we adhere to the thesis that it is of the nature of pleasure to be desired, and of the nature of displeasure to be avoided; and this thesis finds support in the close psychological correlation of feeling and volition. But this correlation, Eisler points out, admits of two interpretations, namely, (a) we desire what is pleasurable, and (b) pleasurable for us is what we desire. However, neither (a) nor (b) can yield an explanation of historical facts; for (a) asserts a merely problematic, not a necessary, relation between pleasure and desire and therefore leaves unanswered the question why we desire pleasure rather than its opposite; and (b) is a tautology.

The difficulties disappear, Eisler maintains, as soon as we discard the ontological conception of values and regard values (goals) as "dependent variables"—as functions, that is, of the prevailing direction of life's activities. To be sure, the value concept has now been reduced to "a merely formal auxiliary concept of the qualitative and quantitative description of historical phenomena" (p. 18), but it has lost nothing of its significance. The change in our understanding of what is meant by value is analogous to the change in the conception of force in physics when the ontological conception of force as "cause of motion" was replaced by the purely formal conception of force necessary for the most economic description of motions.

Eisler now states: "We call a particular group of phenomena evaluated (*bewertet*) when its realization appears to be dependent upon the 'voluntative' attitude of a biological agent. More specifically, we ascribe a positive value to the group when its realization appears to be furthered through the activity of the subject involved. We ascribe a negative value to it when its realization appears to be volitionally hindered" (p. 24). Since every volitional act changes the state of affairs, it follows, in the light of the definition just given, that any change from an initial state to a final state of affairs that is desired has itself a positive value, and the final state is relatively more valuable than is the initial state. Eisler calls this "the law of relatively increasing value magnitudes" (p. 24). What this means is that in every case of an action the final state must possess, relative to the initial state, a certain positive value. Conversely, the initial state of affairs must possess, relative to the final state, a certain negative value. The values involved are thus specifically relative to each other.

But now the question is: Does the initial state of affairs in a situation S_a have a negative value only relative to the final state S_b, or does it have a negative value also with respect to any other actual or possible state of affairs, and in any situation whatever? If the latter is the case, the state of affairs in question may be said to have an absolute negative value. Similarly, the final state of affairs may be said to have an absolute positive value when it possesses this value not only relative to an initial state of affairs S_a, but relative to any actual or conceivable initial state.

Eisler's detailed and, at times, purely formal analysis of various possibilities need not concern us here (pp. 25–65). It suffices to note that his conclusion depends on his interpretation of the nature and validity of value judgments.

As we have seen earlier, according to the first and most primitive conception, rooted in the associative relation of feelings and volitions, values are the objective properties of things for the sake of which the things are desired; and it is true, of course, that our valuations do depend upon the nature of the value-objects. It was rather easy, therefore, to distinguish between "value-feelings" and the "values themselves" in the very same sense in which we distinguish between "sensing a color" and "the color sensed." And it was easy, also, to go a step further and to regard value as the cause of the value-feeling. If this step is taken, then a value judgment is an inference from "value-feelings" as effect to "value" as the cause. When such an inference is correct, the value judgment is true. When it is not correct, the judgment is false (p. 73). This position, however, can be maintained only as long as the value-feeling is not seen as independently variable relative to the value. Once the value-feeling has been seen to be so variable, either the "objective value" loses all significance for the subject and thus no longer serves the purpose for the sake of which it was introduced in the first place, or determination through the value-object is but a partial cause along with complementary subjective conditions, and again the objectivistic value concept has been surpassed. Moreover, since the objective value is accessible to us presumably only in our value-feeling, there is no way of determining in any given case whether or not "value" and "value-feeling" correspond to each other.

These difficulties and incongruities of our value experience are frequently covered up (1) by assumed *a priori* and universal value judgments ("Valuable—beautiful, good—is whatever possesses the qualities a, b, c, d, . . .": or "Whatever possesses qualities a, b, c, d, . . . causes pleasure or elicits desire"); (2) by introducing levels of valuations ("Of two contradictory value judgments, A and B, involving the same object, one is correct, the other false, because A reflects good taste, B does not"); (3) by the accusation of insincerity—the false judgment is taken to be an instance of intended deception, bluff, or the like; and finally, (4) by appealing to the "authority of the majority" (pp. 74–83).

The whole situation changes when we discard the idea that values are objective entities and recognize their dependence upon the valuing subject. The whole of man's cultural history—especially the history of art—supports such a position. The more we know about the various cultural epochs, the more impressed we are by the changes in direction and in styles. Only rarely do we find evidence of a constant line of development. To be sure, in the midst of all the cultural changes and transitions certain valuations remain relatively constant. The Principle of Symmetry, for example, is an important factor in the aesthetic valuations of most cultural periods; and apparent deviations from it (e.g., Japanese decorative art and aspects of the Barock) can actually be understood only in terms of the Principle itself. But to recognize the fact that values are subject-dependent does not mean that we must neglect the role which the object plays in any actual valuation. As Eisler puts it: "Value must be thought of as dependent upon the nature of the object as well as upon that of the subject" (p. 86).

When we now view value judgments in the new perspective, we must, first of all, determine their precise value-theoretical content. That is to say, we must determine in just what sense such judgments are meant. Consider, for example, the assertion "This is beautiful." It may mean (1) "This pleases me" (in contrast to "This does not please me" or "This displeases me"); or it may mean (2) "This object is such as to please" (in contrast to "This object is not such as to please" or "This object is such as to displease"); or (3) "This is beautiful" is meant in distinction from "This is good," "This is useful," etc.

If (1) is intended, the judgment is descriptive of a value-theoretical feeling-state; i.e., it asserts that a particular subject has a specific kind of experience in relation to some object. Eisler calls it a *descriptive value judgment.*

If (2) is what is meant, then the judgment asserts that a particular object possesses the kind of qualities which can serve as partial condition for the occurrence of a specific value phenomenon. Eisler calls it a *justificatory (begründendes) value judgment.*

Understood in the sense of (3), the judgment characterizes the value phenomenon involved as belonging to a particular class of valuations. Eisler calls it a *subsumptive value judgment.*

Value judgments in any one of the three meanings cover, of course, multiple aspects of value experience, and each type allows further distinctions to be made. Also, the evidence for the validity of each type of value judgments is different; and the problem of evidence is especially important in the case of the justificatory judgments because they involve the past and the future as well as the present. But such details need not concern us here (pp. 88–104).

There is one problem, however, that demands further attention. It is this: In the interrelations of value and value judgment which has priority—the value or the value judgment? In the history of philosophy this problem is well known as the controversy between "intellectualism" and "voluntarism." As Eisler sees it, the issue is not a question of which one of man's faculties has priority, but of whether values are to be understood as dependent upon the purely "presentational" contents of consciousness or whether they are the result of value judgments.

In discussing this issue, Eisler points out that, unquestionably, if value-theoretical objectivism were correct in its interpretation of values as objectively "given," then value judgments would have priority over all "presentational content" of experience, for valuation would in that case depend upon our knowledge of the object as the cause of our value experience, and the value itself, as motive for action, would be proportional to the validity of our value judgments. But, as we have seen earlier, value-theoretical objectivism is an untenable position. This is so because of the crucial role which feelings play in value experience. When value-feelings are accepted as value-theoretical criteria, value judgments can play only a secondary role. They have a descriptive and a communicative function, but not a constitutive one (p. 106).

However, there is another aspect to the role which value judgments may play. It pertains to the special case of "value-transference" (*Wertübertragung*)—such as ascribing a value to an object because it does or can serve as a "means" to an "end." The indispensable presupposition of such a transference is an empirically based knowledge of the dependence-relation that exists between "means" and "end"; and this knowledge is, in principle, always a matter of judgments. However, since our knowledge of "means" is empirically based, the truth-value of the judgments involved may vary with the advances made in our understanding of the nature of things—with advances, that is, in science and technology.

And it must also be noted that the judgments upon which the value-transfer depends are not themselves value judgments but are descriptive of the objects that serve as "means." The value ultimately ascribed to a "means" depends, of course, on the primary value of the "end."

What all this amounts to, according to Eisler, is that our technological progress is "historically significant in so far as it makes possible the realization of values through the most 'suitable' means (*die 'zweckmässigsten' Mittel*)." But "the dream of creating new values through a value theory—a dream which, as nucleus of the intellectualistic world-view has been basic to all attempts so far made to achieve more-than-descriptive (i.e., normative) insights—must be abandoned once and for all (*endgültig*)" (p. 109).

V

Arvid Grotenfelt begins his discussion of "historical value standards" (1905) by considering briefly the task of the historian who must select and evaluate what is relevant to the events that are to be dealt with in the historical narrative, for it is obvious that such selection and such evaluation presuppose value standards that are of basic concern in the field of value theory. It is true, of course, that, as a rule, the historian does not explicitly state his value commitments; that, as a matter of fact, he may not even be fully aware of them, for the standards he applies usually reflect prevailing valuations and are part of the "intellectual climate" of his time.

Among the value standards applied by historians and, more often, by philosophers of history is that of Progress—the favorite idea and challenging slogan of modern times. The far-reaching intellectual and cultural changes entailed by Renaissance and Reformation enhanced where they did not engender the idea of Progress. Scientific discoveries and a technology based upon science held out the promise of man's ultimate mastery over the forces of nature, and of an unending improvement in our human situation here on earth. A natural consequence of these developments was that the idea of the historically valuable became closely associated with change and, more importantly, with the idea of individual and personal independence, autonomy, and freedom.

Grotenfelt traces this growth of an idea from the time of J. Bodin (who was next to Macchiavelli the most important political thinker and philosopher of history during the 16th Century) to the end of the 19th Century; but we can spare ourselves the details of this historical account. A brief consideration of Kant's position will suffice but is also necessary because that position is basic to the idealistic tradition of the 19th Century.

In his *Idee zu einer allgemeinen Geschichte in weltbürgerlicher Absicht,* Kant had argued as follows: (1) "All natural capacities of a creature are destined to develop themselves completely and to their purpose." (2) "It has been the will of Nature that man, by himself alone, should produce everything that transcends the mechanical ordering of his animal existence, and that he should partake of no happiness or perfection other than that which he himself, independently of instinct, has achieved through his own reason." (3) "The means which Nature has employed to bring about the development of all of man's capacities is their antagonism in society. . . . Man wants harmony; but Nature knows better what is good for his race: Nature wants conflict. He wants to live comfortably and pleasantly; but Nature wants that he should rouse himself from sloth and passive contentment and plunge himself into labor and toil. . . . The natural urges to do this . . . reveal the plan of a wise creator." They do this because in and through conflict and struggle man develops his capacities as a human being. It must not be assumed, however, that the task is an easy one. Kant himself specifically states that "the problem is at the same time the most difficult and the one which the human race will solve last" (pp. 62–63).

Kant's basic idea that the true value of historical existence lies in the development of the natural endowments of man is central to all idealistic philosophies of history in modern times—and it is so especially when we take into consideration Kant's further statement that man's innate capacities are good only when they are supported by a good will; for only as a moral being is man the ultimate purpose of creation.

It is Grotenfelt's contention, however, that the highest values with which history is concerned cannot all be projected into the future; for if the present has value only as a moment of transition to the future and has no value in itself, then it is impossible to ascribe a value to any historical event as such; and this, in effect, does away with any value within the whole of history.

It is at this point that the Hedonism of the mid-19th Century and after provides a corrective—see Bentham, John Stuart Mill, H. Th. Buckles, G. Grotes, and the Positivism of Auguste Comte. Grotenfelt maintains, however, that the presumed evidence in support of Hedonism is "a great deception," for, as he sees it, it is a fact that volition is frequently called into action by motives other than pleasure or pain—by a sense of duty, for example.

More recently, and in various formulations, Kant's basic theme has been re-echoed—the theme, namely, that the goal and ultimate purpose of mankind's strivings in terms of which all historical achievements must be evaluated can be but the full and complete development of man himself and of all his capacities as a human being. This view is held, for example, by Friedrich Paulsen, W. Schuppe, and Rudolf Eucken, and it is reflected in the idealism of Carlyle.

In 1905, Grotenfelt could write: "Our times are known most

specifically as the Age of National Egoism" (p. 138). But there were times, he adds, when universally human ideals were acknowledged; when the ideas of a common humanity, of freedom, justice, and a universal brotherhood were projected as the unconditionally valid goals for all of mankind. Unfortunately, painful and shameful historical events have, in actuality, contradicted these ideals. "All the beautiful words about justice, humanity, and common cultural tasks . . . have proven themselves to be empty phrases as soon as a nation had the opportunity to attain a great advantage or, through robbery, to annex large territories" (p. 139).

Despite all this, however, the ideals of universal justice and of a common humanity, of universal education and welfare remain effective forces in the historical conflicts of today. "Even the most inveterate *Realpolitiker* and nationalist does not fail to appeal to such ideals in support of his wishes and demands" (p. 140). "And when a historical idea, a great historical movement, inspires the masses, it derives its strength, at least in part, from the fact that it is actually felt to be a high and holy cause. The human-all-too-human and the sublime are intertwined in every moment in history in such a way that it is difficult to distinguish between them" (p. 141). It is the mark of the statesman that he adjusts the interests of his nation to the great ideals that move mankind. And "numerous historical experiences testify to the fact that a policy of humaneness and tolerance, when persistently carried through, is capable of solving successfully difficult political problems" (p. 150). If history, at least in part, is still a cruel and gruesome drama, it is so through human failure.

When we now ask, What, ultimately, is the truly valuable in history?, Grotenfelt endorses Kant's thesis that it is "the development of personality," the recognition of the dignity of man as a person.

It is true, of course, that the views vary as to what is the essential nature of man that is to be developed, that gives him the dignity which, as the highest value, demands our respect; and Grotenfelt is well aware of the different views. By and large, however, there is sufficient agreement on a dominant theme which Grotenfelt states this way: "The valuable within culture is ultimately the

enhancement and enrichment of the spiritual life of the individual human beings"; "the development of a 'refined' and 'spiritualized' life of the emotions"—especially of the humane and altruistic feelings; and the cultivation of aesthetic taste, the forming
of a person's character and of his will as autonomous. "Culture
has a real value only when, in the manner indicated, it becomes
an inner good" (p. 165).

Moreover, the spiritual life of mankind and of individual nations remains vigorous (*lebenskräftig*) and healthy only when all
aspects of its culture—the economic, the social, the political along
with the scientific, the artistic, the moral, and the religious—are
being developed together. According to Grotenfelt, however,
the moral attitude and a genuine religiosity are the real values.
"If it could be shown that the historical development of culture
actually enhances these values, that would be its most significant
achievement" (p. 167). But on this point Grotenfelt is skeptical.
As he sees it, the whole of existence is purposive and rational
or it is senseless and irrational, depending on whether the intrinsic potentialities for a rational and harmonious development are
transformed into actuality or are destroyed; but the actual course
of history provides no proof one way or the other.

If it were possible to show the the highest values which we project are at the same time the goals of a rational world order, then
we would at least have a criterion for the evaluation of historical
events. The required proof, however, is not possible, and the identification is entirely a matter of faith—of a faith that may or may
not be justified. If we have this faith, then it follows that our task
is to make every effort to help realize the divine within us and
within mankind as a whole. But if we believe that, in an ultimate sense, existence is "impenetrable and irrational," that we
cannot fathom its essence or true meaning, we may still accept—
through a free decision and on pragmatic grounds—a particular
world-view that provides reasonable justification for our higher
values. We must not forget, however, that this is and remains a
matter of faith, and we must not overlook the fact that in the actual course of history events and developments occur which are
disastrous distortions (*verhängnisvolle Missbildungen*) of human
potentialities. We must recognize "the evil as well as the good

effects of civilization," the malevolent as well as the benevolent aspects of human activities. And we must realize that "perhaps the meaning of the whole historical development consists in this: that the battle for the ideal must always be fought, and must be fought in various and ever enhanced forms" (p. 187). The conviction that, in the end, our highest values will be realized is and remains a faith on our part—or a postulate. It is not knowledge derived from historical observations or grounded in theoretical considerations. What ultimately matters is the degree of devotion to the ideal and of our being absorbed by it.

V

Walter Strich has stated his basic position rather succinctly: "The solution of the value problem must begin with the meaning of value statements. . . . We do not ask what actual facts are referred to by the statements, but what the expressions themselves mean. This meaning science cannot discover; it is a matter of the feeling for language (*Sache des Sprachgefühls*)" (p. 23). And again: "Our feeling for language, not a value theory, must disclose to us what the term 'value' means" (p. 25). Value theory is concerned only with what is meant, and thus is a secondary matter.

When we use the word 'value,' so Strich continues, "we mean a very specific character of a thing—just as we do when we use the word 'existence'." Hence, "to maintain that value is something subjective makes exactly as much or as little sense as does the assertion that reality is something subjective" (*ibid.*). Value, like existence, is neither a relation to a subject nor a quality in the usual sense of that term, but a determinateness *sui generis;* and just as 'existence' is a category of thought, so is 'value' such a category. "As in the act of affirmation we acknowledge the fact of existence, so in the act of valuing we acknowledge the significance of that existence" (p. 26).

Also, "value is closely related to the idea of an *ought.*" In fact, "the *ought* is the extreme of a value"; and "the acknowledgment of a value is the acknowledgment of the demand that the valuable exist—i.e., that it be or become real" (p. 27).

Having thus stated his position, Strich now turns to a criticism of various value theories. The theories of Meinong and von Ehrenfels, in particular, are submitted to a searching analysis.

Strich points out (with special reference to Meinong) that "valuing is not the same as experiencing pleasure." Although both may be involved in the same experience, they are "never identical." The assertion, for example, that a certain painting pleases me is by no means the equivalent of the assertion that the painting is valuable. And neither is the feeling of pleasure always the basis for a valuing. It is possible, for example, "to acknowledge the will of God as absolute value even where there is no relation to pleasure as the ground for the acknowledgment. In fact, phenomenologically, a pronounced feeling of displeasure—of remorse or self-accusation—may accompany the valuation" (p. 30). What all this amounts to is that we must clearly distinguish between valuing and the grounds for valuing. Thus, we may ascribe a value to an object because of the pleasure we derive from it. But we may also value an object for no reason other than the "purely suggestive influence" of our environment. We may value something because of its relation to an acknowledged purpose, or we may value it because we experience satisfaction in the belief that it alone has value. We may creatively project an ideal as the value per se, as that which *ought* to be, compared with which any reference to pleasure and pain is but a triviality (as Nietzsche maintained); and such ideals reflect the creative power of him who values.

Also, we do not call things valuable because we desire them (as von Ehrenfels did); nor is value always the reason why we desire something. To be sure, we may desire a thing for the very same reason for which we value it; but desiring and valuing are, and remain, different acts. Moreover, to maintain that it is the goal of every desire to achieve a particular feeling-state is a distortion rather than an explanation of the experiential situation. "Desire always involves an awareness of the unreality of the desired object. The intended goal is that object's realization (*Verwirklichung*)—either in the sense of its actually coming into existence, or (if it is already in existence) in the sense of its coming under my control" (p. 36). But this means that "desire is closely related to an *ought:* What I desire *ought* to be or, more precisely, it *ought* to become" (*ibid.*). This fact, however, clearly shows (so Strich maintains) that desiring and valuing are not the same. Desiring is directed toward something which as yet is not; valuing, on the other hand, pertains only to what is. It "stands in the middle between the purely theoretical act of acknowledging a reality and the practical act of desiring a particular realization. . . . Desiring is, as it were, the *practical ought-to-be,* valuing is the *theoretical.*" We thus may acknowledge the value of things—i.e, we may acknowledge that they ought to be —without actually desiring their realization (*ibid.*).

A special problem arises, of course, when we try to determine the degree or magnitude of a value. As Strich sees it, "all intellectual constructions of pleasure-magnitudes (*Lustgrössen*), their summations and substractions, and the summations of the intensities of actual and imagined pleasures are theoretically contrived. They have no longer any connection with the realities of living" (p. 38). Actual experience discloses no such calculations—although we do value some objects more than we do others, and desire some more than others. But it is also a fact that "trivial things may please us very much even though we do not value them highly, and that, when thinking of things which we value very much, we feel no particular pleasure"—which is but further proof that, "in the case of value judgments, valuing and feeling are not the same" (p. 39). The fact is, so Strich maintains, that, psychologically, there is no difference between valuing and evaluing. There is no valuing and, in addition, "a calculating of the real value through the summation of intensities." "When we actually value, we always comprehend the real significance of the object" (*ibid.*).

But there is still a problem here; for we do value some things more than we do others, and the question is, In what do the acts of "valuing" and "valuing more" differ? A difference in intensity of our feeling-states, so we have seen, is either not relevant or not decisive, and the respective acts themselves reveal no differences in intensity. That a value has meaning only relative to a valuation Strich regards as self-evident, and he sees a parallel here between our cognitive and our valuational experiences. "An object is red," he points out, "because it can be experienced as red. Never-theless, the judgment, This rose is red, is not synonymous with, Someone sees a red rose. It is the same with values. Something has value because its existential significance can be acknowledged," even though at a given time no one actually acknowledges that significance. Whether the object has a "high" value or a "low" one is simply a matter of its own nature in its existential situa-tion. And Strich adds: "Neither logical considerations nor a feeling for language (*Sprachgefühl*) nor experience of any kind can prove the contrary" (p. 42). "We therefore continue to maintain that in the value judgment an objective factual situation (*Sachverhalt*) is being asserted; that 'reality' and 'value' are two categories in and through which we understand the world" (p. 46).

But still a problem remains. When we deal with cognitive judgments, we can rely upon various criteria of their correctness. Such criteria are not available when we deal with value judg-ments. Here, will and commitment dominate; and "there is noth-ing that enables us to transcend this relativism of valuing" (*ibid.*).

Still, Strich suggests a further consideration. It is this: A factor common to all human experience is the awareness of one's own self. No matter how much we may belittle the difference between animals and human beings or insist that this difference is simply a matter of degree, reflective self-consciousness remains a distinc-tive mode of human existence. The knowledge that, as individu-als, we experience a world to which we respond is basic to all our actions. Not that animals do not respond to the world. They do. But the meaning of self-consciousness is an awareness of the dif-ference between the "I" which has the experience and the "what" which the I experiences. This awareness is basic to value theory no less than it is to science, for it entails the possibility of think-ing of the "what" as other than it appears to be. In becoming aware of this possibility and making the most of it we escape any rigid determinism through "brute facts." In this experiential sit-uation there are present "the two roots of pure volition": (1) the Will to Power and (2) the Will to Form.

As far as the Will to Power is concerned, "the task is so to transform the world that it no longer confronts us simply as co-

ercive force, and to oppose to the power of the non-self the power
of the self" (p. 85). This power of the self is the Will to Power
come into consciousness as the drive for self-preservation—"the
will to preserve, to emphasize, and to assert the specific individuality." This basic drive (*Grundtrieb*), Strich maintains, we can
trace "from its primitive beginnings." It manifests itself, for example, in man's need to adorn his body, to surround himself with
the mysterious. However, Strich speaks of the "assertion of personality" only when the individual's self-respect no longer depends on purely external matters and on the stress placed upon
the bodily self but finds an "inner justification" (*innere Rechtfertigung*) through the values that satisfy a pure will—knowledge, creativity, "being loved by those we love," accepting more
duties rather than claiming more rights. This Will to Power is
trans-personal (*überpersönlich*) because it is a manifestation of
"the universally-human consciousness of self" (p. 86).

The Will to Form refuses to accept individual experiences in
isolation or merely because they occur. It is, first of all, a "drive to
find causes" (*Ursachtrieb*). Science here has replaced mythology.
Perceptual relations have given way to conceptual ones, and descriptive laws have taken the place of an empathetic understanding. Each law is analytic and, therefore, necessarily true. But each
law, also, has an integrative power and through the formulation
of laws we achieve the purpose of "accepting as little as possible
of the tyranny of brute facts" (p. 88).

In art, "the most profound sense of necessity touches that of
freedom" (p. 89). The necessity here is that of our subjective experience, not that of objective events; but subjectively necessary
is only what is willed by the self, not what is imposed upon it.
Hence, in experiencing a work of art, everything depends on
whether or not what we experience is a unity in which all parts
flow freely into one another to form the whole. When such is the
case, "artistic truth" has been achieved and the Will to Form finds
satisfaction in the achievement. This satisfaction is "the absolute
value of art" (p. 90).

The same principle—the principle, namely, which renders
trans-personal the value of a work of art—is effective also in
the realm of ethics. What counts here is not what society calls

good or evil, but whether or not the satisfaction we take in an action is trans-personal. The subject must take the same attitude of approval or disapproval toward his own action that he is taking toward the actions of others. That is to say, it is not our own particular personality that is decisive, but "being a personality as such" (*das Persönlichkeit-Sein überhaupt*) (p. 91). The very nature of personality, however, finds expression in the attitude toward, and the valuation of, life and the world around us. "What is decisive here is that ultimate and most profound ground of our experience of the world concerning which no argument is possible (*undiskutierbar*). Only where an action is understandable in terms of that ground is it for us self-evident" (p. 92).

Although their respective demands may in some respects coincide, social ethics and individual ethics differ fundamentally. In the case of the former, only that which is useful for social coexistence is important, and society has the right to demand the subordination of the individual whenever that individual partakes in the general welfare. No absolute values are here involved, for all social valuations are grounded in the purpose of living together and are relative to that purpose. "Valuation in accordance with the absolute principle begins only when the individual, entirely on his own, desires to be satisfied by his own actions; . . . when he can conceive of his life and actions as other than they are, . . . and when he realizes that an action is not justified just because all act that way. Only when man wants to establish a necessary context among his own actions has pure volition awakened in him; and this alone constitutes an ethic of the individual. Only now something absolutely valuable is involved" (p. 92)—to wit, the unitary personality which is "to appear in our actions as does the idea that is essential to a work of art" (p. 93).

Whether or not religion involves an absolute value depends on what is meant by religion. But as Strich sees it, "our valuation of the spiritual character of personality is justified only when we feel ourselves to be a part of what is unconditionally valuable in the world of an Absolute—or whatever we want to call it" (p. 94). The spiritual, however, must stand in unified context (*in einheitlichem Zusammenhang*) with matter, for otherwise matter would for us be a meaningless accident. Only when matter shares in some way in the spiritual is the total world-process no longer a "brutal fact" for us but is self-evident. "And therein lies the absolute value" (*ibid.*).

However, pure volition finds its profoundest fulfillment in love. Here, satisfaction is not an increase in an individual's personal pleasure but is rooted entirely in the trans-personal desire. The individual no longer feels himself alone in the world but finds himself in another self that is as self-evident to him as is his own self. Love alone, thus, could become the symbol of the verities of the mystic experience and of religion.

And so the profoundest unity which encompasses all absolute values lies in the realization that the world is not something foreign and coercive, but something amenable to interpretation and evaluation and, in this sense, is subordinate to our deepest-rooted volition: the object of a Will to Power and Form.

BIBLIOGRAPHY

Eisler, Robert, *Studien zur Wertphilosophie*, Leipzig, 1902.
Grotenfelt, Arvid, *Geschichtliche Wertmassstäbe,* Leipzig, 1905.
Krueger, Felix, *Der Begriff des Absolut Wertvollen,* Leipzig, 1898.
Naumann, Moriz, *Die Lehre vom Wert,* Heidelberg, 1893.
Ritschl, Otto, *Ueber Werthurtheile,* Leipzig, 1893.
Strich Walter, *Das Wertproblem in der Philosophie der Gegenwart,* Berlin, 1909.

CHAPTER VIII

THE THEORIES OF VON HARTMANN, OSTWALD, LESSING, AND MÜLLER-FREIENFELS

The four philosophers whose value-theoretical positions will be presented in this chapter do not share a common point of view. They are here brought together primarily because this juxtaposition of diverse interpretations of the value problem will emphasize, as nothing else can, the great variety and the complexity of the issues involved in our valuations. Von Hartmann, for example, gives us an essentially metaphysical interpretation of the whole problem—one based on his conception of The Unconscious. Ostwald, on the other hand, keys everything, and especially the valuations inherent in our culture, to the basic idea of energy. Lessing represents a transcendental point of view, and Müller-Freienfels stresses the role which "fictive elements" play in all aspects of value-theoretical interpretations.

Also, all four men published their key value-theoretical works within a few years of each other. The order in which I discuss them here is that of their temporal sequence.

I

In his speculative *Philosophie des Unbewussten,* Eduard von Hartmann had made the attempt to clear Schopenhauer's pessimistic interpretation of human existence of some of its excesses, to limit its positive contributions to a basic eudaemonism, and to provide new inductive and deductive proofs of its validity. These efforts, however, were generally misunderstood. Von Hartmann was taken to be merely a Schopenhauer disciple and was therefore largely neglected. His *Grundriss der Axiologie* (1908) was intended to correct this situation.

The basic thesis underlying the whole of von Hartmann's argument is that the world is so constituted that it is knowable to us; and that our cognitive faculty is so constituted that we can know the world. World and cognitive faculty thus are in that essential harmony which makes our cognition of the world possible. That is to say, existence and cognition involve the same categories and are subordinate to the same principles of logic. They are correlates that correspond to each other, and their correlation assures us of the validity of our knowledge of the world although this knowledge is neither complete nor adequate but only "capable of progressive completion."

Now, indubitably, our knowledge of the world has for us a positive value. This fact, however, does not entail a positive value of the world itself; for we find in that world not only what is good, useful, agreeable, and noble, but also what is evil, harmful, repugnant, and base. Moreover, "the world as a whole, the universe, is neither beautiful nor ugly. Aesthetic standards are, in fact, inapplicable because we have no unified sensory conception of the universe as a whole" (p. 4). But the world is so constituted that in the subjective appearances of particular aspects of it "a maximum of beauty comes into existence." The creator of this beauty is that "absolutely unconscious genius" that manifests its creativeness in nature, in history, and in the imagination of the artist." Beauty is thus "a revelation of Absolute Spirit—of the creative Will—by means of which a microcosmic idea shines forth from the concrete aesthetic phenomenon without becoming a logical concept" (p. 7).

"If the world were an embodiment of wickedness, a monstrosity or even hell, it would still be valuable for the scientist as an object of cognition, and would still be beautiful for the artist—be he a painter who studies the light-effects of this hell, or a poet who wants to describe the sufferings of the condemned" (p. 8). In matters of value, therefore, the standard of beauty is no more the final word as is that of cognition. Both standards are of great significance, to be sure; but both must remain subordinate to other values.

Also, taken as a whole, the universe is neither moral nor immoral. In fact, moral standards are entirely inapplicable, for moral concepts refer to relations of individuals of the same kind to one another or to individuals of a higher order. Thus, a human being has duties toward other human beings, toward his family, his community, his nation; and, indirectly, he also has duties toward himself. But the universe, being all there is, can have no duties toward some other universe; and neither does it have duties toward itself. To be sure, the world is so constituted as to make possible "noble intentions and actions"; but this does not make the world itself morally valuable because the world is also so constituted as to allow even more "immoral intentions and deeds" (p. 11).

Still, as von Hartmann sees it, "man's moral inclinations unconsciously intend something rational, and the realization of what is moral is the most rational that is conceivable in the world of personal spirits as that world exists" (p. 13). Moreover, moral consciousness must postulate an optimism as its own presupposition because it must regard the realization of a moral world-order as necessary to the solution of the ultimate and trans-moral (*über-sittliche*) task of mankind—the fulfillment of the ultimate purpose, the *Endzweck,* of the world-process itself. The moral standard is thus "dependent upon the truth of a developmental optimism" (*Entwicklungsoptimismus*).

Moreover, "man and world are so constituted," von Hartmann maintains, "that they are capable of salvation in the religious sense." More specifically, "the world as a whole and all creatures in it, find true salvation through mankind, and find it as soon as mankind itself has achieved its own ideal salvation" (p. 14). This positive character of the value of salvation is as much a demand of the religious consciousness as it is evidence of man's and the world's need for salvation; i.e., it is evidence of the presence of guilt and of evil in the world. Put otherwise, in so far as man's longing for salvation is the center of his religious life, it reflects the inherently tragic character of the world-process and reveals it as "a divine tragedy in which man is involved only because mankind is of a divine race (*göttlichen Geschlechts*)" (p. 15). Such a view, however, is but "a religious conception of the absolute teleological world-order," culminating in a religious or teleological optimism.

Now, the world is process. It is a becoming. And this process is neither circular nor straight-forward on the same level. It is, instead, a "spiral-like movement whose circles become larger and larger as they rise to ever higher levels, while the circles themselves are averages of countless waves formed by the oscillations of the various branches of the process" (p. 16). The enlargement of the circles means that ever more areas of human activity are affected by the development of culture, while the rise to higher levels means that the level of culture itself is elevated—at least in its most qualified representatives. If this is at all a true picture of the world-process, then the value of the world, measured in terms of development, is positive and "the evolutional optimism is justified." That this is a true picture of the world-process is the basic postulate of the cognitive, the moral, and the religious consciousness—a postulate without which "the cognitive, the moral, and the redemptive value of the world would be illusory, and the aesthetic value would be greatly reduced" (*ibid.*). But the developmental value of the world depends on whether or not the world-process has a goal which can be attained by the elevation to higher levels, and which will not be attained when such elevation does not take place. To put it differently: The justification of the assumption of a positive world-developmental value depends on whether or not it is justified to believe that the world-process is teleological; to believe, in other words, that every phase of that process stands in the relation of purpose to means to every preceding phase, and as means to a purpose to every phase which follows (p. 19).

It must be noted, however, that he who is a teleological optimist must also be an evolutionary, cognitive, aesthetic, moral, and religious optimist, and must extend his optimism even to economic, social, and political matters. But he who repudiates the teleological world view must in every one of these respects be a pessimist, a sceptic, or an indifferentist. He cannot be an optimist. Von Hartmann himself, however, stands committed to an optimism in all these areas. That is to say, his world view centers in the affirmation of "the highest possible positivity of the world-value (*Weltwert*) as determined by all logical standards" (p. 21).

But von Hartmann also recognizes the presence of volitional and emotional factors in the world; and with respect to them the situation is rather different.

Turning first to the emotional factors, von Hartmann points out that the "standard of pleasure" (*Lustmassstab*) is immanent in the world, but that now "the positivity of the value of the world depends on whether pleasure or displeasure is predominant in the world" (p. 31). An examination of this problem leads von Hartmann to the development of a "calculus of pleasures" (*Lustwägungslehre*) (pp. 32–137). The formalism of this calculus is similar to that of other calculi of this type, and is equally meaningless. However, a few points may still be made.

It is von Hartmann's contention, for instance, that each of the feelings to be compared with others can serve as the measure for all. No special standard is needed. Similar and equally weighty feelings of opposite character (plus or minus) compensate for each other mathematically. On the average, however, we would demand a preponderance of pleasure over displeasure. Intensity and duration are purely quantitative aspects of the pleasure-displeasure experience and suggest an easy comparison of pleasures. However, the qualitative dissimilarities of various types of feelings militate against that. "For the world-process a lesser spiritual pleasure may be more valuable and nobler than a great sensuous pleasure; but for the calculus of pleasures the large sensuous pleasure must count for more than the lesser spiritual pleasure" (p. 38). The comparison of one's own feelings with the feelings of others is especially difficult and would be impossible were it not for the fact that we can infer the feelings of others from their emotional responses and their actions.

Axiology as the calculus of pleasures is concerned with feelings but is itself a matter of "cold, sober understanding, unaffected by feelings" (p. 44). Yet, the null-point between positivity and negativity, between dominance of pleasure and dominance of displeasure, is determined entirely by feeling. It is doubtful, however, that such neutral feeling is ever experienced. Moreover, as a social being, man cannot fail but compare his own feelings with those of his fellowmen—his friends, neighbors, colleagues, etc.— and adjust to them.

Experientially we must distinguish between various groups of feelings—groups that range from feelings involving only displeasure (e.g., envy, grudge, anger, pain, remorse, hate, vindictiveness, etc.) to those involving pleasure only. But viewed realistically, "life sees to it that the illusions with which man begins it are gradually destroyed. . . . In general, old age looks back with melancholy to its own youth and recognizes too late that the happiness looked for in vain in the future is already possessed as far as that is ever possible in the illusory hope itself and so long as that hope was not yet seen to be an illusion" (pp. 60–61). From a rational point of view, however, "death cannot be called an evil" because, "as long as one feels anything, one is still alive, and when one is dead, one no longer feels anything and therefore also no displeasure and no pain." "Only from the irrational point of view of a blind will to life and the instinctive drive for self-preservation is death an evil, and the fear of death a displeasure" (p. 63).

Still, it is of the nature of man that his needs and demands grow more rapidly than do the means to their satisfaction. Moreover, all progress depends upon a selection of the ablest in the struggle for existence; it depends, therefore, upon the employment of the greatest possible strength in order to overcome others and to obtain the means for survival in the struggle yet to come. And in this struggle even the victor does not attain an enjoyment of his victory undiluted by the sacrifices that were necessary to achieve it. "The higher the culture, the more must man become convinced that the struggle against suffering is a vain effort because suffering in one form or another is as inescapable as is death" (p. 69).

It is possible, of course, to admit the surplus of displeasure in our "natural life" and yet to affirm that there is a surplus of pleasure in our total existence. It is possible provided one is of the opinion that man's spiritual life in science, art, morality, and religion supplies a surplus of pleasure greater than the surplus of displeasure of the "natural life." Von Hartmann, however, argues in some detail (pp. 69–96) that, considered on empirical grounds, man's spiritual life also entails a negative valuation of human existence, and that we must reconcile ourselves to encountering "a surplus of displeasure in the whole of life" (p. 96).

But human existence is not the only aspect of reality that is relevant to the issue. Nature herself is cruel and in "unconscious indifference" (*in bewusstloser Unbekümmertheit*) "tortures her own creations through hunger and thirst, fire and water, earthquakes and volcanic eruptions, crushing, dismembering, burying alive." "The worst of all is what living creatures inflict upon one another" (pp. 120–121). The surplus of displeasure found in human existence is thus increased immeasurably when we take animal existence into consideration. The negative balance for the whole earth and its inhabitants far surpasses that for our human existence alone.

Does this fact per chance reflect accurately the balance for the universe as a whole? Von Hartmann proceeds to show that it does.

Let us assume here that he has established his point. What are its metaphysical consequences? Von Hartmann deals with them in his "axiology of the Absolute."

The Absolute, he tells us, is not an object of cognition—neither for itself nor for others. We can know it only indirectly through its relations to what is relative, and as, discursively and reflexively, we infer back (*zurückschliessen*) from appearances to the essence, from products to the producer, from functions to the bearer of these functions. Cognition thus means "to posit relations," and "it is a contradiction to try to reach that which is beyond relations by positing relations" (p. 138).

But neither is the Absolute accessible through aesthetic or moral considerations; for it is "the source of all that is true, beautiful and good, but is itself above (*erhaben*) all such relative determinations" (p. 140).

To be sure, the Absolute is object of the religious relationship, "not, however, as Absolute but as the absolute subject which is already in relation; i.e., only as immanent in the world is the Absolute God," and "the standard of development can be applied only to the world posited by the Absolute, not to the essence of the Absolute itself, for that essence must be conceived as unchanging" (pp. 141-142).

But if the standard of development is to be applied to the world, then, as we have seen earlier, there must be a purpose intrinsic in that world which is of sufficient value to justify the creation of the world.

So long as a eudaemonistic optimism was accepted as valid, this problem was solved, for it could then be maintained that the true purpose of creation was the happiness of all creatures. However, because of the surplus of displeasure in the world, such a view is no longer tenable. And every attempt to attribute the preponderance of evil in the world to some non-divine principle or Being entails the denial either of God's Absoluteness, of his omnipotence or of his omniscience; and, surely, "a genuine religio-moral consciousness would be repulsed by a God who could himself indulge in serene bliss even though he had created a world for lamentation and permitted it to continue in its misery" (p. 148).

The problem which von Hartmann faces is, therefore, this: What must be the nature of the Absolute that will explain the existence of a world of positive teleological and negative eudaemonological value? As he sees it, *the positive teleological value of the world* implies that "there is a principle in the Absolute which, responding to a given motive, is capable of teleological action"; and "this can only be a logical principle that can unfold itself to an intuitive idea." *The negative pleasure-value of the world* implies that "there is a non-logical principle in the Absolute which, in a blind urge and without foreseeing the tragic consequences of its action, plunges into activity" (p. 156). Both principles are of the very essence of the Absolute and are one and the same within the Absolute (*sie fallen in Eins und werden in Eins zusammengefasst*). They are but different aspects of the same relation as seen from two one-sided points of view.

Von Hartmann admits, of course, that this interpretation of the nature of the Absolute is purely hypothetical and that the world-value as such is not affected by accepting or rejecting his interpretation. "The teleological optimism and the eudaemonological pejorism with respect to the world remain valid even if the metaphysical monism . . . should be proven to be untenable" (p. 164); and from this fact certain practical consequences follow.

The more firmly a man believes in the possibility of achieving happiness, the more eagerly will he pursue that goal, and the more vulnerable will he be to unavoidable disappointments. He will face this fate uncomprehending and without sufficient strength to bear it. Furthermore, eudaemonological optimism is also the greatest hindrance to cultural progress. The principle of "the greatest happiness for the greatest number of people," when adopted for any society, leads necessarily through Communism to a universal barbarism. All progress requires sacrifices in the comfort and pleasure of individuals; but as long as pleasure is regarded as the goal to be achieved, "the tragic hero must appear to be the greatest fool" (p. 173). The knowledge that happiness cannot be attained through changes in the external circumstances; that peace of mind is an inner achievement; that it is much more important how we respond to things than what the things are— "all of this teaches us how much less depends on a change in the external circumstances than we are accustomed to think" (p. 181). Eudaemonological pejorism and the conviction that it is true are thus the best remedy for all disappointments and all the suffering that are entailed by the collapse of a false optimism.

On the other hand, the most favorable effects of a teleological optimism are encountered, "where the objective purpose is related to the intellectual, aesthetic, moral, religious, etc. development of mankind, be it with the inclusion or the exclusion of an enhancement of happiness" (p. 191); for this optimism is guaranty that the goals projected by our moral inclinations are not just as illusory as are the goals assumed by a happiness-thirsty self-centered will.

As von Hartmann summarizes it: "It all amounts to this: We must combine the two-fold insights, first, that the self can get rid of its suffering only by finding its peace in God, and, secondly, that the absolute Will itself, in order to regain its lost peace, must relinquish the foolish search for a lasting and complete satisfaction external to that peace itself" (p. 198).

II

It is, of course, a well-known fact that Wilhelm Ostwald's whole philosophy was keyed to the conception of energy and its transformations. Energy, he maintained, is the indispensable condition for all that happens and for every activity in the universe. "The idea of value arises wherever there exist a plus and a minus of needs, and where the exchange of one object for another is desired. . . . But a system of values is developed only through the social activity of man through which a far-reaching particularization (*Vereinzelung*) of the functions and, with it, a corresponding system of the exchange of valuable objects is effected. These value-objects attain their value exclusively through human labor—through the personal expenditure of the energy necessary for their acquisition or production" (*Die Philosophie der Werte,* p. 262).

In this perspective, "culture is the highest intensification (*Steigerung*) of the organism's capacity for work in the realm of conscious intellectual activity (*bewusste Geistestätigkeit*); a higher form of intellectual work is not known" (p. 263). Culture is, thus, limited exclusively to the realm of man; and even here various stages in its development from the lowest to the as yet highest can be discerned, depending on the technological, scientific, and artistic achievements. The "height of a culture" (*Kulturhöhe*) depends (1) on "the mass of raw energy (*Rohenergie*) employed in the service of mankind," (2) on "the quality-relationships with which raw energies are being transformed into purposive forms (*Zweckformen*) of energy, and (3) on "the perfection of the organization or co-ordination of the separately developed functions when each is individually brought to highest efficiency" (p. 266).

Ostwald admits that Humanists—such as Winckelmann and Burckhardt—would repudiate such a standard. All would agree, however, that it is the purpose of culture "to heighten (*erhöhen*) the level of our existence." Differences arise only when the issue is: Through what and in what way ought our existence to be heightened? Ostwald's answer to this question is his value theory.

There are aspects of human existence, so he argues, which are crucial for its continuation. They are the most elementary of all needs: man's needs for food, clothing, housing, and (within a certain age-bracket) for sexual gratification. Superimposed upon these are certain "higher needs." Thus, man eats not merely in order to still his hunger but also in order to enjoy the fine flavor of the food. He builds houses not merely for protection from the inclemencies of the weather but also to satisfy his desire for comfort and for beauty. Along with all this goes mans' desire for a healthy body and for everything that will maintain "the normal life of the organism." We must therefore demand of a culture, and of the highest culture in particular, that it contribute to the satisfaction of man's needs and desires (p. 271).

But when we apply this standard to existing cultures, we find that only some of the basic needs of man are fairly well taken care of, and these only in a very uneven manner. There is still hunger in the world. Housing is inadequate. Public health remains a problem. Where progress has been made, it is "entirely and exclusively" the result of an improved technology. The conclusion, therefore, is inescapable (so Ostwald maintains) that "a really higher culture is not possible without this techno-mechanical foundation"; for "the greater the proportion of mechanical labor which the increasing development of technology allows us to turn over to the machines, the greater is also the proportion of free, voluntary and, therefore, happiness-bringing activity which man can choose in accordance with his wishes and his needs (pp. 273–274).

Underlying the whole development of technology is the basic "Principle of the Most Appropriate Utilization of Energy." And this Principle, Ostwald insists, retains its significance even at the highest levels of cultural achievement, including the aesthetic and the scientific. "Every particular form of our systematic development of culture finds its justification and its value-level in the degree to which the problem has been solved of achieving the greatest possible result with the least possible expenditure of energy" (p. 277).

What this entails can be readily seen when we consider Ostwald's answer to the two questions: What is the purpose of man's existence? and Why is he interested at all in the development of culture?—the answer, namely, that "the joy of living (*die Freude am Leben*) is considerably (*erheblich*) larger than the sum of the sufferings one must experience" (*ibid.*). Also, "the ability to feel happy, not only to be satisfied with life but positively to enjoy it, is an ability which gives those who possess it a distinct advantage in the struggle for existence. . . . Happiness, therefore, is the goal of all of man's strivings and, in consequence, happiness must also be acknowledged to be the goal of all culture" (p. 278).

But when we now ask, What is happiness?, Ostwald finds it

necessary to introduce certain distinctions which, together, give us a happiness-spectrum that ranges from "hero-happiness" (*Heldenglück*)—"the happiness of activist and victorious youth" —to "Philistine-happiness" (*Philisterglück*)—"the happiness of a tired and peaceful old age." Between these two extremes countless other modes of happiness find their appropriate places.

The very fact that such distinctions can be made means, as far as Ostwald is concerned, that happiness depends on at least two variables. On the one hand, "happiness increases in direct proportion to an increase in the total expenditure of energy on the part of the living being,"—a fact which explains why "happiness is pre-eminently the feeling of young people—of persons, that is, for whom even "mere existence is full of happiness" and who give expression of this feeling "through dancing, singing, laughing, etc." On the other hand, human beings unquestionably experience also strong feelings of happiness that are not related to such "surplus of energy," and, on occasion, all men experience unhappiness. The difference, Ostwald maintains, lies in the form or mode of the expenditure of energy.

To be more specific: Ostwald distinguishes between an expenditure of energy that is in harmony with one's own will and inclinations—let us call it "volitional" (*willensgemäss*)—and an expenditure that is necessitated by external conditions and is contrary to one's own will and inclinations—the "counter-volitional" (*willenswidrige*) expenditure. The former is a positive factor, the latter a negative one. Their "sum" is the basis for our feeling of happiness. If the positive factor outweighs the negative, then we are happy. If the negative factor outweighs the positive, then we are unhappy. That is to say, happiness increases and diminishes along with the value of the product consisting of the total expenditure of energy and the "volitional" surplus. The "total expenditure" is always positive. The "surplus" can be positive or negative, depending on whether the obstacles that have to be overcome are smaller or larger relative to the "volitional" expenditure of energy. "The essential factors that determine happiness have thus been found" (p. 280).

Since, according to Ostwald, "happiness must be acknowledged to be the goal of all culture," it follows at once that, in developing their culture, men ought to try to reduce the "counter-voli-tional" expenditure of energy to a minimum. This can be done in many different ways. All of them, however, involve, in princi-ple, either "internal" or "external" factors, or both. That is to say, men either engage in activities which are not dominated by a concern for material things, or they so arrange matters that the external conditions under which they must live include a mini-mum of obstacles to the "volitional" expenditure of energy. When, in specific situations, the latter course has proved to be impossible, men have succeeded in changing their mental attitude toward the obstacles to such a degree that the feeling of unhappiness has been minimized if not actually transformed into its opposite. The great religions all prove this fact.

One last point should be considered. Since energy alone is that which cannot be created or destroyed, and since the world we live in, our own life included, is but a manifestation of diverse trans-formations of energy, it is not surprising that, according to Ostwald, "the basis of all values will be found in the conception of energy." Ostwald does not mean, however, that energy *per se* is a value. "When everything around us is energy, then energy is present in such immeasurable quantity that we can do nothing or refrain from doing anything, we can not acquire anything or throw anything away, without handling each time a greater or lesser quantum of energy. And we know also that an unfree or dissipated energy—energy which is no longer capable of trans-formations—can have or can represent no value because it is no longer usable for the activities of life. Therefore, we can find the source of values only in the free energy which is yet capable of undergoing transformations" (pp. 314–315).

But another factor must also be taken into consideration. Let us suppose that, as organisms, two human beings absorb equal amounts of chemical energy within a period of 24 hours. And let us suppose, furthermore, that one of these men is a day-laborer, the other a renowed artist. How can we account for the great difference in the values ascribed by society to their work?

A first answer to this question is that the creations of the great artist are very much scarcer than are the achievements of the day-laborer; that they thus possess a "scarcity value." Scarcity alone, however, does not entail a special value. It does so only when what is scarce is desired by a sufficiently large number of persons. Only the two factors together—scarcity and demand for that which is scarce—establish the value.

Keeping this fact in mind, Ostwald now describes a "sequence of energy-values." The very lowest value is that of the radiating energy of the sun, the primary source of all free energy. Since this radiation is "unavoidably necessary" for life on earth, "its value cannot be overestimated"; but it is not a scarce item. Since the immediate product of the radiation-energy is the chemical energy of the organic matter in plants, this will have to be put in second place in the scale of values. Considerably higher is the level of the "mechanical work" made available to man through heat and through cascading water. Above this are the forms of energy available to man through the least expenditure of energy on his part. Upon these man depends for his continuous existence and well-being. Still higher in the value scale are "all quantities of energy produced by man himself." And the highest level is "that form of energy which cannot be replaced by a machine—man's intellectual achievements" (pp. 327–328).

Further details of this theory Ostwald leaves for his readers to develop.

III

The first edition of Theodor Lessing's *Studien zur Wert-axiomatik* was published in 1908 as Volume XIV of the *Archiv für Systematische Philosophie*. Shortly after its publication Lessing devoted much of his time to an intensive study of Nietzsche. The result was that he found it necessary to revise and clarify some of his own ideas about values. The changes have been incorporated in the second edition of *Studien*. It is this edition, therefore, that gives us the definitive version of Lessing's value theory and is the basis for the discussions that follow.

Lessing's interest in value-theoretical problems arose as a critical reaction to Kant's ethics and, in particular, to the questions of validity and of evidence which Kant had raised. What, specifically, is the basis for the validity of the moral law? Kant's answer had been the repudiation of all empiricistic approaches and a recourse to "practical reasons" as the only possible foundation for the validity of moral obligation. And as Kant had asked, How is knowledge possible?, and had given a transcendentalist answer, so Lessing now asked, How is value possible?, and maintained that, far from providing an adequate answer to this question, all psychological approaches miss the point, for they already presuppose what they set out to prove. What is at issue is the normative aspect of our value experience—the "being-valued-with-justification" (*das Mit-Recht-Geschätztsein*)—upon which depend "all aesthetic, logical, moral, and practical values" (p. xvi).

Kant had shown, so Lessing points out, that the objective validity of our experience depends upon certain broad *a priori* principles; that such principles are foundational to what is objectively true, objectively good, and objectively beautiful; that far from describing the acts of judgment, of moral approval or disapproval, or of aesthetic preference, these principles are trans-temporal and trans-psychical rational norms. "They represent the sum-total of all the axioms of thinking, acting, and approving," and, together, constitute "the realm of the pure ideal" (*das Reich des reinen Ideals*) (p. 18).

Opposed to this pure or transcendental value theory are (1) the psychological phenomena of valuing, evaluing, prizing, affirming, etc., and (2) the concrete and actual valuations in the real world: the valuations and theories in the field of economics and in applied biology—valuations which stress the values of life itself and of the enhancement of life.

In developing a "pure value theory" we must—initially at least—disregard both (1) and (2). We start by assuming that there is a phenomenon "value," and we ask: "What relations can be discerned that are *a priori* valid in the same sense in which logical axioms (Principle of Contradiction, of Identity, etc.) are valid for everything that we know to be true?" (p. 20). But are there purely formal relationships that are distinctive of the value phenomena, or are the purely formal aspects of the objectively true and the objectively valuable actually identical—namely, laws of correct judgment? Lessing's thesis, of course, is that they are not; that "the value-laws are indeed a specific kind; that they are

toto genere different from the laws of logic; and that they are
laws pertaining specifically to the objective phenomenon value"
(*ibid.*).

Inspection will show, Lessing maintains, that this is so; for the
value-laws (*Wertgesetze*) pertain specifically to values, and
"value" is a predication which assumes that there is a content
of experience which can be said to have value. Hence, (1) "being
relatively material laws, the value-laws presuppose the more
formal correctness of the laws of logic." (2) "The laws of logic
are immediately self-evident and analytic" (e.g., A is A). But
"self-evidence in this sense is not encountered in axiology . . .
because there are no isolated values. . . . Every 'value' occurs within
a system of 'higher' and 'lower.' Or, stated otherwise: Every value
contains a 'compared with.' The value-laws, therefore, pertain
always to competition or to an order of rank." (3) "No truth can
be 'truer' than any other. Values, however, must always stand
to one another in a relationship of degrees. That is to say, the act
of valuing is, in its very nature, a preferring or detracting. The
a priori value-laws, therefore, can be nothing other than norms for
the correct preference or detraction of what is to be valued." As
norms they are "valid for every value-consciousness." What they
mean is not that value A is actually being preferred to value B,
but that one value is *a priori* preferable to another and thus ought
to be preferred. (4) "A truth is true even when nobody understands it." In the realm of values, however, it is otherwise. "A
realm of completely secure objective values, comparable to the
immediately evident logical truths, does not exist" (pp. 20–24).

Continuing his detailed analyses, Lessing distinguishes between
"value as such, value, and disvalue." But since every value is
either a plus-value or a minus-value, we shall use the term
'value' to mean a plus- or positive value, and the term 'disvalue'
to mean a minus-value. And we shall note also that every value
(disvalue) is either absolute or relative, either a value (disvalue)
in itself or by virtue of a relation.

Having recognized these distinctions, we now turn to the
a priori value-laws themselves. We must keep in mind, however,
that "value" always implies a relation to objects of valuation and
that, therefore, an analysis of the value phenomena can yield an

insight into the nature of value relations only. In itself it does not disclose "what is truly valuable," nor does it reveal whether or not there are "empirical values" at all. This formal analysis is thus, in a sense, simply a "game"—a "game" just as symbolic logic is a "game." (p. 26; footnote). The formualism itself comes to this (pp. 27–34):

I. *Value Axioms* (the Principles of value-identity, value-contradiction, and the excluded third)
   1. If V is a value, then V is valuable.
   2. If V is a value, then it cannot be in the same respect a positive value, *A,* and a disvalue, *a.*
   3. If V is a value, then it must be either a positive value, *A,* or a disvalue, *a.*

II. *First Law* (the Law of the specific value-relation)
   Of any two values (or disvalues) one must be higher, the other lower.
   a. First Consequence: All values (or disvalues) stand to one another in a relationship of degree of valuableness.
   b. Second Consequence: Only one "highest" (i.e., ultimate) value exists (value as such, *summum bonum,* "God").
   c. Third Consequence: All values (or disvalues) occupy a place within a system.
   d. Fourth Consequence: The valuable in itself does not lie within the system of all values.

III. *Second Law* (the Law of value-summation)
   a. If *A* and *B* are both values, then *A* plus *B* is more valuable than *A;* and *A* plus *B* is more valuable than *B.*
   b. If *a* and *b* are both disvalues, then *a* plus *b* is a greater disvalue than *a;* and *a* plus *b* is a greater disvalue than *b.*

IV. *Third Law* (the Law of value transference)
   If (*A* plus *B* plus *C*) is a value, then (*A* plus *B*) *A, C,* (*C* plus *A*), etc. are also values.

V. *Fourth Law* (the Law of value-exchange)
   a. *A* plus *B* is the same value as *B* plus *A.*
   b. *a* plus *b* is the same disvalue as *b* plus *a.*

VI. *Fifth Law* (the Law of surplus value)
   a. If *B* is a value because *A* is a value, then *A* is a greater value than *B.*
   b. If *b* is a disvalue because *a* is a disvalue, then *a* is a greater disvalue than *b.*

VII. *Sixth Law* (the Law of univocal value determination)
   a. If *B* is a value because *A* is a value, then (in the same respect) *A* cannot be a value because *B* is a value.
   b. If *b* is a disvalue because *a* is a disvalue, then (in the same respect) *a* cannot be a disvalue because *b* is one.

These Laws, Lessing points out, must be accepted as criteria for our volition—at least as "ideal orientations, as 'rational ideas' (*Vernunftideen*)." However, an intermediate link is required "between the purely theoretical, *a priori,* absolutely objective laws of value-mathematics (*Wertmathematik*) and the normative *a priori* laws concerning correct volition and counter-volition, concerning a correct ranking of "goal" and "means"—in brief, concerning the demands of correct attitudes. And here, too, *a priori* principles are involved—albeit principles of a lower order. They are the *a priori* and intuitively known principles pertaining to the interrelations of both realms, the purely formal realm of values, on the one hand, and the range of volitions and valuations, on the other. Among these principles are: "A good will is directed toward the good"; "A correct valuation is one that accords with the appropriate laws of values"—principles, in other words, which say nothing but that "the good will ought to will the good," and that "the good man is he who wills according to the laws of correct valuations" (pp. 36–37). Thus, it is reasonable that he who desires goal *A* must also want means *B,* and that he who wants to avoid goal *a* must also avoid means *b.* "The intended 'goal' is always a higher value than the intended means; and the avoided 'final end' is always a greater disvalue than is the avoided evil of any transitory stage" (pp. 40–41). Moreover, if *B* is the means to *A* and *C* is the means to *B,* then it is reasonable that *C* must be willed before *B* is willed and *A* is willed. "Actually, the realization of the last and highest value must have as its precondition the realization of all intermediary goals" (p. 42).

The laws and principles here referred to represent, of course, an *ought* rather than any actual determination, and they do so in the very same sense in which the laws of logic are an *ought.* But it is not some specific kind of *volition* that is demanded in these laws; it is rather a "something," i.e., an ideal object (*ideale Objektivität*), that ought to be willed; and this object cannot be found in the realm of the factually real, "least of all in the empirically given psychological person" (p. 76). To put it differently: The purely formal laws pertaining to values tell us nothing about specific and concrete goals, nothing about intentions, and nothing about the specific character of an action; but they allow us to pursue now an egoistic and now an altruistic goal as that which ought to be. No particular state of affairs, no particular function or attribute in itself can be regarded as valuable (or as valueless). It is only in context with everything else that anything is acceptable as valuable (or is rejected as valueless).

In itself every norm and every category is "empty." It has content only when it is applied within the context of concrete experience. But let us not forget that, according to Lessing, our world is the product of our minds (*Geist*). Our reason has formed it; and so we find it to be rational. We are the interpreters and the exploiters of all there is, and of life in particular. Our very nature constrains us to measure the inexhaustible and the infinite in terms of our own "positings," our own *a priori* principles. All values and norms but reflect this fact, and it explains the complete failure of all philosophers who have tried to derive values from the world of nature and of facts. He who confuses the study of values with the study of valuable real objects or, worse yet, with a study of the acts of valuation, finds himself in the position of a man who, because he learned arithmetic by counting apples and nuts, takes arithmetic to be a branch of botany.

It is "the tragedy of value theory," Lessing believes, that the term 'value' has been put to so many different uses. The economists use it when they speak of "goods," while in the field of religion values are "ideals." We speak of the value of parental love, the value of diamonds, the value of a good meal and of the immortality of the soul. A ton of iron ore is a value, and so is the moral character of a person, so is human dignity. Is there anything that is common to all these usages?

As Lessing sees it, "value is what is justly prized" (*mit Recht geschätzt*); but never can the act of prizing or success, self-preservation, validity, or the *consensus omnium* be even a part of that justification. To be sure, we value knowledge, the beauty of form, the purity of heart, the good intention; but how can we justify this? It is Lessing's contention that no compelling justification can ever be given. It is possible, for example, that only that which sustains life is or can be a value; but why must life be preserved? Where is the justification of its existence in the world? We are here face to face with realities that divide men into two groups—one which maintains that it is "better to be a slave than to be dead"; the other that it is "better to be dead than to be a slave." But who can prove one of these groups right and the other one wrong? It is nonsensical to say of life that it is valuable or that it is without value, that in itself it is meaningful or that it is meaningless. Reality merely is what it is. The normative and the valuational aspects of experience are but expressions of the "practical ideal" so to live our lives that in all our actions demands of pure reason serve as a compelling *ought* (p. 115).

IV

Müller-Freienfels begins his investigations with an analysis of the value-phenomenon, making the obvious distinction between the subject which values—the "value-subject"—and the object that is being valued—the "value-object." What relates a value-subject to a value-object is the process of valuing (Grundzüge," p. 320).

As we have seen, this process has been taken by some to be essentially a matter of feeling, and by others to be a matter of desire. Müller-Freienfels, however, finds both of these views to be inadequate. As he sees it, it is not sufficient for a valuational experience that the subject respond emotionally or volitionally to an object. What is also necessary is that the subject affirm or acknowledge the relation and thus "posit it as a value." Only both aspects together—the basic response to an object and the positing of a value—constitute a valuation in the true sense. Pleasures and desires or, more in line with the facts of experience, attitudes involving pleasures and desires become a basis for value only when augmented by the positing of a value. That is to say, "a fullfledged value experience occurs only when both, value-basis and value-positing are involved" (pp. 323–327).

An obvious question now is, What is meant by the positing of a value? Wherein does the positing consist? One might be inclined to say that it is a matter of judgment. Müller-Freienfels, however, denies that it is. He takes a judgment to be "the linguistic formulation of an attitude" and therefore not as the positing of a value; and he points out, furthermore, that in certain circumstances the positing of a value may be essentially a matter of feeling and of desire, not of judgment. As he sees it, the positing of a value is itself the taking of an attitude—of an attitude, namely, toward an attitude, toward the emotional or volitional response of the subject to its object. And since attitudes can be given expression in a judgment, the positing of a value may, but need not, take the form of a judgment. It may also be a matter of the emotions and desires.

Taking the act of valuing as a whole, we can say that "valuing is an emotional reaction of the subject plus the taking of an attitude toward that reaction" (p. 330). Such a valuation, however, is a genuine value experience only when the primary response to the object finds full acknowledgment in the attitude taken toward it. Unfortunately, the ability to have such primary experiences of values is perhaps less general than is usually assumed. Original value experiences are as rare as is genuine creative power. It is, however, pre-eminently manifest in the lives of the great innovators in religion, morality, art, and other value fields. These individuals have asserted their own value experience, and the values rooted therein, against the conventional and often rigid value positing of their cultural environment.

If a valuation is imposed from the outside, the experience is not really a value experience because the value-basis is either a demand confronting the subject to make adjustments in his primary attitudes, or it is feigned. If the former is the case, the extraneous valuation confronts the subject as an *ought*.

It is implicit in what has been said that every value is relative. It is a value for someone, for some particular subject; and that subject is undergoing manifold changes. An absolute sameness of the same individual in the course of time is just not a fact. And, depending on the dominant "subjectivity" at any particular time, the "same" person acts in very different ways. We encounter here a certain duality within the subject itself. There is, on the one hand, the self-identity of the subject; but there are also its momentary phases.

When we now ask, What is the self-identical subject?, Müller-Freienfels replies that it is the conception which, more or less distinctly, every person has of himself—the conviction, that is, of a unitary "true" self which persists in the midst of all changes. But this "substantial self," this "unitary self," is a fiction (p. 336). Despite this fact, however, the "unitary self" is important in connection with the dualism between value-basis and value-positing, for the value-basis is an experience we have here and now as this "momentary subject," whereas it is the substantial or unitary self that posits the values and is the bearer of all valuations taken over from our human environment. To the extent, therefore, to which the unitary self is the "ideal subject" it is also the ground for the suppression of the emotions and desires of the momentary self, subordinating them to its own valuations.

It is impossible, however, according to Müller-Freienfels, to project in the same way a "real and universally human value-subject as the 'normal' self" and, therefore, as standard for everyone and at all times (p. 340). To be sure, men can and do value in the perspective of some particular conception of subjectivity—such as the "Classic," the "Gothic," the "Barock"; but this does not entail the reality of a "normal subject"—of a subject, that is, whose valuations are universally binding and valid. Even Kant's categorical imperative reflects unmistakably the individuality of Kant and of the intellectual climate of his times. In other words, the idea of a "normal subject" is and remains an abstraction.

Frequently, however, it is suggested that a further step be taken; for if all subjects can be regarded as being identical in their ultimate nature, then, surely, we can disregard the subject entirely. That is to say, if things exist which necessarily please all subjects, then it is no longer necessary to refer to a subject at all. Unfortunately, this step cannot be taken because the assumed identity of all subjects is simply not a fact. What is a fact, however, is that the individual actually encounters "the social valuations made by social subjects"—by the family, the clan, the nation, and the trans-national cultural communities. But these valuations are always "external" to the individual who may or may not accept them as his own. If he does not accept them, he finds himself in a value-conflict with the social group—a conflict which reveals the ultimately coercive character (*Zwangscharakter*) of the social values.

Since to every value-subject there corresponds a value-object, the problems just indicated with respect to the subject recur when we consider the value-objects. Since the relationships are rather clear, it is not necessary to go into details here. Only one point is of special significance for an understanding of Müller-Freienfels' position. It is this: Just as we need a fictive unitary subject (*ein fiktives Einheitssubjekt*) so we also need fictive unitary objects and unitary values (*Einheitswerte*) (p. 350). Moreover, corresponding to the transition from the unitary subject to a "normal subject" we find on the object side the transition from a unitary object to a "normal object" (*Normalgegenstand*). Even though we cannot always make it stick, we speak of our own valuations as "normal," and we speak of "beautiful" things and of "good" acts as if the fictive "normal subject" were actually real. We thus create "objective" value-objects which, of course, can be regarded as such only so long as the convention underlying our positing remains acceptable. The danger is that all this leads to hypocracy or to a conscious or unconscious self-deception; for, often at least, the subordination of the subject to the objective valuations takes place in such a way that the subject accepts the extraneous valuations without making an effort to create the appropriate value-basis in his own experience.

One last point must be considered—the fact, namely, that values are judged to be "either 'correct' or 'false' values" (*entweder richtige oder falsche Werte*), and that some values are "subordinate" to others. As Müller-Freienfels sees it, judgments concerning the correctness and the order of rank of values reflect an "evaluation of values" and, thus, represent a "tertiary attitude"—an attitude toward the positing of values when this positing itself is the taking of an attitude toward our primary (i.e., our affective-conative) responses to objects.

The question is, Is there some ultimate standard, some "final basic value," relative to which our judgments pertaining to the correctness of values and to the order of rank of values can themselves be justified? This question, Müller-Freienfels maintains, can be answered only in the negative; for, upon analysis, all suggested standards or "ultimate values" turn out to be themselves but relative positings (pp. 361; 366; 368, 369). "So long as there are human beings, there will also be different valuations and the conflict of valuations. Again and again values will be posited with the claim of their absolute validity; but again and again, also, the concealed relativities will be uncovered. This, however, is no reason for sadness. On the contrary, we believe that all the fascination and the charm of life is derived from the conflict of values" (p. 370). Without that conflict the world would be "boring and desolate," "an ideal for a narrow dogmatism," unbearable for persons having a "spark of life" within them.

And so we come to the seemingly paradoxical conclusion that "the positing of absolute values is itself a relative value which consists in this that—although in conflict with reality and therefore fictive—it has practical significance." Even as fiction the presumed absoluteness of a value raises that value to a level of special dignity and thus enhances its significance for human living (p. 379). However, positing the absoluteness of a value is necessary only for persons who lack insight into the true nature of all valuations. It is so in religion, in ethics, and in aesthetics.

Under certain conditions, the destruction of the "nimbus of absoluteness" can be as much of a value as is positing it. "And it cannot be the task of a scientific philosophy to build up an impossible system of absolute values through dialectical craftiness. On the contrary, its true task is to demonstrate the relativity of all valuations. And such insight need not have less dignity than have those deceptive creations which assume for themselves a spurious eternity" (p. 381).

BIBLIOGRAPHY

I. von Hartmann, Eduard, *Grundriss der Axiologie oder Wertwägungslehre,* Bad Sachsa, 1908.
II. Lessing, Theodor, *Studien zur Wertaxiomatik,* revised edition, Leipzig, 1914.
III. Müller-Freienfels, Richard, "Grundzüge einer neuen Wertlehre," *Annalen der Philosophie,* I, 1919, 319–381.
IV. Ostwald, Wilhelm, *Die Philosophie der Werte,* Leipzig, 1913.

CHAPTER IX

RICKERT AND VALUE AS VALIDITY

It will be remembered that Brentano attempted to establish his value theory in terms of certain subjective experiences whose objective validity he believed to be demonstrable. His key concepts were "right loving" and "right hating." Both refer to actual affective-conative experiences and thus suggest a psychological approach to values. Meinong, von Ehrenfels, Kreibig, and others followed this "psychologistic" trend.

Brentano himself, however, understood "right loving" and "right hating" as also implying a norm. "*Right* loving" and "*right* hating," so he maintained, have an objective validity which transcends the merely psychological level of interpretation. Heinrich Rickert regarded this aspect of Brentano's thesis as crucial for value theory and developed his own interpretation accordingly. As he saw it, any psychological approach is condemned to failure because the more consistent a psychological theory is—i.e., the more it is confined to an interpretation to mental phenomena—the more it is concerned with facts rather than with values, with what *is* rather than with what *ought to be.* Value problems, so Rickert now argued, must be solved, not within the confines of a particular science, but within the framework of an all-encompassing philosophy that attempts the clarification and interpretation of the whole of human experience. Such a philosophy Rickert takes his own transcendental idealism to be.

As he sees it, in order to be adequate, a value theory must include all aspects of human experience that involve decisions and the pursuit of goals. It must include, therefore, all "practical" concerns of human beings—the economic and social along with the cognitive, and the ethical as well as the aesthetic and the religious. Rickert admits that it may not be possible to give a compelling proof of the presence of values in all of these areas; but, he argues, if there is at least one field in which such proof is possible, one field in which the meaning and the role of values can be definitively established, then, by analogy, we may acknowledge corresponding values in all other fields as well. And there is one field, he believes, in which the desired proof is possible—the field of cognition.

I

It is Rickert's contention that a philosophy centered exclusively on the object of cognition—which is the orientation of the sciences—is as untenable as is one centered exclusively on the subject. Only a philosophy which recognizes and preserves the essential role of both can deal effectively with the facts and values in human experience. Such a synthesis is impossible, however, so long as subject and object are taken to be nothing but "real entities"; for in that case the essentially Cartesian dualism of "physical reality" and "mental reality" disrupts the idea of "the whole of reality." Once the dualism has been introduced, it cannot be eliminated from our interpretation of the real. It is important, therefore, that we avoid it from the very beginning. The question is, How can this be accomplished?

In his attempt to answer this question, Rickert argues that "there is a something which lies beyond subject and object" and this "something," too, must be taken into consideration if we truly want to understand "the whole of reality." Instead of speaking of "the I and the non-I," the subject and the object, we ought to speak of "the real and the non-real," including both, subject and object, in "the real," while "that which is other than the real, when interpreted positively, is value and meaning" (C, p. 102).[1] Not to distinguish "being and meaning, existence and significance, reality and value leads to no end of confusion" (C, p. 103).

The fact that not everything is either physical or mental becomes evident, so Rickert maintains, when we consider objects which must be called unreal—objects which do not exist in space (as do bodies), and objects which do not exist in time (as do mental processes). Mathematical objects represent what is meant here. Although mental processes are involved when we think of mathematical objects, those objects themselves (such as triangles

[1]The capital letter preceding the pagination identifies the work in the BIBLIOGRAPHY.

and squares) are neither mental processes nor physical things; they are *ideal* objects with a mode of being that is all their own.

But even this reference to ideal objects is only part of the story because in our experience we also encounter the *meaning* of true statements. That such meaning is not identical with mental processes is obvious, for the processes differ from person to person whereas different individuals who understand a true statement understand the same "theoretical meaning." Moreover, mental processes occur in time, whereas the meaning of a true statement is timeless. It is not a process at all. And neither is it identical with the object the statement is about—be that object real or ideal. The meaning of the statement, "An equilateral triangle is an acute-angled triangle," for example, is itself neither an equilateral nor an acute-angled triangle, nor is it the identity of the two or any triangle at all. It is thus evident that, in addition to real and ideal objects, we encounter in our experience "something" that does not exist at all and yet *is* "something" rather than nothing. This means, however, that we cannot rest satisfied with the conception of the world according to which "everything is either subject or object" (be the object real or ideal). We must allow for a "third" which transcends subject and object but, in itself, is not real at all. As Rickert sees it, "no science is possible unless the world includes the non-real (the 'third') along with the real," for "no science is possible without an understood true meaning" (C, p. 112).

II

The question now is, How are we to understand this "third" that is neither a real nor an ideal object, nor even a subject, and yet is not nothing?

Only two terms, Rickert maintains, are available for designating the "third," namely "value" and "validity." What this means Rickert hopes to demonstrate, first of all, in the realm of cognition; for only values basic to cognition, so he believes, can be strictly proven. Rickert does not deny that statements such as "This odor is pleasing," "The picture is beautiful," "This act is moral," and "This statement is true" are value judgments. He takes for granted that they are. But what he means to demonstrate is that even judgments which contain no "value words"—i.e., judgments of reality, such as "This piece of paper is real"—are intrinsically "acknowledgments of a value" (A, p. 191), and that it is precisely this fact that is the key to the whole problem of values.

III

It will be granted, Rickert believes, that only judgments can be said to be true (or false). Judgments, therefore, are inseparable from cognition. "Every cognition starts with a judgment, advances through judgments, and can culminate only in judgments. As actual, cognition consists in nothing but acts of judgment" (A, p. 184). A cognitive judgment, however, is never a matter of "indifferent contemplation." Its truth is not simply "there" but is also of interest to us. As persons engaged in the pursuit of knowledge we cannot brush it aside. "Truth grips us and compels us to take an attitude toward it" (C, p. 115). And this would be impossible, Rickert argues, "if truth were not *that* value without which there would be no cognition of what exists"; if in our investigations of the real and the ideal we did not value and therefore seek it. Cognition itself would have no value if truth were not a value. In fact, it would not be cognition at all if truth did not make it such.

It is evident, therefore, Rickert believes, that a cognitive judgment is not simply an affirmation or a denial but is at the same time an approval or a disapproval—"the taking of an attitude toward a value." That is to say, it is a valuing. "What I approvingly affirm I can affirm only because of its value; and what I disapprovingly deny I must deny because of its disvalue" (A, p. 186). This means that "in its intrinsic logical sense, cognition is an acknowledgment of values or a rejection of disvalues; and erring must be understood as a rejection of values and an acknowledgment of disvalues" (A, p. 188). Stated otherwise, "wherever we speak of truth, there we speak of a value," for truth and value are here one and the same "unreal something" (C, p. 113).

But something else is also evident; for if truth is a value which

demands acknowledgment—which demands approval and realization—if there is to be cognition at all, then it confronts us as an
ought. This does not mean that value and the *ought* are one of
the same, for the *ought* is merely the way in which at least some
values force us into taking an attitude. But the fact that a value
can thus confront us as an *ought* underscores the further fact that
a value differs in principle from anything that exists, for "that
which merely exists can never assume the form of an *ought*"
(C, p. 116). And this implies that only the real, the ideal, and
the values—all taken together—constitute the whole of the
world. This, however, quite obviously leads to the question of
the status or mode of being of the values.

Realistically inclined thinkers in the Platonic tradition tend to
regard values as "something real"; and their point of view is
largely in harmony with ordinary linguistic usage according to
which "real things with which values are associated are themselves referred to as 'values'" (A, p. 194). In the interest of
clarity, however, it is imperative that here a distinction be made.
To be sure, objects exist which are said to have value. A work of
art is such an object. But it is obvious that the value of these objects is not identical with the physical objects themselves or with
any of their constitutive qualities. In the case of a painting, for
example, the canvas, the paint and the laquer are not part of the
value which the painting has. They belong to the purely physical
sphere—although the value of the painting would not be "there"
if they did not exist. In order to avoid all possibility of confusion,
Rickert suggests that the "real objects" which have value be called
"goods" in order to distinguish them from the value which they
have. If this terminology is adopted, then all "values" with which
the economists are concerned are goods rather than values, for
they are objects or things that *have* value. The mode of being of
values, however, has as yet not been solved.

Values are, of course, always related to a subject. More specifically, they are related to an act in and through which the subject
values an object. And this seems to suggest that a real object is
transformed into a good if and only if a subject "ascribes a value
to it" or "values" it. Does this mean that the act of valuing and
the value merge into one? The question has often been answered

in the affirmative. In all such cases, however, value has lost its independent significance and has been transformed into a purely mental phenomenon. This "psychologistic" interpretation, though widely accepted, is in Rickert's view one of the most confused and confusing "philosophical prejudices" and an obstacle to a successful solution of the value problem. It is necessary, therefore, to emphasize the distinction between values and the mental acts of the valuing subject no less than that between values and the things that have value. But this means that values, qua values, belong to a "conceptual sphere" other than that of real existents. Values do not exist—not even in an "ideal sphere"; they are *valid* (A, p. 195).

IV

Rickert's use of the term *gelten,* here translated as "being valid," may cause linguistic difficulties for the English-speaking reader; for it may be translated in various ways, of which "being in force" is perhaps the most relevant here but, by itself, does not quite express Rickert's meaning.

Also, we must distinguish Rickert's use of the term *gelten* from Lotze's use of it. The latter spoke of the "validity" of Platonic ideas in contrast to the "existence" of the world of things and events. Rickert, not being a Platonist, points out that it is a violation of linguistic usage to say of anything "which is simply there" or which "exists" that it is *valid.* This holds with respect to ideal objects no less than with respect to real things. An equilateral triangle, for example, "exists" as an ideal object; but it cannot be said to be valid in the sense in which theorems concerning it are valid. "Even an insight or cognition is not valid insofar as it exists as a mental event but only insofar as it expresses a true meaning, i.e., a value" (C, p. 122).

But the term "validity" has a perfectly good meaning outside the cognitive situation as well. A ticket to a theater, for instance, may be valid or not valid. If it is valid, it is valuable—valuable, not because it exists (although it must exist in order to be a ticket at all), but because it is valid. The same may be said of any contract or law or similar "object." Rickert proposes, therefore, that we interpret the meaning of "validity" as being co-extensive with the meaning of the term "value." "Aside from the term 'value' we have no better term than 'validity' for the designation of that which is neither a real nor an ideal object or event" (C, p. 126). And just as value always remains a value and never becomes something real, so validity can never coincide with anything real. In every true judgment, however, we acknowledge value and validity.

It must be noted, furthermore, that true judgments are valid not merely for some particular individual or group of individuals, but absolutely. They are valid in a "metaphysical perspective" which transcends any and all subjective restrictions. The situation is similar, so Rickert points out, when we deal with values and their validity. But we must not interpret this in a simplicistic manner.

Relative to value-free conditions, even individually subjective valuations are a "positive value-something" (*ein positives Wert-Etwas*); but, being purely subjective, they have no objective validity. Rickert places them in parallel with sensory illusions. There are other values which all subjects pursue and which, therefore, appear to be universally valid. Their validity, however, depends upon actual valuations and therefore is as subjectively conditioned as are the valuations of the first type. Sensuous pleasures exemplify the values here involved. But what Rickert aims at is to ascertain whether or not there are values that are truly objective—objective in the sense that they do not depend upon actual valuations but have a validity that is universal and provides a standard for all other valuations as well. The problem is how to interpret the status and the nature of such "absolute values."

Rickert approaches the problem by first attempting to clarify the status of the subject in its relation to values. To what extent, for example, are values merely subjective valuations? Are they simply our human and, perhaps, all-too-human projections or are they independent of our volitions? What is actually at stake here, Rickert finds, is man's position within the context of reality, and the meaning of human existence itself.

It may, of course, be argued that moral, aesthetic, and religious values have validity only insofar as they are "posited" by us; and, strictly speaking, such a thesis cannot be disproven. The situation is different, however, as far as the "theoretical values" are concerned; for to maintain that they, too, depend on our positing them and on nothing else entails consequences that are totally unacceptable.

As Rickert sees it, a denial of the objective validity of "theoretical values" is at the same time a denial of the possibility of attaining true knowledeg about the real world. This is so, he points out, because the validity of statements concerning that world cannot possibly depend on the volitions of any actual subject. At least the statement that there exists a subject capable of volitional acts must be objectively valid or true; otherwise it makes no sense to maintain that the validity of values depends on the will of such a subject. This inescapable dilemma suffices to disprove the thesis that the validity of all values depends on the will of a subject, for it shows that "the objective validity of theoretical values is the presupposition of our knowledge of the objectively real world," that "the validity of values is here basic" (C, p. 144). Proceeding from this vantage point Rickert now argues that the more consistent we are in interpreting reality objectively, the more evident will also be the primacy of objectively valid values. Our cognitive acts transcend mere subjectivity and achieve "transsubjective significance" insofar as they are directed toward the attainment of objectively valid values. In the area of cognition the conception of such values is therefore a necessary supplement to our volitions. It is in the pursuit of such values that cognitive acts cease to be merely mental phenomena and in truth become acts of cognition.

But man pursues not only knowledge. His whole history is evidence of cultural achievements in a much broader sense; and all of these are also manifestations of his commitment to values. We find ourselves enmeshed in social situations of many kinds, for we are members of families, communities, nations and, ultimately, of the whole of the human race; and our relations to all of them are determined not only by the fact of our existence here and now but also, and more importantly, by our valuations and value-determined responses. Add to the social patterns and conditions the large areas of aesthetic and religious activities, and the cultural context within which we find ourselves is inexhaustible in its complexities. But values acknowledged as valid are basic to it all. They alone give meaning to our very existence as human beings. They alone are the key to cultural living. And a value theory must deal with them all.

V

But let us return for a moment to Rickert's thesis that only the values that are basic to cognition—the so-called "theoretical values"—can be strictly proven, and that every cognitive judgment is not only an affirmation or a denial but also "the taking of an attitude toward a value," toward truth (A, p. 186; B, p. 676),

When we judge anything, so Rickert's argument is, we are restrained by the value revealed in our "sense of certainty" (*Gewissheitsgefühl*). That is to say, if our affirmation or denial is to be cognitive at all, it cannot be arbitrary. The restraint we experience is well known in logic and in epistemology as *Denknotwendigkeit*—as the necessity, that is, to think in a certain way rather than in some other. Not only do the laws of logic impose such a necessity, but the recognition of even the simplest fact is an acknowledgment of the necessity to judge in a particular way and not just in any way we please. If something is rightly to be called "red" or "real," the cognizing subject must be under the necessity so to judge it; and this necessity—this *Urteilsnotwendigkeit*—extends to all cases of genuine cognition. Indeed, our thinking is cognition only when it thinks its object the way that object really is. In cognition, therefore, the subject is under a kind of compulsion, under "the necessity of an *ought*" (A, p. 201; B, p. 677).

If the reader should hesitate to concede that the "object" of cognition imposes an *ought* upon the subject, Rickert suggests that he may find it less objectionable to regard the *ought* as that factor in cognition which gives judgments their "objectivity" (*Gegenständlichkeit*). But this is merely a change in terminology which alters nothing as far as the facts are concerned. It remains true that in all cognitive situations the subject is confronted with an *ought* as the standard which must be acknowledged if there is to be cognition at all (A, p. 222; B, pp. 678–680).

The assumption of a transcendent reality existing "beyond" or "behind" the world of phenomena, Rickert continues, could never serve as a basis for knowledge because, being transcendent, such a world could never be encountered in experience as something to be "affirmed." What is "given" is at all times but a content of consciousness. But we can ascribe "the form of reality" (*Wirklichkeitsform*) to such a content when, in a judgment, we combine that content and that form which in any particular case "*ought* to be combined affirmatively" (A, p. 223)—when we affirm in a judgment what *ought* to be affirmed. The *ought*, therefore, is foundational to all cognition, including that of reality itself (B, pp. 686–687).

In a sense, Rickert's position here is an "immanentism." As he puts it: "As far as the *content* of cognition is concerned, there is no reason for transcending what is immanent; in fact, there is no possibility of doing so" (A, p. 223). Rickert, nevertheless, repudiates (Machian) positivism and all forms of immanentism, asserting that "in truth, we can speak of *cognition* . . . and not merely of a 'convenient' arranging of the contents of consciousness." The difference lies in the fact that "every judgment is the acknowledgment of an *ought*—of an *ought,* that is, which is grounded in the necessity of judging in a certain way and in no other" (*Urteilsnotwenigkeit*). This *ought* "stands opposed" to the "merely thinking subject"—to the subject, that is, which merely arranges the contents of its own consciousness—and in this sense is an "object" (A, p. 224).[2]

But if the very foundation of knowledge is, thus, an *ought,* then it follows at once that the theoretical aspects of cognition, as theoretical, lie entirely within the sphere of *values;* for "only a value can function as that *ought* which, as necessarily valid, demands an affirmative acknowledgment on the part of the subject" (A, p. 225). Value, in the form of an *ought* is thus constitutive

[2]The translation of *entgegenstehen* as "to stand opposed to" and of *Gegenstand* as "object," although the best possible, does not reflect the interrelation of the terms in German: *gegenstehen-Gegenstand,* though, of course, the Latin verb *objicere* of which *objectus* is the past participle shows the same relationship.

of the "theoretical object" and, therefore, of all knowledge as well. However, we must not overlook the fact that there is a difference between *value* as such and the *ought*.

This difference becomes quite clear when we analyze the basic cognitive situation. In that situation a subject, responding to the *ought* of a judgmental necessity, combines a given content of experience with its appropriate form. "Form and content belong together": this particular "content" *ought* to have this particular "form"; and the subject, aiming at knowledge, must acknowledge the *ought*. All true judgments are affirmations of it, and all objectivity (*Gegenständlichkeit*) consists in the true judgments. But when we now take the subject out of the cognitive situation, then the "form" which the experiential content *ought* to have becomes a value. That is to say, "the *ought* conceived as separated from a subject" is what Rickert calls *value*. It persists as potentially an *ought* for *any* subject that may enter into a cognitive relation with the "object" in question; and it persists whether it is actually acknowledged by a subject or not. It must be noted, however, that the "value accent" has now been shifted. It no longer lies between "form" and "content," as heretofore, but lies entirely on the side of the "form." "Form, as theoretical value, now stands opposed to a formless—i.e., a value-free and theoretically indifferent—content." And thus "there is, after all, a crucial difference between value and the *ought*" (A, pp. 226–228).

VI

When we now ask what, precisely, is the status of a value, Rickert replies that values do not "exist" but are "valid"—*sie gelten* (A, p. 260). The *ought* reveals their "unreality" (*Unwirklichkeit*) but also their validity. Still, "without a will that acknowledges or demands this validity there are no values that are valid." The will, of course, belongs to "the realm of the real" and thus constitutes a basis within that realm for what in itself is not real—the values. "If the subject and its volitions were to disappear, so would the value as value" (C, p. 128).

If this interpretation is to be meaningful, then a criterion is needed which enables us to distinguish between what exists or is real and what is valid. Such a criterion, Rickert maintains, is the principle of negation; for negation is unequivocal when it pertains to existence but is ambiguous when applied to values. Thus, the negation of the existence of something always means simply the affirmation of its non-existence; the negation of a value, however, although it may mean merely the absence of a value and thus a value indifference, may also mean the affirmation of a negative value, of that which is not valid, and therefore of an *ought-not* or an "injunction" (*Verbot*) (A, p. 261; C, pp. 117–118). This contrast between positive value (or value in the narrow sense) and negative value (or disvalue) has no counterpart in the realm of existence.

Various counter-instances which might be cited involve ambiguities that actually strengthen Rickert's argument. Thus, if it be said that the negation of "human" (*menschlich*) may not be merely a negation of human existence but also the affirmation of the negative value "inhuman (*unmenschlich*), Rickert points out that the term "human" is itself ambiguous. On the one hand, it is a purely existential concept. On the other hand, however, it is also a value concept, a norm. The negation of it in its existential meaning simply asserts the non-existence of something human —be that a quality or a human being. The negation of it in its value-meaning, however, is the acknowledgment of a disvalue— "inhuman" (A, p. 265).

Similar to the dichotomy "human-inhuman" is the dichotomy "sense-nonsense" (*Sinn-Unsinn*). In its broad meaning the term "sense" encompasses both, "positive sense and negative sense or nonsense," and stands in contrast only to what is "sense-indifferent." In its narrow meaning, however, the term indicates "positive sense" only and thus stands in opposition to "negative sense" or "nonsense" no less than to the "sense-indifferent"; and this, too, is a value contrast. We must note also that only statements have "theoretical meaning"; that their meaning is either "positive sense" or "nonsense"; that true statements always have "positive sense" and that their "sense" therefore is "necessarily a positive theoretical value" (A, p. 267). Moreover, since a true statement is universally valid and therefore independent of any particular act of judgment, its meaning is understandable only as a "theoretical value-pattern" (*theoretisches Wertgebilde*) having "transcendent validity." It is a "transcendent value."

Rickert makes it clear, however, that here—as everywhere in transcendental philosophy—we are dealing basically with a "problem of form" (*Formproblem*). That is to say, "if any statement whatsoever is to be true, its objective content must have the form of the positive theoretical sense" (A, p. 268). And since logic is "the *a priori* of the theoretical meaning of all true statements about the real," its concern is with the values that must be accepted as valid if we are to attain knowledge of a real world. Such values, of course, do not themselves "exist" but are the "transcendentally valid" presuppositions of our behavioral and cultural sciences no less than of our natural sciences. If they were not valid, we could not even speak truly or meaningfully of "real things."

Kant's much-discussed conception of the *a priori* finds here a new interpretation and a new significance. As Rickert sees it, the *a priori* is not a "psychological reality," not a "certainty," not a "predisposition" or a "force" that engenders knowledge. It is "neither an ideal nor a real existent" but the "form of meaning" —a "theoretical value" that is transcendentally valid and without whose validity no statements concerning real or ideal objects or events would have any meaning. There would not even be "perceptions or other cognitions *a posteriori*"; for "the object of cognition is always a content of experience in transcendentally valid theoretical value-form." This means, however, that "only a value which is self-contained, which in its validity is independent not only of every actual demand or acknowledgment but independent also of every relation to a subject for which it is valid, is the transcendent object *in its formal aspect*"; and this means that in the area of cognition the essence of what is transcendent consists exclusively and entirely in its "absolute validity (A, p. 274). This absolute validity is value as such—"pure value," as Rickert calls it—value antecedently to its being an *ought* for a subject.

If we begin our investigation with an analysis of actual cognition, we become entangled in psychological processes and "the object, the value, the theoretical meaning has no validity." It occurs only as a *norm* for man and "everything appears anthropo-morphically tinged." In its absolute validity, however, value "lies high above everything human and therefore also above all judging and all acts of acknowledgment" (A, p. 276). Norm and validity are thus by no means one and the same. This fact is im-portant for Rickert's position—as may be seen from the following consideration.

According to a widely held view, every normative discipline has a theoretical foundation the construction of which is the task of epistemology. Norms, however, cannot be deduced from "what exists"; and even if they could be so deduced, this would not eliminate the antecedent value-basis, for, as we have just seen, all cognition—including that of epistemology itself—presupposes the validity of values. This means that "the 'theoretical foundation' of norms can be laid only by a value theory." "Certain it is," Rickert points out, "that every normative discipline presupposes purely theoretical results which, in themselves, are not norms. . . . But equally certain it is that the theoretical foundations of a normative discipline are values that are valid, and that only be-cause of the validity of these values the *ought* can serve as a guide to acts of judgment" (A, p. 277). And this means that the norms and the *ought* are in this sense derivative or secondary.

VII

Every act of cognition, so we have seen, is characterized by the intrinsic certainty of a true judgment. This certainty, however, in its "transcendent significance"—i.e., in its reference to some ideal or real object—cannot be accounted for in terms of mental processes as merely mental. And neither can we explain why an *ought* arises which, on the one hand, is connected with a mental state and which, on the other hand, is valid though independent of every actually existing subject. It simply is a fact that the "sub-jective real being"—the subject and its mental acts—is assurance of a trans-subjective non-real necessity. As Rickert puts it: "An immanent mental state discloses the transcendent validity of an *ought* that is acknowledged in a judgment" (A, p. 291). To demand an explanation of this, he argues, makes no sense because every conceivable explanation depends itself upon the very fact to be explained.

It is, of course, possible to deny that certainty is a "feeling," an immanent mental state; and it is equally possible to avoid the term "certainty" altogether or to deny that cognition is always a matter of "necessary judgments." But this, Rickert argues, is merely a matter of terminology; for it can not be denied that cognizing is always a mental process in which there must be given that which assures us of what is "more than merely mental," namely, "the independent meaning or content as a valid value," "the affirmation of an *ought*" (A, p. 292). In other words, cognition is never merely a passive observation. It is "the taking of an attitude, a valuing," and is thus "in line with the moral and the aesthetic and, perhaps, the religious attitudes which, despite their difference from cognition, are also the taking of an attitude toward values" (A, p. 293).

The parallelism is especially clear in the case of cognitive and moral attitudes; for "in both cases the values toward which an attitude is taken are unconditionally or 'categorically' valid." No "if" is involved. "In both cases a value is acknowledged simply because it is a value; and an *ought* is acknowledged simply because it is valid" (A, p. 293). This does not mean, however, that aesthetic and religious experiences do not involve values that are valid; for they do (C, pp. 151–152). It merely means that in these fields the evidence is not so compelling.

To be sure, if there should be someone who never asserts anything or who does not want to know truth, he would not have to acknowledge the "validity of the transcendent *ought*"; but he also would have to abandon all hope of ever attaining knowledge. Cognition and, therefore, knowledge presuppose the "will to cognize or to obtain knowledge," "the will to discover truth." This will is the acknowledgment of truth as a value to be attained and the acceptance of an *ought* that necessitates certain judgments rather than others because they alone are true. Once the subject has committed himself to the pursuit of truth, he can neither alter nor abandon the *ought* or its transcendent validity (A, pp. 309–311). We can now generalize this fact and say (with Rickert) that an *ought* is encountered when, and only when, a subject acknowledges a positive value; and, correspondingly, an *ought-not* is encountered when, and only when, a subject faces a negative value—e.g., nonsense or error (A, p. 337). But it is clear also that only that which is understood as a value can have the "dignity" of an ultimate principle determinative of an attitude toward it (A, p. 357); and only in acknowledging a value that is valid does the will of the individual empirical subject rise above mere subjectivity (C, pp. 146–47; B, p. 690) and does the individual himself attain the "dignity" of a human being. "The absolute value of the autonomous will derives from the fact that the will is the presupposition of every possible realization of unconditionally valid or absolute values" (B, p. 692).

This interpretation of the human scene entails Rickert's repudiation of every empirical realism which regards reality as "self-contained" and as in every respect independent of the cognizing subject; and it entails, furthermore, his commitment to a transcendental idealism which understands "everything that goes beyond the content of perception as the totality of imperatives which demand that the actually "given" be ordered and structured in accordance with certain forms (A, pp. 294–295). Seen in this light, the "object of cognition" is the terminus of a judgment which, guided by an *ought* that reflects an "absolutely valid theoretical value" (truth), combines an experiential content with its appropriate "logical form" (A, p. 432). The whole of reality (*Wirklichkeitstotalität*) thus permits only a value-theoretical, not an ontological, interpretation.

In this correlation of a valid value and a valuing subject epistemology transcends itself. Not only has the opposition of theoretical and practical disciplines been eliminated—since all of them involve the pursuit of a value and therefore an *ought*—but the possibility has been revealed of developing a unified interpretation of the whole of human existence—an interpretation which is concerned with values that are valid and with their realization through subjects that acknowledge them. It is here that we encounter the very meaning of our existence.

VIII

When values are realized, they are realized as "goods" and are encountered in any given culture. In fact, culture itself is a "good" and "cultural goods" are, as it were, the "precipitate" of values (C, p. 320). It is "cultural history," therefore, rather than natural science or psychology that is pre-eminently relevant to value problems. The danger in this fact is that, in avoiding psychologism or a reductionistic naturalism, we may now fall victim to an equally untenable historicism. In order to escape this fate, we must clearly understand that value theory is not history; that history merely provides subject-matter for value theory.

Now, history shows clearly that all culture presupposes a communal or social existence in the broadest sense. Not only does a culture arise as the result of social interactions, its continuation, its very "life," depends upon them. Culture separated from all society is simply a fiction. This implies, however, that culture is the common concern of the members of any society; that the acknowledgment of its values is *expected* of all individuals who wish to "belong"; and that the "unity" of a cultural community lies in the fact that the members accept shared values as "norms" for all. To be sure, not all members of a community share all of the "cultural goods," for culture is much too complex and there are degrees of "participation" as there are degrees of appreciation. Perhaps no individual ever accepts all values that are acknowledged in his society.

There is one field, however, (so Rickert points out) in which "every mature and reasonable person participates to a certain degree, accepting its values as binding for him." This is the "realm of the mores," of "customs imbued with an ethical significance" (*das Reich der Sitten*). Of all aspects of man's social existence this is the most important, for it is constitutive of every cultural community, and the problems we face with respect to all cultural values—the problems of their validity—are most readily discernible here.

History shows that wherever human beings live together there certain customs and modes of behavior are developed and the members of the community are expected to conform. Non-conformance, because it is disruptive, is disapproved. The facts seem to indicate that the validity of the customs depends entirely on a general consensus and lacks a truly compelling or objective significance. Such an interpretation, however, misses what is crucial in the situation. Also, if compliance with customs and mores is simply a matter of habituation, it is not really a moral action. It is the latter only when it is the result of a conscious and deliberate choice; when compliance is recognized and accepted as being "right." That is to say, we act morally only when our will is determined by what we believe *ought* to be done. Basic is here that we recognize and acknowledge an imperatival necessity which transcends the prevailing customs and mores but is valid just the same. Only when we respond to this transcendent *ought* do we act autonomously and, therefore, morally. As Rickert puts it: "Man is moral in the widest sense of the term when he does what *ought* to be done by acknowledging in free decision a given value as valid" (C, p. 327) and when in the light of this value he evaluates the customs and the mores themselves; when he accepts particular modes of action, not because they are the established mores which most (if not all) members of his community happen to accept, but because he sees in them *objectively valid* norms which, being objectively valid, *ought* to be accepted. The idea of morality is thus inseparable from that of "objectively valid values" (C, p. 329), and ethics is not a social science but, basically, a value theory.

In addition to the moral values, we encounter in every human community also certain non-moral "goods"—"goods" that "lie outside the sphere of action" and whose "valuation is not transformed into a deed" (C, p. 323). These are the "works of art"—the "edifices, statues, paintings, poems, dramas, musical compositions" and the like—whose values are "constitutive of aesthetic objects and of the artistic significance of these objects," values that are comprehended only in "contemplative intuition" (*Schauen*) (C, p. 334).

Contemplation and intuition, Rickert continues, are words describing an attitude which, "in its intrinsic meaning, does justice to the harmony, the self-containedness, and the wholeness of a work of art just as in the realm of ethics a will which determines itself to action expresses best the nature of moral freedom as autonomy." More precisely, Rickert holds that "with the same necessity with which moral man strives toward practical activity of his whole personality within the social group, the value of beauty restrains all volition and action and demands a withdrawal of the subject from social activity in the interest of a calm contemplation and an impersonal surrender to the object" (C, p. 334). Whosoever speaks of "art" thus presupposes "the objectivity of a special species of validities" (C, p. 335)—validities which are not subjectively grounded and therefore do not depend on the whims and wishes of individuals or groups of individuals. To determine what these values are is the task of aesthetics and does not concern us at the moment. Suffice it to have pointed out that in the realm of the arts we encounter a third type of values and validities alongside the cognitive and the moral.

But the cultural life of a community finds expression also in religion. Whether or not religion can be understood entirely as a matter of values may remain a moot question. It cannot be doubted, however, that values are deeply involved in all religious attitudes and activities. The key concept here is that of the "holy." Although this embodies the ideas of infinite perfection and of the divine, and thus of a value which far transcends what is merely human, it has validity for human beings as the supreme standard of all valuations. History shows that wherever and under whatever circumstances men have regarded human beings and human affairs as imperfect, they have acknowledged the validity of values which transcend the human sphere—even if the existence of God as the embodiment of such values has remained problematic.

The very meaning of the concept "holy" implies absolute perfection. It implies, in other words, that the realization of the "holy" is ever unattainable for man but that, nevertheless, it is an "unavoidable ideal" (*ein unvermeidliches Ideal*); that the religious person accepts it as "necessarily binding," as an absolute norm. And wherever there is faith in this ideal of the "holy," there is religion in one form or another.

If this religion is essentially contemplative—i.e., if it envisions the self-abandonment of the individual in the divine (as is the case in Asian mysticism)—then the religious life is akin to our aesthetic experience. The difference between them is essentially one of degree only. "What fills but a moment in the life of aesthetic man—the impersonal abandonment to the object and the dissociation from all social problems and events—now involves the whole of man's existence" (C, p. 342). But if religion is of a different kind, the ideal may demand action—working cooperatively with one's fellowmen toward the realization of the "Kingdom of God" even on earth. Religious life is then akin to man's moral existence, although again there is a difference in degree. "God himself is now conceived as active, personal and social, and through his communion with God man's whole existence takes on an eminently personal, active and social character" (C, p. 342).

Two basic types of religion must thus be distinguished—the contemplative and the activistic—one stressing the withdrawal from the world, the other emphasizing personal effectiveness in the world; one advocating the depersonalization of the individual, the other insisting upon the development of the personal self. Unless these differences are taken into account, so Rickert points out, we fail to understand the nature of religion and of its intrinsic values. Significant is the fact that religion is never "just another facet" of human existence; that, on the contrary, it demands total involvement. This may mean that religion enhances other cultural activities and values; that it furthers the arts and the sciences without destroying their independence. But it may also mean that religion tends to "despise the world" and all that is in it; that it tends to suppress free inquiry and artistic creation. This latter fact in particular shows that religious values are never indifferent relative to a given culture and the values inherent in it; that, in fact, they themselves can be subsumed under the broader category "cultural values" (Kulturwerte), along with the theoretical, the ethical, and the aesthetic.

Within a given culture we may, thus, respond to four types of values which, taken together, give meaning and significance to our existence as human beings. As we acknowledge the validity of these values we free ourselves from all forms of naturalism and from every psychologistic conception of the value structure. We exist as members of a cultural community. That different individuals in different cultures (or in the same culture, for that matter) may and do mean something different when they speak of "the true," "the good," "the beautiful," and "the holy" is, of course, a fact; but it is not crucial. What *is* crucial is that in every culture, from the most primitive to the most advanced, certain valuations imply the claim (*Anspruch*) that the values toward which an attitude is to be taken have an objective validity that is trans-subjective and trans-cultural as well and is thus a challenge for the whole of mankind. This is crucial because it implies that the development of man's cultural existence, as reflected in his history, has a significant objective meaning (B, pp. 694–703).

IX

One final problem must now be considered. Rickert deals with it in his essay "Vom System der Werte"—Concerning the System of Values.

The time of the great speculative systems of philosophy, Rickert believes, is a matter of the past. If philosophy, nevertheless, is to interpret the sense and the meaning of human existence, it must find a new approach to that existence. It must still aim at a systematic integration of all aspects of human experience and especially of the values accepted as valid; but it must realize also that the "material" to be included in any system is historically conditioned; that it is in development and, therefore, essentially incomplete. Nobody can anticipate what the future will bring. We do not know what new values will be acknowledged in time. Even the search for truth for the sake of truth is a relatively late phenomenon in human culture. "The only thing certain is that so far man's historical development has always brought forth something new" (D, p. 298).

Under these circumstances the system aimed at by philosophy must always be an "open" one. How is this possible? How can we construct a system which, on the one hand, is comprehensive and all-inclusive, and which, on the other hand, can accommodate all that is new in the future course of history? It can be done,

Rickert points out, if the system remains "open" with respect to the historical aspects of culture but is structured in terms of factors that transcend all history without coming in conflict with it. A merely classificatory scheme could be such a system; but classification alone is insufficient. If the system is to disclose the sense or meaning of human existence, then we need also an "order of rank" (*Rankordnung*) of values, or at least a criterion by means of which that order can be determined. That is to say, a systemic integration of human experience must enable us to subsume under the necessities of an order of rank the "accidentals of the merely historical," and must enable us to do so in such a way that "within the closed context of values there is still room for the openness of historical existence" (D, p. 299).

The difficulties of such an approach arise, of course, from the fact that the "material" which alone discloses the values is in ceaseless development. More precisely, it is the idea of development itself that apparently entails elements of uncertainty. We must realize, however,—so Rickert argues—that, although everything is in development, development itself is not. Whatever is valid as presupposition of any development is itself beyond development and, therefore, is of an a-historical nature. "Absolute evolutionism" is thus an untenable position.

Applied to the basic problems of value theory this means that even though the historical culture patterns are continuously changing, their "formal presuppositions" are not affected by that change. Among those presuppositions are "certain values that are valid," "certain actual goods which embody the unreal but valid values," and "subjects who take a valuing attitude toward values and goods, for only for such subjects can there be a world-view as interpretation of their life's meaning." These concepts are as yet indeterminate as to "material content." Insofar, however, as they refer to factors that are present in every cultural situation and are in this sense trans-historical, it may be possible with their help to derive "formal concepts of levels in the realization of values which stand in a definite order of rank for all subjects that must take an attitude toward them" but remain "open" as far as "historical content" is concerned (D, p. 300).

Since the "meaning of life" depends upon the order of rank

of values and is always "meaning for a subject," Rickert suggests that we begin our attempt at integration with an analysis of the "valuing attitudes" of the subject. When we do so, we find that, in his efforts to actualize values in "goods," everyone presupposes a goal and finds his actions to be meaningful only when he achieves that goal or when he at least approaches its realization. In other words, he aims at an "end"; and when that has been reached, his action is also "at an end." But this final stage is attained only when the "end has been *fully* realized." We can say, therefore, that intrinsic in our goal-directed actions there is a tendency toward a "full ending" (*Voll-Endung*)[3] (D, p. 301); and insofar as this tendency is of the very essence of every value-realization it is also "determinative" (*massgebend*) for every order of rank of values and may therefore be regarded as one of the "formal factors" that possess "more than merely historical significance."

It is true, of course, that every realization of a value involves a "content" that is made "valuable" in the process. This "content" may be conceived as consisting of a "whole and its parts," and let us assume that the "whole" is "boundless" (*unübersehbar*) in the sense that it consists of an indefinite and therefore perhaps an infinite number of parts. If we then correlate the contrast of the "un-ending whole" and its finite parts with the tendency toward "full-ending," several kinds of value-realizations in "goods" are possible. Thus, if the tendency toward "full-ending" is directed toward the "inexhaustible whole," no finite subject can ever complete the task. Whatever goals may be attained are but stages in an unending process. If, on the other hand, the tendency toward "full-ending" is restricted to a finite part of the whole, then the goal may be attained and we are dealing with a range of "goods" that can be characterized as "full-ending particularities." But a third "realm" is also at least possible—namely, the synthesis of the two that have been identified; and this third "realm" may be

---

[3]Rickert here takes advantage of certain peculiarities of the German language for which there are no parallel devices in English. The intended relationship between *Voll-Endung* (full ending) and *Vollendung* (perfection) is obvious in German; but I have not been able to find an English equivalent. Of course, the Latin *perfectus,* past participle of *perficere,* "to finish," suggests the same root meaning.

referred to as "full-ending totality" (*voll-endliche Totalität*), and this, Rickert maintains, is the ultimate goal that any striving toward value realization can have. At the same time, this completes the number of types of "goods" that necessarily exemplify values (D, p. 302).

To be sure, the concepts of the three levels that have just been indicated tell us nothing about the specific "content meaning" (*Inhaltsbedeutung*) of human existence. In their empty formalism, however, they are trans-historical; and this alone is now important, for it implies an order of rank of values. In order to see that this is so, consider first the first two levels. If the highest goal is the forming of the totality, we, as finite beings, must project this goal into the indefinite future and must be satisfied with some stage or stages in the on-going process. But if the "full-ending" is to be achieved in the present, then we must abandon the "whole," the totality, as our goal and must be satisfied with only a "part." Both alternatives have their respective advantages as also their deficiencies. They are in a sense co-ordinate alternatives. But the third value realm—that of the "full-ending totality"—combines the advantages of the first two and eliminates their deficiencies. "It therefore contains the highest good that we can possibly conceive." It also casts new light upon the relationship of the first two levels to each other, for it is evident that "the possibility of an approach to the full-ending totality of future goods possesses the highest dignity" (*Würde*) (D, p. 304).

But another perspective must now be considered. As Rickert sees it, historical events involve persons, social contexts, and various activities; and these three factors are interrelated. Every personal action ultimately concerns some other person—even if it does so only in an indirect manner. Every action, therefore, has its social aspect. This fact, so Rickert points out, justifies us in grouping together those "cultural goods" whose values pertain to "social persons," i.e., to communities. But this group does not include all cultural "goods." It does not include, for example, the "goods" available to contemplative and essentially a-social attitudes. The two groups together, however—the social and the contemplative or a-social—include all the "goods" there are, for it is inconceivable that there could be "goods" which are neither social nor a-social. Furthermore, the aesthetic and the logical values are characteristic of things, whereas the moral and social values pertain to persons; and this distinction also exhausts all possibilities.

But what is important in all this is the fact that in the perspective of contemplation the conception of the "whole" is one thing, and in the perspective of social action it is another. The former reveals a tendency toward monism; the latter does not. Wherever persons are involved as embodiments of values their individual differences must be reckoned with. Value realization in the social sphere is therefore intrinsically pluralistic (D, p. 306).

As far as Rickert is concerned, the distinction just made suffices to define six specific areas of "goods" that reveal an "order of rank" of all the values involved.

Since, "so far as possible, philosophy is to be scientific," Rickert considers, first, the area of science as a special part of culture. As he sees it, the scientific attitude is one of contemplation, and science itself is a "thing" rather than a person. It is one of the "social goods," but its value proper, truth, is not strictly a social value. Science aims at an understanding of the whole of human experience and, in this sense, is monistic in its basic tendency. But the "material content" with which science is concerned is inexhaustible. Science, therefore, can never achieve "full-ending." Every one of its achievements is but a stage in an unending process that aims at "un-ending totality." Opposed to its monistic tendency are two dualisms that can never be eliminated. One of these is the contrast of form and content. To be sure, only the combination of the two constitutes a "theoretical object," and in a true judgment this combination is affirmed; but this is precisely what emphasizes the contrast because, in order that their combination can be affirmed, they must be thought of as distinct.— The second dualism is the contrast of subject and object, and this also cannot be eliminated because, if there is to be cognition at all, the subject must be confronted by an object that is independent of it, otherwise there is no object that is to be known.

The second realm of values is that of the "works of art." Like science, art also is essentially contemplative. No matter how important a role art may play in the personal or the social life of man, its value, beauty, is essentially impersonal and a-social. However, unlike science, art does not point to the future but has its full significance in the present. Indeed, for many persons the aesthetic value is identical with "full-ending." Artistic form integrates part of the content of man's experience in such a way that it is separated from the rest of the world and from every progressive development. The work of art, in other words, is self-contained as a "full-ended" (*voll-endeter*) part of experience. The dualism of form and content has been overcome. "The norm is valid but silent," for in the aesthetic experience there is, strictly speaking, no judgment that combines form and content; there is only integrative contemplation—contemplative intuition (D, pp. 308–309). The contrast of subject and object, however, remains.

The question now is, Can the aesthetic level of "full-ending particularity" be surpassed? Rickert finds that it has been surpassed in some forms of religious mysticism—in Buddhism, for example. Here the claim is made that "the world in its totality is comprehended in contemplation" and that the subject is "totally absorbed in the All." Every form of dualism has thus been transcended. "All is the one God." Not only does monism attain its "full-ending" in such pantheism, but the impersonal and the a-social character of values also finds here its "purest expression." The individual is as nothing. Every social relation that presupposes at least two persons is submerged in the "All-One." "God alone is Everything" (D, pp. 309–310).

Rickert has thus distinguished three forms of contemplation and their respective "goods" or values as stages in a system that is emerging in man's cultural history. Leaving aside for a moment any reference to the personal, the social, and the activistic aspects of human existence, he points out that, in the perspective of "full-ending," those three forms exhaust all possible types of contemplative experience and that therefore the contemplative aspects of any future development in man's history must find their place in one or another of those three types (D, p. 310). The question is, Can similar distinctions be made when we consider the "activistic" areas of human experience, notably the moral and the religious?

Rickert finds that man's "moral life" is not as easily definable as are science, art, and pantheistic mysticism. He suggests, therefore, that we begin our investigation by considering what is indisputably relevant to moral issues: "the duty-conscious will of the autonomous person who voluntarily obeys the law" (D, p. 311). As a delimitation of the whole field of "the moral" this may be too narrow; but it must be admitted that the reference is at least to facts actually encountered in man's cultural existence, and that the values involved must find an appropriate place in any value system.

The situation is this: Wherever human beings interact, there emerges something we call "custom" (*Sitte*). Certain modes of behavior are expected of every member of the community. Through them the individual is bound to his society. As long as observance of such customs is essentially "instinctive" or merely habitual, it is of no further interest here. But when a person takes a deliberative attitude toward the customs—"explicitly approving some and rejecting others"—then "morality" (*Sittlichkeit*) comes into being as the autonomous acknowledgment of "duties" in the life of a community. This is an "attitude of will" that leads to actions of significance to all communal living— even when the actions are "anti-social" in tendency. What is at stake here is the value of the autonomous person as a person. Man's entire social life—in the family, the state, and the whole of his cultural history—must contribute to the enhancement of that value. Decisive in this situation is the "social interaction of persons." But since generations die and new generations take their place, ever new combinations of interrelationships emerge. The result is that the "totality of individual persons" and of social institutions is never complete. The tension between what *is* and what *ought to be* persists. Moreover, since the basic moral value is the duty-conscious person himself, the *ought* not only persists, it ought to persist; for without the acknowledgment of a norm, of an *ought,* there can be no freedom in the sense of personal autonomy and, therefore, no morality. But this means that man's moral existence implies an "un-ending totality" in the sphere of moral actions, of personal and social "goods" (D, pp. 312–313).

Man's inherent "tendency toward full-ending" presses on beyond any achievement in the moral sphere just as it does in science. But neither morality nor science suffers any dimunition of value because of it. A special problem arises, however, because, actually living only in the present, man is made "problematic" in his innermost being by a persistent concern with the future. So long as he works toward the realization of "trans-personal goods" (as he does in science), he may find inspiration in the thought that he is "working in the service of the future." But when his own person is at stake, then the thought that everything in his existence is but a "preliminary stage" (*Vorstufe*) becomes unbearable. There arises, therefore, most poignantly the necessity of finding an area of values in which man can come to a total "full-ending" but which, nevertheless, preserves the values of moral action and communal living. Is there such an area—such a special level of "full-ending"?

To this question Rickert gives an affirmative answer. It is necessary, however, to distinguish between "goods of the present personal life" and "socio-moral goods of the future." The former stand out in their "full-ending particularities" like "islands in the stream of an endless cultural development" but without becoming "works of art" or existing in timeless transcendency. Examples are love, kindness, friendship, and other personal relations that play important roles in the lives of individuals and that can be pursued to "full-ending" without disrupting the socio-cultural context or its development. But even anti-social attitudes find in this sphere an "eminent significance." Thus, we avoid "society" in order to "come to ourselves" in our solitude. Everyone knows the value of such "hours of loneliness," Rickert believes.

The examples given may suffice to indicate that the values of the "full-ending present of our personal existence" must not be omitted when we try to understand what gives meaning and significance to our lives. If it be argued that much of what is involved here is simply a matter of ordinary daily existence, Rickert replies that it is high time for philosophy to concern itself not only with what saints, heroes, and geniuses of science and art have regarded as the meaning of life—for they all have looked to the future for the justification of their work—, but also with what the average person feels and values here and now. That conflicts may arise between "moral duties" and the "goods of the full-ending life of the present" is perhaps unavoidable, but it supports rather than disproves Rickert's contention that we deal here with a new and specific level of values.

It is not possible to consider all the problems that arise here. One point, however, needs emphasis, for it transcends the "goods of the mere present" (*die reinen Gegenwartsgüter*) and, thus, is important for the structure of the whole system; it is this: The personal meaning of the life of one person is determined more by the "goods of the future" and the "endless labor" in pursuit of them, whereas the meaning of the life of others depends more on the "goods of the present and their full-ending." In actual fact, the valuations of the male pertain more to the values of the future, the valuations of the female to those of the present. But only a "one-sided moralistic fanatiscism of development and progress" will value the status of the woman lower than that of the man. Indeed, "femininity" is an especially important value in the sphere of "personal goods of the present." The woman's life has significance more because of what *is,* the man's life because of what he *does.* But only man and woman together are "the full human being." "Full-ending" consists in the union of what is essentially different in them and what, in this difference, is supplementary. In this sense, therefore, the "principle of love" is the highest value in the "full-ending personal life of the present" (D, p. 319).

But this idea of synthesis carries us a step further. As in the case of contemplative experience, so there opens up here the perspective of a third level which combines the first two without retaining their deficiencies. It is a perspective which "earthly love," despite its union of present and future, does not yet disclose; for "earthly love" is still afflicted with the "finitude of particularity." What is lacking is the "necessary connection with the whole of the personal universe." We thus face the problem of the "full-ending totality" of the values here involved. How are we to conceive the "terminus of this personal sequence"? A comparison with the levels of contemplation will give us an answer to this question.

There is the "monistic tendency toward full-ending" advanced from the theoretical dualism of form and content and the dualism of subject and object to the idea of the All-One. Here the "full-ending particularity" is a resolution of the tensions of the autonomous moral *ought,* but, at the same time, it has emphasized the manifoldness of individual existences. Every individual finds a particular "full-ending" in his own special way. The situation is therefore pluralistic, and this pluralism must be preserved. That is to say, we cannot find a resolution of the problem in an all-embracing pantheism. On the contrary, we must preserve the ideal of personal "self-full-ending"—which culminates in the idea of a personal God that must yet preserve the autonomy of the human individual. In this perspective, God and the world are separate and must remain so despite all tendencies toward a unification. God now is the "full-ending total person" relative to which human beings retain their independence. This type of religion supports life in the present no less than in the future by imbuing it with a value which that life cannot attain by itself. It brings the eternal down into the temporal, the divine into the human, the absolute into the relative, the "full-ending" into the "end-less" and the infinite, the "totality of the person" into the particular; and in doing so it gives meaning to what remains incomplete or even irrational in personal existence when viewed in the light of the perspectives previously discussed.

What Rickert means to argue here is not which particular religion is "true," but that the multitude of autonomous persons and the "personal God" of theism finds as readily a place in his value system as does an all-absorbing pantheism. Just as pantheism is the culmination of the "full-ending totality of the object," so theism is the "full-ending totality of the subject." In pantheism, however, man's personal, active, and social existence is ultimately submerged in a "poverty-stricken monism," whereas in theism the full pluralistic richness of human existence is deeply rooted in the eternal. The individuals work toward the realization of the "Kingdom of God on Earth" and, in doing so, rise above mere finitude. "In every respect—the personal, the activistic, and the social—the believer can hope to be redeemed from the curse of finitude" (D, pp. 319–321).

Rickert thus finds that the six categories of values which are a problem for philosophy have been brought into one system. To be sure, the arrangement is purely formal; but the system is "open" in the sense that all values which may yet emerge in the un-ending process of cultural development can find a place in it. But the system is not only "open"; it also provides a criterion for an "order of rank" of values in two forms—i.e., as viewed from the perspective of contemplation or that of action, respectively—each form consisting of three distinct levels. However, this "order of rank" is as yet purely formal. It is still an open question as to which of all the "goods" is to be regarded as the highest or the most central. And it is also still a question as to which of the two sequences of levels provides the best possible chance for the development of a unified world-view. Is monism or is pluralism the ultimate truth? It is not even certain at this point that philosophy can decide once and for all this particular issue or others of a similar nature. Perhaps it is up to each individual person to accept that point of view which gives most meaning to his own existence (D, pp. 322–323).

But let us assume for a moment that philosophy has been successful in solving all those problems. That is to say, let us assume (with Rickert) that philosophy has achieved a unified world-view which gives meaning and direction to human existence. The question then is, Where does philosophy itself fit into such a system of values? It cannot be classified with the sciences because their respective orientations differ radically, philosophy aiming at "full-ending totality" whereas the sciences, being entirely object-orientated, do not. But neither can philosophy be grouped with the arts, for its "full-ending" is totality while theirs is particularity. And, of course, philosophy cannot be placed in a class with religion because its aim is knowledge rather than faith. According to Rickert, however, the history of philosophy gives us a clue as to the solution of our problem; for, as he sees it, the history of the great philosophical systems is not—as it might seem to be at first glance—a "graveyard" of misconceived efforts. The "factual" materials which have served in the past as a basis for the integrative interpretations of the world are, of course, essentially obsolete; we now have to deal with new "facts." But this is a minor matter. What is of importance is that the system-builders of the past did attain (each in his own way) an "end"—a "full-ending"—and "therein lies their greatness." "They tower high above the flood of endless happenings" and "out of the darkness of the past" they cast light even upon our own problems. Seen in this perspective, the "full-ending particularity of a closed system" remains ultimately "in the service of the un-ending totality and partakes of its value." When philosophy understands itself in this sense, then it adds "the copestone to the structure of the value system and completes that system in its formal aspects" (D, p. 327). The specific contents of the system are a matter of cultural development and will become evident only as we progress in that development.

BIBLIOGRAPHY

A. Rickert, Heinrich, *Der Gegenstand der Erkenntnis,* Tübingen, 1892. Revised 6th edition, 1928. All references to this work are to the 6th edition.
B. ——— *Die Grenzen der Naturwissenschaftlichen Begriffsbildung,* Tübingen, 1902. 5th edition, 1929. All references to this work are to the 5th edition.
C. ——— *System der Philosophie,* Volume I: *Allgemeine Grundlegung der Philosophie,* Tübingen, 1921.
D. ——— "Vom System der Werte," Logos, IV, 1913.
Messer, August, *Deutsche Wertphilosophie der Gegenwart,* Leipzig, 1926.

CHAPTER X

MÜNSTERBERG'S THEORY OF
ABSOLUTE VALUE

Rickert, so we have just seen, regarded validity as the very essence of value—of "pure value," that is; and he spoke of value as being antecedent to any *ought*. As he put it: In its validity value lies "high above everything human." Rickert himself did not pursue the issue further than this; but he did say that values considered as the basis for any *ought* probably do constitute a "realm" such as Münsterberg discussed in detail. In a very specific sense, therefore, Münsterberg's theory may be regarded as a supplement to Rickert's thesis.

It is this fact, of course, which fully justifies our inclusion of Münsterberg with the German-language group of value-theorists. The fact that his basic work in value theory was written and published simultaneous in German and in English is no argument against this inclusion.[1]

I

It was Münsterberg's aim to derive all values from a single principle inherent in human experience. He was convinced that such a principle can be found in a "basic act of the will" and that, when it is found, it will entail a well-integrated system of values. The construction of such a system should therefore be the ultimate aim of all value theorists. His own work was to be regarded as a pioneering effort.

In our search for that "basic act of will," our natural sciences are of no help; for, as interpreted by these sciences, the world around us is completely value-free. Whatever happens in that world is causally determined, and the causal nexus precludes an

---

[1]The English version, *The Eternal Values,* 1909, is not a translation from the German. Münsterberg wrote both versions at the same time. However, in the English version "much is newly added and much is omitted" from the German text. Nevertheless, the German version is basic and all references in what follows are to that version; and all translations are my own.

intrusion of values. Within the framework of our natural sciences, therefore, the existence of man (for example) has no more value than has the existence of a pebble on the beach. Both are simply the product of cause and effect relationships. Even pleasure and pain are but "natural" occurrences which have neither value nor disvalue. They, too, are part of the causal chain of relationships. And within that same causal nexus moral excellence has no more value than has the pungent odor of sulfuric acid.

This is so, Münsterberg points out, because all valuations presuppose a will capable of "taking an attitude," and no such will is acceptable as an explanatory factor in the natural sciences. Still, the very existence of the sciences themselves, and their historical development, depend upon a will—upon the will to know. That is to say, science is what it is only because men value truth more than error, and pursue it. Even to think of nature as value-free assumes a selective interpretation of experience and, thus, an act of will. It follows at once that reality, in so far as it includes science itself, is more than a causal interrelation of value-free events, and that, in order to discover values, we must transcend the world of science and must turn to the world of practical affairs in which human volitions play a decisive role. In this world things are not merely objects of knowledge but are "goals" and "means" requisite to the realization of goals. They are something desired or feared.

But if values are encountered within the realm of human volitions and desires, the question is, Can they be fully understood in terms of desire only? In answer to this question Münsterberg points out that, for certain purposes, especially in the field of economics, "value" and "desired goal" may indeed be identical. But before we call everything which someone may desire a value, it will be necessary to distinguish between dependent or relative values and independent or absolute values; and it is Münsterberg's contention that the philosopher should reserve the term "value" to designate absolute values only.

But let us first use the term "value" in the broad sense in which it includes both, relative and absolute values. The question now is, Do we find absolute values among the objects of desire? Do we encounter in the realm of desires values which are "valuable in themselves without reference to this or that individual or to his wishes"? (p. 23). The answer to this question, Münsterberg maintains, must be negative. From desire we can derive only such values as depend upon the desire for their very existence; and these are relative, not absolute values.

Attempts have been made—in the field of economics, for example—to get around this conclusion by speaking of the desire of a group of individuals, or of a community, rather than of the desire of some particular individual. The exchange-value of goods in the market place, for example, is determined in this way. In a sense, of course, we may here speak of "objective" values because the valuations of the group transcend those of the individual and provide a "norm" for his valuations. But "objective" values in this sense are still only relative and not absolute. Since they depend upon human needs, any shift in those needs entails of necessity a change in the corresponding valuations.

Value theories which are primarily psychological in orientation do not escape this relativism. Whether values are defined as the desirability of objects or as related to feelings of pleasure and displeasure, they remain dependent upon our subjective experience and are therefore not absolute. It may be granted that, depending on the duration and/or intensity of the desires or feelings, values can now be arranged in some order of rank. And when we take into consideration also the "depth" and the manifold interrelations and entailments of desires and feelings, we may be able to project even a "highest value"—a value, that is, which we prefer to all others. Such a "highest value" may be the peace that comes to us when all our desires cease; or it may be the harmonious realization of all our desires. Once we accept such a "highest value"—no matter how we define it—that value serves as a norm relative to which all other values can be "ranked." In principle, however, we do not escape value relativism even here; for there is no transition from the personal to the transpersonal in such an acceptance of a "highest value." Even the idea of the greatest possible happiness of the greatest possible number is and remains a relative value.

After all is said and done, the conclusion is inevitable that, if we accept feeling or desire as basic to all values, then we can never apprehend independent or absolute values. The plight of relativism, or pragmatism, and of positivism stems from this very fact.

II

Having thus dealt with various approaches to value theory which entail a value relativism, Münsterberg next turns to the development of his own value theory—a theory keyed to the conception of absolute values. His starting-point is the thesis that, as values, truth, beauty, progress, and morality are not derivable from, or dependent upon, the inclinations or desires of individuals or of groups of individuals; that they are, therefore, not merely trans-subjective but absolute. Truth, for example, is what it is and does not depend upon human desire or human feelings.

One might argue, of course, that Münsterberg's thesis here rests upon a basic confusion; for no matter how we define truth— be it in terms of a "correspondence with reality," in terms of an "integrative interpretation of experience," or in some other way— it designates a condition of knowing, not a value. In terms of the correspondence theory, for example, a proposition is true when what it asserts corresponds to the facts as they are; and in terms of the coherence theory a proposition is true when what it asserts contributes to a coherent interpretation of the whole of our experience. In neither case does the term "truth" denote a value. We can, of course, speak of "truth" and the "value of truth," but these two terms do not have the same meaning; and our pursuit of truth is the pursuit of a valued goal in the very same sense in which we pursue other goals that we value.

In a similar way we may value beauty and progress; but such valuations, too, have significance only relative to our experience and to our endeavors. They are not independent of that relation. When we say, for example, that an object is beautiful, we do so because that object affects us in a certain way. It elicits in us a feeling-response of a specific kind. In the case of progress, the situation is even more complex; for the very meaning of progress itself assumes a value standard which has significance only within the reach of our desires and volitions, and which we accept as valid for us. If a development continues in the direction of our highest hopes and greatest aspirations, we are pleased and value it because it contributes to our own self-fulfillment. The reference to our experience is again unavoidable.

Such facts, however, Münsterberg does not discuss. He confronts us at once with a dilemma: Either we live in a world in which trans-personal or absolute values prevail, or we have no "world" at all but merely a stream of experience within which the search for truth and morality is meaningless. This dilemma, Münsterberg believes, forces us into the acceptance of absolute values.

Let us assume for the sake of a faithful exposition of his position that Münsterberg is right in his initial belief. Then various questions arise: What is the essential nature, the "mode proper," of absolute values? How do we come to know them? What do they contribute to our personal existence? How are they interrelated? What is their deepest significance, their most profound meaning?

III

The causally determined system of nature, so we have seen, is value-free, and human desires and volitions involve relative values only. Münsterberg argues, however, that it is meaningless, because self-contradictory, to doubt the existence of universally valid or absolute values—of values, that is, which belong to the realm of the trans-personal and are deeply embedded in the very nature of reality itself. Such values, however, must still be accessible to us; and the question is, How is this possible without enmeshing them in the relativity of experience?

In his answer to this question Münsterberg adopts (as did Rickert before him) what might be called a Kantian principle of interpretation. The absolute values, he maintains, are "norms" whose validity is binding for every intelligent being who thinks and shares with us our world. As norms the values are independent of every act of desire or volition, be it an act of a particular individual or of billions of individuals collectively (p. 40).

Moreover, as norms the values entail an *ought*—but an *ought* that must not be confused with the merely prudential "ought." The latter simply indicates what is useful as a means to our personal well-being and therefore has nothing in common with absolute values. Even social norms, as embodied in the mores and the laws of a society, impose a merely prudential "ought," for they but reflect our communal experience.

Münsterberg's interpretation here depends upon, and is conditioned by, his essentially neo-Kantian epistemology. The "being of reality," he maintains, is given only in judgments whose sole ground and justification is their necessary validity which imposes an *ought* upon our will. Such judgments can not be arbitrary; but neither are they determined by some unknowable "Ding an sich" or by a sequence of cause and effect relationships. Their necessity is deeply rooted in thinking itself. That is to say, he who thinks truly subordinates himself to an absolute *ought;* and he who does his duty does likewise. Indeed, in this trans-personal necessity the difference between cognition and morality vanishes. We are confronted by an *ought*—really by an *ought to be*—which, in cognition, confronts us with a world for action in which duty itself is deeply rooted (p. 48). And in that same world we also encounter the aesthetic *ought* which, for the artist, is also a form of the *ought to be.* In substance, therefore, whenever we think, will, or feel *as we ought to,* we observe norms and encounter values that are absolute (p. 49).

If this interpretation is accepted, then truth is valuable in an absolute sense; and so is beauty, and so are morality, historical progress, and religious fulfillment. But there is as yet nothing which unifies these diverse ideals. We have no unitary standard of values but a multiplicity of standards. What, for example, does the logical *ought* of the mathematician have in common with the aesthetic *ought* of the landscape painter or with the moral *ought* of our daily existence? Instead of obtaining an integrated system of values, we are now confronted with a value chaos. Recourse to an *ought* evidently does not provide an ultimate basis for values. In fact, such recourse entails a vicious circle, for we now find valuable "that which we ought to do, and we ought to do that which is valuable" (p. 51). And there is the further danger that an interpretation of value in terms of an *ought* introduces elements into the conception of value which do not belong to it; for, in the last analysis, there is no *ought* in the value itself (p. 52).

However, if we hope ever to attain a unified world-view, we must demand that, in the end and despite their diversity, all values be derivable from a single principle. The question is, Can such a principle be found?

IV

In order to understand absolute values, Münsterberg now argues, we must try to understand how our will, as distinguished from every particular *ought,* can itself become a trans-personal or pure will—a will, that is, which, "without reference to personal pleasure or displeasure, finds satisfaction in the true, the beautiful, the moral, and the holy" (p. 59). If we succeed in this, then and then only are we in a position to "deduce a complete system of pure values from one 'basic act' " (p. 68).

It is evident at once that the world of nature—i.e., the world of space-time relations and causal interactions—is irrelevant to our problem, for that world is self-sufficient. It does not depend upon a will and it is value-free. Hence, if we are to discover values at all, and their ultimate foundation, we must examine the world of immediate experience, not that of science—the world of actions and of practical affairs.

In this world, human beings are not simply objects or things among other objects or things, but are themselves subjects endowed with a will. They are persons whom we understand or fail to understand, whom we acknowledge and accept or whom we fight and reject. And in this same world of action, even things are not merely value-free entities. They are objects with which we are concerned and which are part of our valuational experience. They attract or frighten us; and, in turn, we desire or reject them—either as ends or as means. Our attitude toward them is rarely that of a passive spectator.

The question now is, How, in view of our value-accentuated activities, are we to understand the normative character of values?

Let us assume, to begin with, that we call "value" everything that is an object of desire, and that we can distinguish between "conditional" and "unconditional" values. We call "conditional" any value which depends completely on the desire of a particular individual in particular circumstances. Such values can be fully understood in terms of desire. We call "unconditional" or "absolute" all those values that are independent of circumstances and of the desires of any particular individual. The crucial question now is, Do we encounter "unconditional" or "absolute" values among the objects of desire? That is to say, Do we encounter in our experience values which are "valuable" universally and without reference to any particular subject and its particular desires?

The question is crucial because no "unconditional" value can be derived from purely personal or individual desire. Hence, if we do encounter absolute values in our experience, desire in the subjective and personal sense cannot be their basis. The problem is complicated by the fact, which Münsterberg clearly recognizes, that we cannot even talk about values which, without any relation whatever to human experiences of pleasure and pain and to human desire, presumably exist in pristine purity in objective reality. A completely transcendent realm of values is and remains inaccessible to us.

A first clue to the solution of the problem Münsterberg finds in the field of economics. In the exchange of goods, he points out, the basic fact is the interdependence of competing desires. Because of this interdependence, goods can be put into classes of interchangeable items. The exchange-value of each item now no longer depends upon some happenstance of personal interest or desire. It has been generalized and "objectified" in the "market place." This "price" is largely independent of any one particular purchase; but the buyer has to pay it if he wants the goods in question. In the last analysis, however, even the "market value" of goods is not absolute. It is conditioned by human needs, on the one hand, and by the usefulness and the availability of the goods which satisfy those needs, on the other. Our search for absolute values must therefore go on.

Münsterberg considers next a psychological approach to the problem, pointing out that in this search it makes no real difference whether we define value in terms of desirableness or in terms of feelings of pleasure. Once we have selected a certain value as "the highest"—no matter how this was accomplished on psychological grounds—that value henceforth serves as an "objective" point of reference, as a standard, relative to which all other values can be "ranked." Despite this fact, however, the transition from relative to absolute value has not been accomplished. It is no more possible on psychological grounds than it is in terms of economic activities. Even the greatest possible happiness of the greatest possible number of people remains a relative value, for it depends on the feelings or desires of peoples. And nothing more than a relative value can be obtained even when we define value in terms of the feelings or desires of an "ideal" person (p. 76). There simply is no logical bridge from values which are relative to feeling or desire to values which are "unconditional" or absolute. If we are to justify an acceptance of absolute values, we must do so on radically different grounds.

V

There is one act of the will—so Münsterberg continues his argument—which, in principle, has nothing to do with pleasure or pain, or with desire. "It is the will that there be a world"; that the content of our experience be not simply a stream of experiential data but have an independent existence as a real world. This crucial act of affirming the existence of a world gives even our own existence meaning and significance. Without it, "life would be an empty dream, a chaos, a Nothing" (p. 94), and all values would be but relative. To be sure, nothing has validity beyond the fact of its being experienced; but if we do affirm the world as an independently existing reality, then every "disclosure of a self-identity within experience" must, of necessity, satisfy our "will to a world" and must satisfy also every other will that "wills a world." This "universally valid satisfaction" of the "will to a world" Münsterberg regards as a "pure value" and, he maintains, in so far as the world provides this satisfaction, it is in itself valuable (p. 96).

If we now ask what else is entailed in "the act of world-affirmation," a whole system of values will be disclosed. To begin with, we must accept "truth" as a norm, as a value; and truth, not being dependent upon individual desire or preference, is an absolute value. Even a "proof"—should one be offered—that truth is relative to the individual's desires or feelings assumes that the proof itself is universally valid and, thus, not relative to an individual. Were it otherwise, a contrary "proof" would be just as valid; and such a condition would effectively destroy any "proof" as proof. But if the objective validity of a proof must be admitted in at least one case, then the possibility of an unconditional truth has been established and complete relativism has been disproven.

Our "world-affirmation" has, of course, other consequences as well. As Münsterberg sees it, that act entails a whole system of values, and at least three kinds of absolute values may be distinguished. There is, first, the "value of preservation": In the flux of experiences every part of the world must remain identical with itself. There is, secondly, the "value of harmony": The various parts of the world must co-exist harmoniously. And there is, thirdly, the "value of activity": The world is a going concern and full of changes.

However, if the world is to maintain itself completely on its own, the three values just mentioned must be so interrelated that each is realized by itself alone as well as in conjunction with all others. And this fact entails a fourth value: Perfection (p. 97).

If we will the world, then (so Münsterberg argues) we must also will the four "pure values." We must will them as assurance of the self-containment and the self-sufficiency of that world. We thus face the crucial alternative that either our experiences are nothing but the ephemeral phenomena of a stream of consciousness and all values are relative to our feelings and desires, or there exists a real world in which absolute values play a decisive role. As far as Münsterberg is concerned, the choice cannot be in doubt.

At first, however, our affirmation of a real world is rather naive, stressing the requirements of life in its immediacy. In time, this naiveté gives way to more critical and more systematic interpretations and valuations. Our volitions become increasingly surer of the ends to be achieved. This development, Münsterberg holds, is the result of our growing culture. And if this interpretation is correct, then a distinction seems to be called for between naively posited "life-values" and critically discerned "culture-values" (p. 98). Each group will then be found to contain three sub-groups of values, depending on whether we are concerned with the "external world" as such, with the "world" in interaction with us, or with our own "internal world."

Münsterberg thus recognizes 24 distinct species of values—all of which, however, are entailed by the one value (the existence of a world) which consists in the total satisfaction of that basic will which posits or affirms the world.

We must now consider this uniquely derived system of values in greater detail.

VI

Our first concern is with the values pertaining to the "self-preservation of the world." They are the "logical" or cognitive values and consist of two groups: (1) *Daseinswerte* or "values of existence," and (2) *Zusammenhangswerte* or "values of context."

To be sure, the bare existence of an object, its factual "givenness," is value-free. It elicits no "admiration" but must be acknowledged or affirmed. However, when we distinguish the real from the non-real, we take a first step beyond mere acknowledgment and, in doing so, we posit the value of existence: The real is better than the non-real. Beyond this, however, we also want to know how the real is structured and how its component parts are interrelated. Inspection will then show that, while the affirmation of existence is direct and immediate, the delineation of interrelations and, therefore, of "context" is not. The discovery of causal, historical, or logical interrelations presupposes "goal-conscious labor" on our part; i.e., it presupposes an act of will directed toward the uncovering of the connections. It follows at once that, existence being basic to all interrelations, the value of existence is the indispensable presupposition of all other valuations; that it is an absolute value in the sense that it satisfies the demand of the "pure will" that there exist something self-identical as its object (p. 99).

However, as factually given and as acknowledged by us, reality encompasses at least three distinct levels. It encompasses (a) the world of things, (b) the world of human relationships, and (c) our own inner world. All three levels must be considered when we deal with the values of existence.

(a) What is significant in our experience of the world of things is the fact that, in different experiences, identical objects recur. The tree yonder which we saw yesterday we may see again today and the day after tomorrow. Such recurrence in our experience is "satisfying" and, therefore, "valuable." It is what Münsterberg means by "existence-value." If the tree were chopped down tomorrow, we would not encounter it the day after tomorrow. That is, we would lack the satisfaction that stems from recurrence. What is decisive here, however, is not our own particular experience or even the experience of our fellowmen, but the fact that, in principle, the self-identical object (in our example the tree) can be experienced—and can be experienced recurrently—by *every* possible subject. Only when this condition is fulfilled does the object exist in the true sense of the term. Only then does it exist independently of our feelings and desires, and as a self-identical entity. It is by virtue of such an existence that the object in question has an "existence-value" and that this value is absolute (p. 101).

It is the task of science, Münsterberg maintains, to determine specifically which objects of experience are real and which are not. This problem, therefore, need not concern us here. What alone is important at this time is the basic fact that our experience entails the necessity of positing a real world, and that the persistent self-identity of the real things in that world is itself a basic value. Münsterberg's value theory rests upon this premise.

One might now argue against Münsterberg that perhaps not all existence is an absolute value, for disease germs, leprosy, arteriosclerosis, and the like, though only too real, are generally experienced as disvalues rather than as values. Such an argument, however, makes human feelings and human desires the arbiter of values and thus makes all values relative to our needs. It is not an argument which effectively meets Münsterberg's thesis—a thesis which entails the conclusion that, by virtue of the fact that they exist, even the "dreadful" things mentioned have an "existence-value," and have such a value no matter what our human reactions to them may be.

(b) In the world around us we encounter also our fellowmen; and the question now is, In what sense do we attribute existence to them?

There is, of course, the obvious fact that human beings, like things, are perceivable objects, and that, in some respects, we can apprehend even ourselves as "things" in an external world. However, such an "external" view of ourselves and of our fellowmen is a distortion of human existence.

As we act and have experiences, we know ourselves in a way that is crucially different from the way in which we know "things," for we "feel" rather than "perceive" ourselves to be the center of our experience. Our actions are not simply occurrences observable "from the outside"; they are "deeds" expressing an attitude we take. It is we who decide upon and determine them. In fact, we *are* the taking of an attitude, the making of a decision. We are the will that manifests itself in all our actions. In our volitional experiences we thus know ourselves in a way which differs radically and in principle from the way in which we know "objects" (p. 104).

Moreover, in our actions we directly—i.e., not by way of analogical reasoning but immediately—encounter the will of others. We know their will because we understand their intentions, their decisions; and we approve or disapprove. The world of our fellowmen is, thus, a world of volitional interactions in which one will immediately responds to some other will, and in which all wills are characterized by intentions and decisions, compelling favorable or unfavorable responses on our part. Existence in this world has its own limitations; but it also has its own mode of "existence-value" (p. 105).

(c) The limitations of the will just referred to are found not only in the external world of things or in our encounter with our fellowmen; they exist also in our own inner world. Such "inner limitations" are the restraints imposed upon our merely subjective needs and inclinations by our trans-personal (*überpersönliche*) valuations—valuations which are unavoidable so long as we will that there be a world; and this will we can give up only when we abandon all hope of achieving reality as a person. That is to say, our "inner limitations" arise from the fact that we exist as human beings only when we affirm the existence of a real world and find our place in it. This and this alone, according to Münsterberg, is, in the end, the real meaning of "existence-value" and is foundational to all other values and valuations (p. 108).

VII

In addition to the "existence-value," we also encounter "context-values" (*Zusammenhangswerte*). It is the never-ending task of the scientists to delineate and define the various "contexts." The philosopher, on the other hand, is concerned with clarifying the values inherent in each "context."

Since "contexts" transcend the actualities of any given individual here and now, they all possess a trans-personal "reality-value." However, since every "context" is rooted in the interrelations of objects of the same kind, three and only three basic "contexts" are possible. They are (a) the "context of things," (b) the "context of persons," and (c) the "contexts of valuations" (*ibid.*). The "context of things" depends upon a cause-and-effect relationship and encompasses the whole of nature. The "context of persons" depends upon human interactions. It is "the world of history and of culture." The "context of valuations," finally, is determined by logical interrelations. It is typified by "the rational system" (p. 109).

The Realm of Nature.—Only "things" enter into the context known as "nature." Human beings are part of it only in so far as they, too, can be regarded as "things." The context of nature is value-free. This is so because valuing presupposes a subject that approves or disapproves, and neither approval nor disapproval has a legitimate place within a context that consists exclusively of cause-and-effect relationships.

However, nature itself and taken as a whole can be valued from the outside and may therefore be said to have a value. It actually has a value for us when we realize that, in comprehending things in their context, our trans-personal striving after personal identity is satisfied. This occurs when, at a certain level of experience, we acknowledge things as existing, and when, at a higher level, we discern and comprehend ever more fully a lasting order or context of things. The realization that nature is a context, that all changes in nature are but modifications of a "given" which endures—all of this entails an encounter with values—i.e., with cognitive values—that are objectively binding and are "a source of pure satisfaction" (p. 112).

The Context of History.—The world we live in is a world of interacting persons. It is "the world of history." In this world no person exists or remains in isolation. Each produces effects beyond himself in a context of interactions with others. At the same time, however, the volition of each person is also identically itself and remains so in the midst of historical changes. And this self-identity of volition within the historical context, Münsterberg maintains, is itself a value (p. 115).

As a psycho-physical object, man, like every other "thing," exists as part of that causal nexus which constitutes the realm of nature and is value-free. But man is also a "comprehending subject," and one that wills certain ends. He pursues goals which he sets himself as tasks to be fulfilled; and in doing so he rises above the causal nexus and transcends nature. Man thus lives at a special level of existence. And it is at this level that he specifically interacts with other persons.

Basic to that interaction and to his relation to other persons as persons is the "act of comprehension." The interrelations, however, are very complex. I may, for example, comprehend the intention of another person whose intention already reflects his comprehension of, and reaction to, my earlier intentions. The historical context must include all of these complexities, for they are essential to the "dialectic of history."

In order for us to understand the historical context, it may be necessary that we distinguish specifically definable aspects or phases within the total range of human volitions. We may thus speak of a person's political, judicial, economic, social, scientific, artistic, religious, and moral volitions; and each and every one of these groups of volitions may itself constitute a context and may reflect its own values (p. 117). All of them together constitute our historically developed culture.

The Context of Rational Systems.—As far as Münsterberg is concerned, we encounter "rational systems" in various fields of endeavor—in logic, in aesthetics, in ethics, in metaphysics, etc. Activity in these fields discloses our basic volition to achieve integrative unity and, thus, the persistence of our "deepest self"— the "deepest depth of our inner world," where the will to be itself and to have a world is most efficacious (p. 119). The rational system, thus being an expression of our will to a world, not only constitutes a "context of identity," it reflects our highest values.

XIII

In Sections VI and VII we have considered in a cursory way the general framework within which Münsterberg develops his more specific and essentially systematic interpretation of values. We shall now deal briefly with some of the details of that interpretation.

On the basis of what has gone before, Münsterberg distinguishes six basic types or classes of values: (1) values of unity, (2) values of beauty, (3) values of development, (4) values of achievement, (5) values of religion, and (6) values of philosophy. In each area numerous more specific values are interrelated and thus constitute a "realm of values." But since all values ultimately depend upon our "will to a world," they are all derivable from that will and, therefore, constitute one integrated and integrative system.

Values of "unity."—When we deal with "things," we give objective significance to the contents of our experience by relating them to a space-time framework. Thus, what we "perceive" to be a tree is indeed a tree "out there"—if it finds its proper place within the space-time pattern of the external world. Similarly, our "inner" experiences take on an objective significance when they occupy a place in an appropriate "framework." That "framework," Münsterberg maintains, is "the Absolute." "It corresponds to the primordial demand of our deepest self that our life be, not an incoherent dream, but part of a real world" (p. 120). By relating our experiences to this demand, we objectify and verify them, and, in doing so, we attain the "unity of self" for ourselves.

But we also experience, immediately and directly (i.e., without reasoning from analogy), our fellowmen as subjects like ourselves with whom we can communicate. And, similarly, we experience immediately and directly the melancholy or the joy that is in musical tones. "If we are to hear merely 'sounds' to which we then attribute our feelings by way of empathy, we must first kill the soul that speaks to us directly" (p. 121). And what is true of musical tones is true of aesthetic objects in general. In each of them there speaks to us, immediately and directly, the "harmony of an inner diversity." That is to say, the aesthetic objects "express their own essential being—their loveliness or dignity, their agitation or calmness, their pulsating vitality or resignation, their gaiety or dreaminess" (p. 123); and they do so immediately and directly. When we use words to describe or interpret them, we have already distorted the experience. What the aesthetic object has to say, and what it says in itself and directly, cannot be adequately expressed in any other way. This is so because the aesthetic object is itself an integrated, indivisible "one," a "unity." Its "unity"—its basic value—is that of an inner harmony.

In interacting volitionally with our fellow human beings, we experience another form of the value of "unity." It manifests itself in love, in friendship, in peaceful co-existence, and, ultimately, in the brotherhood of all men (p. 123).

Beyond this, however, the world itself is more valuable—and more valuable in a trans-personal sense—because in it "happiness illumines the souls of men" (p. 126). And this, too, is a value of "unity"—the "unity" of man and his world.

Values of Beauty.—Beauty, of course, is not limited to the realm of the arts. It is found in nature as well. But the arts play a special role in our aesthetic experience; for it is the aim of the visual arts to give revealing expression to the harmony inherent in the external world; and it is the aim of the musical arts to do the same for our inner world. In the successful realization of these aims are grounded all "values of beauty"—i.e., the aesthetic values.

But we must contemplate "the unreal content of a work of

art" free from any desire; for it is the absence of desire that allows
the aesthetic intent inherent in the art object to come to full
effectiveness in our experience. Whether or not that intent is
fully realized in the art object itself depends, of course, on whether
or not the "genius of the artist" has achieved full and compelling
expression of his own aesthetic intention (p. 127).

Values of Development.—Whatsoever is valuable because of
its own development attains its value precisely because it is in
transition from a "given" actuality to something "as yet not
given." This means, however, that, inherently, development is
action. It is a "deed" (*Tat*).

If the "deed" aims at a goal, Münsterberg calls it "performance." If it deliberately aims at the realization of values, he calls
it "culture." The values of development *per se* are so-called "life-
values" (*Lebenswerte*). The values of performance, transcending
the "life-values," are the "cultural values" (*Kulturwerte*). Let us
consider the "life-values" first.

Mere change—i.e., the transition from one state or condition
to another—is not valuable. Change is valuable when it is a
"becoming"—when what emerges is the actualization of what
originally was not fully "given"; when it is the realized "intent"
of the "given"—as the full-grown plant is the "intent" of the
seed (p. 128).

Strictly speaking, so Münsterberg holds, there is no development, no progress in the "nature" with which our physical scientists are concerned because in that world there is no room for
values. And to comprehend the development of the universe as
a whole is not within the reach of finite minds. In the causally
determined sequence of events which we do understand, man is
but a "small growth upon the crust of the earth" and the earth
itself but a speck of dust in the universe.

Still the universe has brought forth man—a unique being who
can live his life in freedom. And if he is the realization of what
was originally but potentiality or "intent," then the world has
developed and is developing and, in this respect at least, it is
valuable as well. The question concerning the sense and the
value of historical changes cannot be brushed aside (p. 132).

As Münsterberg sees it, genuine development advances from

the personal to the "more-than-personal," the latter, surpassing the valuableness of the accidental and the particular, being the valuable *per se*. It is valuable for everyone. And because progress brings forth values that are valid for all, it contains an element that is imperishable. The great achievements even of vanished cultures have thus become part of our human development. Without them our own culture would not be what it is.

A special problem is, of course, our own personal development. When and under what conditions is that development valuable?

In discussing this topic, Münsterberg assumes that volition is the very core of our being and that our self "wills" itself to unfold and to enhance its very being but, in the midst of this development, remain self-identical in its volitions. Our development, therefore, must be the volitional unfolding of our persisting self-same self. Only thus does our self achieve significance as an independently existing being—as a self.

Conducive to such self-development is everything that can be achieved through patience, diligence, persistence, self-restraint, courage and, especially, through the creative deed. In such achievements the whole of our personality finds an ever-enriched expression and, in them also, it lives its life to the fullest.

However, if we are really to speak here of a "development," then the "new"—i.e., the newly achieved—must lie in a direction that is already implicit in the "old." The "new" must be the "old" more adequately or more fully realized. This means that, in the last analysis, the "genuine value of our development" is attained when our particular will to self-enhancement is in harmony with those ideals of reason which are the manifestations of man's deepest will to values"—his *Grundwollen zum Wert* (p. 134). Only in the pursuit of these ideals do our particular volitions rise to the level of the "more-than-personal"; and only to this extent is there real development in our personal existence.

Values of Achievement.—If development is guided toward projected goals, it culminates in values of achievement—i.e., it culminates in "culture-values" (*Kulturwerte*). In these, all self-directed activity finds its highest realization.

Münsterberg distinguishes three kinds of "culture-values": (a)

In the material world we encounter the values of man's economic achievements; (b) in the world of human co-existence the
values of law and order prevail; and (c) in our own inner world
the values of moral achievement stand out as unique.

(a) Basic to man's economic achievements is the assumption
that, inherent in the external world, there is a "will to serve man";
that, in fact, "service to man" is the goal of the external world.
Man's own task is simply to help bring about the realization of
that goal, and to surpass each particular achievement by project-
ing a still higher goal to be served. This and this only, Münsterberg insists, is the "meaning of the economy" (p. 135). Through
its full realization the economic values as such are realized.

As far as (b) is concerned, law is that order regulating human
co-existence through which the realization of the will of the
community is enforced and made secure. This is not a matter of
legal codes alone, however. It involves the whole organizational
structure of a society through which the will of the community
is translated into an obligation for each member of that community.

When we consider (c), the values of moral achievement, the
situation is somewhat more complex; for morality, Münsterberg
maintains, is the development of our inner world in the light of
projected goals. It is an achievement, in other words, for which
the self-determination of the person is a task that is being pursued consciously and deliberately. And if this is so, then the values
of law and the values of morality are quite different. The former
pertain to our world of co-existing individuals; the latter involves
only our own inner world. That is to say, law is always concerned
with the realm of communal living, morality with that of the individual person. It is desirable, of course, that the stipulations and
demands of law conform to the moral will; but whether or not
they do has no bearing upon the value of the law *per se.* Even
if it should be argued that it is moral to subordinate oneself to
the law, the subordination in itself would not be a value of law.
What, then, is the nature of moral value?

A pre-condition of morality, Münsterberg holds, is a positive
valuing of the happiness, the well-being, and the community-life
of "others." But this is only a pre-condition. He who is incapable

of such positive valuation of the interests of others is not *im*moral but *a*-moral—i.e., he is incapable of morality (p. 137).

In order to attain the level of morality, it is necessary that, in harmony with the pre-condition just stated, we project ourselves as persons who attain realization in and through their actions. If we lie or steal, we may attain what, selfishly, we desire; but our own selves suffer in the act, for we are now no longer identical with the selves that fulfill the pre-condition of morality. Moral value thus lies in the identity of our actual deeds with what is demanded from a "more-than-personal" point of view. This means that it is not our action but the person being realized in and through it that is morally valuable (p. 138). To see that this is so is something that we have to learn as we develop. And it is for this reason, Münsterberg holds, that morality is a "culture-value."

One other aspect is important. The moral value itself lacks "material" content, for it makes no difference, Münsterberg maintains, which action we choose in conformity with the pre-condition of morality. We are moral when we "really will" it *as this action,* and not because of its consequences. It is our intention, not the success or failure of the action, that counts.

The specifically moral valuation of the self as the subject of action entails our sense of duty. That is to say, the *ought* of morality is encountered whenever our volition is confronted with an awareness that, because of the volition, the true value of our self is in danger. To be more specific: The awareness of danger is experienced whenever we face two possibilities of action, one of which we "will" as being in harmony with the pre-condition of morality; the other of which we do not "will" in this sense but like to perform because of the desired results to which it leads.

In confrontations of this kind, Münsterberg maintains, there can be but one moral *ought*: "You ought to perform that action which is the realization of your own true will" (p. 139). What particular action this may be in any given situation depends on the level of your own moral development. Nobody else can impose an *ought* upon you. "To remain true to yourself is thus the only moral value, the only moral *ought*" (*ibid.*). To be active, to remain true to oneself in freedom, and thus to preserve the identity of will and action means that in our decisions and actions an "independent reality" unfolds itself which is not merely experience but value.

The Religious Values.—Experience confronts us again and again with conflicts of values. The world of actuality, for example, and the cognitive values pertaining thereto often negate the demands of morality or the desire for an inner harmony; and, on its own part, the world of morally valuable actions may destroy happiness and be a hindrance to cognition. The conflicts are genuine, Münsterberg holds, and cannot be solved by placing one group of values above the other. Yet, since an inherently contradictory world cannot exist, it must somehow be possible to overcome all value conflicts by integrating the various groups.

Moreover, only a world which maintains its essential self-identity in what is true, beautiful, or good can be itself valuable. This value of the world as a whole—this ultimate value—is encountered in its immediacy in religious experience—provided the experience reflects a truly living faith. It can be discerned in philosophy only when philosophy is a sensitive interpretation of the whole of man's culture. What this amounts to is that only a world broadened and enlarged by a demand for the "more-than-personal" can and does transcend the apparent conflicts of values in our experience; and only such a world can manifest itself as one world—as a persistent unity in the changing flux of values.

It is true, of course, that the religious and philosophical augmentations of experience are not apprehensions of an actually existing entity. They are, rather, content of convictions—i.e., they are a matter of faith. But since conviction or faith is the most secure basis for action, the broadened meaning of "realization" is here completely fulfilled. That is to say, action based upon faith actualizes what was previously only potential. And so, according to Münsterberg, the experienced world—which is in danger of disintegrating into the special worlds of logic, ethics, and aesthetics—finds its total realization in the all-encompassing "last world" that is rooted in our religious and philosophical convictions—a world in which the divisive conflicts of values have been overcome. Our convictions yield "reality" because the world thus augmented is the basis for our actions and "dominates our lives" (p. 143).

Religion finds an "over-arching level," a "superstructure" (*Oberbau*), for the world of experience in the conception of God, and finds therein also the specifically religious values of "holiness" and "eternity." Philosophy, on the other hand, is searching for a "foundation" of the world of experience in some "first cause" and, ultimately, in the Absolute—a search which entails "foundational" or metaphysical values. Both groups of values, the religious and the metaphysical, supplement and stand in contrast to the logical, the aesthetic, and the moral values.

It is impossible, however, to distinguish clearly between a "metaphysic of religious feelings" and a "metaphysic of philosophical reason." Both are concerned with the same ultimate goal: An integrative conception of reality. If this goal is achieved through "goal-conscious intellectual work" (*zielbewusste Gedankenarbeit*), then philosophy is involved and the result is a "culture-value" (*Kulturwert*). But when the goal is achieved without such "goal-consciousness" and, essentially, on the basis of feelings, then religion prevails and the goal is a "life-value" (*Lebenswert*). It is this latter value which now concerns us.

Religious value manifests itself in three distinct forms. With respect to the external world, it is entailed by our faith in "creation." With respect to the world of co-existence, it is encountered in our faith in "revelation." And with respect to our own inner world, it is rooted in our faith in "redemption." Let us briefly consider all three forms.

(1) Religious faith must and does hold that the "creator" of the world is spirit, and that the reference to the act of creation is not an attempt at a causal explanation of the world but an interpretation of its meaning. To accept the world as God's creation means, therefore, so to understand that world as to find in it an appropriate place for every value. The opposition of "nature" and "morality" is in that case suspended, and the world is seen as one coherent whole. This faith, which draws strength and life-sustaining power from a conception of reality that is profoundly meaningful, is at the center of all great religions.

(2) "Revelation," as Münsterberg interprets it, supplements

human interactions as encountered in history. In it, faith compre-
hends the historical context of events as leading back to God in
whom the order of nature, the realm of morality, and the state of
eternal bliss fuse into "unity." The "more-than-personal" aspects
of communal life are thus rooted in "revelation"—a "revelation"
which ever anew recociles man's contradictory valuations and, in
doing so, provides a secure basis for man's communal existence
and gives that existence a value-determined direction. Every
"miracle," every new discovery of social values, is in this sense a
"revelation." What characterizes such a "miracle" and gives it
significance is not the absence of a causal explanation but the relation to a transcendent will that governs man's destiny and gives
meaning to his existence (p. 146).

(3) Our inner world, too, is full of conflicts and contradictions.
But out of this situation there arises within us the desire to attain
personal integration—to attain "redemption." This desire may be
combined with a belief in immortality; but immortality is not a
pre-condition for "redemption." Genuine "redemption," so Münsterberg holds, lies in the triumph of an act of will through which
we overcome all value conflicts within us and attain the complete
unity of the true, the beautiful, and the good. "Redemption," so
understood, is "timeless bliss." We achieve it when, through our
own efforts, we advance to a "higher, a purer life"; and it remains
a religious achievement so long as the "redemptive deed" is itself
an act of faith—of a faith in the value-unifying power of the
divine (p. 147).

The Philosophical Values.—These, so we have seen, are the
basic values. We encounter them only within that unity of values
which is the result of our conceptual clarification of all values—
the result, that is, of a "goal-conscious" intellectual effort. Viewed
in this perspective, experience itself becomes problematic; and so
does the "given." Both must be analyzed critically. And when we
do this, we are led from "experience" to the "subject" having the
experience, from "value" to the "subject" that values, from the
"world" to the "self" and its "rationality," our analysis culminating ultimately in an investigation of "the inner unity of all valuations." It is only through such an integrative interpretation that
the world itself becomes a value; and only then do we achieve

a world-view which gives meaning to our own lives as well (p. 148).

But here we face a dilemma: Either we abandon all hope of ever achieving the integrative synthesis or we derive all values from one basic idea. Actually, of course, we have little choice in the matter; for to relinquish the ideal of an integrated system of values would be equivalent to our regarding the world itself as in principle self-contradictory and, therefore, as valueless.

The situation is complicated by the fact that the values cannot be regarded as something actualized or "given." They are "tasks which ought to be fulfilled." But as "tasks" the values are not simply encountered in experience, for "he who finds them is also he who creates them" (p. 149). It is, therefore, in itself a task so to interpret the world as a whole that all values which we acknowledge find a place in that world, and that, nevertheless, the world remains unified within itself.

It is true, of course, that relating the diverse values to something which lies beyond our experience is not an act of cognition but an act of faith—of a faith, however, that is rooted in "the deepest depths" of our personality and is closely allied with religious faith. But it is also true that without this profound involvement—i.e., without a crucial commitment on our part—no ultimate philosophy is possible and the logical, the aesthetic, the moral, and the religious values exist side by side and remains in conflict with one another. Only the conviction that, in the end, all values derive from one and the same source, that they are but varying forms in which the Absolute manifests itself, gives unity to them all.

But when we view all values as manifestations of the Absolute, we have relinquished our own empirical selves as the basis of values. That is, we have relinquished as irrelevant to our interpretation of values what is purely accidental and particular in our experience. "What remains is what is common to all conceivable selves: namely, the realm of values" (p. 151).

At the same time, however, our own selves have been enlarged into a "more-than-self"—a "more-than-self" which is not a "thing" that exists but a striving—a "primordial striving" that transcends every goal that has been reached and which, thus, is self-enhancing. As Münsterberg sees it, the whole development of human culture is an expression or manifestation of this "primordial striving," this basic volition. "The ultimate meaning of mankind is that, through the realization of values, it represents the self-preservation and self-enhancement of volition in an eternal primordial deed" (p. 157). In this perspective, the universe as a whole is one unique drama within which each event has its necessary place. And in this perspective, too, our own actions are our participation in that drama; and we are accountable for them. At the same time, however, our own selves take on significance and meaning as participants in the process of "building a world of values," and become themselves tasks to be fulfilled.

That the "primordial will" to realize the "more-than-personal" is real, and that our own selves attain meaning only as participants in the on-going process of "building a world of values," is not subject to scientific proof. It is a matter of commitment. It requires a decision, an act of will on our part. But we must make the commitment unless we are willing to abandon ourselves as human beings (p. 158). Moreover, only when we make the commitment do we become fully involved in human affairs as human. Only then do we encounter friends and enemies, models after which to pattern ourselves and imitators, co-workers and opponents, well-wishers and the envious ones. Only then do we encounter the whole complexity of values and valuations (p. 163).

IX

In Section VII, brief reference was made to Münsterberg's distinction between the "context of things" or nature, the "context of persons" or history, and the "context of valuations" or the rational system. These distinctions, however, do not imply a diremption of our experience as such. They are but discernible aspects of the complexities of that experience. The objects of desire, for example, *as objects of desire,* do not belong to the "context of things" *per se.* Only when we think of them as separate from all volition and as merely perceptual objects are they "things" and part of a value-free nature (p. 172). It must be noted, however, that it is not sufficient merely to separate them from our own volitions. Basic is here as everywhere the "primordial will to a world," and our aesthetic experiences disclose that will as intrinsic to the objects themselves. As manifestations of that will the objects "express their own nature, their own charm (*Lieblichkeit*), their own dignity, their repose, their vitality (*Lebensdrang*) and their quiescence (*Lebensverzicht*), their gaiety and their dreaminess." "But every word here," Münsterberg adds, "leads us astray: Nature composes no program music. What the swan has to say in its gentle motion through the dark waters cannot be said in any other language" (p. 212). And "just as the starry heavens at night in their eternal beauty foreshadow with infinite sublimity the meaning of the value of unity, so we encounter the value of unity in its infinite magnitude also whenever, through rapture and pain, two souls have become one in eternal loyalty" (p. 219). The trans-personal value here, too, lies in the fact that two separate realities have, in a sense, become identical.

If by "happiness" we mean pleasure—i.e., if we mean by it the satisfaction of merely personal desires—then it obviously has no trans-personal or absolute value. Such a value can be attributed to it only when happiness is taken to be the complete harmony of all our volitions. Its value is in that case a universally valid value of unity—just as the unity of things in the beauties of nature, and the unity of persons in genuine love are such values. But in that case, also, happiness presupposes a constantly effective volition— a volition that is manifold yet one, and that progressively advances towards it goal (p. 229). Happiness so understood is "a pure and independent self-value." But it is aesthetic rather than moral in character; and, "in a trans-personal sense, the world itself is more valuable because happiness illumines men's souls" (p. 233).

However, the values of unity and of beauty are essentially values of static conditions in the world. They are values of existence (*Dasein*) and of the existential context of things and persons. But we have seen already (Section VIII) that there are also values of development and of achievement—the "life-values" and the "culture-values." They are in evidence when what emerges as the result of any change is the realized "intent" of what was but potentiality in what was initially "given." But the unity of continuity must be preserved in the process, for only then can we speak of a world at all. We must note, however, that the value here lies *in the becoming* (*im Werden*), not in what has been realized. It is of value, in other words, that that which has come into existence is what was "intended" from the very beginning.

It is in this sense, Münsterberg maintains, that nature itself has developed, "not in order to bring forth unfree man," but in order to provide an abode for man in his freedom. "It is the will intrinsic in nature to become the dwelling-place and the tool for man" (p. 316). Without this relation to human volition it would be nonsensical to attribute a value to the development of nature or to speak of progress in that development.

At the human level, however, development is a matter of historical or cultural changes. And "just as the biologist must explain both, health and disease, life and death, so the historian must relate and try to understand with empathic sensitivity the heights and the depths, the Ages of Nobility and the Ages of Horror in the history of mankind, and must help us to understand how it all came about. The purpose of the historian is not to evaluate; for that which has emerged in freedom is for him already an unchangeable sequence of actualities which he views in retrospect in order to understand the context" (pp. 321–322).

Still, the question concerning progress or regress in the historical development cannot be brushed aside. However, in order to find an answer, we must transcend the historian's interests and must strive to attain a point of view from which valuations attain universal validity. Such a point of view would be the projection of a goal toward the ultimate realization of which every individual, as member of a community, would contribute his share (p. 334). But can such a goal be projected as a meaningful norm for all mankind? Historical development, as we actually encounter it, "knows no great universal Yes or No, but only an unending game of Up and Down" (p. 336). It is, nevertheless, no accident, Münsterberg maintains, that man continues to believe that, seen as a whole, his own sojourn on earth has been an irresistible ascend;

that every retrogression has been surmounted; and that progress is real—a progress that moves from the subjective and personal to the trans-personal.

This "self-development" (*Selbstentwicklung*) is, to begin with, an essentially unconscious drive and its value a "pure life-value" (*reiner Lebenswert*). Still, the very essence of the self involved in this development is an ever-renewed volition that presses on to its own enhancement, its own enrichment. Its very nature is the drive toward an ever greater achievement, toward the "creative deed" (*die schöpferische Tat*). The person as a whole finds in it an ever richer and ever more varied expression. The process as a whole, however, is a development only when "the new" is already contained in the "the old" as the latters potentiality; and it is a genuine development of man only when the volition which enhances itself in the process knows itself to be in harmony with the ideals of Reason—i.e., when it is our most profound will to value (*Wille zum Wert*). When this is the case, and when the development is consciously directed towards its goal, then the "development-values" become "achievement-values" and the process itself becomes man's cultural development. In it "the self-activity of the world" (*die Selbstbetätigung der Welt*) attains its highest goal.

Involved in this cultural development are, of course, the three "realms" or levels previously distinguished: the world of things, the context of human relationships, and the realm of our inner experiences. And corresponding to these three areas we encounter in our culture the achievements in economics, in law, and in morality.

As we have seen earlier, nature (which is but the world of things in its unity), having brought forth man, wants to serve him as his dwelling-place and his tools. It is the purpose and the meaning of man's economy not only to assist nature in the realization of that goal but to enhance infinitely its fulfillment. The value of the economy, therefore, does not lie in the fact that some particular needs of individual human beings are being satisfied (an activity which would at best yield relative values only), but in the trans-personal realization of the true purpose of nature itself.

At the level of human co-existence and human relationships, law is the important aspect; for "law is the orderly arrangement (*Ordnung*) through which the realization of the common will (*Gemeinschaftswille*) is assured and imposed in the interaction (*Wechselverkehr*) of the members of the community" (p. 375). This orderly arrangement and this security constitute the universally valid value of law (*Rechtswert*).

Our inner experience constitutes the realm of morality—the realm, that is, in which our specific task is the self-activity (*Selbstbetätigung*) and the realization of personality. Law, so Münsterberg emphasizes, must always remain within the realm of communal living, whereas morality pertains to the individual person. To be sure, Münsterberg adds, it is desirable that the demands of the law be in harmony with the moral will, and that we do all we can to bring about that harmony; but this has nothing to do with the value of law *per se*. And neither is the fact that it is moral to subordinate oneself to the law a value of the law. But be that as it may, we are here concerned with the specifically moral value, and how it is to be defined.

Münsterberg maintains that the specifically moral value is not simply a matter of preferring certain lines of action (such as telling the truth and contributing to the welfare of others) and of repudiating other actions (such as lying and stealing). Concern for the welfare and the happiness of others and for the life of a community is but a pre-condition of the moral. It is not the moral value itself; for he who is incapable of such concerns is *a*-moral rather than *im*moral. That is, he is incapable of morality. Decisive for the moral realm proper is that in the process of our "universally valid self-development" a trans-personal value standard is increasingly accepted; that we learn to see ourselves as "an absolutely valid value" that is to be realized in and through our actions. When we lie or steal, we may achieve a purely egoistic goal, but our own self, as we truly value and intend it, has not prevailed. We are no longer identical with ourselves and, thus, have become valueless, for "not the action is valuable, but the person who realizes his own proper and intended self in the completed action" (p. 389). When we carry out an action that is not an expression of this "truly intended," this ideal self but is designed to achieve some particular and merely selfish end, we are immoral.

We must note, however, that, according to Münsterberg, the moral value proper is independent of any specific material determination. In other words, for the moral value proper it is immaterial what particular action we decide upon so long as it is an action which, *simply as action* and not because of its results, we truly intend or will. In the last analysis, therefore, there is only one moral *ought:* Carry out that action which you truly will. What action you will in any given situation depends upon the stage of your development as a person. This "categorical imperative" can be translated into an hypothetical imperative by simply adding: "if you do not wish to betray your own true self." However, so Münsterberg maintains, we can never really will that our selves should not remain identical each with itself. And from this it follows, Münsterberg points out, that being true to oneself is the only moral value, the only moral *ought.* "To be active oneself, to remain true to oneself in freedom, and thus to posit willing and acting as identical—this means for the community as well as for the individual person that in them [i.e., in the community and in the person] an independent reality unfolds itself; that they are not only an experience but are values" (p. 394).

X

We have considered, if ever so briefly and inadequately, three "trans-personal value-worlds" (*überpersönliche Wertwelten*): the world around us or nature, the world of human interactions or history and communal existence, and the world of our inner experiences. All three are involved in the development of culture and are thus related to "achievement-values." What is common to the three worlds is that in all of them value comes into being through the ever increasing realization of an identity; that "the old" is preserved, fulfilled, and confirmed in "the new"; and that every stage in the development is but origin and anchorage for further intentions and volitions. Despite this common aspect, however, the three worlds are and remain three distinct "value-worlds," and the question is, Can they be brought together in such a way that their respective characteristics are preserved while, nevertheless, they form one integrated system? If this cannot be done, then, so Münsterberg maintains, internal diremption threatens our volition and, therefore, our very existence as persons; for the meaning of our life depends on the fact that, in an ultimate sense, the world we live in is self-identical and one, and that this trans-personal "oneness" retains its identity in the true, the good, and the beautiful. Only such a world can have for us an ultimate value.

This ultimate value of the "world-totality," of the One World, is "given" in *religion* in its immediacy as a "life-value." It is achieved in *philosophy* as the result of deliberate and goal-directed effort. Religion and philosophy are thus supplementary in our search for ultimate values. As Münsterberg puts it: "The world of experience—split up as it is in the irreconcilable special worlds of the logical, the moral, the asethetic—'realizes' (*'verwirklicht'*) itself in the all-encompassing ultimate world (*in der umfassenden letzten Welt*) that is given support (*getragen*) in our religious and philosophical conviction and in which every conflict disappears" (p. 403). This ultimate conviction gives us "reality" because what here supplements our actual experience is precisely what gives meaning to our whole existence.

In religion, the "Ultimate" that transcends the world as experienced by us is, of course, God. In philosophy it is the Absolute. The difference is that God is the culmination of a developing Reality, whereas the Absolute is its "primordial ground" or foundation (*Urgrund*). In line with this distinction, Münsterberg speaks of "God-values" (*Gotteswerte*) and "Foundation-values" (*Urgrundwerte*). The former center around the value of "holiness," the latter around that of "eternity."

The religious orientation manifests itself, with respect to the external world, as belief in creation; with respect to the world of human interactions, as belief in revelation; and with respect to our inner world, as redemption.

As "Creator," God must be Spirit and akin to our own "life of the spirit"; for the act of creation (*die Schöpfungstat*) is not meant as a causal explanation of the world, but as interpretation of its meaning. "To believe in God the Creator means so to understand the world that in it and by virtue of a transcendent (*jenseitige*) power any conflict between the order of nature, happiness, and morality is suspended (*aufgehoben*)" (p. 414). And this faith through which all values are brought into harmony is the very essence of Religion that is basic to all historically developed religions (p. 415).

Just as "creation" supplements the causal nexus that is constitutive of nature, so "revelation" supplements the historical context of interacting human beings. The conflicts and apparent contradictions which we discern in the historical process can be surmounted only when we are certain that, despite everything that has happened, the historical context itself, the development, is ultimately sanctioned by God in whose holiness all order, all morality, and all blessedness are finally unified. "The trans-personal demand for the perfect unity of all values must thus relate man's communal life to a divine revelation" (p. 423).

Our inner life is also full of conflicts, and the drive toward a universally valid value of unity is a "yearning after a redemption" (*Erlösungssehnsucht*) that transcends those conflicts. "The true redemption in the meaning of Christianity is thus the triumphant occurrence in us of that deed (*Willenstat*) through which every conflict of values is overcome and there is achieved in our soul the complete unity of the true, the harmonious, and the good. It is redemption through timeless bliss" (p. 435). Such redemption comes about, not through God's intervention "from outside," but through our own advance to a higher and purer mode of living. What is "transcendent" in our inner world thus actually lies in ourselves. And because this is so, religious thought here turns into philosophy.

It is the task of philosophy to establish the unity of values conceptually, for philosophy finds its own completion only through the all-inclusive unification of the world we live in, and only its unified world-view can give meaning to our own existence. To relinquish this aim at an integrative interpretation would mean to regard the whole of Reality as ultimately and intrinsically contradictory and therefore as valueless. "The world as a whole," Münsterberg holds, "has value only when, in the last analysis, the diverse realities are but forms or modes (*Gestal-*

tungen) of one inherently self-identical primordial Reality (*Ur-wirklichkeit*)" (p. 442).

The values, however, are not simply "given"; they are tasks (*Aufgaben*) that are to be fulfilled. And the relating of the various and separate values to a something that transcends experience (*ein Erfahrungsjenseits*) is not a matter of cognition but an act of commitment that is rooted in the deepest, the most profound nature of the person—an act akin to committing oneself to a religious belief. "Without this deepest decision, without committing one's whole person—in brief, without conviction—there can be no ultimate philosophy" (p. 444). And the value of this conviction (*Überzeugungswert*) alone is superordinated to the logical, the aesthetic, the moral, and the religious values. In fact, every logical, aesthetic, and moral experience attains its full meaning only through its relation to this ultimate and primordial Reality" (p. 445).

But, in the perspective of that value, everything that is merely incidental to our existence as a person and that varies from person to person and from situation to situation loses its significance. There remains only "a striving that has itself as content and that strives to hold on to its content" (p. 448).

Moreover, "my experience is that of my own personal self, and whatsoever is conceived as experienceable (*erfahrbar*) must be capable of belonging to a self" (p. 446). When this condition of the possibility of experience is denied, then "the worlds of my values" (*die Welten meiner Werte*) can no longer be experienced. But when I thus relinquish the relationship of those worlds to myself, "my own self relinquishes itself" and, "with the I, the thou also vanishes." That is to say, when all relations to persons are denied, the "distinction between I and things" no longer exists and "reality" has become a meaningless term.

The constructive alternative, according to Münsterberg, is that the self rise to the level of a trans-personal Self (*Über-Ich*), a "Super-Self, and that the self find tranquility, security, and the sense of belonging to the Ultimate Whole in that conception (p. 452). But when we proceed from the actual self, then the trans-personal "Super-Self" is itself but a posited value, the culmination of an act of faith— of a faith, however, that is "a universally satisfying act of will which, as yet, has no inner relation to an *ought*" (p. 453). Still, through this act of faith "the necessity of context, the unity of harmony and of progress in the world are reconciled." All are manifestations of "a free deed of the primordial will" (p. 461). And so is the whole cultural development of mankind (p. 463). "We ourselves are that striving and, at the same time, the whole deed as well" (p. 465).

Viewed in this way, "the world is a living, striving, doing, not a dead accidental happening." "Our own deed is a responsible and irreplaceable participation" in the primordial volition (p. 468). "To build up the world of values (*Wertwelt*) is now not only the necessary will of every being that wants to be acknowledged as a self, but is a task antecedent to becoming a self which alone gives meaning to the self itself and to the context of its experience" (p. 469).

Even on empirical grounds it can be asserted that the development and the achievements of mankind are something valuable. How much more, then, will the history of mankind gain in depth and dignity when we now view it as the "unfolding of an eternal volition." "Every truth and every work of art, every just action and every moral victory, every scientific progress and every religious exaltation now becomes an enhancement of an eternal volition. Every cooperation of human beings in some value-producing activity—be it in the family, the community, the state, or in the broadest cultural area—now manifests itself as a steady growth of the one living, world-positing (*weltsetzende*) power. In every pioneer of a new value, in every leader of mankind there wells up something from the deepest depth of Being. From the obscure subconscious of mankind it arises" (p. 469). And the significance of our individual self lies in the degree of our participation in the development of the values. "Only as co-creators of values (*Wertmitschaffer*) do we fulfill the task intrinsic to the will to value—a task which that will realizes in and through mankind" (p. 471). As such co-creators, our self is enlarged through its own deed into the "Super-Self" and our whole life is part of a world struggling to rise to ever higher values (p. 477). In this fact lies "a joyous affirmation" of life itself; for "he who posits the value carries within himself a joy which, of necessity, renews itself with every pulse-beat of life; and volition itself turns into an infinite source of satisfaction" (*ibid.*). But it would be senseless to expect more of life than the fulfillment of one's own volition; for nothing other than the realization of our own volitions can give us satisfaction. The fact that the fulfillment of our volition is not an unattainable goal but is realized in every step toward the goal—this makes our life "the best and the most fulfilled" (*zum besten und erfülltesten*) (p. 478). The ultimate issue, therefore, is "to remain true to oneself." But this means "so to enhance our will by creating what we will in the very depth of our being, and thus to help build a world of values in which the universally valid becomes an expression of our personal volition." "The history of mankind thus becomes an infinite unfolding of our most personal volition" (p. 480).

However, "that the Super-Self is real; that its will determines unalterably our value-world; and that therefore our duty-bound life is really infinitely valuable—all this is not a matter of knowledge. Our certainty here is based upon the rock of conviction (*Überzeugung*); and upon this conviction, this faith, depends every value of truth, of unity, of activity, and of perfection. But the conviction itself is, ultimately, our own deed. We cannot avoid it if we do not want to abandon ourselves; for only through this deed are all our values unified" (p. 481). But it remains our own deed, nevertheless. "To remain true to ourselves in eternity—all values of the world are securely grounded in such a deed" (*ibid.*).

BIBLIOGRAPHY

Münsterberg, Hugo, *Philosophie der Werte*, Leipzig, 1908.
———— *The Eternal Values*, Boston and New York, 1909.

CHAPTER XI

THE "EMOTIONAL INTUITIONISM" OF MAX SCHELER

In the Preface to the second edition of *Der Formalismus in der Ethik und die Materiale Wertethik,* Scheler himself tells us that this work is "central" not only to his ethics but to his whole philosophy; and he states, as a matter of principle, that "all values must be subordinated to person-values" (*Personwerte*) (p. 14). It is this principle, incidentally, which Scheler means to emphasize when he calls his "emotional intuitionism" (his own term for his position) "a new attempt at finding a basis for an ethical personalism" (p. 15).

During the five years between the publication of the second edition of *Der Formalismus* (1922) and the third (1927), Scheler modified his metaphysical views in important respects. Thus, in 1927 he no longer regarded himself as a theist. However, in the Preface to the third edition he stresses the fact that those changes have in no way affected his views as set forth in *Der Formalismus;* that, in fact, these views were in part responsible for the change in the rest of his philosophy (p. 17). Some of the changes, by the way, can be traced in *Die Formen des Wissens und die Bildung* (1925) and *Die Wissensformen und die Gesellschaft* (1926). For our purposes, however, it is not necessary to consider the nature of such changes, for they do not affect Scheler's approach to values as developed in *Der Formalismus* and as stated in the first edition. All references, however, are here to the third edition which is actually but a reprint of the first.

I

Scheler's basic assumption is that Kant has definitively disproven every form of ethics keyed to the idea of a "highest good" or an "ultimate purpose" (*Endzweck*) (p. 29), and that the task now is to eliminate Kant's own "formalism" as well. It is crucial for Scheler's argument, however, that he here regards the "highest good" as but a special kind of "good" among other "goods" and, therefore, not as a value *per se*. As he himself puts it: "In their very essence goods are valuable *things*" (Wert*dinge*) and not values" (p. 32).

If the moral quality of man's will were made to depend upon "goods" (such as "the welfare of an existing community" or "cultural possessions" (*Kulturbesitz*)), and upon the degree to which an individual tries to preserve or to further these "goods," then a radical relativism in moral matters would be unavoidable; for changes in the "world of goods" would entail changes in the meaning of "good" and "evil." That meaning would therefore depend upon the course of history and could have empirico-inductive validity only. Moreover, we would have no standard whatsoever by means of which to judge—and judge morally—any currently given "world of goods" (p. 32). Kant was right in rejecting such a basis for morality.

It is Scheler's contention, however, that Kant thought he had accomplished more than he actually had; that he thought he had demonstrated not only that all theories of ethics which are keyed to the preservation of "goods" are untenable, but that all theories keyed to "values of a material nature" are also untenable. Kant himself had put it this way: "All practical principles which presuppose an object (material) of the faculty of desire as the determining ground of the will are without exception empirical and can furnish no practical laws. By the term 'material of the faculty of desire' I understand an object whose reality is desired" (*Kritik der Praktischen Vernunft,* Pt. I, Chpt. I, Theorem I).

As Scheler sees it, Kant's argument would cover "values" (along with the "goods") if and only if values were derivative and were obtained from the "goods" by a process of abstraction or were encountered as the effects which "goods" have upon our pleasures and displeasures. But values, Scheler maintains, are non-derivative and are in themselves "independent phenomena." It is this thesis which Scheler must now substantiate.

II

The crux of Scheler's argument in support of his thesis can be stated quite simply: Just as we can conceive a certain *red* as merely an extensive quality (e.g., as a pure color of the spectrum) without taking it to be the color of an object or even something space-like, so there are accessible to us (in principle, at least) such values as agreeable, charming, lovely, friendly, noble, without our thinking of them as qualities of things or persons. That this is so, Scheler maintains, can readily be seen when we consider, for example, one of the simple values—the agreeableness of certain sensory experiences. We then find, for instance, that every delicious fruit—a cherry, a peach, an apricot—has its own kind of agreeable taste. The agreeableness is in each case qualitatively different from all others. It has its own characteristic value quality. As far as Scheler is concerned, this means that the distinctive value qualities of the various kinds of agreeableness are "genuine qualities of the value itself (i.e., of agreeableness)" (p. 35), and are not definable in terms of value-free attributes.

What is true at this elementary level is true also, and even more so, in value spheres which transcend the merely agreeable. In the case of aesthetic experiences, for example, the values designated by words such as "lovely," "charming," "sublime," and "beautiful" are not definable in terms of, or derivable from, value-free qualities which things possess. On the contrary, we must already know what the values are before we can say that they are realized in such and such objects. That is to say, each of the value-words mentioned integrates into the unity of a value concept a qualitatively graduated series of value phenomena and not some value-indifferent attributes.

What is true in the field of aesthetics is true also in the moral sphere. In fact, it is true generally. Wherever we speak rightfully of a value, there we find it impossible to derive that value from attributes of objects and things which are not themselves values. But this means that a rightfully asserted value must be directly given or intuited as a value.[1] It is non-derivative.

But if this is so, then the genuine or true value qualities must

---

[1] We must note here a similarity between Scheler's view and that of G. E. Moore. In the Preface to the second edition of *Der Formalismus* Scheler himself has called attention to it.

constitute a sphere of "objects" of some sort within which the values stand in specific relations to one another, thus forming a context within which some values could be said to be higher than others. If there actually were such a distinction, there would then prevail an order of rank of values—an order of rank that would be independent of the existence of "goods" and would, in fact, be determinative of the various value levels of the actual "goods." What Scheler underscores here is the fact that value is one thing and a "bearer of a value" (*Wertträger*) is quite another. This distinction underlies his whole argument.

Of equal importance for Scheler's argument is his insistence that values, simply as value phenomena, are not "feeling-states" (*Gefühlszustände*) but genuine objects—albeit "ideal objects." Only in "goods" are values both, objective and real. Every creation of a new "good" thus means a real increase of value (*Wertwachstum*) in the real world, and the creation of a world of "goods" is always guided by an order of rank of values.

This interpretation of values, Scheler argues, casts a new light upon the specifically moral values, good and evil. Kant had maintained that good (*bonum*) and evil (*malum*) always pertain to a will insofar as that will is determined by a law of reason to pursue certain goals; but he had interpreted the law of reason in a purely formal sense. This formalism Scheler repudiates by relating man's rational will to the order of rank of values. As he sees it, an act is morally good if it tends to realize the higher rather than the lower value in any given situation. But this principle, Scheler maintains, has validity also beyond any narrowly conceived sphere of morality and, in connection with the idea of an order of rank of values, it is basic to the following set of axioms:

Ia. The existence of a positive value is itself a positive value.
 b. The non-existence of a positive value is itself a negative value.
 c. The existence of a negative value is itself a negative value.
 d. The non-existence of a negative value is itself a positive value.
IIa. Morally good is that value in the sphere of volition that is connected with the realization of a positive value.
 b. Evil is that value in the sphere of volition that is connected with the realization of a negative value.
 c. Morally good is that value in the sphere of volition that is connected with the realization of a higher (highest) value.

    d. Evil is that value in the sphere of volition that is connected with the realization of a lower (lowest) value.

  III. The criterion for "morally good" (and "evil") consists in the agreement (disagreement) of the value whose realization is intended with the value that ought to be preferred (*Vorzugswert*), or in the disagreement (agreement) with the value that ought not to be preferred (pp. 48–49).

We must be clear on this point, however: The value "morally good" ("evil") is always a quality of the will itself, never an object of the will. The object or "matter" is a non-moral value. But since acts of will are always acts of a person, the existence of a person is a necessary presupposition of all volitional acts, be they morally good or morally evil. Keeping this in mind, we can now define good and evil as "person-values" (*Personwerte*); and the prevailing "directions" in which a person carries out good acts or evil acts are then that person's virtues or vices, respectively.

After all that has been said so far, it seems fairly clear that values and their order of rank are relevant to all our purposive actions—to actions, that is, which involve deliberate decision and which thus differ from actions prompted by innate drives and by desires. The question is, Precisely how are the values involved in all this?

Values, Scheler maintains, are "given" in our feelings. But does this mean that we must first feel the values before we pursue them? Or do we feel the values in the pursuit itself? Or, finally, do we feel them only as we reflect upon what we are pursuing? One thing is certain, Scheler believes, it is not our "feeling-state" (*zuständliches Gefühl*) that causes our action. And neither is a "feeling-state," such as pleasure, the goal of our action. Where the facts seem to be otherwise, closer examination will show that the distinction between "feeling-state" and value has been overlooked, and that it is the value involved, not the "feeling-state," that prompts us to act. Even the "pursuit of pleasure" is actually not a pursuit of pleasure as such but of pleasure regarded as a value. Hedonism in all its forms thus rests upon an untenable assumption. But the question still is, How are values related to our pursuit of goals?

Scheler points out that the "givenness" (*Gegebenheit*) of values is not bound to our pursuits—either in the sense that positive value is identical with "being pursued" (*Erstrebtwerden*), negative value with "being avoided" (*Widerstrebtwerden*), or in any other sense. We are perfectly capable of feeling values without pursuing them or finding them to be immanent in our pursuits. Similarly, we can prefer one value to another without, at the same time, deciding on a course of action. That is to say, values can be "given" and can be "preferred" without our actually pursuing them.

However, to every value that is "given" in our actual pursuits there corresponds the possibility of its being "given" in our feelings also. It is because of this fact that a value that is being pursued can be identified with a value "given" in our feeling. Actually, a value-feeling (*Wertfühlen*) is basic to every one of our pursuits—in the same way in which, for example, a perception is basic to perceptual judgments. And this is so even if, at times, we apprehend in our pursuits values which we would never have encountered had we not pursued some goal.

What all this amounts to, however, is this: All purposive actions are directed toward goals which are selected and projected on the basis of value considerations; that values and their order of rank are the indispensable presuppositions of all deliberate and rational actions.

III

The broad outlines of Scheler's value theory so far presented must now be augmented in several important respects.

To begin with, if values and their order of rank are indeed the indispensable presupposition of rational choices and deliberate actions, and if they are non-derivative and not demonstrable inductively, then they must be *a priori* and must be knowable through "immediate intuition" (*unmittelbare Anschauung*).

Kant identified the *a priori* with purely formal aspects of experience; and this, according to Scheler, was his basic error. It is too narrow a view when values are involved; for the very essence of values is "specific content," i.e., it is "material" rather than "formal."

Kant's second error was to identify the *a priori* with the rational, i.e., with thought, and the "material" with sensory experience and the *a posteriori*.

In repudiating the Kantian position, Scheler asserts that emotional experience—"feeling, preferring, loving, hating, and willing"—also has "an original *a priori* content (*einen ursprünglichen apriorischen Gehalt*) that is not borrowed from thinking." As Scheler puts it: "There is an *a priori* 'ordre du coeur' or 'logique du coeur,' as Blaise Pascal said so aptly," and this "emotional *a priori*" is basic to all value experience (84). "Pure logic" must therefore be augmented by a "pure value theory"—by a "phenomenology of values," that is, as a totally independent (*völlig selbständiges*) field of investigation (p. 85). And it is intuition (*Wesensschau*) rather than inductive generalization that is the key to our understanding of values and their interrelations. The "locus proper" (*der eigentliche Sitz*) of every value *a priori* is intrinsic to that intuition.

What is disclosed in emotional intuition is, of course, the objective character of the values and of their interrelations; and, as objectively valid, values can and do justify an *ought*. They are the basis of it. Moreover, the same objective nature of values and of their order of rank implies that the subject, the human being, is only a "bearer of values" (*ein Träger von Werten*) and not the precondition of there being any values. That is to say, the subject does not create the values through an act of valuing but finds them as "given" in value intuition. And that intuition discloses to us a whole realm of objectively "given" values.

Within that realm a characteristic order prevails: Some values are "higher," others are "lower." This order of rank, Scheler argues, like the distinction between positive and negative values, is grounded in the very nature of the values themselves. It is apprehended by us in a special act of value-cognition—the act of "preferring" (p. 107). This act, however, must not be confused with "choosing," i.e., with an act of deciding on a course of action; and neither does it determine which value is "higher" and which is "lower." It but discloses that values stand in this characteristic relation to one another. That is to say, the order of rank of values is "given" just as the values themselves are "given," and is objective and invariable (p. 108).

Being rooted in, and reflecting, the very nature of the values, the order of rank is, of course, not derivable from anything else. But there are characteristics of the values themselves that are related to the degrees of higher and lower. The lowest values, for example, are the most ephemeral; the highest are eternal. But whether or not this fact can serve as a criterion of higher and lower remains a mute question.

Another aspect of the interrelations of values is involved when we consider the values of material "goods," on the one hand, and values of the intellectual or spiritual realm, on the other. The former can be shared by a number of subjects only when the material bearers of the values are distributed among them. However, because of the limited number of material bearers available, the pursuit of these values may in some situations lead directly to a divisive conflict of interests. This is not so in the case of the other values—i.e., in the case of the values of the intellectual or spiritual sphere, the values of knowledge, of beauty, of the holy. It is of the very essence of such values that they are available, without diminution in value, to any number of people; that, in fact, they tend to unite rather than to divide those who pursue them. And the most unifying pursuit of all, Scheler argues, is the communal veneration of the holy. What separates here and entails conflicts, such as the "religious wars," are the symbols and the techniques of veneration rather than the value of the holy itself.

But again it is a mute question whether or not the aspects of value-interrelations just referred to can serve as a criterion of higher and lower.

It is different, however, when we consider the relationship which Scheler calls "founding" (*fundieren*). A value of the type B is foundational to a value of type A when a particular value A can be "given" only when some particular value B is already "given." And when such a relationship exists, then the "founding" or foundational value—i.e., the value B—is always the higher value. The value of what is "agreeable" is thus foundational to the value of the "useful" and is the higher value, for what is useful has value only as means to what is "agreeable." But the value of the "agreeable" is, in turn, "founded" in a "life-value"

(*Lebenswert*)—i.e., in the value of a felt vitality, strength, and well-being. But the value of life is also not ultimate. It is "founded" in the spiritual values—the values of knowledge, of beauty, and so on. In the last analysis, so Scheler maintains, all possible values are "founded" in the value of an "infinite personal spirit" and the "world of values" which that spirit encompasses (p. 116); and this value alone is absolute (p. 120).

That the higher values give us a deeper or more profound satisfaction than do the lower ones is an empirical fact. In itself, however, it is not a criterion of the height of a value. But there are other aspects of value relations that are germane to the problem and must be considered here.

As Scheler sees it, we must distinguish between two kinds of *a priori* "orders" of values: one which determines the height of values in accordance with their essential bearers, and one which pertains to the value qualities themselves. As far as the first order is concerned, Scheler distinguishes between "person-values" (*Personwerte*) and "goods-values" (*Sachwerte*). The "person-values," having persons as their bearers, include the value of the person himself and of his virtues (*Tugendwerte*). The "goods-values" include not only the values of material goods (both, goods of consumption and goods that are "useful"), but also the values of "spiritual goods," such as the values of science and of the arts— i.e., values of the cultural goods proper (*die eigentlichen Kulturgüter*). Since the "person-values" are foundational to the "goods-values," they are also higher than the latter.

Moreover, *acts* (such as cognitive acts, acts of loving or hating, and acts of the will), *functions* (hearing, seeing, feeling, and so on), and even *reactions* (including responses to other human beings, such as sympathy and revenge) can be bearers of values. But their values are subordinate to the "person-values" and are therefore lower. However, among these values themselves there prevail *a priori* relationships of higher and lower. The value of *acts* are thus higher than the values of *functions,* and both groups are higher than the values of mere *reactions.* That is to say, the values of spontaneity are higher than the values of merely "reactive responses."

Within a communal relationship of persons we must distinguish three types of bearers of values: the persons themselves, the form of their relationship, and the relationship as actually experienced. In the case of marriage, for example, the three types of value-bearers stand out quite clearly: the persons married to each other; marriage as a special type of communal relationship; and the way in which the persons married to each other actually experience their relationship. As the value-bearers differ so do the values of which they are the bearers; and the types of values here discernible are not reducible to one another or, all of them, to some other type. Yet, the interrelation of the values is obvious.

A further distinction among values is that between values whose value character is independent of all other values— Scheler calls them "self-values" (*Selbstwerte*)—and values whose very nature includes a "phenomenal" (i.e., an intuitively felt) relation to other values and that would cease to be values without this relationship—Scheler calls them "consecutive values" (*Konsekutivwerte*). We must note, however, that things necessary for the causal production of goods which, because of this fact, are *judged* to have "means-value," do not therefore also have "consecutive value," for "consecutive values" are intuitively felt, not ascribed to a value-bearer in a judgment. As Scheler sees it, all "tool-values" are genuine "consecutive values," for a tool has a value that is intuitively "given" in its nature as a tool, and is not derived, via a judgment, from the value of any "product" for the realization of which the tool might be employed, although without the relation to a "product" the tool would not be a tool. All specifically "technical values" are, in this sense, genuine consecutive values. And so are also all "symbol-values" (*Symbolwerte*) —the flag of a nation, for example, which symbolizes the honor and dignity of a people; or the *res sacrae* (to give another example) which, in sacramental functions, are the bearers of a special kind of values that is independent of what is being symbolized but which the "sacred objects" would not have if they did not function as symbols.

More important for the order of rank of values than the relationships just indicated are the interrelations of the value qualities themselves—the "value modalities" (*Wertmodalitäten*), as

Scheler calls them. They constitute the "material *a priori*" (*das materiale Apriori*) for our insight into values and value preferences, and thus are the real disproof (*die schärfste Widerlegung*) of Kant's formalism (p. 125).

One of the clearly delimitated value modalities is the polar opposition "agreeable-disagreeable." To it there correspond the functions of our "sensuous feeling" (enjoying and suffering) and the "feeling-states" (sensuous pleasure and pain). That is to say, we must distinguish here (as we must in the case of every other value modality) between an "object-value" (*Sachwert*), a "function-value" (*Funktionswert*), and a "state-value" (*Zustandswert*). This entire value-sequence is relative to the nature of a sensuous being but not to any particular organization of such a being, such as man; and neither is it relative to the particular objects or events in the external world which are agreeable or disagreeable to a being having some particular organization. The value-difference "agreeable-disagreeable" is in itself absolute. It is not affected by the fact that the same object or event may be agreeable to one person (or animal) and disagreeable to another. In fact, its meaning is clear before such differences are recognized.

Also, that the agreeable is preferred to the disagreeable is not a fact that depends upon induction from experience but is grounded in the very nature of the values involved and in the nature of sensuous feelings. Moreover, no evolutionary theory can explain the difference between the agreeable and the disagreeable. What alone can be explained in terms of "usefulness for survival" is the fact that specific "feeling-states" of pleasure and pain are induced by particular objects in the environment. But such "feeling-states" are not the same as the values "agreeable-disagreeable," nor are they a "preference-relation."

A second value modality includes all values of "vital feeling" (*Werte des vitalen Gefühls*) that range from "noble" (possessing excellent qualities) to "ignoble" (possessing base qualities). Subordinate to them are the "function-values" belonging to the sphere of "welfare," and the "state-values" of an enhanced or a declining vitality: the feeling of health and of sickness, of strength and senescence. These values constitute an independent value-modality because they can be derived neither from the values of the agreeable or the useful, nor from any spiritual values. They are rooted directly in the very nature of "life" itself.

The third value modality, that of the spiritual values, is characterized by a detachment (*Abgelöstheit*) and independence vis-a-vis the whole sphere of the body and its environment. The acts and functions in and through which we apprehend them are functions of "spiritual feeling" (*Funktionen des geistigen Fühlens*) and acts of "spiritual preferring and loving and hating" which differ phenomenologically from their biological counterparts and cannot be reduced to them (p. 128).

At least three distinct types of values are here involved: the values of the aesthetic realm that range from the beautiful to the ugly; the values basic to any judicial order that range from just to unjust; and the values of cognition *per se* (*Werte der reinen Wahrheitserkenntnis*) to which the values of science are consecutive. Consecutive to all the spiritual values are the so-called "cultural values" (*die sogenannten Kulturwerte*) which actually belong to the sphere of "goods-values" (e.g., art treasures, scientific institutions, positive law). The correlative "states" are feelings, such as joy and sadness, which are phenomenologically distinct from any feelings that depend on "states" or conditions of the body, and which vary as the values of the objects vary—not as the vital or sensuous "feeling-states" vary. Included are here the values of response-reactions, the values of approval and disapproval, of respect and contempt, and of a "spiritual sympathy" that is basic to friendships.

The last value modality, that of the "holy-unholy," is sharply separated from all others. The values involved all share one specific condition of their "givenness": they all occur only in connection with objects which, at least in intention, are given as "absolute objects" (*absolute Gegenstände*). However, the modality is independent of everything which, at different times and by different people, has been called "holy." That is to say, it is as independent of the purest conception of a personal God as it is of the crudest fetishistic images or objects. The value difference "holy-unholy" is thus independent also of all specific cultural conditions or situations.

The experiential "states" corresponding to this value modality are the feelings of "heavenly bliss" (*Seligkeit*) and of "utter despair"—experiences which differ radically from feelings of "happiness" and "unhappiness." The "response-reactions" are "belief" and "unbelief," "reverence" and "irreverence," "worship" and "blasphemy." But the act in which we truly apprehend the "holy" is an act of a particular kind of love and which, being love, is, in its very nature, directed toward something "that has the form of a personal being" (*das von personaler Seinsform ist*). The "self-value" in the sphere of the "holy" is thus a "person-value" (*Personwert*) (p. 129). The corresponding consecutive values are the "value-objects" and the "forms of veneration" encountered in public worship and in the sacraments. They are genuine "symbol-values" (*Symbolwerte*), not merely "symbols of values" (*Wertsymbole*).

Now, as Scheler sees it, the value modalities just distinguished stand in an *a priori* order of rank relative to one another—an order of rank which is intrinsic to the respective series of value qualities themselves and is therefore valid for any "goods" that are bearers of these values. The values of the modality "noble-ignoble," for example, constitute a dimension of values higher than that of the modality "agreeable-disagreeable." Similarly, the spiritual values constitute a value dimension that is higher than is that of the "vital values," and the values of the holy are higher than the spiritual values, for they are the highest of them all (p. 130).

IV

In the Preface to the first edition of *Der Formalismus* Scheler explicitly affirmed what the title of the book suggests: His intention to develop "a positive basis for a philosophical ethics" that would replace all purely formal theories, such as Kant's. His approach and method were those of a phenomenological analysis of our value experience. That analysis has been briefly described in the preceding pages. However, additional details will become evident when we now examine at least some of the aspects of Scheler's ethics itself.

The first point we must note is that, for Scheler, the ultimate bearer of moral values is the "disposition" (*Gesinnung*) of a person insofar as this disposition includes wish, intention, and resolve. "Without a good disposition there can be no good action" (p. 134). Action, however, not being part of the disposition, is an additional bearer of moral values. That is to say, it has a value all its own.

It is of the nature of an action that it aims at the realization of an intended "state of affairs" (*Sachverhalt*). To intend to do something and to intend to realize a particular "state of affairs" are but a unitary experience in which the "content"—i.e., the anticipated "state of affairs"—is basic to the act through which its realization is intended; and it is basic because it is experienced as a value. However, experiences of this type merely reflect the "value structure" (*Wertstruktur*) of the agent's disposition. His intention to realize particular value-contents and the "world" in which he intends to realize them thus "fit together" (*passen aufeinander*) because both depend upon the value-qualities and their order of rank inherent in his disposition. But this means that the "world" in which an agent acts is not "a value-free universe." Instead, it is "milieu"—"the exact counterpart of his drive-dispositions and their structure." His own "feeling-states" depend upon his drives as elicited by the objects of his milieu after those objects have already been selected by his drive-dispositions as part of the milieu. That is to say, the "feeling-states" are the result, not the cause, of the agent's drives.

When we now consider more specifically the problem of moral values, Scheler maintains that here, too, we must begin with the facts as experienced. When we do so, we find that value qualities —such as noble, magnanimous, and just—differ, one from another, just as nuances of red (as perceptual contents) differ from one another. And we must note also that value-words are not employed simply to express feelings. They are not equivalents of Ah! and Oh!; for value-words have cognitive meaning, whereas mere expressions of feelings have not. Thus, when we assert that one action is just and another ignoble, our feelings about them reflect essential differences in the value qualities. Our approval in one case and our disapproval in another is always rooted in, and warranted by, our apprehension of the value-content that is inherent in the actions themselves. Variations in the degree of our emotional responses do not affect the quality of the values. Thus, when we recognize a moral value—magnanimity, for example— in the character of our enemy, we may grudgingly admit its presence. Our lack of enthusiasm, however, does not affect the nature or quality of the value itself (p. 188).

Moreover, value statements are neither disguised pleas nor commands to act in certain ways. And neither are they expressions of wishes or desires. They are instead propositions asserting and designating something objectively given, namely, values (p. 190).

But it is also a fact of human experience that, at times, the same actions and attitudes are both, approved and disapproved, praised and condemned. Thus, one person may call an attitude "unassuming," when another calls it "servile"; one may regard a person as "proud," when someone else regards him as "arrogant." Such differences of opinion may be, and often have been, taken as proof that approval and disapproval depend upon the interest we take in the actions, not upon the values of the actions themselves, and that therefore approval and disapproval are devoid of objective significance. Scheler, however, argues that the facts in the case are not only reconcilable with, but actually demand, an objective interpretation of values. Why, he asks, is it that, instead of expressing their interests and desires directly, human beings disguise them as value judgments? Why do they say that certain actions are "good"—i.e., worthy of approval—and others are "bad"—i.e., deserving of disapproval? Scheler's answer is that, because it is of the very essence of all moral values to demand approval, we find it useful for our own purposes to call a person "morally good" when what he does coincides with our own interests, and "morally bad" when what he does is in conflict with our interests. That is to say, we make use of the demand for approval that is inherent in all moral values to serve our own private interests. To put it differently: The interest we take in an action does not explain the moral value of that action but conceals it. It explains only how we can be deceived about values (p. 192).

To argue, as Rickert does, that the very essence of a value is an *ought* misses the crucial point. The meaning of such statements as "This picture is beautiful," "This action is morally good," is not that this picture or this action *ought* to be something; for the statements assert what already is the case. This means that value statements cannot be reduced to, or derived from, *ought*-statements. On the contrary, whenever we assert an *ought,* we presuppose a value that *ought* to be realized. Every *ought,* in other words, is grounded in a value (pp. 200–201)—as are all norms, imperatives and demands, if the latter are not to be entirely arbitrary (p. 202). And we must note that insofar as it is the intent of value statements to assert what is the case, such statements are either true or false in the very same sense in which all cognitive assertions are either true or false. What Scheler denies, however, is that value statements refer to experiences of pleasure or displeasure, or that they relate objects to such experiences (p. 256). Values, he maintains, are not "feeling-states," and they are not relations. They are qualities directly apprehended through our feelings—just as blue, for example, is directly experienced as a sensory quality and not as a "state of sensing."

Scheler also repudiates the thesis that man, desiring pleasure, ascribes value to those objects which, by virtue of their intrinsic qualities, elicit his pleasure. "Feeling-states" he argues, are always causally induced. Values, however, are not causes that are in themselves objectively real. Experientially they are, of course, effective; but they are effective as motives rather than as causes. The beauty of a landscape, for example, and the fascination it has for us are two entirely different experiences—the former being the reason for the latter. That is to say, the beauty of the landscape is not the experienced effect of a value-free landscape upon us. On the contrary, it is the beauty of the landscape that affects us, and its effect upon us manifests itself as a "feeling-state" (p. 262).

It must also be noted, Scheler points out, that the actual feeling which an object causes in us may not correspond to the value of that object. We may take pleasure in evil, and goods may elicit displeasure. Moreover, whereas the experiences of pleasure (or displeasure) are always passing events and, as actual, are also individual, the values involved are permanent and inter-individual (*interindividuell*). We thus encounter here an important incongruence between "feeling-states" and values which, according to

Scheler, militates against the thesis that we ascribe value to objects because of the "feeling-states" which they arouse in us.

And we must not overlook the fact that our experiences of pleasure and displeasure have themselves a value. Not only may pleasure be taken in the vulgar, but there is also a vulgar pleasure —as there is a noble sadness, etc. We must distinguish, in other words, between the value disclosed in our feeling and the value quality of that feeling itself; and the latter, Scheler maintains, is further evidence against the thesis that we ascribe value to objects on the basis of our feeling-states. He concludes that, no matter how we interpret the relation between pleasures and objects, it is not possible to deduce from such a relation the fact that there are values. Values are an irreducible phenomenon (*Urphänomen*) and, as such, are not amenable to reductive explanations (p. 267).

V

If this thesis is accepted (even if only for the sake of argument), a crucial question arises—the question, namely, of how or in what way are values given in our experience? The difficulty we encounter here stems from the fact that in the long tradition of Western philosophy reason has been taken to be the truly cognitive faculty, and that the non-rational aspects of experience —notably all feelings and desires—are regarded as essentially non-cognitive. Very few thinkers—among them St. Augustin and Blaise Pascal—have held different views.

Reference has already been made (III, above) to Pascal's "logique du coeur." It is now necessary, however, to guard against certain misinterpretations of Pascal's (and, therefore, of Scheler's) position.

When Pascal says that "le coeur a ses raisons"—so Scheler points out—he means to say that there is an order intrinsic to our feelings, in our loving and hating, that is as absolute as is that of pure logic—an "ordre du coeur" that cannot be reduced to the laws of intellectual reasoning. It is a mistake, therefore, to take Pascal's thesis to mean that, after reason has reached its conclusion, our "heart"—our feelings—may also affect our experience. The "reasons of the heart" are not "needs" of our emotional self which, as factors in our experience, must find an appropriate place in any comprehensive world-view that is rationally constructed. What Scheler means—and what he takes Pascal to mean—is this: There is a mode of experiencing whose objects are inaccessible to reason —objects to which reason is as blind as the ear is to color; a mode of experiencing, nevertheless, which reveals to us "genuine objective objects" (*echte objektive Gegenstände*) and an eternal order among them: the values and their order of rank. This order and its laws are as definite, as precise, and as understandable as are the laws of logic and mathematics. They are the basis of all our valuations and our preferences (p. 269).

It is important, however, that we distinguish between mere "feeling-states" (*Gefühlszuständen*) and the intentional feeling of something (*das intentionale Fühlen von etwas*). Since Scheler maintains that only the latter discloses values, the question is, Are intentional feelings discernible in our experience? In defense of his affirmative answer to this question, Scheler points to experiential situations in which both, "feeling-states" and intentional feelings, are involved—situations, in other words, in which intentional feelings are directed toward "feeling-states." Such situations are by no means rare. Consider what indubitably are sensory "feeling-states"—pain, sensory pleasure, the agreeableness of a taste sensation, etc. Such "feeling-states," however, by no means determine the mode of feeling; for the experiences are quite different when, for example, I simply suffer a particular pain or put up with it or bear it patiently or even take pleasure in it. What varies here is not the "feeling-state pain" but the quality of the intentional feeling concerned with that pain. The pain itself is content of experience; the intentional feeling is a function or mode of experiencing it.

Also, as Scheler points out, we experience "feeling-states" which, at first, seem unrelated to any objects. If we wish to account for them, we may have to search for whatever causes them. The "feeling-states" as such do not refer to or "mean" something beyond themselves. Past experience involving comparable situations may obfuscate this fact by suggesting causal connections. But this does not alter the non-directional character of mere "feeling-states."

It is quite different in the case of our intentional feelings; for these are closely related to what is felt in them. As Scheler puts it: "Here there exists a primary self-relating (*ein ursprüngliches Sichbeziehen*): the feeling directing itself (*ein Sicheinrichten*) to something objective—i.e., to *values*" (p. 271). Such feeling is not simply a "state" which can be associated with, or related to, objects, but is a "goal-determined movement" (*eine zielbestimmte Bewegung*), an activity which has the same relation to a value-correlate that perception has to an object—i.e., it has an intentional or cognitive relation. In the act of feeling, feeling itself is not the object; but in and through it value qualities are revealed as "given" and the world of objects is encountered in its value aspects. Given with these value aspects is also the experience of value preferences as a mode of cognition.

Loving and hating are the highest forms of this intentional or cognitive character of our emotions.[1] The act of loving, in particular, leads to the discovery of new and higher values (*spielt die eigentlich entdeckerische Rolle*).

It is, of course, true that human beings, simply as human beings, are the place and the occasion (*der Ort und die Gelegenheit*) for the appearance of felt values. This dose not mean, however,—so Scheler maintains—that the values are relative to, and dependent upon, the biological organization or even the existence of the human species. Nor does it mean that man himself is the highest value. On the contrary, a human being is but a bearer of values; and when we ascribe a value to him, we already presuppose that value as "given." But man is a being which, in the pursuit of ever higher values, can always transcend himself. He is "the living X" (*das lebendige X*) which, in the pursuit of spiritual values and of the values of the holy, can rise far above mere biological existence (p. 305).

VI

It is not possible to develop here Scheler's phenomenology

---

[1] I omit here the detailed analyses of love and hate which Scheler presented in *Zur Phänomenologie und Theorie der Sympathiegefühle und von Liebe und Hass.* I also refrain from tracing connections between Scheler's thesis and Brentano's conception of "right loving" and "right hating," although such connections are unquestionably there—as are also unmistakable differences.

of our emotional life to the point that all questions of value theory and of ethics can be answered. Certain basic facts, however, must still be considered. They concern the answers to two questions: (1) What is the connection between the "feeling-states" and the value of a person, of his volitions and his actions? Is that connection crucial or empirically accidental? (2) What is the role of the "feeling-states" and their various forms or modes, not as *goals* of our intentions to realize values, but as *sources* of such volitions—especially insofar as the rank of values is also involved?

That we experience a "stratification" (*Schichtung*) in our emotional life that is reflected in our valuations but does not depend upon the accidental occurrence of an emotion or upon such purely quantitative aspects as the duration and intensity of the emotions is undeniable. Even the language we use is sensitive to it; for we speak of experiences of "bliss," "happiness," "gaiety," "joy," "well-being," "sensuous pleasures," "agreeableness," etc.; and of experiences of "despair," "unhappiness," "sadness," "the disagreeable," and so on. Such differences in our "feeling-states" obviously imply corresponding differences in the "value-situations" (*Wertverhalte*).

But it is not sufficient merely to acknowledge the differences here indicated because some of the distinct feelings may occur together in one and the same experience. Thus, a person may well experience a sensory pleasure in a period of deepest despair; or he may be serene though bereft of all pleasures. In such situations the various "feeling-states" do not simply alternate, if ever so rapidly; and neither do they "fuse" into one total "feeling-state." They remain distinct and are experienced as distinct That is to say, they are experienced in different ways. But this is possible only because the feelings involved are experienced at difference levels of our existence.

Scheler distinguishes four such levels: (1) that of our sensory feelings; (2) that of our "body-state" feelings or, in the case of body-functions, our "feelings of vitality"; (3) our feelings of "self" or "pure ego-feelings" (*reine Ichgefühle*); and (4) our "spiritual" (*geistige*) feelings, i.e., our "person-feelings" (*Persönlichkeitsgefühle*) or the feelings pertaining to ourselves as persons (p. 344). Despite their differences, however, the feelings of all four levels are experienced relative to ourselves; but this relation which all feelings share is, in principle, different from our other experiences—i.e., it is other than our perceiving, willing, and thinking. But the relation also varies specifically from level to level, involving specifically different aspects of our whole being (p. 345).

Now, if this is so, and if feelings play so crucial a part in our knowledge of values as Scheler maintains that they do, and if, furthermore, man himself is but a "bearer of values," not a value itself, then it becomes necessary to consider more fully just what it means to be a human being, a person.

As Scheler sees it, a person is not only a living, conscious being, but a being that is capable of intentional acts. He is a being, furthermore, that reflecting upon his own intentional acts experiences himself as responsible for those acts. In this felt responsibility as an ultimate fact of experience is rooted his moral responsibility which, at the same time, is also the precondition of all responsibility he has before God and men (pp. 484-492). It follows from this that, when we morally judge another person, our judgment is truly adequate only when we take into consideration not only generally accepted norms and our own ideals, but also, and perhaps primarily, the ideal reflected in the basic value-intentions of the other person. However,—and this is crucial for Scheler's position—the value-ideal of the other person is not attainable through induction. Only an "understanding love" (*eine verstehende Liebe*) can discern in the mass of empirical detail the distinctive features of the ideal, of the "value-essence" of the other person.

What, then, is the "value-essence" of a person?—the "individual-personal value-essence" (*das individualpersönliche Wertwesen*), as Scheler calls it (p. 494).

Essence *per se,* Scheler holds, is neither universal nor individual. This distinction arises only in connection with objects of experience. That is to say, the distinction arises when essence is considered to be the "essence of something" and in that case it is the essence of an individual. It is in this sense, therefore, that we can speak of "the individual value-essence of a person"—that we can speak of a value-essence, in other words, that is personal and individual and, thus, is the "authentic" value-essence of a particular person (if I may so translate Scheler's phrase *persönliches Heil*).

The experience of my own individual value-essence *as mine*— i.e., as my own "authentic self"—is basic (so Scheler maintains) to an *ought* which, as a "call" (*ein Ruf*), is directed specifically to myself—and is so directed irrespective of whether or not it is also directed toward others. Seen as the value-ideal of my own self, my own value-essence is thus a goal to be realized in my actions. Not to pursue this goal would mean the denial of my own authentic existence as a person, the abandonment of my "personal redemption" (*ibid.*).

But now the question is, How are the universally valid values, and the norms derived from them, related to the personal value-essence and to the *ought* that is entailed by it?

As Scheler sees it, the proper relationship between value-universalism and value-individualism can be preserved only when every individual moral agent subjects to "special moral cultivation" the values accessible to it alone, but does so without neglecting the universally valid values. And this, Scheler continues, is an *ought* not only for individual persons but for "collective wholes" as well—for families, nations, and whole civilizations (p. 497).

All of this presupposes, of course, the "autonomy of the person"—"the autonomy of personal insight into what is good and evil," and "the autonomy of personally willing what, somehow, is 'given' as good or evil" (p. 499). Autonomy, however, is but the pre-condition of the moral and the value relevance of the person, not his essence. The autonomous person, merely as autonomous, is by no means the highest value. He is only a bearer of values. What this entails will become clear when we compare Scheler's position here with that of Kant and Nietzsche.

Despite some radical difference in their general philosophical orientations, both, Kant and Nietzsche, had maintained that the value of a community and of the historical process itself depends upon the degree to which they provide the best possible basis for the existence and activities of human beings *as persons*. The ultimate goal of history (according to Nietzsche) is the emergence of "the highest exemplars" of men, and (according to Kant) it is the development of a community of free, self-legislative and rational beings. Neither Kant nor Nietzsche was willing to subordinate the person to some "trans-personal higher value-bearer," such as a community, a culture, or even a moral world-order. In this all-important respect Scheler finds himself in complete agreement with Kant as well as with Nietzsche. The value of the person, he maintains, is "the value of all values"; and "the glorification of the person—in the last analysis the glorification of the person of persons, i.e., of God—is the meaning of every moral order" (p. 508).

But now a point crucial for Scheler's position must be noted. Briefly stated it is this: The *conditio sine qua non* of a person's value-growth—i.e., his growth in "person-value"—is that that person never directly intend his own moral value. To put it otherwise: It is a mistake to believe that, when person-values are to be realized, these values must also be intended. To intend them is, in fact, the surest way of preventing their realization; for the person as the subject of all his acts can never himself be the object of his own acts. He grows and develops morally by focusing upon and directing his activities toward the objectively given values and the possibilities of their realization (p. 511).

As bearers of their respective person-values all persons are ultimately unique, differing from others in their attitudes and their actions; and their person-value is higher than any other kind of value. But let us be clear here. For Kant as well as for Nietzsche, the person is not only a bearer of values. Being himself the highest value, he *posits* values as values. That is to say, he determines what is and what is not a value. He is the ultimate norm. The individualism of these two thinkers is thus bound up with subjectivism and with a value nominalism—a transcendental subjectivism for Kant, an empirical subjectivism for Nietzsche. For Scheler, however, the person is exclusively a bearer of values, not a "positer" or creator of them. The values are objectively given (like Platonic Ideas), and the person grows as a value-person in and through the pursuit of the highest of those values.

But something else also distinguishes Scheler's position from that of Nietzsche and Kant. Inherent in the philosophies of both, Kant and Nietzsche, is a "singularism" which does not allow for what Scheler calls the Principle of Solidarity. No person, Scheler points out, exists or acts in a vacuum. In the very idea of a "great" person, for example, are intertwined the existence, the ideal image, and the effectiveness of that person within a segment of man's historical experience. And the same is true in the case of every other person, although perhaps to a reduced degree only. This means, however, that the indispensable conditions of a person's existence include, as a matter of principle, the situations and tasks which elicit the person's responses and permit his active pursuit of value-goals. And this experiential context includes man's experience of a necessary membership in a human community and his co-responsibility for common actions. Since the intention to a possible community is inherent in, and therefore essential to, certain actions, the meaning of a community and its possible existence is not simply a postulate or an assumption but is as essentially and primordially a part of the meaning of a person as is the distinction between inner and outer world. The individual experiences himself not merely as a part of historial events and as a member of a social group, but also as a participant, a fellow human being, and as co-responsible for what is relevant to the values of the whole, of a "total person" (*Gesamtperson*). Put briefly, every finite person is at once individual person *and* total person. His world is total world *and* individual world. And both are intrinsically necessary (*wesensnotwendige*) aspects of a concrete whole that encompasses person and world (p. 525).

To be sure, not all social groups are "total persons." The "masses," for example, although effective at times in action, lack all characteristics of a person. The basis of "solidarity" is here mere association; and the individual loses his self-identity. As far as Scheler is concerned, a "social unit" is a person only when the solidarity of its members is rooted in an experience of co-responsibility for the valuations, the decisions, and the actions of the group as a whole, and when this "lived community" (*Lebensgemeinschaft*) is so structured that making decisions and setting goals for the group are tasks assigned to an agency which expresses the will of the whole. The locus of moral responsibility is thus essentially the community itself. But its members all share in that responsibility—and share in it as mature and responsible persons. Their stature as persons is preserved within the whole. This, however, implies that the communal whole is co-responsible for all its members. The co-responsibility between individual and "total person" is thus a two-way affair—a matter of mutuality (p. 537).

As mentioned before, every finite person is (and experiences himself as being) both, an individual and a member of a "total person"; and both, individual and "total person," are responsible to "the person of persons," to God. They are responsible to God in both, their self-responsibility and their co-responsibility. This means that, in examining his own role in the scheme of things, each individual must ask himself: What positive values would have been realized in the world, and what negative values would have been kept from being realized, if I, this particular person, occupying this particular place within the social structure, had acted otherwise than I did; if I had intended and actually realized more than I did? Viewed in this perspective, the "principle of solidarity" is seen as basic to any "cosmos of finite moral persons." Its validity assures the integrative wholeness of the entire moral order; and it does so irrespective of the space and time dimensions of the moral world. To put it differently: The inclusion, on the basis of the "principle of solidarity," of all possible finite persons in my welfare (*Heil*) and of my welfare in the welfare of all finite persons is of the very essence of any volition that is directed toward the realization of the values of an absolute value-sphere.

Still no matter how rich in detail and how complex the relationships may be in which every person is woven (*eingeflochten*) into the whole of the value-cosmos, and no matter how diverse the directions of a person's co-responsibilities may be through which that person is bound to the fate and the meaning (*Sinn*) of the whole, no person is simply the sum-total of such relations, nor can its responsibility as a person, its *Selbstverantwortlichkeit*, be reduced to nothing but co-responsibility. That is to say, despite all interrelations with the whole, each person is and remains his own particular self and is responsible for himself. Each person has his own "intimate sphere" as well as his "social sphere" (p. 563). Both spheres are of an ontological rather than an epistemological nature; but only the undivided concrete person is bearer of the highest, the moral values (p. 571).

VII

The preceding discussion of Scheler's value theoretical position has been based exclusively upon his formidable and fundamental work, *Der Formalismus in der Ethik und die Materiale Wertethik.* This limitation is justified, I believe, because the thesis set forth there is crucial and is basic to all of Scheler's thinking. It has not been modified in any important respect in his later writings. Most relevant to the discussions here is perhaps the essay "Zur Idee des Menschen," published in *Vom Umsturz der Werte.* There we are told that, "understood in a certain way, all central problems of philosophy can be traced back to the question: What is man, and what metaphysical place does he occupy in the whole of Being—relative, that is, to the world and to God?" (Vol. I, p. 273)—a question reminiscent of Kant's famous four questions in the Introduction to his *Logic.* Scheler's answer to the question: "The passion to strive beyond himself—be the goal called 'Superman' or 'God'—that is man's sole and true 'humanity' " (p. 311). But this, of course, is an answer already implicit in the arguments set forth in *Der Formalismus.*

Scheler himself regards the earlier work as *a break in principle* with the subjectivistic and relativistic value theories generally accepted at the turn of the century. To be sure, he also regarded Brentano as in some sense a precursor. He thus states, for example, that it was Brentano who first formulated the axioms that are basic to any order or rank of values (see Section II, above). Yet, the difference in the views of Scheler and Brentano is evident even here; for where Scheler states that "the existence of a positive value is itself a positive value," and that "the non-existence of a negative value is itself a positive value," Brentano declared it to be axiomatic that the existence of *what has been recognized as being good* is to be preferred to its non-existence, and that the non-existence of *what is known to be bad* is to be preferred to its existence. What Brentano here regards as axiomatic is reconcilable with a subjectivistic interpretation of values; what Scheler asserts is not.

It is also of interest here that Nicolai Hartmann's monumental *Ethik* (three volumes in the Coit translation!) assumes the validity of Scheler's thesis of an emotional *a priori* which discloses to us all values and their order of rank, and that he makes explicit what is implicit in Scheler's position—namely, that, in their mode of Being, all values are Platonic Ideas; that they are metaphysical "entities" having an "ideal in-itself-ness" comparable to that of logical and mathematical "objects" (*Ethik,* Chapter 16). Hartmann, however, is concerned exclusively with problems of ethics. At no time does he develop a general theory of value. There is, of course, much that is suggestive and important in his meticulous formal analyses. But this is not the place to go into details. Our topic is value theories, not ethics.

BIBLIOGRAPHY

Scheler, Max, *Der Formalismus in der Ethik und die Materiale Wertethik,* first published in *Jahrbuch für Philosophie,* 1913-14. The text used here is that of the fourth edition, which is Volume II of Max Scheler's *Gesammelte Werke,* Bern, undated.
———— *Vom Umsturz der Werte,* two volumes, Leipzig, 1919.
———— *Die Formen des Wissens und die Bildung,* Bonn, 1925.
———— *Die Wissensformen und die Gesellschaft,* Leipzig, 1926.
Hartmann, Nicolai, *Ethik,* Berlin, 1926. Translation by Stanton Coit, London, 1932. Relevant here are volumes 1 and 2.

CHAPTER XII

WIEDERHOLD: VALUE AS AN INTEGRATIVE CATEGORY

Since the days of Lotze, so Wiederhold informs us, the value concept has played an increasingly important role in "scientific philosophy." In fact, it is not amiss to speak of a "value-philosophical movement" in modern philosophy. Unfortunately, however, so Wiederhold continues, the concept "value" has not yet (1920) been sufficiently clarified to warrant its employment as integrative category in a system-centered philosophy. The attempt must therefore be made to bring about the needed clarification, and Wiederhold proposes to do just that.

I

Common usage reveals a bewildering variety of meanings of the term "value." Thus, "we value a piece of bread because it alleviates hunger; we speak of the aesthetic value of a symphony and of the market value of some merchandise; we value a ring as an heirloom; we discuss in sober factuality the use-value of a particular kind of wood; and when we lose a friend, we are aware of the value he had for our own development. We simply value everything conceivable which we, as psychophysical individuals, encounter in our lives" (p. 1). And the question is, Does the term "value" retain a unique and unified meaning despite such diversity in linguistic usage?

In his search for an answer to this question, Wiederhold finds that (disregarding Aristotle) the first clarifying distinctions in the field of economics were made by Adam Smith, who introduced the important terms "use-value" and "exchange-value" to designate basically distinct aspects of economic valuations. Marx added to this the conception of "surplus value," and the Austrian economists (Menger, von Wieser, and others) contributed the idea of "marginal utility." This development in the field of economics provided the impetus for a psychological approach to value and valuations as we have come to know it in the writings of Meinong and von Ehrenfels. In the meantime, however, Lotze had recognized the central position of the idea of value in any comprehensive and systematic interpretation of reality. And it was in this sense that Rickert tried to deal with it.

These historical facts, however, do not in themselves clarify the meaning of the term "value." That clarification can be achieved only through an analysis of the relevant aspects of human experience. When we attempt such an analysis, we find that the value of an object is identical neither with the object as such nor with any of its constitutive attributes; for it is we who "posit" the value. It is we who establish a "value-relation" with the object. This presupposes, of course, that the object exists or is assumed to exist. The "value-relation" is thus superimposed upon a purely factual judgment concerning an object. And now the question is, How is such superimposition possible? What is its warranty?

It is possible, Wiederhold replies, whenever the experiencing subject relates the (actual or assumed) object to a "third," to a "standard." "Value" can then be defined as "the relation posited by a consciousness between an object and a standard." But only the "tri-unity" of consciousness, object, and standard "constitutes the meaning-complex we call value" (p. 6). Because this is so, a psychological approach—keyed either to feelings or to desires as basic—can never lead to a real understanding of the nature of value. It is at best concerned only with an analysis of the act of valuing.

To be sure, many of our valuations pertain to actually experienced pleasures or displeasures. This does not mean, however, that, in principle, all valuations are but emotional reactions. We know, for example, of instinctive drives that aim at the gratification of appetites "even when prior emotional experiences most strongly oppose them" (p. 7). And desires alone are insufficient because we very much value certain objects—art objects, for example— without desiring them. We must acknowledge at least a reciprocity of feeling-based and desire-based valuations. Actually, of course, much more is involved, for cognition—i.e., our understanding of the nature of the valued object—also plays a part in the valuing process, and the "relative constancy of direction" of our deepest feelings indicates that we ourselves as persons, and in the totality of our being, are the ultimate ground of all valuations (p. 9).

The definition of value given above is, of course, empty and abstract. It refers to no specific consciousness, to no specific object, and to no specific standard. In this emptiness it is a mere "thought-form" (*Denkform*) and differs radically from the concrete content of the psychological interpretations—from the references, that is, to specific feelings and specific desires. But we know (at least since the days of Kant if not since Aristotle) that only the combination of form and content can give us full-bodied experience. "Thought-forms" are "the conditions of the possibility of experience"; but they "authenticate" their function only when they attain realization in concrete content. "Content and form require each other" (p. 10).

The question now is, In what sense is it possible to speak of value as a "thought-form"—i.e., as a category?

In answering this question, Wiederhold starts with Windelband's distinction between "constitutive" and "reflexive" categories, and argues that value is neither constitutive of an object—of an object of nature, for example—nor purely formal or reflexive in the sense of the categories of logic. It presupposes both types of categories. It is not a condition of the possibility of experience—as the other categories are—but is "the basic form (*Grundform*) of an attitude which a subject may take toward an object." As this basic form, however, value transcends the subjective as well as the objective particularity of any given situation and claims universal validity (*objective Allgemeingültigkeit*) (pp. 11-12).

II

The general meaning of the term "value," as just presented, may be analyzed into five sub-forms.

1. The form of the most restricted validity has pleasure and displeasure as its standard—a standard that is actually limited to subjectively individual valuations.

2. The "positing of values" may be a matter of "convention" —i.e., the value standard is either specifically agreed upon or posited by a smaller or larger number of people, or is part of their

historically developed tradition. An example of the former is the "exchange value" of the market place. An example of the latter are the mores of a given culture.

3. Objects that are useful in the realization of valued goals have "use-value." Usefulness is here the standard for the value-relation. It is a standard which, together with the idea of "marginal utility," plays an important role in the field of economics. Seen in psychological perspective, "use-values" are essentially "volitional valuations." Actually, however, they readily become valuations based upon feelings. Their validity may assume all forms of generality—with the sole exception of universal validity.

4. The "value of totality" (*Ganzheitswert*) is first encountered in the "everyday affairs" of our existence as human beings. We thus speak of the value which a certain period of our life has had for the whole course of our development; and we speak of the value of a person to the whole of a community. In all of these cases a "totality" (*Ganzheit*) is taken to be the standard. This "totality" may exist in the present (static form) or it may be the distant goal of some particular development now of concern to us (dynamic form). In both of these sub-forms the "value of totality" plays an important role in our culture and, therefore, in all the sciences dealing with that culture (*Kulturwissenschaften*).

As mental events the valuations here at issue are essentially conceptual and intellectual. The categorial nature of the "value of totality," however, is not so apparent. The value concepts previously identified all pertain to objects "given" in experience. It is not necessary first to "create" the objects. The situation is quite different, however, in the case of the "value of totality." The historian, for example, selects "the historically significant events" on the basis of specific valuations. He does not accept just any event as part of history but chooses and arranges what he regards as relevant in the light of some "totality" which he posits and the conception of which he deems justified. This means, however, that the value of the projected "totality" is "the constitutive category of the relevant reality for the historian" (p. 15). And what is true in the case of historiography is true in all sciences dealing with human culture: the value-relation is constitutive of the objects. If we did not envision a "total culture" as the projected ideal for all mankind, we could also not speak of progress of the human race. The categorial or constitutive function of the "value of totality" is here beyond dispute. But when we consider the diversity of points of view in historiography and in the other cultural sciences, it is evident that the "value of totality" lacks universal validity; that, in effect, it is but a manifestation of subjective valuations. The situation will change only when it is possible to prove beyond all doubt that the "totality-goal" (*Ganzheitsziel*) of all mankind is objectively grounded in Reality itself. But such proof cannot be anticipated.

5. The last sub-type of value, according to Wiederhold, is the "norm-value." The standard is here a "norm which transcends our individual choice and experience" (p. 16). The autonomy of such a norm is more or less clearly indicated in our daily concerns. Thus, an action that is judged good (or evil) is related to an ideal "whose dignity does not depend on our individual wishes and desires." Seen from the point of view of psychology, the "majesty of the moral norm" manifests itself in the phenomena of conscience.

But the "moral norm" is not the only one that must be considered here. A work of art, for example, has aesthetic value in proportion as it measures up to some norm. It makes no sense, so Wiederhold maintains, to say that the value of a work of art is intrinsic to that work itself. Precise usage of the value term requires that we say: "This work of art has a high value because it conforms in a high degree to the aesthetic norm" (p. 17). Such a judgment quite clearly transcends the subjective and merely accidental elements of the value experience. In popular usage, however, the "norm" remains vague and "mysterious." It is in philosophy, where the idea of a "value norm" plays a particularly important role, that the problem of the norm must be clarified and, if possible, be solved.

III

Following a great tradition, Wiederhold holds that the ultimate aim of philosophy is an integrative interpretation of the whole of human experience—the achievement, that is, of "an all-inclusive system of what can be known and conceived." The history of philosophy, however, is not merely a record of systems that have been surpassed and abandoned. It is also the history of the categories that were employed in the past in the interpretation of the world—categories which in each case reflect the most profound meaning and the content of the systems based upon them. The philosophically most fertile periods in human history have thus incorporated in a few basic concepts what seemed most important at the time in man's increasing understanding of reality. "Truth is disclosed in the succession and through a multiplicity of categories" (p. 19).

But if such is the case, then it is also evident that not all concepts accepted in the past as basic were indeed true categories; and the question is, What criteria are we to employ to make the necessary distinction between what is of timeless validity and what is not. Wiederhold believes that there are criteria which may serve our purpose. There is, first, the purely formal criterion of the correct (*sinngemässe*) employment of the concept within each system; and there is, secondly, the question of content—the question, that is, of "the systematic productiveness (*Tragfähigkeit*) of the concept" (p. 19). The significance of the first criterion is obvious. It is the demand for logical consistency in the employment of terms. The second criterion is the demand that the concepts be adequate to the facts in the case. Both demands are commonly disregarded —even if only quite subtly—in the great metaphysical systems. The efforts at solving metaphysical problems lead to ambiguities and shifts in the meaning of terms, and to attempts to deal with the inexhaustible richness of human experience in terms that are inadequate to the task. But since we are here not concerned with metaphysical problems, the two criteria may be of some help in our attempt to view value as basic to an integrative philosophical system.

Let us consider, first, pleasure as the basic category. The standard is here the empirically real feeling of pleasure. In a strict sense it is, of course, the "quantity of pleasure" that counts. But aside from the fact that it is difficult, if not impossible, to determine the exact quantity involved in any given experience, we cannot fail to observe that a qualitative element is also present in every experience of pleasure, and that the pleasure itself is indicative of the depth of our feelings; that it affects us only superficially or that it involves the very core of our being.

In its extreme form as a quantitative and individualistic hedonism which sees in the pleasure of the moment the meaning of human existence, we encounter the identification of the standard of value with pleasure in Cyrenaicism. It was Epicurus, however, who developed the most comprehensive justification of hedonism. But he stressed freedom from pain, an inner harmony and peace, and the absence of violent passions throughout a life-time rather than the indulgencies and pleasures of the moment. In his doctrine the value standard is no longer the quantity of pleasure but the quality of the experience. The more spiritual, the more refined the pleasure is, the less it disturbs inner harmony and peace. Aesthetic enjoyment, therefore, occupies the highest rank in the order of pleasure-giving experiences. Even so, however, the hedonism of Epicurus (like that of Aristippus) is essentially individualistic in orientation.

There was a revival of hedonism during the 16th and 17th centuries; but the pleasure-principle was no longer set forth in its pure form. It was now increasingly related to the idea of "utility for the general welfare"—a movement in philosophy that culminated in the utilitarianism of Jeremiah Bentham which made the greatest happiness for the greatest number of people central to all evaluations. But what interests Wiederhold here is not the historical development of an idea but the fact that the concept of pleasure by itself is no longer regarded as sufficient as a basis for a normative ethics—be that conceived as a strictly personal or as a social ethics. This is not to deny that the pleasure motive plays a large part in human affairs. It merely means that pleasure can never serve as a constitutive category of the realm of morals. And if the pleasure concept is taken to be the basic category of an all-comprehensive philosophical system, its inadequacies are especially glaring. A system of philosophy is concerned with more than the question of whether or not our experience in this world yields more pleasure than pain.

Historically, the hedonistic conception of pleasure as the standard of value has largely given way to the utilitarian's thesis that "utility" in the pursuit of happiness is the standard. But this conception, too, is too narrow to serve as the constitutive category of an all-inclusive philosophical system. At best it might provide a basis for ethics; but even then it is inadequate—as Kant has convincingly demonstrated.

We have seen earlier (II, 2 above) that the value standard may be a "convention"—either posited and agreed upon or historically developed. So interpreted, value can certainly serve as constitutive category for any theory designed to explain the origin and development of our social institutions. But is this problem of origin really one with which "systematic philosophy" should be concerned? Is it not rather a problem for sociology and history? This does not mean that a value for which some convention is the standard might not serve as constitutive category for those sciences. But sociology and history are not philosophy. Their problems are not problems of systematic philosophy; and what is constitutive for sociological and historical theories is not, for this reason, also constitutive for philosophy.

The point Wiederhold here insists upon is that values for which pleasure, utility, or convention is the standard may all find a place in systematic philosophy; but they are not and cannot be constitutive categories of philosophical systems. When we now consider values for which "totality" is the standard, the situation changes radically. We have seen already that the idea of "totality" plays an important role in historiography; but there it is no metaphysical concept. In philosophy this is different. If the "value of totality" (*Ganzheitswert*) is to function as the constitutive category of a philosophical system, "we cannot avoid a teleological metaphysics" (p. 27).

Suppose now that we are willing to accept this metaphysical orientation. The question then is, Can the value concept be correctly (*sinngemäss*) employed in this context; and if so, to what extent is it "productive" (*tragfähig*) as integrative concept and, therefore, as constitutive category of a philosophical system? The answer to the first part of this question is affirmative—provided that the valuations involved are either those of an individual subject or those of all empirical subjects taken together. If they are the former, they have, of course, subjective validity only; and if they are the latter, they have general but not universal validity. The moment it is claimed that the valuations do have universal validity, they "must necessarily be related to a universal consciousness" (p. 28). But since the conception of such a consciousness can be justified—if justified at all—only on metaphysical grounds, the "totality value" (presupposing, as it does, the universal consciousness) cannot be the constitutive category of the system. And this is the inescapable answer to the second part of the question raised above. The standard of "totality" for our valuations can have only relative validity. This fact, however, does not deprive it of its empirical significance in our daily affairs.

IV

There is now left for consideration only the "norm-value" (*Normwert*).

In the sense intended by Wiederhold—i.e., as a category constitutive of a philosophical system—the concept "norm" has played an important role in the "value-philosophical movement since the time of Lotze" (p. 29). The problem of the "norm" simply *as* norm has, of course, been recognized much earlier. It arises because human beings in all they do or suffer—in all their actions, desires, thoughts, and indulgences—are part of a context and a process in space and time. Whether this context is regarded as in some sense capricious or as determined by rigid laws, the understanding and interpretation of it are themselves part of the process. Whether we smile or weep, act or refrain from acting, accept a proposition or reject it—all this is from one point of view but a manifestation of mental and/or physical processes whose full meaning consists in their space-time function here and now. From a different point of view, however, the question arises, *Ought* we to think or act the way we do at any given moment? And this is the question of "norm." Consciousness, though itself an occurrence in the process of events, has now risen to a new level —to a level, that is, which in its true meaning is essentially trans-subjective. But this is precisely what creates the problem. How can we justify the trans-subjective or "normative" aspect of experience in which the subject recognizes an *ought* which he himself is to impose upon his actions?

The more we ponder the interrelations of the "natural" and the "normative" the more we realize how complex they are. Both aspects—the "natural" and the "normative"—are unquestionably present in consciousness. Neither can be reduced to the other without doing violence to the facts of experience. But how can the validity of the "norm" be justified vis-a-vis the factual content of experience?

The Sophists struggled with the problem and came forth with an untenable subjectivistic "solution" which, in effect, destroyed the validity of every norm. Plato projected his "Realm of Ideas" as basic to what is normative in human experience and thereby attempted a metaphysical justification of the validity of norms. Although his "theory of two worlds" had a profound influence throughout the history of Western philosophy, it actually is but "a typical attempt at a solution," and not a solution that stands up under criticism. The key concept of "anamnesis," in particular, was unacceptable. Plotinus and Origenes already stressed the active and synthetic function of consciousness. Descartes, making the "principle of self-certainty" basic, came to the conclusion that the validity of spiritual reality, grounded in God, is "necessarily given." The philosophers of the Enlightenment aimed at a psychological solution, arguing that the so-called "eternal truths" were either empirically derived (Locke) or were innate (Leibniz). Kant, finding empiricism as untenable as he did traditional rationalism, proposed a solution of the vexing problem within the framework of a transcendental idealism according to which categories are the conditions *sine qua non* of the possibility of experience. But it is evident that the ultimate framework here, too, must be a metaphysic. Fichte, Schelling, and Hegel each provided one. The negative reaction to their speculative systems was inevitable and not long in the coming. It took the forms of positivism, evolutionism, and pragmatism—whose originators again aimed at a psychological explanation of all norms. But only after the repudiation of materialism and a "return to Kant" did a truly normative point of view make any headway. Philosophy once more became an inquiry into the "meaning and value of life." It was the time, also, during which value theory was developed as an independent philosophical discipline (pp. 29–36).

As we know, it was Lotze who, attempting to reconcile the methods and results of the natural sciences with the "needs of the mind," raised the problem of values in its modern form. His basic assumption was that all science stands committed to a mechanistic interpretation of the world. What he tried to demonstrate was that this mechanism and the whole of reality as subsumable under causal laws is but "a necessary organization of means for the realization of the highest purpose of a spiritual reality." His "teleological idealism," therefore, demanded not only a scientific investigation of the laws of nature but an explication of the "highest purpose" as well. The whole system is thus "value-centered." The details of the system are, however, highly ambiguous, and Lotze's arguments fall short of providing the required proofs. The conflict between a psychological and a metaphysical approach to values remains ultimately unresolved. The reason for this, Wiederhold maintains, is not an indecisiveness on Lotze's part but the very nature of the problem which defies resolution (pp. 39–40).

In Rickert's philosophy, so we have seen, "the value problem is the problem of philosophy"—of *Philosophie überhaupt.* Any integrative interpretation of reality must take full account of both, the subject experiencing a world of objects, and the objects thus experienced. But such an interpretation is not possible if either the subject alone or the object alone is assumed to be basic. Rickert argued that there must be a "third" which transcends both; that this "third" is a "realm of values," and that the very essence of a value is its "validity" as an *ought.* It follows from this that the ultimate ground of all that is experienced as real is neither empirically given within experience nor hidden in some "transcendent Reality." It is conceivable only as "transcendental ideal." Knowledge is knowledge only when it is as it *ought* to be—namely, true. An action is moral only when it is as it *ought* to be—namely, good. And a work of art is indeed a work of art only when it is as it *ought* to be—namely, beautiful. The concept of value is thus the key concept, the constitutive category, of Rickert's whole philosophy (pp. 44–50).

This idea of value as constitutive category in philosophy must now be further examined.

V

In Section III, above, Wiederhold's two criteria by which to determine what is of timeless validity and what is not were briefly stated as "correct employment" (*sinngemässe Anwendung*) and "systematic productivity" (*systematische Tragfähigkeit*) of any concept. These criteria must now be applied more specifically to the concept "value" as that concept is being used in various philosophical systems. The results will be especially illuminating when the so-called "absolute values" and their validity are at issue. In what sense, for instance, is it at all possible to speak of "absolute values"? Was the justification of such values and their validity in the value-philosophical movement since Lotze metaphysical? And if it was, was it necessarily so? Any attempt to answer these questions entails inevitably a critical appraisal of the whole value-philosophical enterprise. But it is not sufficient for such an appraisal simply to point out the ambiguities and the limitations of various systems; it is necessary also to clarify what appear to be lasting insights and the "factually justified motives" that inspired the whole movement.

An examination of Lotze's writings will show, Wiederhold points out, that here value is indeed the key concept, the focal point of the whole system; but the meaning of the term "value" undergoes noticeable changes as that system unfolds. At first, Lotze regards pleasure as the standard of value. We ascribe value to things because they elicit in us a feeling of pleasure. Such a position is perfectly tenable—provided one is willing to accept its intrinsic limitations, which Lotze was not. The whole conception of his system required that values be not empirically grounded; for as so grounded they can have only relative validity, whereas value as constitutive category of an all-comprehensive system must have universal validity.

In order to justify this second meaning of the term "value" Lotze attempts to relate it, not to an empirical subject, but to "a rational consciousness *per se*," so that the standard of values is now "something universal, unperishable, and in itself valuable"

—an idea which Lotze himself had repudiated as meaningless. The term "value," therefore, is no longer "correctly employed" (pp. 60–62).

Rickert made much of the fact that value is validity and that it therefore confronts any subject as an *ought*. His whole theory was keyed to this idea. The value of any act, he tried to show, lies in the fact that the act—be is cognitive, moral, or aesthetic— is what it *ought to be*. If we accept this as the "correct" use of the term "value," then it is difficult to see that it is also "correct usage" when Rickert later indicates that only "a world of values provides a secure standard for our judgments," for the implication here is that only a "self-sufficient realm of values" which transcends subject as well as object is the ultimate ground and justification of all valuations. The shift in meaning is obvious; and it is Wiederhold's contention that Rickert cannot have it both ways (pp. 63–65).

But when philosophers of the stature of a Lotze and a Rickert are thus driven into ambiguities, it may not be amiss to ask, Is there perhaps something intrinsic in all value-theoretical considerations that necessarily leads to unacceptable ambiguities?

What all value-theoretical efforts ultimately aim at, so Wiederhold believes, is to transcend mere subjectivity and to find a basis for values that will support and justify their objective, if not their universal, validity.

But if such is the goal, then it seems clear that no empirical derivation of values is adequate to the task. Psychologism, historicism, and evolutionism must regard values as temporal phenomena conditioned by accidental circumstances of heredity and environment, and therefore as purely relative. No *ought*—not even one valid or binding for a single individual—can be derived from empirical observations alone. To understand this fact is, of course, already a value-theoretical achievement. But two questions remain: (1) What does it mean to speak of "absolute and universally valid values"? And (2) what are the conditions upon which the absolute validity of values depends?

The answers to these questions that have been given by the philosophers concerned with the problems of value since the days of Lotze differ a great deal; and, what is more important, no trend toward agreement is in evidence. One aspect, however, seems clear: The ultimate solution of the problem of universal validity must be found—if it can be found at all—in the realm of metaphysics. Even Rickert's thesis of the value-imposed *ought* is, in effect, a metaphysical notion—and it is so despite Rickert's protestations to the contrary.

It is Wiederhold's contention that (a) philosophers do indeed intend to provide a tenable basis for "the necessary and universal validity of values," and that (b) they can do it only within the framework of metaphysics. So far, however, "the realm of values as the realm of unconditional validity is but the hypostatization of an empty abstraction" (p. 74). Indeed, to speak of the "valid in itself" as an "absolute realm" unrelated to experience is to employ an "impossible concept" (*Unbegriff*). Concepts such as "consciousness in general," "normal consciousness," "universal validity," "transcendent validity" and "value in itself" lose all meaning within a philosophical system if it is impossible to assure us of their "metaphysical dignity." In logic or epistemology they may serve a good purpose as "limiting or boundary concepts" (*Grenzbegriffe*); but within an all-comprehensive system they are merely hypostatizations—unless they are metaphysically justified.

In all our experiences we face an objective and meaningful content (*Sinngehalt*) which "stands against us in its autonomy." We do not create it; we simply acknowledge it as an *ought* whose fulfillment is a task for any subject having the experience. This fact, however, entails certain consequences. We can no longer say that it is the subject which "creates truth and beauty" even though truth and beauty "dwell in our experience." There remains a "tension" (*Spannung*) between experienced content and experiencing subject as the "primordial duality" (*Urdualität*) which cannot be eliminated. And since the subjective aspects of experience cannot be derived from the objective content, they retain their significance as subjective. But the objective content is a "demand" (*Forderung*) that must be complied with if there is to be valid experience at all. "The moral, the beautiful, the true, and the holy are but special forms of that basic demand which confronts us and which we, in brief, designate as the idea of humanness" (*Menschlichkeit*) (p. 77). The specialized demands can then be understood as emanating from the objective content of an Absolute—call it God or World-Ground. In so far as a subject measures up to the "demands"—in cognition, in moral matters, in aesthetic creation, etc. —it participates in the essence or content of that Absolute. But the question still is, What role does value play in all this?

One answer to this question is that the World-Ground itself is identical with Absolute Value. But such an interpretation, according to Wiederhold, is irreconcilable with the notion that value is a relation between a subject and an object; and the idea that the World-Ground itself is value is rather vague and borders on the mystic. This is so because value, meaningfully interpreted, can never be separated from a basic relation to a subject. And even if we were to accept the idea of a "consciousness in general" as fulfilling the role of the subject, it would be merely a more subtle or "sublimated" reference to a subject that could not possibly create the objective content.

As we examine the value-theoretical systems since Lotze, we find the various philosophers struggling with the insurmountable difficulty of making a transition from the valuations of individual subjects in their empirical reality to a valuing but abstract rational consciousness (*Vernunftbewusstsein*). In order to justify the unconditional validity of values, they advance from empirical facts to "the hypostatization of an empty abstraction" which yet bears unmistakeably traces of its psychological origin. There may be reasons which justify the introduction of such an abstraction as an "auxiliary concept" (*Hilfsbegriff*) in the field of epistemology. As a metaphysical concept it is unacceptable (p. 80).

The term "value" has at times had an "intoxicating effect" even on philosophers. It has been used as referring to the "sublime" without an awareness of the fact that the same term was employed with reference to the human-all-too-human and banal affairs of man's daily living. What Wiederhold suggests, therefore, is that the term "value" be employed only as a scientific concept in the fields of economics and psychology, where it has a precise meaning; and that philosophers refrain from using it as constitutive category of some all-inclusive philosophical system. To speak of aesthetic and moral valuations as psychological events cannot be misleading so long as the restriction to the field of psychology is clearly understood. Such limited usage would be appropriate to the original idea of value as a "context of meaning" (*Sinngefüge*). This does not, however, eliminate the basic problem of value theory. On the contrary, it but underscores that problem and presents its solution anew as something demanded by the facts of human experience—a solution which can be provided only by a "critical metaphysics" which surmounts all subjectivism and establishes an adequate ground for all "objective content" of experience as well as for its demands upon the subject (p. 84).

BIBLIOGRAPHY

Wiederhold, Konrad, "Wertbegriff und Wertphilosophie," *Kant-Studien*, Ergänzungsheft No. 52, Berlin, 1920.

CHAPTER XIII

THE METAPHYSICAL PERSONALISM OF WILLIAM STERN

In the Preface to his *Wertphilosophie* William Stern states: "What distinguishes the personalistic value-philosophy from related systematic value theories of our times is, above all else, its explicit metaphysical character. The axiological apriori of faith: 'I believe in something objectively valuable,' stands at its beginning; the 'introception' of objective values into the value proper (*Selbstwert*) of every human being stands at its end as the object of a moral demand (*sittliche Forderung*). This arrangement is characteristic of the guiding idea. Not man is the beginning; not even mankind or the culture within which mankind lives and realizes itself. Value-philosophy, in its very nature, is neither anthropology nor philosophy of culture; it is metaphysics. The category 'value' reaches far beyond the narrow limits of what is human— even though it unfolds its whole richness and greatness only in its application to human and cultural affairs" (p. xiii).

No better summary of Stern's value-theoretical position could have been given in so few words. But we must not overlook the fact that he developed this view only as the concluding part of his "Critical Personalism," and that he regarded it as the "touchstone" for his philosophical position as a whole (p. xvi).

The presupposition of this philosophy is Stern's acknowledgment that man is not simply an observer and "theoretician" but also, and perhaps primarily, a doer; and that the world is not merely a panorama of changing events but also, and most importantly, man's home or the arena of his struggles. Man's view of the world, therefore, has an eminently practical significance. It is a guide in his efforts to give his own life significance and meaning and to come to terms with the world. Small wonder, therefore, that the quest for a satisfying world-view has been a powerful motive in human affairs ever since the pre-dawn of man's history and that it encompasses the whole of his existence—the religious and moral aspects no less than the aesthetic, the political, and the economic. Once man wondered about such matters and began to ask questions, there was no stopping until, in the end, he had found his answers in a well-constructed "philosophy of values" (p. 4).

It remains a fact, however, that in all his actions man is really in interaction with an objectively real world—even with a non-human and non-moral world. An interpretation of his existence is therefore impossible if that external world is not taken into consideration. How, for example, could one understand human actions as determined by "personal causality" without coming to terms with the problem of the "non-personal, mechanical causality" that determines the events in nature? Or how could one be either optimistic or pessimistic about man's future without taking into consideration the whole of evolution?

Furthermore, since all values are "attached" to value-objects and value-objects are real, any science dealing with the real world is relevant to the problem of values. This is so, not because such a science is itself concerned with values, but because it provides an understanding of the "factual presuppositions" of all valuations and, by giving us a new insight into the nature of things, may bring about a re-valuation as well. There is no area of valuation that escapes such influence. The moral assessment of a criminal act, for example, has been greatly modified by the findings of modern genetics and psychopathology, and by a better understanding of the influence of the environment upon the development of a person. And, to mention but one other example, the value we assign to an historical epoch or personality may change markedly as historical research uncovers new facts that are relevant to our valuation.

The sciences are, thus, relevant to the problem of values. In themselves, however, they do not provide a solution for it. Only metaphysics can do that. The next question, therefore, must be: Is metaphysics at all possible? And to this question Stern gives a firm and affirmative answer: "Metaphysics is possible and must be possible because it is necessary. Even science is possible only when there is metaphysics; and value-philosophy is possible only when there is metaphysics. Hence, if there are to be science and value-philosophy, then there must be metaphysics. There is no other justification for metaphysics than this necessity" (pp. 24–25). Put differently, the necessity that there be metaphysics is a faith—"I believe in a world which is real and in which there are values (*ist werthaltig*)"—and a "deep-rooted drive" (*urwüchsiges Streben*) to come closer to the object of that faith: "I seek the world which is real and in which there are values" (p. 25). That is to say, as metaphysician man faces not a world that is "completely given" in his experience, but one that is an "eternal task." In his efforts to come ever closer to the "unity of being and value," he must cultivate the sciences and, at the same time, clarify ever more fully the "validities" and the "norms" inherent in the "value-sphere."

Because of the duality of "being" and "value," metaphysics—though the *conditio sine qua non* of all the sciences—cannot itself be a science. This has the advantage, as Stern sees it, that the metaphysical foundation of the value-sphere does not entail a "rationalization" of that sphere. There is now no necessity of trying to deduce what is valid in religion, morality, art, law, etc. from a logical context of ideas; the task is to comprehend what is valid in those fields within a "context of meaning" *Sinnzusammenhang*) that is more than logical and actually is a presupposition even of logic.

I

In developing his value theory, Stern starts with the "value-theoretical apriori": "I believe in something objectively valuable." This premise asserts a necessary relation between subject and object: "A subject which believes in values—or, briefly, which 'values'—relates itself to objectivities that are valuable, i.e., it relates itself to 'values'" (p. 34). The value-theoretical apriori is, thus, bipolar: "I value, therefore I am a value," and "There are values." In accepting this bipolarity, the subject assigns to itself a meaningful place within a meaningful cosmos. It accepts itself as "value-center" of a "value-cosmos," and in doing this, it values itself. "Its faith in values is at the same time a faith in its own dignity as a person" (*Selbstwert*) (p. 35).

The relation between the subject and the object, so far identified simply as an act of valuing, is experienced in various forms. Of these the most basic are the acts of "positing values" (*Wertsetzungen*) and the subsequent acts of "valuation" (*Wertschätzungen*). The difference between them is the fact that acts of valuing always involve an affirmation or denial, an approval or disapproval, and the expression of a preference, whereas acts of "value-positing" do not involve such alternatives. We experience them as a comprehension, an acknowledgment, or a creation of values.

The immediate and simple comprehension of what is valuable is a "believing" that is basic to metaphysics as well as to value theory. But value comprehension is more than the mere acceptance of what is "given." "It is the conviction that the given is intrinsically significant." Value comprehension is thus a "primordial affirmation" (*Urbejahung*) for which the dichotomy of affirmation-denial does not yet exist (p. 36).

Such a comprehension, however, is but the subject's "first step into the realm of the objectively valuable." The second step is "the acknowledgment of values." It involves the positing of a "value in itself" and of its objective validity as an "ought" that is determinative of our actions.

The third step into the realm of the objectively valuable is the "creation of values" (*Wertschöpfung*). The very existence of the values is now dependent on the acts of the subject, and the subject itself attains its own "full reality as a person having his own intrinsic value" (p. 37). The whole development of man's culture is here involved; for whenever someone builds a factory, creates a work of art, makes a discovery in science, or modestly does his daily work he adds something to the objective value-content of the world. And he adds to it even when he merely tries to develop his own potentialities or to perfect himself.

It is only after values have thus been "posited" (comprehended, acknowledged, or created) that acts of valuation are possible— acts, that is, which establish relations among the posited values. And these acts, too, occur in three forms.

The first are acts of "qualitative co-ordination." Whether we call something "aesthetically valuable," "morally valuable," "economically valuable," or anything else "valuable" no longer depends exclusively on the object valued but on its relation to other valued objects and to the context of interrelations of these objects. But it is only because a given object has already been "posited" as a value that it can be placed into a value-context which, as such, is qualitatively distinctive. The moral, the religious, the aesthetic, the economic, the political, the legal are examples of available contexts. Within each one of them more narrowly defined qualitative distinctions prevail. In the field of aesthetics, for instance, we encounter "the categories of style, of form, of content, of harmony, of symmetry, and so on." These "narrower categories" in all value-fields are the presuppositions of the remaining two forms of valuation and serve as their "value-standards" (p. 39).

Once valued objects have been qualitatively related to a "value-context," they can also be arranged in an "order of rank of values" (*Wertrangordnung*) as being "higher" or "lower" than some other value, or as of "equal" rank with it. Although such "quantification" of values—the second way of establishing relations among values—is, theoretically, a tertiary step (following the "positing" in any of its forms and the "qualitative valuation") it is of crucial importance in the "practice of daily living"; for the "order of rank of values" is the basis for rational decision-making.

"The third derivative form of valuation represents a peculiar combination of qualifying and quantifying attitudes. It is a placing of values in opposition (*Wert-Entgegensetzung*)—a polarization of values" (p. 40). From the point of view of quality there is no greater difference between values than that of good and bad, true and false, beautiful and ugly, useful and harmful, etc. At the same time, however, these contrasts are but extreme poles of a scale that centers in a "zero-point." Here we encounter a form of value-affirmation which is strictly correlative to a negation. The relationship, however, is obviously derivative and not primary (as some value-theorists would have us believe).

II

Up to this point we have dealt only with half of what Stern calls the "value-theoretical apriori." That is to say, we have dealt only with how the subject relates itself to values. We must now consider the other half of the apriori—the assertion, namely, that "there are values."

To begin with, Stern points out that the term "value" cannot be defined because there is no other elementary concept in terms of which a definition might be given. The best we can hope for is a somewhat circuitous clarification of its meaning. Analysis will then show that "value" is "an attributive concept" and that value itself is not a "substance," that it is always "attached" so something—to a "value-bearer" (*Wertträger*). Strictly speaking, therefore, "we cannot say that this or that is a value—but only that it has a value, that it is valuable" (p. 41). Stern thus repudiates "the strong tendency in modern value-philosophy to substantialize values." Values, he insists, have no independent existence.

The "value-bearer" may be anything that has "objectively demonstrable existence" (a work of art, a human being, a nation, a factory, an area of culture, money), but it may also be something that itself is an attribute of something else. We can thus speak of the value of virtue, of power, of technological progress. But whatever the "value-bearer," value is always an "accent of significance" (*Bedeutungsakzent*). Significance, however, is a relation: A has significance for B; B endows A with significance. That is to say, B is the point of reference for the significance of A. It is what Stern calls the "value-goal" (*Wertziel*). To illustrate: Money is a "value-bearer," but it is this only because of its relation to such "value-goals" as individual profit, the national economy, or the general welfare of mankind. It is evident, however, that no value could be derived from a relation to a "value-goal" if the latter itself had no "significance." This means that the "value-goals" themselves must be "value-bearers."

But now a difficulty arises. If B is "value-goal" for the "value-bearer" A but is itself also a "value-bearer," then there must be another "value-goal," C, from which B derives its value—and so on. We seem to be caught in an infinite regress and, therefore, in a total value-relativism according to which "value" always means "value for some other." The only way out of this difficulty is "the complete identification of 'value-bearer' and 'value-goal'" (p. 43). The relation of A to B can then be preserved; but it is now immanent rather than transient: the "value-bearer" has become his own "value-goal," has attained "self-value" (*Selbstwert*).

To be sure, the "self-value" of the valuing subject is, initially at least, quite different from the "self-value" of anything that is not a subject. Both types of "self-values" are necessary, however. They are entailed by the two poles of the value-theoretical apriori. We shall return to this problem in the next Section.

Once "self-values" have been acknowledged as legitimate, they provide the anchorage for all other value-attributions. But further distinctions must now be made. If the bearer of a "self-value" is not absolutely simple but is a "whole" having a multitude of parts, characteristics, modes of self-manifestation, fields of action, etc., then every one of these "elements" or aspects may become a "value-bearer" without being itself a "self-value." Its value but reflects the "self-value" of the whole. Stern calls it a "radiated value" (p. 44).

If the bearer of the "self-value" is not "absolutely rigid," then there is within that bearer "a movement toward its various parts." "The bearer becomes a totality of purposes the realization of which requires the employment of means," and whatever serves as means —be it an object, a process, a power, or anything else—receives a "value-accent" by virtue of its contribution to the realization of whatever purpose is involved. Stern speaks here of "service value" (*Dienstwert*) (*ibid.*).

The distinctions just made between "self-value," "radiated value," and "service value" provide the decisive orientation for the whole of Stern's value-philosophy. But one other aspect must also be taken into consideration. It is the problem of the absoluteness or relativity of values.

"Self-values," Stern holds, must be regarded as absolute in "the only possible sense" of being in themselves "points of origin" (*Ausgangspunkte*) and "goals" of value-meanings. This absoluteness, however, is not in itself identical with the universal validity, the immutability, the eternity, and the timelessness of the values. Only metaphysical considerations can establish those aspects.

"Radiated values" and "service values," being derivative, are, of course, relative only. The full significance of their relativity becomes evident when we realize that one and the same "value-bearer" may stand in indefinitely many value relations to other "value-bearers." A particular coin, for example, has different kinds of value for a person using it to purchase something, for the collector of rare coins, for the miser who hoards it, for the person for whom it has some sentimental significance, and for the state for whom it is part of the national wealth. The relativity of values thus entails a basic ambiguity which affects the values of all "value-bearers"—even the values of the bearers of "self-values" (God excepted), for there is no finite bearer of "self-values" that is not also a bearer of values relative to some other bearer of "self-values." Such relativity, incidentally, pertains to both, the qualitative and the quantitative aspects of the values.

However, the fact that values differ with respect to quality and quantity does not in itself indicate an "order of rank" of values. Such an order emerges only when the values in question are seen in their relations to a principle or norm that serves as a standard. Actually, every "order of rank" of values depends upon three factors: (1) the type of the values to be arranged according to "rank" ("self-value," "radiated value," "service value"); (2) a principle or norm; and (3) the point of view which determines how the values are to be related to the norm—i.e., the "criterion" of the "order of rank." Analysis will then show that the principle or norm and the criterion—and therefore the whole meaning of the "order of rank"—are different for the three types of values. "Self-values," for example, can be ranked only in terms of their common relation to the "value-cosmos"—to the totality, that is, of all "self-values"—and only in accordance with the criterion of "self-value abundance" (*Selbstwertfülle*). "Radiated values" form an "order of rank" relative to the particular "self-value" to which they belong, and in accordance with the criterion of "nearness" to the "self-value." In the case of "service values" the relation to some derivative value provides the principle or norm; the criterion is the degree of usefulness (p. 49).

The large cultural realms of value—religion, morality, science, art, law, the state, society, etc.—which other value-theorists have regarded as providing the basic distinctions and "rank order" of values, Stern considers to be secondary. As he sees it, the demarcations of these areas depend upon complexly interrelated "motives" that can be clarified only as the metaphysical point of view is fully developed. Only this much need be said now: The principle of value is infinitely more far-reaching than is human culture and its subdivisions. Value-metaphysics is therefore something decidedly other than philosophy of culture—although human culture must ultimately find its appropriate place within the metaphysical framework.

III

Up to now we have dealt with preliminary matters only. We turn next to a consideration of the basic metaphysical problem. This means that we turn to a discussion of Stern's conception of "self-value" as "the ultimate value-category"—the key to his whole system. As he puts it: "To have self-value means to-have-meaning-in-itself; but meaning-in-itself can have only that which in itself has being. The question concerning the true self-value is, therefore, at the same time also the question concerning true being. At this point of metaphysical connections, value-theory becomes a philosophy concerned with the meaning of Being" (p. 56).

The question arises at once, Is there only one "self-value" or are there many? If there are many, is there, nevertheless, a unifying principle that brings all of them together in one integrative system? The question is important because, if there should be no "ultimate unity," then no coherent metaphysical system can be developed.

If a radical view were taken of the subjective aspect of the value-apriori with which we started—i.e., the assertion "I value, therefore I am a value"—the inescapable result would be an extreme form of solipsism: Only my self—this particular individual —has "self-value." But we know already that even this "self-value" is meaningful only when the "self" is understood to be interacting with a world in which values have validity. In its radical form, therefore, solipsism cannot be taken seriously as a value-oriented philosophy.

However, the "ego-principle" may also take another form: "Every self is the bearer of a self-value; and only selves are bearers of values"; and human beings alone are such selves (p. 58). It is Stern's contention, however, that in this case the restriction of "self-values" to human beings and the multiplicity of co-existing human selves prevent us from viewing the world as a "value-totality."

A one-sided concentration on the object-side of the value-apriori also leads to difficulties, for it entails the thesis that "only the All-Being (*das Allseiende*) has self-value," in consequence of which "everything finite is devalued." If the idea is consistently carried through that only the whole of reality has "self-value," then there may still be "radiated values" and "service-values" short of the whole; but there can no longer be the "self-values" of human beings. Man is then stripped of his "dignity" as a person and his valuations of the world of objects make no sense (p. 60).

An adequate value-philosophy must preserve the multiplicity of "self-values" within a monistic framework. "*Unitas multiplex* must be its goal." In other words, we must acknowledge that there are "infinitely many self-values"; but we must view them as "forming a system, an exhuberantly powerful order" (*über-schwenglich gewaltige Ordnung*) (p. 61). What Stern has in mind here is a "hierarchical monism of self-values"—"the synthesis in which both, the radical value-monism and the chaotic value-pluralism, are suspended" (*aufgehoben*), but what is true in them is preserved (p. 62).

The presupposition of such an interpretation is that "self-valuableness" (*Selbstwertigkeit*) and genuine Being (*echtes Sein*) belong inseparably together. This means, however, that not everything that exists is also a bearer of a "self-value." A scrap of paper, for example, exists; and so in some sense does a language. But neither the piece of paper nor the language can be said to "be" in any ultimate sense. What, then, is meant by "genuine Being"?

The reference cannot be to ideas; for ideas have only derivative value and they are abstractions. The concept of an "abstract Being" is nonsensical (*ein Ungedanke*). Genuine Being must be something concrete, and the distinction between bearers of "self-values" and bearers of "derivative values" must pertain to the realm of the concretely real. As Stern sees it, the distinction in question is that between "value-creating Being" and "value-receiving Being," between the "being of persons" and the "being of things." And in the perspective of this distinction Stern now formulates what he calls "the value-faith (*Wertglaube*) of critical Personalism": *"Only persons have self-value* and *all persons have self-value"* (p. 65).

Stern means by "person" a complex existent which, despite its many parts, is a characteristic and real unity and which, as such a unity, is capable of unified, purposive, and autonomous action. That is to say, a "person" is *Unitas multiplex;* a "thing" is not, for it is inherently incapable of autonomous and purposive action. Moreover, a "person" exists only as a whole. Its genuine being is that of a whole; whereas the parts have derivative being only: their being consists in their being parts of the whole. But having genuine being, the "person" also has "self-value."

Even in the perspective of time is the living person a whole within which every phase of existence derives its significance from the personal-historical or biographical context. Every person is unique, is *sui generis.* And it follows from this that, in their "here" and "now" and in their particular quality, "self-values" are not subject to rational explanation. "They are because they are, and they are as they are." Neither their being nor their quality is derivable from something else (p. 68). But this concreteness of the "self-values" entails also their limitation. As this particular concrete quality a "self-value" excludes all other qualities. As concretization in space it has the overwhelmingly large part of the world "outside" itself; and as concrete manifestation in time, it has a beginning and an end. But despite all such limitations the "self-value" loses nothing of its positive quality as a value. There is no contradiction in the thesis that something which, in itself, has significance and which, therefore, represents an "absolute value" (*Wertabsolutheit*) is finite in time. "With every human being that is born a new self-value which previously did not exist comes into being. And with every human being that dies there disappears a wholeness (*Ganzheit*) and there ceases to be this particular self-value" (p. 69).

However, not every whole encountered in experience is already that "primordial wholeness" which we must acknowledge as a person and, therefore, as a "self-value." Only a whole whose "essential wholeness" (*Ganzcharakter*) is irreducible and inexplicable in terms of anything else can be said to be a person. This means, however, that we must have a criterion which enables us to determine what is and what is not a "genuine whole"; and this criterion, to be objectively significant, must be rooted in the essential nature of the objects themselves.

A first suggestion of such a criterion is, of course, the "unity of consciousness" of the experiencing subject. All attempts to explain this unity as nothing but the "summation of experiences" are bound to fail, for the subject experiences itself as unitary and indivisible and as distinct from the objects experienced. Accepting the experienced "wholeness" of consciousness as irrefutable fact, Stern now hypostatizes that "wherever this unity of consciousness exists its bearer must be acknowledged to be a person and, therefore, a self-value" (p. 72).

It must be noted, however, that Stern does not say that consciousness is the person; he says that its "bearer" is, and that consciousness is but a symptom of this fact. He elaborates this theme by stating explicitly that the "totality" of what, on the subject-side, is related to the unity of consciousness—the unconscious, the physical, the objective pattern of meanings—this, and only this, is the real person.

Even so, however, the criterion of what is and what is not a genuine person is inadequate. We must take into consideration also "the realm of the objects." And here the criterion is "the wholeness of the configuration" (*Ganzheit der Gestalt*). What is significant in this conception is that in a "configuration" the various objectively existing parts are so interrelated that they become subordinate to the whole and derive their meaning and significance from that whole, and that the wholeness of each configuration is distinctive and clearly separated from the wholeness of every other configuration. Also, the configuration is distinctly more than the sum of its parts. A work of art exemplified what Stern has here in mind.

However, significant as the conception of configuration is, by itself it, too, is inadequate as a criterion of what is and what is not a "genuine person." Its deficiency lies in the fact that a configuration is essentially static. What is needed is a criterion that does justice to the dynamics of a person. Stern finds it in what he calls the "wholeness of function" (*Ganzheit der Funktion*): "Only what produces effects is real, and only what as a whole produces effects is a whole." Hence, "effective existing wholeness—that is the person" (p. 76).

Such effectiveness, however, is found only where a "whole" autonomously determines its own actions. "Self-value," therefore, is found only "where a whole exercises self-determination." And this may take place where animals, human beings, and human communities are involved. But if such is the case, then it is also evident that a "whole" need not exclude the existence of other "wholes," that, in fact, it may contain them. And this relationship may be extended upward and downward *ad infinitum.* The interrelation is then hierarchical.

Although we started with the conception of "person" as a human being, we now find that, in the meaning of "self-determining whole" (*Selbstbestimmungsganzes*) everything "merely human" has been left behind. We now must distinguish "unities of being" (*Seinseinheiten*) which are sub-human, co-human, and super-human—all of which are capable of self-determination. That is to say, the principle of self-value must be accepted as valid wherever a "whole" maintains or develops itself. Each such "whole," "be it a molecule or a cosmic constellation," is an "irreducible primordial value (*Urwert*) of the world" (p. 79).

This hierarchical interrelation of self-acting "wholes" implies that the opposition of "person" and "thing" is by no means absolute. Indeed, what is but "factual" from one point of view is a "whole" that possesses "genuine personal existence" from another point of view. This is true, for instance, in the case of a cell in relation to an organism, of the human individual in relation to a community, and of a community in relation to the whole of mankind. "Person" and "thing" are not two distinct kinds of substances but are two modes of viewing the same facts. "The one view is 'from above' and is directed toward the wholeness of the object; the other is 'from below' and is directed toward the parts, the phases, and the means" (p. 81).

IV

So far Stern's arguments have culminated in the equation: "Self-value = Person = Self-determining Wholeness." But he cannot rest here, for "self-value" must also be seen in its relation to a "world"—to a "world" that is encountered (a) as "the totality (*Inbegriff*) of what is objectively given and what is happening"—as a system, that is, of causally interacting forces within which the person himself acts and is acted upon; and it is encountered (b) as "an infinite system of self-values" within which the "self-value" of the individual person has to find its appropriate place. The relation in the sense of (a) Stern calls convergence; that in the sense of (b) he calls introception. His point is that "only through convergence with the world is self-determination possible"; that "the influence of the external world is necessary" in order to "transform a broad dispositional goal-directedness into univocal reality." "There is no part, no condition, no process in the life of a real person that is not also the result of convergence." This fact, however, does not reduce the person to a mere thing. On the contrary, the person is and remains "directedness toward goals." It is and remains the agent that imbues what is external and accidental and, therefore, but a "part" with a direction toward a wholeness that is envisioned as complete. In brief, the person is and remains "what Aristotle has called an entelechy" (pp. 82–84).

But the "world" is also "a cosmos of self-values," and each person has its own appropriate place in that "cosmos." In fact, it is precisely this "relation to the world as the value-cosmos that assures the person of perfect wholeness and that reveals the ideal personality within the person." Moreover, in the "cosmos of self-values" every "self-value" is "a center relative to which other self-values are either superordinated, co-ordinated in various degrees of nearness, or subordinated." For every "self-value," therefore, "the whole value-cosmos is, as it were, a perspectival constellation" within which any "self-value" posited as "center" occupies a place that is uniquely its own (p. 85).

In view of this fact, the "central person" may posit its own "centro-value" as absolute and regard all other values as derivative—as "radiated values" or as "service values." But the "central person" may equally well take the opposite point of view and regard himself as a "tool," a "sacrifice," a "part"—i.e., he may regard his own value as derivative (p. 86). It is Stern's contention that only a fusion of these two points of view can yield a tenable interpretation of the facts. No person can realize his own "centro-value" without involving "radiated" and "service" values —without, that is, of involving "excentro-values"; and the latter depend for their realization upon a "self-value" that is also a "centro-value." The synthesis here demanded Stern calls "introception"—"a real fusion, a making the 'other' into one's very 'own'" (p. 87). And this, for Stern, is the "basic value-philosophical category" upon which the development of a *Lebensanschauung* depends. "Only in introception is an altogether positive relation between value-center and value-cosmos possible" (p. 89).

If every "self-value" were in itself simply and entirely a "value-world"—if it were a "value-monad without window"—then we would have no standard by means of which to determine the height of one "self-value" with respect to that of any other. There could then be no "order of rank" of values. An amoeba would rank no lower than a human being, an idiot no lower than a genius. Every attempt to compare their respective "self-values" would be meaningless.

But "self-values" are not self-sufficient (as windowless monads would be). Despite their uniqueness and indissoluble unity they are "open" to the "value-cosmos" within which, through introception, they derive an inner richness which, in varying degrees, reflects their relations to other "self-values." This "inner richness"— this "self-value-fullness" (*Selbstwertfülle*)—serves well as a criterion of the "order of rank" of all "self-values." In his "self-value-fullness" man thus ranks high above the animals, for "fused" in his "self-value" are moral, religious, social, and aesthetic values. In fact, only this "infusion" of those values makes his own "self-value" real.

The highest "rank" belongs to "the self-value of infinite self-value-fullness for which there no longer exists any difference between the act of introception and the state of completed introception becaues all other values are contained in it—in the divine All-Person" (*Allperson*) (p. 91). Through its relation to this highest "self-value" and as part of the general value-context every "self-value" attains its own cosmic rank.

V

The "order of rank of self-values" has now been indicated *in principle*. It is an ascending scale that ranges from the simplest existing "whole" through a hierarchy of interrelated "self-values" to the "All-Person" which is no longer a subordinate part of any other "self-value" but is the all-inclusive "whole." "The hierarchy of self-values has thus found a pantheistic completion." Stern calls it "personalistic pantheism" (p. 85). "God and the world are not external to each other," for God is but the ultimate "whole," the "All-Person," in which the hierarchy of all concrete "self-values" finds its completion.

So far, however, we have dealt in abstractions only. Let us now turn to the essentially concrete content of Stern's value theory. Our task will be simplified if we begin by considering what is most familiar to us: the position of the human being within the value-cosmos.

Analysis will then show that the human being possesses unity of "configuration" (*Gestalt*) and of consciousness. Its functions are inherently goal-directed. Its autonomy is real in two forms, as self-preservation and as self-development. Its incomparableness expresses itself as individuality. Through introception the human person lifts himself to the level of personality. In brief, the human being meets in every respect the criteria of a self-value (p. 106).

Co-existing with human beings there are other "individual persons"—"configurational wholes" (*Gestaltganzheiten*) which also have the power of "determining themselves as in an integrative process of living: the animals and the plants." Their functioning is integrative because the many partial functions are coordinated in such a way that they preserve and develop the organism as a self-identical whole. "In this sense, every plant, every animal is a person and, therefore, a self-value" (p. 107).

When we trace the levels of animal and plant life downwards, we finally come to unicellular beings that are not yet differentiated as plants and animals but which, as organisms, are nevertheless "personal beings." Theirs is the lowest level of "personal" existence and of "self-value."

When we trace the "sequence of wholes" in the opposite direction, we come to "trans-individual levels of persons" of which at least two still remain within the realm of "manifestations of life" in the narrower sense: species and communities.

The various species of animal and plant life, each comprising many individuals, maintain themselves as self-identical trans-individual "wholes" through their gene-determined phylogenetic development. In one respect, however, the species are deficient in their "wholeness": They lack the functional interrelation and interaction of all their members as "agents" in the service of some "total goal" (*Gesamtziel*) to be achieved by the species. As Stern puts it: a biological species is a "person in itself" but not yet a "person in itself and for itself"; it is not a "personality" (p. 111).

What is true in the case of plant and animal species is, of course, true also in the case of *homo sapiens* as a biological species, and of its subordinate "races." At the level of man, however, the phylogenetic "wholeness" is superseded by social and cultural "configurations," by the development of "communities." The question is, Are communities "self-values"? The answer to this question may depend on what is meant by a "community."

Not every association of human beings is already a community. Most of them have no "self-value." What value they do have is either a "service-value" or a "radiated value"; and these derived values may depend either on the "self-value" of individuals or on the "self-value" of a "higher community." If an association has "service-value" only, it is a "service organization" rather than a community. Even within a "service organization" there may, of course, develop important human relations —friendship, love, etc.—and there are therefore given certain possibilities for introception. The values of one person may, through introception, enrich the values of another. The "service-value" of the organization is thus augmented by "radiated values";

but even this fact does not raise the value of the organization to the level of a "self-value."

It is Stern's thesis, however, that there are communities which, "in themselves, create and maintain their value because, as wholeness (*Ganzheit*) they possess an immanent teleology." "Classical examples of these personal levels are . . . the family, the nation (*Volk*), mankind" (p. 113). Here, "all activities and expressions, no matter how diverse they may be, are subordinated to the whole and directed toward the realization of its goal" (p. 114). To be sure, the whole does not determine the existence and the actions of its component individuals down to the last detail. If it did, the individuals would cease to be persons in their own right. But the whole, nevertheless, "participates" in it all. Common fate and common history broaden individual existence and create a solid foundation of traditions, mores, and veneration in and through which the self-preservation of the super-individual whole proves itself. Common ideals and shared tendencies of development point to progress, reform, and expansion in the future. Biological and trans-biological relationships are here intertwined in such a way as to constitute "a genuine communal person" (*eine echte Gemeinschaftsperson*). A family, for example, is not simply a means for the preservation of the species but is, beyond that, also a whole within which the interests of the individual members and their introceptive interrelations find recognition and accommodation as parts of shared goals.

A nation, so Stern maintains, is also a "communal person." And here, too, the broad biological basis—not a racial one—is indispensable. But a nation is not the same as a state. Taken by itself, a state is but a "service organization" and has no "self-value." What has "self-value" is the nation—i.e., it is the people organized in a state and working through the machinery of the state to realize shared goals.

When next we consider mankind as a whole, we find that here, too, the biological basis is present; that, in fact, because of this basis mankind, being a species, has the wholeness of a species. But we also find that mankind is "on the way" of achieving a "communal unity" (*Gemeinschaftseinheit*) which transcends but includes all nations. As Stern sees it, it may be precisely this tendency of mankind to develop "from the status of a slumbering person into a wide-awake personality" that has placed such great emphasis upon the very idea of a common humanity and has intensified international efforts to make it a reality. But even here the principle of a hierarchical order prevails. The "self-values" of nations and of humanity as a whole do not exclude one another —although the "self-value" of the whole of humanity, being all-inclusive at the human level, is far higher than the more limited one of any particular nation or of all of them individually.

One final point should be considered here; for we must not forget that all life is but a manifestation of evolutionary developments that are cosmic in extent. When we view in this perspective the origin and development of our earth and the life it supports, then we are actually dealing with the unique process of "a whole forming itself" (*ein sich selbst gestaltendes Ganze*)—a process, that is, of "personal self-unfolding" (*personale Selbstentfaltung*) (p. 121). And is it not possible, Stern asks, that the "awe" which the "starry heavens" inspire in us reflects, not the "majesty of the law" (as Kant thought), but the fact that we intuitively comprehend genuine wholeness and truly *personales Sein* "in ourselves and in the stars and constellations"? (p. 122). And this question suggests once more the close connection between value-metaphysics and the meaning of human existence.

VI

Every person, no matter at what level of existence, is *unitas multiplex* and has a "self-value." Every one of its parts derives value from the fact that it is a part of the whole. Its value "emanates" from the whole. Stern, as we know, calls it "radiated value." Relative to the "self-value" of the whole, the "radiated value" is the lower of the two. Relative to "service-values," however, the "radiated values" (because of their integral relation to the "self-value" of the whole) are the higher ones. This fact is of crucial significance, for it means that "the values of morality and religion, of mind and body, of art and justice, of nature and culture, of history and society, of health and wealth" can now be assigned their proper place in the realm of values. They are not primary or "self-values"; but neither are they "service-values." They are valuable, not because they are in the same sense "useful" but because they are "radiated values." The "primary values" (*Urwerte*) "manifest themselves in them" (*stellen sich in ihnen dar*).

A certain ambiguity arises from the fact that the relation of the "radiated value" to the "self-value" can be viewed in two ways: from the "self-value" down and from the "radiated value" up. If viewed from the "self-value" down, the essence of the "radiated value" lies in the fact that its "bearer" is a part of the whole. If viewed from the "radiated value" up, it is essential that the "radiated value" in some way still reflect the whole. If the first of these perspectives is intended, Stern speaks of "participating value" (*Anteilswert*). If the second perspective is meant, Stern speaks of "symbol-value" (*Symbolwert*). Care must be taken, however, that the "participating value" not be reduced to mere factuality, or the "symbol-value" be elevated into a "self-value" (p. 127).

The situation is complicated by the fact that a "radiated value" may also be intertwined with "service-values." A Gothic cathedral, for example, has a religious, an aesthetic, and a cultural "radiated value" as a "symbol of the Divine" and as "manifestation of human and national forms and phases of life"; at the same time, however, it also has a "service-value" as a place of worship and as "effective means for the development of ecclesiastical power" (p. 128). Comparable complexities are encountered in connection with all other "value-bearers"—with the sole exception of the All-Person.

The significance of the "symbol-value" lies not so much in the fact that, as a "radiated value," it depends upon a "self-value," but in the fact that it "points toward" that value. "The radiated value is, as it were, transparent; it permits the self-value to be apprehended through it" (p. 129). The relationship of value and being here takes on a new form; for it is not the immediately real—the flag, the painting, the spoken word—that is valuable, but "the deeper self-value that lies behind it." This fact emphasizes the difference between "symbol-value" and "use-value," between the aesthetic realm, for example, and the "practical."

The danger is that a "symbol-value" will be taken to be a "self-value." If this happens, the "symbol-value" loses its transparency and the identity of "self-value" and "radiated value" is no longer one of meaning only but one of existence. It is unfortunate that no area of human experience is completely free of such confusions, for the confusions can be disastrous. Thus, "are" the bread and the wine at Holy Communion actually the body and blood of Christ, or do they but "mean" them? Embittered battles have been fought over this issue for centuries.

The shift from "symbol-value" to "self-value" is complete when the very functions of the "self-value-bearer" are ascribed to the "bearer" of the "symbol-value." Stern calls this shift—the act as well as the effect—a personification. "Personification as act" is exemplified by man's "myth-forming" activities and, at a more sophisticated level, by the Neo-Platonic elevation of ideas into "potencies" or "personal powers." "Personification as effect" may be seen in the idols and amulettes, the mountains and rivers revered as divine persons.

That the problem of personification is, and must be, of special interest to Stern is obvious because, for him, "true being" is found only in the form of persons. Personification is therefore essential to his version of Personalism—but not every form of personification. Criteria have to be formulated that help us to determine "when and how in a concrete case personification is permitted, which personification yields real persons and therefore genuine self-values" and which does not. But even the naive personifications which culminate in "fictitious persons" cannot be brushed aside entirely, for they are not meaningless "delusions" (*Hirngespinste*) that have no value. They are "symbols: sensory representations of the invisible, linguistic crystallizations of what cannot be expressed in words, projections into the sphere of the perceptible of what transcends all perception." And such personifications have a practical significance. As "transition stages" in the cultural progress of mankind they are convenient and even "necessary self-deceptions"; for only what is directly acknowledged as in itself valuable can have an "inspiring and normative force" for the naive person (pp. 131–132).

Every subject—be it an individual human being, a nation, a cultural Era—must regard as absolute the values determinative of its ultimate goals; and every "activist" is, in a sense, a fanatic—

the pious person who regards religious symbols as "holy"; the revolutionary for whom the ideals of Freedom, Equality, and Brotherhood are "holy"; and the modern engineer for whom Technology is God. It is the specific task of a critical value-metaphysics, so Stern maintains, not simply to repudiate these self-deceptions but to "see through them" and to reveal the "self-value" of which they are but "symbols." Viewed in this perspective, the "radiated values" lose nothing of their "dignity" as values, merely their absoluteness. But he who is searching for the ultimate, as does the metaphysician, must emphasize this difference.

VII

The distinction between "participating values" and "symbol-values" reflects the purely formal aspects of the relation between "radiated values" and "self-values." All further differentiations are conditioned by the qualitative characteristics of the "parts" that are the *multiplicitas* of the *unitas* having the "self-value." The multiplicity of these elements (subordinate wholes and goals, functional directions and phases of existence present in every bearer of a "self-value") entails at the same time the possibility of an "infinite multiplicity of radiated values"—a multiplicity of values which, however, may be arranged in some form of order.

As Stern sees it, there is available a criterion which enables us to compare "radiated values" as to their "order of rank" without affecting in the least their qualitative individuality. This criterion is the "essential nearness," the "intimacy," with which the parts represent the essential nature (*Wesensgehalt*) of the "self-value." That is to say, a "radiated value" stands higher in the order of rank in proportion as its characteristics approach the wholeness of the "self-value" (p. 134).

This criterion must now be elucidated by applying it to the multitude of "radiated values." First, however, let us remind ourselves of the fact that, for Stern, the key to any interpretation of reality and of value is the "person"; that a "person" is "essentially wholeness, activity, purposiveness, self-determining unity"; that every "person" exists in a world of "persons" and thus exists for itself and for others; that its actions are both, "inward-directed" and "outward-directed." The aspects of "inner" and "outer" are characteristic of all "persons," the "outer" being their "physical nature," their "body," in and through which they are "available" to themselves no less than to others.

When we now turn to particulars, Stern tells us, to begin with, that the physical existence of a human being, symbolically reflecting the whole person—the "inner" as well as the "outer"—, is "the ultimate mystery with the acknowledgment of which Personalism stands or falls" (p. 148).

Every physical manifestation is always actual. It exists in the present only; is here and now. The person, however, that manifests itself in the physical reality is "actual and, at the same time, dispositional," having existence here and now and also "continuing potentiality." And since the physical is "expressive" of the whole person, it must represent even the "dispositional and lasting essence" in the actual present (p. 152). This fact leads Stern to distinguish between actual or "phenomenological" and dispositional or "characterological" forms of "self-expression" and their respective values; and it is clear that the values rooted in characterological self-expressions are more "intimately" related to the person as a whole than are the others. Judged by the previously stated criterion, they are therefore the higher of the two types of "radiated values."

But there is another dimension to all this; for the individual human being did not develop (nor does he exist) in isolation. In his whole being and deportment he reflects his human associations past and present—his social status, his cultural environment. But this means that in the manifestations of his own being there is reflected also something that is more than merely individual. A work of art, being such a manifestation, reveals perhaps best what Stern here means. A Beethoven sonata, for example, is of course a significant expression of the unique personality of Beethoven; but it also has value as a manifestation of the culture of the time and, as a genuine work of art, it was the expression of something new and valid that enabled others to translate into tonal configuration what had been inexpressible before.

But forms of expression are characteristic also of "persons" more complex than individual human beings—of the nation, for example, and the whole of mankind. In the case of the nation, the "body" consists of all the people involved in the ceaseless process of "national life"—a process which includes economic and industrial activities, artistic creation, the development of traditions and mores, of language and literature, and whatever else constitutes man's cultural existence. The way in which people act in the market-place or at leisure, in their own homes or in church—all this, and much more, has immediate significance as "person-symbol," as reflecting the character of the nation as a "person" (pp. 173–174).

A particularly important function in all this must be assigned to the state as the expression of the concentrated will of the "communal person" (*Gemeinschafts-Person*). If the state lacks this "communal" basis, it is merely a "service organization." If the people are not organized as a state, they are but a "slumbering," not a real person. In the nation, however, state and people are fused into a whole having all the characteristics of a "person" (in Stern's sense of that term), the form of the state—"constitutional monarchy, democratic republic, congress of soviets"—reflecting the very nature of that "person" (p. 177).

Other manifestations of that same "communal person" are, of course, the "physical creations"—primarily architectural and other works of art. Although every work of art has its own aesthetic value and many of them have a "service-value," they have, in addition, a distinctive value as "bodily manifestations" or "outward projections" of the "self-value" of a community. "Such works are, in intensively condensed form, the independently existing physical embodiment of the essential character of a communal person" (p. 178). Insofar as the works have "service-value," they are products of man's civilization. Insofar as they have "symbol-value," they are products of his culture. The line of demarcation, however, is not sharp; for there exist many objects which are "bearers" of both types of values, and are so in varying proportions (p. 180).

When next we consider the whole of mankind as at least potentially a person, we find that it manifests itself physically in two positive forms and in one negative one. The first of the positive forms is, of course, the human body. Body-form, erect posture, language—these are characteristics of human beings as human. They are what separates man from animals, plants, and rocks. The second positive aspect common to all mankind is man's self-engendered culture. Economic activity, technology, art, science, mores —despite all their diversity in details—are specifically human achievements; and no "expressive value" (*Ausdruckswert*) is more human than is the reality of culture. And there are also signs indicative of the fact that the "slumbering" whole which is mankind is awakening. World-wide interactions of different cultures, the exchange of goods and ideas, the international interests in science and technology, international agreements and compacts, international law, the Geneva Convention, the Declaration of Human Rights, the United Nations—all of these reveal a growing awareness of the ultimate unity of all mankind. Although that unity is still more projection than reality, the idea of a common humanity is at least an "inner symptom of mankind's awakening."

To be sure, there are also the disruptive aspects in international relations—intense nationalism, ideological conflicts, revolutions, world wars; and it may seem that these negative symptoms "outweigh the beginnings of an active solidarity of mankind." But, as Stern sees it, even these negative aspects are indicative of the integrative trends in history. The frightful conflict that was World War II, for example, revealed how intimately the interests of all mankind are interrelated. "Even while the war was still raging, international contexts and interactions in transportation, communication, and economic relations asserted themselves with a necessity that could not be suspended (*paralysiert*) by the political separation of nations." After the war, the development of "world-historical, world-economic, and world-cultural relations" continued the trend toward unification. To be sure, national diversities persist. But this fact is not only reconcilable with, but is demanded by, the conception of a "whole of mankind." "As a person, mankind must be *unitas multiplex.*" All efforts aimed at the elimination of the cultural differences between nations are as much contrary to "the true nature of mankind" as are the attempts to make those differences absolute (pp. 183–185).

VIII

Having thus presented in broad outlines Stern's metaphysically oriented value theory, we shall now consider very briefly some of the values which Stern discusses in detail. We begin with values pertaining to the human person.

The individual human being is a psycho-physical unity, having an "inner" and an "outer." It has a "self-value" from which the values of the "inner" and "outer" emanate.

The "inner" is best characterized as "experience." But "experience" must not be identified with the person as such; it is only "a small segment of the life of a person." "Its value depends on the significance which it has in the total life of the person"—i.e., it depends on its "transcending mere occurrence" (p. 204). This transcendence consists in the fact that experience is in the most literal sense of the term an *Auseinander-Setzung,* a "positing as distinct," of subject and object, and also their "coming to terms" (*Auseinandersetzung*) with one another.

This duality of transcendence implies that experience is concerned with the clarification of "the true self and the true world"; and this, in turn, reveals that there are "two entirely different realms of radiated values: the spheres, respectively, of the subjective and of the objective life of the spirit" (p. 207).

On the subject-side we encounter the felt contrast of pleasure and displeasure and of their many variants: "joy and suffering, love and hate, happiness and unhappiness" (p. 213). That is to say, we experience an emotional polarity which all hedonists have made basic to their interpretation of values. Stern points out, however, that hedonism is untenable. When we are told, he argues, that pleasure is what alone is valuable, that it ought to be pursued and enhanced, we must ask: For whom is it valuable? Who ought to pursue it? If the answer is that "pleasure wants itself," then our retort must be that it is obviously nonsense to say of pleasure that it wants or wills something. A person, however, who wants pleasure "does not want pleasure as pleasure but wants himself in and through the pleasure—and this means that pleasure ceases to be the primary value." The fact is that pleasure and displeasure are not "independent experiential configurations but only aspects or feeling-tones of experience." "The pleasant taste of a morsel of food, the enjoyment of a Beethoven symphony, the joy of seeing old friends, the satisfaction that stems from having finally solved a scientific problem—all these are experiences having a hedonic feeling-tone; but they are at the same time experiences of so diverse qualities and meaningful relations that their reduction to the accompanying pleasure would deprive them of all significance" (p. 215). The facts in the case merely prove that "not the immanence of the experiences but their transcendence is determinative of their value" (p. 222).

In addition to his feelings, the human individual experiences perceptions and thoughts, and these, too, belong to his "inner" sphere. "Their entire meaning, however, lies in the outer sphere." Their transcendence is that they "seek and posit the world" (p. 224). The experiential process is that of cognition, and the "value-sphere" which this process creates is that of "spiritual values." The central value here is that of truth, of a critically progressive objectification of the experiential contents, "an ever-continuing approximation of the Absolute." Since only that which has independent existence can also have "self-value," the value of truth is not a "self-value"—despite all idealistic arguments to the contrary. But truth has an immense "use-value" because true knowledge is basic to technology, to medical progress, and to a multitude of other cultural activities that affect mankind in general no less than the individual human persons. To deny this "use-value" of truth would be nonsensical. But it would be equally nonsensical to maintain that truth has nothing but "use-value," for cognition, in both of its aspects, as belief and as criticism, "belongs to the very nature of a person as one of its highest activities and thus partakes of its personal self-value." Moreover, since cognition is "a never-completed approximation of Absolute Reality," true knowledge is "in some way close to the Absolute and participates therefore in the self-value of the Absolute" (p. 229). The value of truth is thus related to the "self-value" of the cognizing subject and to the "self-value" of the object. It is neither merely "experiential value" nor merely a "reality-value" but comes into being because of the interactions of both spheres, that of the subject and that of the object, and therefore constitutes "a new and unitary sphere of radiated value."

Analysis will show, so Stern continues, that "all cognition is an abstraction; that it means disregarding much in order to concentrate all the more upon something specific" (p. 232). But such abstraction is possible in two forms: as concentration upon an ever-increasing individualization, and as concentration upon an ever-increasing generalization. The former yields the "truth-value of intuition," the latter the "truth-value of ideas."

Intuition "affirms concrete existence." At one level it is "the most primitive starting-point of cognition." At another level, however, it is "the highest, the ultimate completion of the cognitive process accessible to us"—the surpassing of conceptual abstraction through "trans-conceptual concretion," through a "sublimated" or "intellectual intuition" that goes beyond conceptual understanding.

As far as "ideas" are concerned, the process of abstraction is twofold: culminating, on the one hand, in the "universality of the concepts," and culminating, on the other hand, in the "universality of judgments," the "universality of laws." But the two forms are actually inseparable because universal concepts are already "potential judgments" and, therefore, "potential laws." It must be noted, however, that neither the concepts nor the laws have "self-value." Only "self-existent persons" have that.

When "conceptual meanings" and "intellectual intuition" fuse, "ideas" are transformed into "ideals." As Stern sees it: "In the 'ideal,' intuition and idea, concretion and universality, are brought together (*aufgehoben*) in a higher unity" (p. 242). And this "fusion," this emergence of "ideals," is significant for the "self-determination" of every person. It is significant because a person is not simply an "existent" here and now and of such and such character, but is also, and more importantly, a "self-projected ideal but uncompleted task." That is to say, the person is "striving to attain a state or condition (*Zustand*) in which his own self-value and the values of the world are simultaneously affirmed" (p. 243).

Since every person is the center of his own "value-world" (*Wertewelt*), the manner in which he seeks to "fuse" (*einzuschmelzen*) the "objective values" into his own "self-value" is and must be unique. This means that "every person has his own ideal which cannot be subsumed under a universal concept but can only be intuitively comprehended." Despite this fact, however, the intuition of the ideal must also have universality in some form because, "relative to the ideal task of the person, every actual particularity [of the person's existence] appears to be merely provisional and superficial." No "limited present," no particular "Now," can ever contain the ideal task as fulfilled. The "universality of the ideal," therefore, pertains not to that which is never absent but to that which is "never quite real." "It is not the universality of the *must* (*des Müssens*)"—as is the universality of scientific laws—"but the universality of the *ought* (*des Sollens*), of a *demand* (*einer Forderung*)" (p. 243).

What a person posits for himself as an ideal task he imposes at the same time upon everything that belongs to him, making it share in the pursuit of the task. But such an imposition of an *ought* must not be interpreted as being entirely subjective. "Nothing would be a greater mistake," Stern points out, "then to believe that ideals are simply mental experiences of the self, posited by the self as incentive (*Anspornung*) for his own actions." The positing of ideals is, rather, "an acknowledgment of their validity," "a saying Yes! to their demands," "a subordination of oneself to their standards." The ideals thus acknowledged are objective because "they emanate as demands from value-bearers that are not identical with the subject" in its actuality. "This objectivity, however, is one of validity only for those subjects that are subordinate moments of the value-bearers in question. Here the ideals become *norms* (*Normen*)" (p. 246).

IX

The human person exists as a becoming. That is to say, in his existence being and becoming, constancy and change are indissolubly intertwined. As Stern sees it, this bipolarity of existence, important though it is for ontology, is even more important for value theory because there is no area—be it "cosmic, biological, or cultural"—no field of human valuations and actions that is unaffected by the contrast of being and becoming, or by the "dialectic" of their interdependence (p. 249).

In view of this dual aspect of human existence, Stern distinguishes between "values of preservation" (*Erhaltungswerte*) and "values of development" (*Entwicklungswerte*). The former include values pertaining to the preservation of "the absolute personal minimum," i.e., to mere existence, to the preservation of "personal qualities," characteristics, memories, and works accomplished, and to the preservation of "relations or adaptations."

The "values of development" include all values of "growth" and of "self-unfolding" (*Selbstentfaltung*). It is not sufficient, however, to view any given "phase" of development as merely a step (*Vorstufe*) toward some ultimate state or condition, or as a "means" to its realization, and therefore to ascribe to it merely a "use-value." Only "the living whole in its wholeness is the value-center," and from it each phase of development derives its value. This is true for the phylogenetic development of man no less than for his individual and personal unfolding (pp. 250–260).

But only where there is a "linear ascention" (*Aufstieg*) does development have value-theoretical significance; and this fact implies that a criterion is needed if we are to speak meaningfully of an "increase in value" and, therefore, of "progress" in development. This criterion is not "enhancement of happiness or of virtue or, for that matter, of consciousness or of strength—either in the individual or in mankind as a whole." "All of this may be contained in development as a subordinate element but it does not constitute the essence of development" (p. 260). "Only this can be called development: the very nature of a person as *unitas multiplex* is ever purer in its manifestation." A person that unfolds itself takes in ever new contents of experience, lets them become effective and to combine with others, transforms them into a new productive action (*Neutat*), and widens the range and the content of its social and cultural realm. Growth of the person thus means an increase in "multiplicity in unity" (*Vieleinheitlichkeit*) but also of "spontaneity, self-determination, and independence vis-a-vis the world" (p. 261). Because of such increases every development gains "direction" (*Gerichtetheit*), and every phase of the process attains a specific "value-height" (*Werthöhe*).

Such development has its "formal" and its "empirical" aspects. Formally it is simply "the growth of multiplicity in unity." Empirically, however, it is simultaneously an increase in differentiation and integration. Thus, the mature person is superior to the child in inner manifoldness and in the forceful integration of the many into one; and so is the cultural community superior to the primitive. This, however, is only part of the story. The other part is that not just any elements of experience are being combined in the actual unity of personal existence, but that the greatest possible multiplicity of "world-values" and the personal "self-value" are combined by introception into a "value-microcosm" (p. 263).

However, a progress that is nothing but "progress" is in itself "conservative," for it retains as constant the direction of progress (*Fortschrittsrichtung*). "Every genuine unfolding is change, creation, and self-surpassing" (p. 269)—a "dialectic" in which any particular phase of development stands in interaction with the whole of it and contributes to its richness and variety; but a "dialectic" also in which progress is not necessarily uni-directional.

When we now turn to the history of mankind in order to identify the values it involves, we must clearly distinguish between "history as science" (*Geschichtswissenschaft*)—i.e., history as an account or an interpretation of certain events—and "history as the object of that science." Only the former—history as science—is relevant here; and for history in this sense not everything that has happened in the course of time is of significance. The historian selects only a limited few from the infinitely many events that have occurred and, in doing so, he gives them "historical significance." Such selection, however, is possible only in view of certain criteria which the historian accepts. The danger here is that the historian imposes his personal predilections upon the mass of material which he wishes to interpret. Stern argues, however, that what happens in the world is not simply a "formless, chaotic conglomerate" but is inherently "structured." The events themselves are interrelated as "contexts of meaning" (*Sinnzusammenhänge*) and are "delimited by singularities of meaning" (*Sinnbesonderungen*). And these relationships and connections are determined by "value-relations" (*Wertbeziehungen*)— "not, however, by a relation to general and abstract value-principles but by a relation to concrete value-bearers as their center of meaning" (p. 272). Thus, only those events which stand in meaningful relation to the "self-value" of a nation belong to the history of that nation. In general, only "existents" whose meaning is indigenous in them as their own self-determination can be genuine centers of relationships that are historically significant. And this means that only persons (in their different levels of rank) are such centers. They alone can be said to have a history, and facts can be said to have historical value only insofar as they contribute to that history.

The actual phases of historical development, however, are not only "transitional stages" but also, and perhaps most importantly, the "sources" from which the present derives support and "nourishment." The historical value of "wars of liberation," for example, lies not only in the fact that they are a "stage of transition" in the life of a nation, but also in the fact that through them something new comes into existence which has lasting validity for the future.

But it is also true that the historical value of the past always depends on its relation to the present; and that, as the present changes, it becomes necessary to re-evaluate the events of the past. The historical significance of a Plato and a Caesar, of a Jesus and a Goethe is even now undergoing changes as these individuals are seen in ever new cultural perspectives. "The petrified rigidity of the past is a scientific abstraction and not history" (p. 293).

Interrelated with the "historical values" are, of course, the different "service-values" (*Dienstwerte*) of man's economic and technological activities. Such values belong to objects because of the relation of the objects to "meaningful purposes"—i.e., because of the relation to purposes which, in some way, are part of a "whole" which in its very nature (*wesenhaft*) is itself a purpose (*Selbstzweck*). As far as Stern is concerned, only "persons" can be such "wholes."

Since different means may serve the same purpose, and since the same means may serve different purposes, different objects may derive "service-value" from their relation to one and the same "whole," and the same object may derive "service-value" from its relations to various "wholes." Moreover, it is not necessary for an object having "service-value" that it is actually employed as means; it suffices that the object has the potentiality of being so employed. And different objects which are means to the same end may, despite their differences, still be identical in their "usefulness" and thus have identical "service-values." A ten-dollar "Federal Reserve Note" and a valid personal check in the amount of ten dollars are thus identical in their "purchasing value."

"Service-values," it is clear, are all "external" to the "self-value." The "means" to which they are attached "form the environment of the self-value" (p. 306). Within this environment, however, the means differ in how closely or how directly they are related to the purpose which they serve; and their "service-values" differ accordingly. As Stern sees it, such items as home, furniture, clothing, books, tools, the "fruits of the field" and many many others rank highest in direct service relation to particular personal ends. The "service-values" of such environmental factors are essentially universal, potential, interchangeable, and measurable. Still, "in the manner in which a woman chooses her clothes, in the attachment of the peasant to his fields, of the scholar to his books, of a child to her doll we can discern more than the acknowledgment of a use-value; we discern an enlargement of personality beyond the limits of the body. And in this respect no interchange of the objects is possible" (pp. 307–308). The "accent of personal affection" makes the objects in question quite unique; they may become virtually irreplaceable, and their loss entails an impoverishment of the person. Moreover, it may be the case that a means to an end takes on the character of a symbol; that its "service-value" is superseded by its "symbol-value." A book received from a dear friend now dead, the glove of a loved one as reminder of a special occasion, historical memorabilia (a pen used in signing the Declaration of Independence, for example), and religious relics—these but illustrate what is meant here.

A second level in the series of immediacies of "service-values" is that of the "means-means" (*Mittelsmittel*)—of the means, that is, which are needed to produce the means that are directly involved in the realization of a "self-value." Thus, as we have seen, the dress a woman chooses has both, an immediate "use-value" and a "radiated value" reflecting something of that woman's personal "self-value." Because of this "radiated value" the dress is difficult to replace. The universality of its value is limited—as is the value-potentiality of the dress as a means to other purposes. But the dress exists only because of a chain of interrelated means that extends farther and farther away from immediate usefulness. There is, for example, the cloth out of which the dress is made. Its usefulness is wider than that of the dress, for it can be material for other dresses or even for other useful objects, such as coverlets or drapes. This potentiality for a wider use constitutes the "service-value" of the cloth. And then there is the mechanical weaver's loom, the usefulness of which is still broader because it can be employed for the purpose of weaving quite different materials. Beyond the mechanical loom there is the fuel needed to keep the machinery going. The potentialities of this fuel as useful means are, obviously, immensely much broader yet, for it can be used to keep all sorts of machines going. Finally, there are the human beings whose ingenuity and labor make all this technology, and much more, possible.

This "chain of means-means" is the area in which "service-values" are measurable—measurable in accordance with the demand that "use-effect" (*Nutzeffekt*) divided by "cost" equal an "optimum." This formula assumes, however, that the value of the "use-effect" is somehow "given"; it cannot be used to determine that value. A "justification" (*Rechtfertigung*) of the "use-effect value" can be given only in terms of its relation to a personal "self-value." Wherever the formula is applicable, we find ourselves in the area of the "technical sciences." The range of the applicability of the formula defines the range of those sciences and determines their limitations. Such sciences, in other words, are not concerned with "self-values." But "a system of self-values that is prior to and independent of all technology must be established if the technical values are to be justified"—justified by virtue of their relation to those "self-values."

Reference has already been made to the human beings whose ingenuity and labor make technology itself possible, and to their place in the "chain of means-means"; but we have not yet considered what this entails. If the persons involved were merely "means" in the process of production, they would, of course, be deprived of all personal "self-values"—as they are in slavery. The development of mankind, however, has reached a stage at which such deprivation is rightly condemned as immoral. "It would be the height of absurdity," Stern points out, "if the service-values which can never be ultimate goals were to dominate over the self-values of human beings which are ultimate goals" (p. 316). To equate "human labor" with other "means-means" is impossible. And this, Stern adds, is not merely an "academic declaration of protest" without further significance, it is a vital issue in the whole "labor movement" and concerns the scholar and inventor, the writer and the artist no less than it does the manual laborer. It permeates our whole industrial society.

Related to the "service-values" are the "exchange values"; but the two groups are by no means identical. In order that there be "exchange values," three conditions must be fulfilled. (1) A particular person must have at his disposal various "service-values": bodily strength, material goods, diverse "means-means," and so on. Since each "service-value" is in effect a possibility of fulfilling some purpose, every elimination of a "service-value" from the sum-total of such values available to a person means a "lessening" of that person's possibilities of realizing his purposes—unless a substitute for the eliminated "service-value" is available. The demand for a substitution follows from the person's inherent tendency to maintain himself. As a rule, however, the mere possibility of substitution is not sufficient to induce a person to part with a "service-value." A plus of received value is necessary—be it that the substitute object serves better the more urgent purposes or that it serves more general purposes than does the object that is being relinquished.

(2) "Exchange is an inter-personal process," involving at least two persons. The exchange takes place when some particular person, A, values a certain object, O, (which he does not possess) higher than an object P (which he does possess) while another person, B, values P (which he does not possess) higher than he does O (which he does possess). Both participants in the exchange thus gain by the exchange.

(3) The inter-personal exchange as just described is embedded in "an immense network of exchanges"—ultimately in a world-wide market-situation. This complicates the picture but does not affect the basic principle of exchange.

Inherent in the broader aspects of the exchange relationships there is, however, one specific aspect that must be considered, if ever so briefly. It is this: the "plus" attained in an exchange may be experienced as an increase in power and may be desired for this reason—and there is no inherent limit to the power-drive. The drive, however, may turn in various directions. "An individual or a nation which experiences within itself the manifold powers of technological know-how . . . and exercises them in a many-faceted dominance over nature, over economic conditions, over other individuals and nations finds its own self-value enhanced—provided only that the new values find an appropriate place within the total system of radiated values" (p. 332). This transformation of the economic and technical means into expressions of personal life—i.e., this transformation of "service-values" into "radiated values"—changes civilization into culture. And this brings us to a last point.

X

The "value-apriori," it will be remembered, had two forms: (1) "There are values"; (2) "I value, therefore I am—value." Up to now we have been concerned primarily with (1). We must now examine (2) more closely, for the entire "value-cosmos" is centered in a subject or self that values. As Stern sees it, "being centered in a self (*Selbstzentrierung*) is the basic fact (*Urfaktum*) of all axiosophy; it makes it possible that, for man, the objective value-cosmos transforms itself into the value-spheres of religion, art, morality, science; and it makes it necessary that this cosmos imposes itself upon man as a system of tasks, norms, duties" (p. 338). This "ego-centricity" is part and parcel of the very nature of the self, for a person is a self only insofar as, "valuing something other than itself, it posits itself as self-value." This basic fact, however, must not be confused with solipsism or egoism, for service, humility, sacrifice, even self-sacrifice also must find their appropriate place within the over-all value-framework. What Stern does mean by "ego-centricity" is that "the metaphysical value-individuality of the self in its metaphysical value-situation is the pre-condition for every concrete world-view, every life-forming (*Lebensgestaltung*), and every norm-structure" (p. 340).

In this metaphysical situation, "value-introception" plays a decisive role. It is "the act in and through which the person at the center of the value-cosmos affirms its own centro-values and, at the same time, the excentro-values as well." "The self makes the affirmation of the not-I-values a part of its own self-value." In fact, the self "realizes its own self-value only through making the other values its own inner property, thus broadening its point-like being into a microcosmos" (p. 353). The presupposition which makes such an act at all possible is that "self-value" and "not-self-value" are clearly distinguished in experience and that they are antithetical. Introception, although bringing these values together, preserves their antithetical character as a particular "state of tension" (*Spannungszustand*) in experience (p. 354).

Stern distinguishes four basic forms of introception: The most immediate and most subjective is love, the most objective is a scientific understanding of a culture; the purest form is aesthetic enjoyment, the most compelling is the holy which, in religious introception is elevated into absoluteness. These basic forms are augmented by a "practical" introception which pertains to the acts of value-realization.

In its most elementary form introception occurs where one human being encounters another; for here the "not-I-value" is so similar to one's own "self-value" as to be "felt" at once as similar. In some situations this "empathy" turns into love and the together-ness of the value-subjects into a community. But "hate" also is connected with introception. It arises where introception encounters insurmountable obstacles. And so it is clear that "introception is the presupposition of all personal relationships among human beings." Feelings of sympathy and compassion are "but symptoms of the interlacing (*Ineinanderfliessen*) of the essences and values" (p. 358).

That love may take various forms—the erotic, the familial, the social (love of mankind)—is obvious from the facts of human existence and requires no further elucidation. It should be noted, however, that in every one of its forms love is not simply or exclusively a relation between individuals. It is always also the realization of something "higher," of a "whole" which transcends but includes the individuals as constitutive elements.

In some respects the opposite of love is cognitive understanding of the "other." Whereas in love the subjective side dominates—as empathy and as readiness to take risks on behalf of the other—cognitive understanding is as objective as far as that is at all possible within the process of introception. "The purely intellectual comprehension of the essence and the value of another person is the ultimate purpose" (p. 373). However, we must distinguish between two forms of intellectual cognition: the generalizing form exemplified by the natural sciences, and the individualizing form exemplified in the historical or cultural sciences. It is only the latter that concerns us here, and it concerns us because the objects of history, for instance, are individual persons and nations, individual cultures, styles, and institutions. If we really want to understand these in their unique significance, our objectifying cognition must be supported and superseded by an empathetic understanding. A "great personality," for example, is understood and can be made understandable to others only when we know how its unique "self-value" found realization in specific and meaningful relations to the objective "value-sphere" and the metaphysical "world-situation" of its time. It is true, of course, that without respect for the facts in the case there can be no real understanding. But a knowledge of facts alone is insufficient. It is merely auxiliary to empathetic introception. And in this form of introception cognition approaches the nature of an art.

In aesthetic experience the object is taken out of its interrelations with reality and is experienced as a self-contained and self-sufficient "whole" which in every one of its parts is reflected as that "whole." However, as far as Stern is concerned, the apprehension of the "sensorially given" is not yet the aesthetic experience. What is crucial here is the "content of meaning" which the sensory elements suggest or imply. In this respect a work of art is like a person, for the person also is not the body—though that may be present in sense perception; it is the "ideal nature" of which the body is but a space-time manifestation. Wherever human beings are the aesthetic objects—in literature, in the plastic arts, in painting—it is that "ideal nature" toward which the aesthetic experience is directed. The person who has an aesthetic experience is empathically absorbed in the values thus disclosed. He may feel the value qualities of a particular character or of our common humanity in the concrete object of art here and now. Or he may feel an empathetic affinity with plants and animals (if such are the objects of experience), or with "cosmic forces" that are "visible" and "audible" in architecture and music. "There is nothing in the world that, of necessity, is foreign to the aesthetic experience. . . . The dead world of things transforms itself everywhere into a living, personal reality" (p. 388). And he who has had such an experience is the richer for it, for the values apprehended in the aesthetic experience are now his own through introception.

In love as well as in the aesthetic experience we relate ourselves to something "above" us. And the same is true—and especially so —when we introcept the "holy." To posit the "holy" means to acknowledge demands and norms which the individual accepts as valid and therefore as binding for himself. Or, to put it differently, to posit the "holy" means to acknowledge "the hierarchical structure of the value-cosmos" and to see the individual as related to value-bearers whose values are norms for him. But this act of positing the "holy" is an act of introception only when the individual feels a kinship with the highest in the hierarchy—when the individual is not simply a part of the "whole" but "participates" in it.

This "participation in the whole" has been conceived in different ways in the various religions. The differences have varied between two extremes. On the one hand, the self insists upon its own absoluteness and sees God (or Gods) as nothing but protector, savior, counselor and (perhaps) judge. It regards the world as nothing but a "divine contrivance" for the self's own benefit. On the other hand, the self feels the absoluteness of the "Non-Self" so strongly that it cannot assert itself as a person and tends toward its own "depersonalization" (*Ent-Ichung*). The relation to God is now experienced as that of the "infinitely little to the infinitely large, of the absolutely powerless to the omnipotent, of a particle of dust to the universe" (p. 395). A man has religion, so Stern continues, as soon as he understands that the absoluteness of his own self consists in the fact that he can take up into himself the absoluteness of the world, and understands also that for his own self the absoluteness of the world is not something foreign and oppressive but a kindred reality upon which his own absoluteness depends. In this metaphysical situation, God is posited as "holy self-value" raised to the level of absoluteness. "God is the Absolute Person" (p. 398). To put it differently: The "all-Person"—i.e., the all-inclusive cosmic "whole" of intellectual cognition—has here been transformed by introception into "Divinity"—a "Divinity" that cannot be explained rationally but "is the full and completed realization of value-introception." "We understand God when we comprehend in Him as eternally realizing and perfecting itself that which is in ourselves an eternal and never solvable task, when we see in Him the absolute personal model for our own self-development (*Selbstgestaltung*) as a person" (p. 399).

A person not only contemplates the "value-content" of the world but acts on the basis of his understanding and, through his actions, modifies the world. In doing this, the person is engaged in an active affirmation or realization of values. Stern speaks here of "practical introception." As he puts it, "practical introception is that activity through which a self realizes its own self-value by realizing non-self-values" (p. 403). This "realization" of values, however, is either a "manipulation" (*ein Handeln*) or a "creation" (*ein Schaffen*). In the case of "manipulation," the objective value aimed at in the action is independent of the self and is "given" prior to the action. In pursuing it the self realizes itself as a value. Even in "manipulation," therefore, the action cannot be evaluated simply in terms of effects. If it were so evaluated—as it usually is in the field of economics—the human being would be deprived of his self-value and would have "use-value" only, just like a machine.

If the realization of values is a "creation"—and "in the realm of values genuine creation is possible"—then the self imbues the objects involved with his own values but, through the values thus created, gains himself "a new richness." There occurs, thus, a peculiar interaction between the creator and his creation. In creating, man is "nearest to God," and "when his work is done, something absolutely new, something that previously did not exist, something that in itself is valuable has come into objective existence" (p. 408). It is the greatest defect of modern industrialism that it makes it almost impossible for the worker to introcept the results of his own work. It was different in the Age of the Craftsman, and is still so in artistic creation. However, in forming himself as a person, man is also creative; and in this case "manipulation" and "creation" are peculiarly intertwined. "As a real person the human being is a 'given' value the preservation, elevation, and change of which are subject to manipulation. But as ideal personality man is a value which can be realized only in his life as a whole and which, therefore, remains always the goal of his self-creation" (p. 409). And it is this fact that entails the crucial problem of the *ought*.

As Kant has pointed out, with the discovery of the *ought* man entered a new dimension of existence, for the *ought* is basic to man's moral life. Stern, however, interprets the *ought* in a much broader sense than did Kant. For him the "basic imperative" is: "Develop your life so that your attitude toward inviolable values can become part of the fulfillment of your own self-value" (p. 413). Or, more simply stated: "Introcept!" And this imperative, Stern argues, "this purely formal basic norm," is "the presupposition of the possibility of morality as such" (p. 417). That its correlate is "freedom" Kant had already pointed out. Stern merely re-affirms it.

To be sure, the "basic imperative" is not itself a "moral law" but a principle under which specific actions can be subsumed and in the light of which they can be evaluated. The "material content" of morality arises out of the "value-cosmos" in which a person finds himself and which suggests the goals he pursues. Within that "cosmos" the individual encounters values other than his own "self-value"—values such as the "person-values" of family, nation, mankind, and the values embodied in institutions such as the state and the church; and all of these values imply a "demand." Inherent in the "self-value" of a nation, for example, there are demands of the type: "Serve me!"; "Live, and when necessary die, for the sake of the national values!", the traditions, the mores, the institutions. Similar demands are inherent in every other sphere of the "value-cosmos" within which a person exists. They are concrete demands arising out of the concrete metaphysical situation that is determinative of the relationship between the individual and his "self-value" and a "normative value-sphere." Stern calls them "norms intrinsic in the actualities of a given situation," or, briefly, "reality-norms" (*Real-Normen*) (p. 428).

There is one aspect, however, that must be considered. It involves the norms intrinsic in an "ideal" (*Ideal-Normen*)—norms, in other words, which arise out of an individual's own "tendency toward self-unfolding" (*Selbstentfaltungstendenz*). Such norms are not "conservative" (as the *Real-Normen* are) but "evolutional." They are not of the form "Preserve what has proven its worth" but of the form "Help realize a perfection which has never been attained before."

It is evident from what has been said that the "range of validity" (*Geltungs-Umfang*) of a norm depends on the limitations and the "lived-in world" of the individual concerned. A family, for example, "generates" (*erzeugt*) a number of concrete demands which have "validity" only for the members of that particular family. However, such demands are superseded by the demands inherent in a larger "whole" of which the family is a "participating member"; and so on up throughout the hierarchy of "existents" until we come to the all-embracing "All-Person." Here the demand is: "Let the divine determine your will" (pp. 431–432).

As members of an encompassing "whole" all individuals are called upon to act at least in such a way as to preserve the "whole" —both, as to its existence and as to its character or quality. This demand is, as far as Stern is concerned, the gist of the principle of equality—of an "equality of duties." It is also "the moral minimum" (*das sittliche Minimum*) and is perfectly reconcilable with the diversification of particular duties which reflect the different functions that individual members of a hierarchically structured "whole" perform. Thus, relative to the whole of mankind, nations of high cultural attainment have duties other than those which primitive tribes have—although all have the same duty to see to it that mankind survives. A scholar has duties which a day-laborer does not have; and he has these duties because, by virtue of his position within the "whole" of a community he plays a different role in the creation of human values.

But now the question arises, How can we determine which demand or which "norm" should prevail in any given situation? Keeping in mind the distinction between "service-values," "radiated values," and "self-values," we can now formulate at least the following rules: (1) In the sphere of "service-values" degrees of "usefulness" can be distinguished. Hence, that demand should prevail compliance with which would entail the highest "use-value." (2) As far as "radiated values" are concerned, we found that the "essential nearness" to the basic "self-value" determines an order of rank of the derivative values; and this order of rank can be taken as implying a norm. The more essential "radiated value" should always be given preference. (3) "Self-values," so we know, have an "order of rank" that is determined by their "intrinsic richness"—by the total of "self-values," that is, which are constituent elements of the "whole." In this sense the "whole" of mankind has a greater "self-value" than has a nation, the nation a greater one than the family, the family a greater one than its individual members, and the genius a greater one than the idiot. If this order is assumed, then the "order of rank" of demands or of norms is obvious. But it is equally obvious that the actualities of human existence are in important respects much more complex than this; and this complexity increases with the shifts and changes in our human situation. Stern concludes, therefore, that it is impossible to formulate a principle which determines universally how the "norms of rank"—the imperatival demands—ought themselves to be ranked (p. 449).

And there is another dimension to all this. It lies in the fact that every "self," every person, is not only the center of its own "value-cosmos" but, as that center, is also unique and "incomparable"; and this uniqueness is not merely a matter of empirical fact. It is also, and more importantly, an obligation (*Verpflichtung*)—an obligation, namely, to develop his own "self-value" as a "microcosm." Put in imperatival form this means: "Realize your own vocation!" This "vocation" is the "ought-structure" of the self as that grows out of the "is-structure." It is the "justification (*Rechtfertigung*) of the self through its goals," the expression of an inner directedness (*inneres Gerichtetsein*) that tends to fulfill the potentialities inherent in the self. The crucial idea here is that inborn talents and abilities oblige, and that only "when one wills what one is capable of doing does one do what one ought to do" (p. 457). To put it differently: Every person ought to set for himself as his goal the greatest possible introception within the range of his abilities of objective values into his own "self-value." Such goal-setting is his "vocation." The only thing which counts in the end is that a person develop his own life in conformity with that "vocation."

BIBLIOGRAPHY

Stern, William, *Person und Sache: System des Kritischen Personalismus*, Leipzig, 1923–24.
Volume I: *Ableitung und Grundlehre*, 1923.
Volume II: *Die Menschliche Persönlichkeit*, 1923.
Volume III: *Wertphilosophie*, 1924.

CHAPTER XIV

THE PERSONALISTIC VALUE THEORY
OF FOLKERT WILKEN

Despite its "personalistic" character, the value theory here under consideration has nothing to do with metaphysical conjectures a la William Stern. It grew out of Folkert Wilken's interest in economic problems and is the result of Wilken's realization that even so limited an area as the economic life of man can be fully understood only when we consider it in the light of the whole human enterprise.

For a human being to exist means to have experiences, to encounter "objects" as something "given." But does what is "given" also exist when it is not being experienced? Without going into the details of various philosophical arguments and positions, Wilken accepts a form of "realism" which distinguishes between the realities of nature, the realities of our mental life, and the realities of man's cultural existence (*Geistwirklichkeit*). A tree, for example, exists in itself as a part of nature. As experienced, it exists as content of a perception, of a thought, or of some act of the imagination. But it may also play a role in "ideal significance" and may therefore exist within the context of a culture. Value, too—so Wilken argues—is an "object" concerning which the "reality question" may be raised. Is it part of nature? Does it exist only as part of our mental life? Or is its proper mode of existence that of a "culture content"? What are the conditions of its being "given"? Also, a distinction must be made between "valuing" (*Werthaltung*) and "value realization" (*Wertverwirklichung*)—between what a value is and the mode of its existence; and only a fully developed value theory can provide an answer to all of these questions.

I

When we speak of "valuation" and "valuing," the linguistic forms seem to imply that we mean a subjective activity of a "value constitutive kind" (*wertbildende Art*). This means, however, that "whenever objects attain value for man, this presupposes that something human has been brought into relation with them" (p. 10). Every value (*Wertdignität*) ascribed to an object is thus subject-dependent but is, nevertheless, "fused" (*verschmolzen*) with the object into the conceptual unity of a "value-object" (*Wertobjekt*). The value of water, for example, is not a "material" attribute of the water itself but depends upon the existence of a "value-creating" (*wertschöpferisch*) human being.

To be sure, it is possible to maintain that water retains its value as a thirst quencher even when, at the moment, nobody is thirsty. The concept of "use value," which is basic in economics, specifically includes this condition in the meaning of the term "value." Von Ehrenfels, speaking of the "desirability" of an object, and Meinong, referring to "value potentialities," acknowledged in effect the same fact. What actually is involved here, so Wilken points out, is a "value objectification" as "generalized anticipation" based upon the possibility-probability of actual valuations. But even if the subject is thus taken to be the source of all values and if values themselves are regarded as being in some sense subjective, we ought not to preclude *a priori* the possibility of there being instances of values which, transcending the human subject, provide "stimulus and directives for man's creation of values." Values which in their validity confront the subject with an *ought*—as Rickert had argued—might be instances of just such values.

But be that as it may, Wilken proposes that we begin our investigations with an analysis of our "personal, subjective value formation." When we do so, our first question may well be: How does the process of valuation or value ascription arise in our experience? The answer is complex; for the occasion initiating a valuation may be a "need-intention" (*Bedürfnisintention*) or something like it, or it may be an objective stimulus. Generally speaking, it may be a combination of both.

In order to make this point clear, let us assume that, at a given moment, we are without a value experience. Then a certain object enters our field of perception and elicits in us a desire for it. We now value the object as that which "satisfies" our desire. In this case, clearly, the subject is the valuing agent; but the occasion for the valuation is the fact that the object entered the range of our experience. This means that the conditions for the *possibility* of a value experience are in every case purely subjective, whereas the conditions for its *actual occurrence* are objective as well as subjective.

Crucial to an understanding of value experience is thus the distinction between need and valuation. Need is not a valuation but only a "possible basis" for one—i.e., it is a "subjective value ground" (*Wertgrund*). Valuation, however, is "a special kind of reaction of the total personality" (*Gesamtpersönlichkeit*). It is rooted in the "innate spiritual dispositions" of the valuing subject. The "value object" satifies a need. But this fact does not give the object its value unless the valuing subject has taken an attitude (*Stellungnahme*) toward it in consequence of which the need itself becomes part of the value experience and the whole experience is grounded in "the quality of the value consciousness."

In this interpretation the valuing subject is and remains the creator of values (*Wertschöpfer*); but since its valuations are functions of the whole person, the specific stimuli occasioning a particular valuation must be consonant with corresponding facets of personal existence, be these organismic, mental, or spiritual. The value-object—i.e., the object satisfying a need—may therefore be physical, mental, or spiritual. A thought, for example, may satisfy a need as readily as does a change in the physically real world. "Both deserve to be called value-object," and their relation to any particular person is in a significant sense irrelevant (p. 15).

II

As the term implies, valuation is an activity and therefore can have its origin only in a subject; but valuation must not be confused with "motivation," "striving," or similar "mental tendencies." We can speak of it, however, as an intention (cf. Brentano and Meinong). What is important in this connection is to note that the value-object is never the *causa sufficiens* for the occurrence of a value experience; that it is not the cause of a psycho-physiological effect in a simple stimulus-response situation. We must note also that a specific object is not necessarily always valued the same by the same subject or by different subjects. The reason for the variations can be found in changes in the conditions under which the object is being experienced. But more must be said about the subject involved in valuations.

For Wilken's theory the distinction, briefly indicated above, between "valuing subject" (*Wertungssubjekt*) and the "subjective value-ground" (*Wertgrund*) is of utmost importance. To identify the two entails no end of confusion. Pleasure, for example, is a "subjective value-ground," not a value nor a valuing subject. In other words, the "subjective value-ground" is "the mediator (*Vermittler*) between the value-object and the human person." Because of the "value-ground" the subject ascribes value to an object; but the relation of the "value-ground" to the "whole person" can be understood only as a teleologico-rational context of purposes in and through which the person aims at his own realization and into which the object enters as a means toward that realization. Seen in this context, "the subjective value-ground is the index of a necessity of development of the human person" and the "indispensable condition" for the actions which lead to that development and, thus, to the realization of values. To put it differently: "The relation of the value-object to the necessities of personal development as experienced in the subjective value-ground is finalistic (teleological) in character. The value-object is embedded in a context of purposes. However, its relation to the realization of the tendencies inherent in the subjective value-ground is that of cause and effect" (pp. 19–20).

Seen in this perspective, "need is the reaction to a subjective necessity for a change" (*Änderungsnotwendigkeit*); it tends toward bringing about that change. That is to say, need is indicative of the fact that the change has not yet occurred. As subjective value-ground it brings to subjective awareness the necessity for a change; and this necessity becomes a "value" in the strict sense (*im eigentlichen Sinne*). All objects necessary to its realization derive their significance as value-objects from their relation to it.

It must be noted, however,—and this is essential to Wilken's theory—that what is experienced as need is only the "possibility" or the occasion for a valuation. The valuation itself is the act of a person which transcends the merely "given." The valuing subject

as a whole determines the order and direction of the actions required for the realization of a value. It conditions the "state of
need" and anticipates "in idea" the satisfaction of the need, making this anticipation the motive for action, and then acts accordingly. But in wishing and desiring the subject also transcends felt
needs. Need merely reflects a "disturbed equilibrium." The tendency to change the state of affairs is still latent. A wish, however,
indicates a shift in attitude—a shift toward conditions that would
lessen or eliminate the need; but a wish still lacks what desire supplies: the intention to act. Need, wishing, and desiring thus form
a normal continuity of interrelated experiences; and they are encountered in all areas of our mental life—the areas of thought, of
feeling, and of volition (p. 33).

III

It is now clear, I believe, that, for Wilken, the valuing subject
is the agent that ascribes values, that is constitutive of values, and
that provides a standard for values. In accomplishing all this the
subject reacts to its own experiences as the "matter" toward which
an attitude must be taken—and must be taken in conformity with
the subject's own character and needs. Inherent in this value-intention is the will to bring about a "state of fulfillment" (*Erfüllungs-
zustand*) and to bring into existence a "value-object" that will
produce such a state. The existence or non-existence of "value-
objects" is, thus, as important for Wilken's theory as it is for Meinong's: "The good ought to *exist*" (p. 35).

This, of course, raises the problem (extensively discussed by
Meinong) of the "unreal values" of imaginative experiences and
of assumptions; but it is Wilken's contention that no difficulty is
involved here; that a person who vividly imagines or assump-
tively projects a certain object can also take a valuing attitude toward it. What is fictional here is the "value-object," not the valuation or the need which leads to the postulation of fictional objects.
As a matter of fact, any "value-object" plays a twofold role in a
valuation. In the processes leading to the realization of a value it
occurs in some form of reality—be it physical, mental, or spiritual.
Prior to the realization, however, any such reality is merely antici-

pated in representation. As motive for an action it is but the projection of a goal. As anticipated and projected the object is "unreal." When it is finally realized it is "real."

Within this context of projected and realized goals—i.e., within the process leading from the projection to the realization—"usevalue" and "usefulness" have their place. "An object is useful either for the immediate satisfaction of a need or for the production of an object that gives immediate satisfaction" (p. 41). In the latter case, the value of the object is "mediated" through a relation to an object that gives immediate satisfaction. This means, in effect, that acts of valuing can become "specialized," pertaining in particular to various degrees or chains of "mediation." "All special valuings, however, are derivative and depend on the goal-value established in the original valuation. They come into being because of the needs related to the realization of the goal-value" (p. 42).

Since the attainment of a goal may involve many intermediate steps, the valuing person may at any time be directly concerned only with the requirements of the next following stage in the process, not with the ultimate goal or with the process of its realization as a whole—a fact which, according to Wilken, is of special significance for an understanding of the "exchange value" in the field of economics.

So far, however, we have spoken only of "subjective valuegrounds" and have identified these with needs. But Wilken now points out that there is a "sphere of value-grounds" which is not reducible to needs. It consists of "value-grounds of an objective type" encountered in "the realm of spirit," the "realm of transpersonal (überpersönliche) values." In a figurative sense we may speak even here of "needs"—of "spiritual needs"; but the "transpersonal, objective value-grounds" basic to "the true, the good, and the beautiful" are "normative" for the valuing subject in a way in which true needs are not. And only the latter, Wilken maintains, are basic to economic valuations (p. 47).

In the field of economics, the distinction between "use-value" and "exchange-value" is, of course, of special importance. As Adam Smith well knew, things having great "use-value" may have little or no "exchange-value," and things having a great "exchange-value" may have little or no "use-value." The air we breathe, although having great "use-value" (since we can not exist without it), normally has no "exchange-value" at all; whereas a blue sapphire, having little or no "use-value," has a high "exchange-value."

It should be evident by now that "valuing" is as complex as is thinking. "There is nothing that could not become an object for thought, thinking itself included; and, similarly, there is nothing that could not become the object of a valuation, valuing itself included" (p. 48). And in valuing, as in the ensuing realization of values, processes of a "spirituo-psychological" (*geistig-seelische*) character are involved that remain ultimately inexplicable; for whenever a human being acts, he does so not simply as an organism: his thinking, feeling, and volition—i.e., his whole personal self—are involved. Moreover, in order to realize a "value-object," the subject must become effective in the world of realities. Knowing more or less the laws which govern events in that world, he must initiate causal sequences calculated to lead to the valued goal. And if he wants to induce another person to act, he must in some way affect that person's own "value system." If the activity of a person on behalf of his fellowmen is itself an "immediate value-object"—i.e., if it is valued for itself—we speak of an "unselfish action." In order to elicit such an action we appeal to the "sense of charity" of a person—i.e., we appeal to the "subjective value-grounds" as manifested in his feelings of sympathy.

But when we want to induce a person to contribute to the "value-fulfillment" (*Werterfüllung*) of someone else for reasons other than charity, we must so arrange matters that his action is "indirectly" (*mittelbar*) a "value-object" for the realization of his own "immediate" valuations. This simple fact is the basis for the whole texture of "economic exchanges," be these the exchange of "services" or of "goods." The "inducement," however, is here not a matter of causal efficacy but of our having an "influence" upon the spontaneity and the valuations of the other person. This influence may consist in creating the "loss of values" (*Wertverlust*) in the case of non-compliance (as in the case of slavery), or it may depend upon "mutuality"—i.e., it may depend upon our making the action of the other person on our behalf a derivative or indirect "value-object" for his own value-realization. In this sense, an "exchange" takes place because of the dynamic interplay of the valuations and value-intentions of the partners in the exchange. The underlying principle is that of mutuality: Through the exchange each partner achieves the realization of his own value-objective, and the value-realization of each partner is here the ground—the motive but not the cause—for the value-realization of the other.

If this is at all an adequate interpretation of "exchange-value," then it is clear that a conception of "use-value" which identifies "usefulness" with "causally conditioned usefulness" is much too narrow in scope. The blue sapphire mentioned earlier has essentially no "use-value" in that narrow sense; although of a diamond one can still say that it is "useful" (in the causal sense) for cutting glass. Wilken suggests that the term "use-value" be so redefined as to cover not only every "causally mediated material satisfaction of a need" but also every form of "psychological and ideal effects." The diamond thus has a "use-value" not only in the realm of causal efficacy but in the psychological sphere as well; for it has value as an ornament and, in various social situations, as a "symbol" also.

Moreover, so Wilken now argues, the sharp distinction between "use-value" and "exchange-value" of classical economics cannot be maintained. In other words, he argues that "exchange-value" cannot be considered as independent of "use-value."

In an exchange the intention on both sides is to realize or to obtain valued objects and thus to increase one's own possession of "value-objects." It must be noted, however, that an "exchange" is not really an exchange unless the "rights of ownership" have also been transferred. It is this transfer of rights that transforms for the exchange partners that which "others" possess into what "oneself" possesses. In this sense the exchange is a value-productive transaction. It is productive of values for each exchange partner. This productivity, however, depends not on causal efficacy but on a transfer of rights mutually agreed upon. All else would be robbery.

But because in and through the exchange both partners attempt to maximize their own valued property, the exchange situation involves two competitive "value scales." The "value-object" which advances the process of value-realization is what the exchange partner makes available. It represents the effort which the exchange partner is willing to undergo in order to carry through the transaction. And so the question is: Is the value-realization effected in the exchange to be determined by what "the other" offers in the exchange or by the motivation of that offer through one's own counter-offer? This question arises, of course, for each exchange partner. It is what has led to the sharp distinction between "exchange-value" and "use-value." What "the other" offers is the "use-value"; what oneself offers is the "exchange-value." But since the "exchange-value" is actually an "additive" value, it falls within the sphere of "value creation"—as does any "use-value." In this respect the distinction between the two is blurred.

Still, in the exchange, the "giving" differs in principle from the "receiving." The value involved in the "receiving" has for the recipient a place in the predetermined scale of value-realizations. The recipient's counter-offer, however, stands, in addition, in an entirely different "value context" (*Wertzusammenhang*). It has an independent value significance. "It is valuable, on the one hand, because as derivative (*mittelbares*) value-object it contributes to a value-realization; but, on the other hand, it has the possible side-effect (*Nebenwirkung*) of being a value-sacrifice (*Wertopfer*)" (p. 56).

To be sure, it does not always have to be so. But when it is the case, a new problem arises: There occurs a competition of the valuations and of the necessities of value-realizations (*Wertverwirklichungsnotwendigkeiten*) and it is precisely here that the problem of the "exchange-value" arises. As Wilken sees it, the problem does not arise in the opposition to any "use-value" or, better, to any "production of value," for this opposition does not exist. The problem does arise, however, because of the "value-competition" (*Wertkonkurrenz*). "Use-value" performs the function of a direct "value-fulfillment." But "use-value" may be related to other "value-fulfillments" in such a way that the possibility of its realization (*Existenzermöglichung*) entails the loss of other "value-objects" or of their "realizability." Placing the competitive "value-objects" in relation to one another thus involves an element of the irrational. What is called "cost" presupposes the concept of a "negative value," a loss of "value-objects" or, more specifically, the renunciation of certain "value-objects" in order that others "may become existent for oneself." The problem is: To what extent may "value-objects" be relinquished before relinquishing them is value-destructive to a higher degree than it is value-creating? Stated differently, the problem is: What is the ratio of the "positive value-effect" (*positive Wertwirkung*) to the "negative value-effect" (*negative Wertwirkung*) entailed in an exchange?

It is evident at once, however, that this problem is not unique to the exchange situation. It is encountered wherever a personal effort is required to realize a value. The same laws which govern the one case also govern the other. What alone is unique in the exchange situation is the "social" aspect of mutual motivation.

IV

Wilken's basic theme, supported by the facts so far discussed, is that, ultimately, the valuing subject, as a person, is the value-creating and value-sustaining agent. Further analysis must now show what exactly this means. It must show in particular how this "personalistic" theory differs from any value metaphysics which hypostatizes a "superpersonal" source of values, and how it differs also from every "transcendental idealism" that postulates a purely abstract value-basis. However, the analysis required is not easy; for it must begin with the idea of the "ego" or "self" or "I"—admittedly one of the least clarified ideas of psychology and philosophy, which is yet most intimately intertwined with all of our experiences and cannot be completely separated from them.

The "self" is unique in the incomparable sense that every human being can speak only of himself, never of others, as "I." In this self-reference of "I" we express our highest *"An-und-für-sich"*—our reality as a being uniquely distinguished from "the world." To be sure, our experience of ourselves is never total. In fact, it is more the intention rather than the actuality of ourselves as a person that permeates our whole existence.

In dealing with other objects, three questions are basic: What is their essence? What is the mode of their existence? And how are they "given" in our experience? In the case of our own self, such questions can be answered only imperfectly. Whether we stress the psycho-physical aspects or speak of our sensory, affective, volitional, or rational nature—or of a combination of all of them—the fact remains that there is also our reflective self-consciousness relative to which all else is but an "object." It would be a mistake, however, to regard this consciousness as "the person."

Through the psycho-physical levels of our existence we are enmeshed with the causal nexus of the world. At the level of consciousness, we enter "the trans-personal world of the objective realities of reason" (p. 68). But neither extreme provides an adequate interpretation of our existence as a person. We are born with certain hereditary potentialities (or the lack of them). We were born in a particular place at a particular time into particular circumstances that have conditioned our development. And in all this we had no choice. Laws govern even the life of reason. Now we demand only—so Wilken here echoes Lotze—that in the midst of all this necessity "there is at least one point where freedom is present"—one point from which, through our own effort and activity we can transform into our very own possession that which otherwise is merely "given," merely encountered in our experience.

This freedom, however, has its own "levels of being." In the economic sphere it is egoism that provides the motive force for our actions. But "egoistic value-attitudes" extend farther than this and constitute "value-situations" that explain much else in human behavior. And in the perspective of this broader egoism the sense and the meaning of valuations appear to depend upon an understanding of the ultimate goal implicit in the development of the self.

But if the self in its development can approach a specific goal; and if in doing so it can come to terms with the spiritual, the psychological, and the bodily realities of the world it lives in, using them selectively to further its own development; then that self must have the capacity to affect valuationally the world of its experience—the capacity to decide between what ought and what ought not to be; for its own development depends upon the manner in which it takes hold of that world.

In the light of this understanding of the self's basic position in the world, Wilken now defines the "meaning of a valuation" as "a *worthiness of being* in the bodily, the psychological, or the spiritual sphere as determined by a self and rooted in the necessities of the development of that self" (p. 70). The act of valuing is then "the meaning-experience of a self working on its own development" and intending that something having a subject-determined "worthiness of being" actually *be*. The self involved in the valuing experience is, of course, the whole self in its bodily, psychological, and spiritual existence; and the development of this self, so Wilken now maintains, is "the first and ultimate task of being human" (p. 71).

The final goal of this development is not entirely clear; for it involves the human race as well as the individual human being. When Hegel saw world-history as the progress in man's consciousness of the idea of freedom, he came close to an understanding of what it means to be a human being—or so Wilken argues. In our days, however, the individual is struggling especially hard to preserve his values as a person. He is in conflict with his community. This conflict must be resolved. But the manner in which it is resolved determines whether and to what extent the development of the self has been served.

As Wilken sees it, there are two distinctly different ways for the individual to resolve the conflict. Either he subordinates his self to the physico-psychological sphere of existence and to its "subjective value-grounds," or he responds to the "trans-personal objective value-grounds of spiritual existence." The former entails egoism, the latter is idealism. They are qualitatively so different, Wilken finds, that "we must speak here of a lower and a higher form of the self" (p. 72).

V

Accepting egoism means to relate all objects and conditions of experience to one's own psycho-physical existence as the center of the world. In the extreme sense this means that the individual is concerned exclusively with the satisfaction of his own needs.

Egoism does not imply, however, that its advocate must completely disregard the needs and the wishes of others. On the contrary, he may find that in certain situations it is in his own interest to contribute to their satisfaction. Indeed, as Wilken points out, "the English School of national economy saw in such an attitude the ideal and the pre-condition of social harmony" (p. 73). The realization that, "in the long run, one cannot attain one's own satisfactions without serving one's fellowmen" is basic to the moral philosophy of all "social egoism." But as Kant well knew, the whole problem is one of intention and inner attitude rather than of overt action. Egoism exists only where the attitudes and the actions of the self are determined exclusively on the basis of "subjective value-grounds" and, especially, in terms of the "pleasure-displeasure dichotomy" within the psycho-physical sphere.

To be sure, bodily needs always pertain only to one's own bodily well-being, never to that of others. But among the psychological—and especially the emotional—needs there are some that do involve the well-being of others. Love, for instance, externally viewed, is altruistic. However, strictly speaking, egoism and altruism are "value-forms" and, as such, cannot even arise at the psycho-physical level. They presuppose a valuing subject. And this subject may take one or the other of two possible attitudes toward the values of the psycho-physical sphere: It may affirm or deny them. In doing so, the subject either identifies his own value standards with the values in question or he accepts the values of the spiritual sphere—the true, the good, the beautiful—as "ideal standards."

Experientially, so Wilken maintains, the two attitudes are quite different as far as an awareness of freedom is concerned; for if one's attitude toward one's psycho-physical needs is determined by one's "ideals," one experiences that "characteristic awareness of one's mastery over the life of need-conditioned drives." The self is in command over "body and soul" in a way in which it otherwise is not. Psycho-physical needs must still be satisfied—even Christ had to eat and to sleep!—but their satisfaction is now part of a rational pattern of living, and an action thus "born of the spiritual freedom of reason" no longer fits the simple pattern of egoism.

It remains true, of course, that the furtherance of one's own well-being is part of the circumstances of human existence, and that pursuit of this goal is in itself not a disvalue. On the contrary, the positive value of satisfactions that are indispensable to the psycho-physical well-being of the individual can be objectively demonstrated quite as readily as it can be subjectively experienced. But the point of Wilkens' argument is that, in committing itself to the pursuit of the "ideal" values inherent in the life of reason, the self rises above the instinct-determined drives for need-satisfactions and in doing this becomes truly human.

If an egoistic attitude is taken, then the "subjective value-grounds" play a special role in the value experience. To illustrate this let us assume that we experience certain "visceral feelings" indicative of the fact that we are hungry. If food is readily available, our need for it can be satisfied at once and our "hunger experience" ends right then and there. But when food is not readily available, then the degree of certainty of satisfaction determines whether or not the "visceral feelings" become a "subjective value-ground" for actions that are intended to lead to a need-satisfaction. Economic theorists make the most of this. But they overlook the fact that when it becomes evident to a person that a need-satisfaction essential to his existence cannot be realized, the result may well be an "egocentric revolt" that transcends all considerations of pleasure and displeasure alone. What happens during a panic illustrates the point; but panic conditions merely emphasize what is inherent in the circumstances of human existence in general. A threat to one's very existence thus creates a "value-situation" and a "readiness for action" that depend on the degree of certainty of the threat and the strength of one's egoistic commitment, and that must be added to all the other "subjective value-grounds." The person is now concerned about his very being or not being and thus is totally involved, whereas all other "subjective value-grounds" pertain only to special needs.

It is, of course, possible that a long neglected particular need—such as the need for food—may also constitute a threat to the whole person. But when it does, the experience of it as a threat is quite different from the experience of it as simply a need. This difference is of particular significance for the field of economics, for it alone explains why the subjective valuations that presuppose existentially vital needs are infinitely variable; and it explains also how it comes about that the subjective valuations of the same "object" vary so much from person to person and for the same person at different times. The subjective ground for the variations is the degree to which the total "life-reaction" (*Lebensreaktion*) of the person is involved. The objective ground for the variations lies in the "external possibilities of the value-realization" toward which in the last analysis the person adjusts his "life-reaction," his will to self-realization. This "life-reaction" is the actual arousal of the totality of all "subjective value-grounds"—more particularly the arousal of all those "grounds" that pertain to the necessities for continued bodily existence.

Strictly speaking, loss of life is always a matter of bodily non-existence, and threatened by loss of life the person is always "at stake." His bodily needs, however, tend to preserve his existence and to regulate his proper functioning. The psychological and spiritual needs (with the possible exception of the passions) do not play a comparable role in the life of the individual. They do not have the same "compulsive character" (*Zwangscharakter*). But be that as it may, reactions involving the whole complexus of vital needs cannot be identified simply as egoism. It will be helpful to distinguish at least between "self-concern" and "selfishness." The difference is one of quality rather than of degree and is of special significance in the field of economics. "In it can be found the ultmate criteria of the capitalistic economic order based on self-interest" (p. 82). Even if we admit—as we must—that "self-ishness" may lead to excesses, there remains a legitimate "self-concern" in the life of every individual; for there is a vast difference between prudential self-interest and selfishness, between a desire for self-preservation and self-development and a drive for mastery over others, between self-respect and a prideful air of superiority. The "ego-centricity" of the egoist is not only irreconcilable with altruism, it is essentially a-social, if not anti-social; and in this fact is rooted its moral inferiority.

It is necessary, however, not to identify every form of anti-social attitude with ego-centricity. Also, it must be admitted that ego-centricity was a strong force supporting the development of the individualism of the last several centuries. But the very fact that ego-centricity isolates the individual and separates him from the firm basis of the spiritual and broadly cultural values of his community causes a deficiency in his self-development as a human being. This is especially noteworthy in the realm of the emotions. The will to attain personal dominance finds itself in opposition to prevailing social conditions. In his attempt to change those conditions, the individual must suppress within himself basic emotional tendencies—a fact which leads to those "severe disturbances of his personality" which manifest themselves in the "so-called nervous illnesses"—fear and hate—which character- ize our times. If ego-centricity did not exist, fear and hate would not be possible—at least not in the exaggerated and apparently unmotivated form that is widespread today; for hate is the turning of self-love into an aggressive enmity directed toward others, and fear is the reflexive turn of those same aggressive feelings against oneself.

VI

Although every form of individualism involves elements of self-concern, the development of a truly human individuality de- pends on factors and conditions that transcend egoism. One's own development, Wilken maintains, is furthered only as it contrib- utes to the development of others. It depends, that is, on attitudes and a value-orientation whose realization encompasses the well- being of others as well as one's own. And it is in this perspective that the values of man's spiritual existence play their decisive role. It all depends, however, on the attitude which the self takes to- ward the demands of its own psycho-physical and spiritual nature. There is a choice here, a freedom of commitment, and therefore a personal responsibility for one's own development. In this very fact is rooted the crucial problem of what it means to be a human being.

This problem in its ultimate sense is the struggle between an "egotistical orientation" and an "idealistic one." And when Hegel sees history as "progress in the consciousness of freedom," he simply expresses his faith that, in the end, the idealistic orienta- tion will triumph. This is so, Wilken points out, because a com- pletely egotistical orientation is "unbearable" so long as there is freedom (p. 90). This does not mean, however, that the "lower levels" of human existence are without value. On the contrary, they are necessary for self-development if only as providing a "real resistance to development" (*realer Entwicklungswiderstand*) through the overcoming of which alone we attain "access to the higher forms of value-attitudes."

It may be argued that "the ideal absolute values" (in the sense of Stern and Münsterberg) are "objective value-grounds," and should be considered in metaphysical perspective. However, even these values become effective in personal self-development only when some human being acknowledges them, accepts them as valid, and makes them effective in his own life. "Truth in cognition, beauty in aesthetic feelings, moral kindness in volition"— these become standards or norms in self-development only because, through his own commitments, the individual accepts them and identifies himself and his goals with them" (p. 92). In doing this, the individual but unfolds and develops the spiritual capacities latent within his own nature, the potentialities for being truly human.

This fact, however, does not in itself eliminate the struggle between an "egotistical orientation" and an "idealistic one," referred to above, for each orientation is supported by its own intrinsic "value-evidence" (*Wertevidenz*). For the "idealistic orientation" this evidence is the *validity* of values (*Wertgeltung*) as norm or standard for the realization of the "higher self." Opposed to it, but without destroying the validity, is "the time-bound urgency of value-realization"—the evidence, that is, of the "actuality of values" (*Aktualitätsevidenz der Werte*). The "validity-evidence" is timeless. The "actuality-evidence" is the result of the time-dependent conditions and laws of our actual existence. Confronting both forms of evidence is the self whose own "validity" as a person must find realization in response to them. This realization— and therefore the coming to terms with the conflicting evidence— is the problem of human development. Its goal is gradually to give priority to the "validity-evidence" over the "actuality-evidence," for only so can the self realize its own potentialities and fulfill itself as a spiritual being.

It must be noted, however, that the "actuality-evidence" plays a crucial role in the field of economics. It is there identified as the urgency with which needs—individually or in combinatoin—demand satisfaction. When several needs are involved, circumstances may require that some order of priorities or of "rank" be established. Such an order, however, is not necessarily determined by the intensity with which the vairous needs are felt. It may be determined by rational considerations and judgment; and in that case the result may differ markedly from a scale determined directly by the pleasure-displeasure dichotomy.

It is also a fact that, under the pressure of actualities, those needs must be given first consideration which, seen from the point of view of "validity-evidence," would be the last to be of concern. That is to say, the satisfaction of the "lowest level of bodily needs" is, objectively considered, the "least postponable." Starving to death and freezing to death, for example, may at times be a matter of only a few days; hence the urgency intrinsic in the needs. Psychological needs are never quite so pressing or so crucial, although in time they, too, may become "torturous." Man's spiritual needs lack this "actuality-pressure" completely.

The sphere of bodily needs, which is also the center of man's economic activities, is thus distinguished from all other needs by the "highest actuality." As "subjective value-ground," this pressure of needs is so strong that it tempts the self to subordinate itself to the needs and to "place itself in the service" of their alleviation. As far as the "higher" needs are concerned, this "compulsiveness of actualities" diminishes. It is absent altogether in the case of the "ideal values" which constitute our "objective value-grounds" (p. 106).

One other aspect of the facts in the case is important. Whereas the "validity-evidence" of the "ideal values" that are the "objective value-grounds" is absolute, all "actuality-evidence" is relative—and it is so in a twofold sense. In the first place, there are the differences in degree that range from the faint uneasiness identifiable as a barely felt need to the "frightful compulsion" of a "total reaction" in which the very existence of the self is at stake. In the second place, the degree of intensity depends not only on the nature of the need but also, and especially, on the objective factors of the possibility and the degree of certainty of the "need-satisfaction." It is this latter aspect that introduces into the human situation that element of uncertainty which, in the case of vitally important needs, lies "somewhere between zero and infinity." The need for food, for instance, may be barely felt as a need when food is readily available. Under different circumstances, however, it may become the cause of anxiety or panic. The more stable the conditions are under which needs can be satisfied, the more do needs cease to be experiences of "subjective urgencies" of the pleasure-displeasure variety and approach the status of "objectively valid actuality-judgments"—a fact which is of special importance in the field of economics. The difference between subjective and objective value conditions thus deserves further consideration.

VII

All valuations originate with the subject, the self. From there they encompass, on the one hand, the sphere of "spiritual realities" and, on the other hand, the realm of "psycho-physical realities." As experienced, these "realities" constitute the "value-grounds" for the valuing subject and are determinative for the distinction between subjective and objective value conditions. This disinction, however, may be viewed from two different points of view.

On the one hand, "subjective" may be taken to refer simply to the subject, the human being having the experience—in which case "objective" refers to that which is being experienced, to the object. On the other hand, however, the terms may refer to differences in the validity of valuations—"subjective" indicating what is uniquely valid for a particular subject under particular circumstances, "objective" meaning universally valid and, in the extreme, absolutely valid. That the two meanings of "subjective" are interrelated is obvious. The same cannot be said of the two meanings of "objective."

When we consider the actual process of valuing, the contrast between "subjective" and "objective" is essentially that of the causal relation of the "value-objective" to the "value-grounds" that are fundamental to the subject's valuations. When these "grounds" are bodily needs, then the "value-object" is a material thing or situation to which the subject ascribes a value. And what is true with respect to the "immediate value-object"—i.e., with respect to the object that directly satisfies a need—is true also with respect to all objects that are a "means" to its realization. They, too, are material objects to which the subject ascribes a value.

The situation is complicated by the fact that the production of a "means-object" may require "effort" and thus be valued negatively. Actually, of course, the "effort" is valued from two points of view—as immediately experienced disvalue and as contributing to the realization of a desired goal—a fact which plays an important role in the "exchange of goods" in the marketplace, and thus in economic theory. In interpreting the market situation the Classical economists made "effort" or "cost" basic, whereas the representatives of the Austrian School regarded "use-value" as crucial. The actual exchange of goods, however, involves both aspects and depends, furthermore, on "subjective" and "objective" conditions of the market—such as "demand" and "supply." This means that "effort" or "cost" must be viewed from still another perspective.

We found earlier that, as "means" to the realization of a desired goal, "effort" is valued objectively, and that in itself it is valued subjectively. In an industrial economy, however, the "subjective" valuation also involves objective factors—such as the "cost" of raw materials and the wages of workers—and the total process of a national economy ceaselessly fluctuates between subjective and objective valuations. Not to recognize and acknowledge this fact leads to one-sidedness in interpretation. But the facts in the case can all be accounted for, so Wilken believes, when we accept a personalistic value theory—his own—for which "subjective" and "objective" valuations are but complementary aspects of a unitary process in and through which the person develops himself as a human being (p. 116).

So far, however we have dealt with the distinction between "subjective" and "objective" only in connection with the actualities of needs and need-satisfactions. We have not yet considered the problem relative to the issue of "value-validity" (*Wertgeltung*)—relative, that is, to the contrast of "valid for a particular subject" and "valid universally." This problem actually consists of three more specific questions: (1) What is the validity of the "value-grounds"? (2) What is the validity of the "value-reaction" (*Wertreaktion*) of the subject to those grounds? and (3) What is the degree of "generality" of the coordination of some specific "value-object" to a particular valuation?

In discussing these problems Wilken accepts as "given" the existence of a "valuing subject" or self without which there would be no values at all. This self is "the absolute universal (because constitutive) character of the human person." It is a unique individual endowed with the freedom to take either an egotistical or an idealistic attitude, or to alternate between them. Despite this freedom, however, the development of the self as a person tends intrinsically in one direction: the idealistic one; although some persons advance farther than do others.

But there is also a "parallelism of development" and there are similarities in personality structure. As a result, certain Periods in man's history are characterized by a "social generality in value-attitude," be that attitude materialistic, romantic-emotional, or whatever. Individuals taking an essentially egotistical attitude stand opposed to others who adhere to an idealistic world-view. Within these large groups there exist smaller ones, and within them still smaller ones, and so on—each group accepting some more specialized valuation as valid. The facts in the case thus allow us to speak of a "relative social objectivity of valuations"— a group-objectivity—as distinguished from an absolute one. And both of these must be distinguished from a value-orientation that is "subjectively individual" (pp. 116–118).

The "social objectivity" of valuations is grounded not only in the self, is not merely an indication of a parallelism in the levels of self-development, but has its strongest support in the sphere of "value-grounds" which, on the subjective side, includes the psychological as well as the physical "grounds." The psychological "grounds" encompass "feelings of sympathy and antipathy, the needs of the intellect and of volition," whereas the physical "grounds" pertain directly to the needs and responses of the body; and since all human beings have essentially the same kind of body, the "value-reactions" based on bodily needs are basically the same for the whole of mankind. In this fact are rooted the "socially general" value-responses which, depending on particular circumstances, may differ in kind and degree of intensity but are remarkably uniform throughout. It is in this sphere that a distinction must be made between "vitally important" and not so important needs—a distinction that is of great consequence in economic theory.

From the perspective of the "vitally important needs"—i.e., from the perspective of needs deeply rooted in the material requirements of the living organism—the maintenance of life is an "individually and socially objective value in the sense of absolute universality" (p. 120). Hedonic theories which imply the relativity of such values are a misinterpretation of the facts. What alone gives them a semblance of support is that, depending on circumstances, "the degree of actuality of the needs" varies from individual to individual; but "actuality" is not "universality" and "degrees" of actuality are not the same as "variations in universality." Moreover, even the variations in the degree of actuality are determined by intrinsic and therefore socio-objective laws. Gossen's law, the law of diminishing returns, and the law of marginal utility illustrate the point.

Now, if we accept—as Wilken does—the *a priori* rule that to identical valutions there must correspond identical "value-objectives" (*Wertobjektive*), we must accept also the principle that the same "value-objective" may be represented by various "value-objects" (*Wertobjekte*) which, together, are then characterized by an identity of their "value-dignity" (*Wertdignität*). That is to say, different "value-objects" may satisfy the same need; and when they do, their "value-objective" is also the same—which is but another way of saying that such objects have an "objective or universal value" (p. 121).

It is true, of course, that there are many objects which are valued because they are unique and irreplaceable—such as the Kohinoor; whereas other objects are valued because of properties which they share with other objects. Wheat grown in Russia is, nutritionally speaking, as valuable as wheat harvested in the United States, and both may be replaced by other nutriments which equally satisfy human needs.

The difference between "individually valuable" and "generally valuable" objects is rooted in the particular needs of an individual. If such needs have a socio-objective significance, then that significance is transferred to both, the individual and the general "value-objects." But only in the latter case is there a chance that a "recurring socially general need" may find an "inter-personal universal satisfaction." In the conception of the general "value-object" there is thus indicated an element of objectivity—in the form, namely, of the "objective possibilities of value-realization." All the factors involved in industrial production—soil, labor, capital—are socio-objective values and, in their actuality, they are also in the overwhelming number of cases "general value-objects." Individual variations in their respective values depend primarily on their "cost-value" within the framework of some particular process of value-realization, "cost" being an additional valuing that finds its limitation only in the necessity of the original valuation.

VIII

It is obvious that in a valuational situation of the type just referred to the interrelations of subjective and objective factors are complex. Indeed, in analyzing the situation we are struck by the ambiguity of such terms as "subjective" and "objective."

Basically, there is the contrast between the "intrinsic subjectivity" of the valuing subject and the "intrinsic objectivity" of the valued object. But "between subject and object" there are the "value-grounds"—the grounds, that is, upon which the valuation depends and in terms of which it is justified; and of these grounds some are "subjective" and some are "objective." Some reflect the nature and condition of the subject, others involve the nature and condition of the object. On the side of the subject we find "needs" which affect the self only tangentially and concern only some particular subject. But we also find there "needs" that are "universally human" and are essential to human existence. They provide a basis for an "inter-subjective identity of valuations" and do so especially when parallel levels of personal self-development are in evidence. On the side of the subject we thus find objective (i.e., universally valid) as well as strictly subjective (i.e., merely individual) valuations. No analogous distinction can be made as far as objects are concerned.

It must be noted, however, that even the universally valid (and in this sense "objective") valuations involve modalities in the realization of values that may also be called "subjective." Thus, when the realization of a value is not assured there may come a moment when there occurs a value-reaction which, rapidly running through all degrees of involvement, culminates in total involvement—a value-reaction, in other words, in which the very existence of the self is at stake. Böhm-Bawerk's example of the traveler in the desert who, almost dying for lack of water, at the very last moment discovers a refreshing spring, illustrates what is meant. It shows how, normally, subjective needs find their objective counterparts in some "value-object." Water is valued because it satisfies a need. But the example also shows how the valuation varies as circumstances change, and that in the case of "vitally crucial" needs we may encounter an ultimate and total involvement that has its unmistakable bearing upon the valuation involved. The value of the "object" may become equal to that of life itself.

The facts in the case seem to suggest that the "magnitude of the value" (*Wertgrösse*) depends entirely on the subject, not on the "value-object." But, as Wilken points out, the subjective reaction in all such cases can also be explained in terms of the objective circumstances. This means, however, that the "subjective" and "objective" value theories advanced in the field of economics are both justified as "logically equivalent ways of explaining value."

There is still another point of view from which the contrast of "subjective" and "objective" valuations may be considered. The presupposition here is that we regard as "subjective" everything connected with the process of valuation as directly experienced. The valuation can then be called "objective" when the originally personal experience is given the form of an "impersonal rational value judgment." The evidence supporting the valuation is now no longer to be seen in the act of valuing itself but in the evidence that justifies the judgment. "Value-dignity is now transformed into the cognitive dignity (*Erkenntnisdignität*) of the affirmation of the judgment" (p. 126). It remains true, of course, that reason is not the originator of the valuations but only the agency for their rational comprehension. But in a judgment even the most uniquely subjective valuation is "objectified"—just as a uniquely personal perceptual experience is objectified in a judgment of perception. However, reason can also transfer any particular valuation from one object to another and can thus "broaden" the original valuing. At the level of reason, therefore, valuing is not a value experience proper. It is not "constitutive" of value but only a "logical manipulation" of values originated in the primary process of valuing (p. 127).

Moreover, our "rational apprehension" of the valuing process transforms the "value-intention" of the original value experience into the idea of a "goal" that is comprehended as "purpose." The intrinsic teleology of the valuational dynamics thus reveals itself at the level of thought as being "finalistic," and as the basis for all rational actions. Beyond this, however, it is of the nature of thought to generalize. Hence when the qualities of a "value-object" are known, analogical reasoning will attribute a comparable "usefulness" to all objects possessing comparable qualities—even when these objects are not actually encountered. But this is merely another way of saying that reason affirms the possibility that an object may be valued—nay, that it will be valued—when it is encountered under appropriate conditions. And this is equivalent to ascribing to the object itself a value. Reason is thus the indispensable presupposition for our knowledge of "value-possibilities and of the possibilities of their realization in the affairs of man" (p. 129).

In considering the "value-possibilities" and the possibilities of their being realized, reason brings together what belongs together for the purpose of realizing a value, and in doing so it introduces an order of preferences, an "order of rank," of the "value-objects" no less than of the needs of the subject. In accomplishing this, reason serves to separate our valuations from the "irrationalities of the pleasure-displeasure directives." Thus, in matters of economic needs, no one depends today entirely on his immediate and "instinctive" responses. He knows what he needs and he knows or considers the quality of the objects that might satisfy them. "He acts without passion on the basis of his insight" (p. 131).

As Wilken sees it, the whole trend of human development— individually and as a species—re-enforces the increasing emphasis on reason and understanding in matters of value. The result is that the individual not only feels himself but knows himself increasingly in the '"wholeness of his existence." A personalistic value theory merely emphasizes this fact and makes it basic to an interpretation of our valuations. The "rational orientation of life" is now understood as an expression of the individual self-realization of a person in his totality. Where formerly the person found security in the knowledge that he was a member of a clan, of a community, he is now placed on his own and must find security within himself. This inner security he can and does find when his autonomous actions are but expressions of a clear and rational pattern of value commitments that gives direction and meaning to his whole existence.

BIBLIOGRAPHY

Wilken, Folkert, *Grundzüge einer Personalistischen Werttheorie*, Jena, 1924.

CHAPTER XV

BECK'S PHENOMENOLOGICAL
APPROACH TO VALUES

Stated briefly, Beck's fundamental contention is that it is a mistake to view pleasure as merely a subjective mode of experiencing; that, actually, pleasure is an "extra-mental fact" (*ausserpsychisches Faktum*) whose objectivity is constitutive of objective values. This thesis requires, of course, detailed elucidation and proof—a task to which Dr. Beck has devoted 1288 pages! His whole orientation is strongly influenced by the phenomenalism of Alexander Pfänder, even though in his theoretical interpretation of the "given" Beck finds himself in disagreement with his teacher.

I

If we begin our analysis with "the much slandered 'naive experience'," we encounter values as "immediately present in autocratic reality" (*selbstherrlicher Wirklichkeit*): as the beauty of a picture, the agreeableness of the taste of wine, the goodness of a human being. At the same time, however, we are struck by the heterogeneity of these experiences; and the question is, What is the common element in experiences of this type that identifies them as value experiences?

It will not do to identify "value" with "what ought to be," for it makes no sense to say that beauty and goodness are values *because they ought to be*. It is rather the case that they ought to be *because they are values*. Moreover, the qualitative differences of the values—that in one situation they are variations of the beautiful, in another situation variations of goodness, and in still another one variations of the agreeable—cannot be derived from the empty abstraction of an *ought* (p. 4). And neither can values be accounted for in terms of "historical development," for "development" may also take place in the direction of "disvalues"

(*Unwerte*), and the idea of progress in either direction presupposes the goal-values and therefore cannot explain them.

Beck thus comes to the conclusion that what is common to all values must be some aspect or mode of experience; and this he identifies as pleasure—making it clear, however, that what he means by pleasure is not what is usually meant by it: a subjectivistic-relativistic and psychological event. He does not deny that pleasure can be a feeling; but what he does deny most emphatically is that "being felt" is essential to pleasure, that pleasure is nothing but feeling. What he affirms instead is that "*all* objects which have self-value have that value only insofar as the pleasure-element is actually (*realiter*) intrinsic to them" (p. 14). Since feelings are themselves objects, pleasure may, of course, be intrinsic to them; and if this is the case, then pleasure "realizes itself" (*realisiert sich*) in a feeling but does not become identical with it. It can realize itself also in other objects. And it is this thesis which Beck tries to prove.

But if Beck's thesis is to be understood at all, it is necessary to view it in relation to his whole approach to an interpretation of experience. When we do so, we find, to begin with, that, as far as Beck is concerned, our "every-day existence" is existence within an "external world" which is accessible to us only through our body. Although in different situations different organs may be specifically involved in our contact with the world, the experienced interaction is always one of the total mind-body organism with our surroundings. "The self is in the totality of its body" (p. 33). Even though the body differs from the self whose body it is and, being different, is also object for the self, it can, nevertheless, be experienced as "being of the self" (*ichzuständlich*). But this entails that any "sensation" (*Empfindung*)—i.e., any experienced process or condition of the body—can also be "felt" as being of the body. Or, stated more precisely, the "givens of experience" (*Gegebenheiten*) which, as "givens," "*are sensations* (*Empfindungen*) can be *experienced* as feelings (*Gefühle*), i.e., they can be felt" (*gefühlt*) (p. 34).

In actual experience, however, "I never experience myself—this actual ME—as separated from me, as external to myself, or as an object." What is even more important, however, is that, according to Beck, I never experience my sensations as "objects" —at least not as long as I identify myself with them as states or conditions (*Bestimmtheiten*) of my body. In any such identification I remain well aware of the sensations as specific conditions of my body, but I experience them as "of the nature of objects" (*gegenständlich*) only when I "step out of them," as it were,— (*wenn ich aus ihnen heraus trete*)—and view them as something confronting me. But even then the sensations remain what they are: "qualities of my body"; they have merely ceased to be "subjective states" of my self. I am aware of them as "other" than myself (p. 35).

Stated differently, what Beck here asserts is that the "deeper" or more intimately the self lives in the body—i.e., the more it identifies itself with its body—"the more indeterminate in position and content is the quality" of the experience. It is only by becoming aware of it and "objectifying" it that the experience becomes clear and specific. A "vague feeling of pain," for example, is thus recognized progressively as a toothache and, more specifically, as pain in such and such a particular tooth. The ache is then no longer simply "felt" but is "perceived as a pain sensation in this tooth." But to have such a "clarified" experience necessarily requires "distance" (*Distanz*) between what is being experienced and him who experiences it—just as actually seeing an object requires "distance of the eye from the object seen"; and only where such "distance" exists can the self come to know the "other" as other. But it is also the case that, as "complete awareness" (*Vollbewusstheit*) is progressively achieved, the determinateness and the clarity of the contents of experience increase and with them there increases the "distance" among those contents. "Even my own self, clarified in its definiteness (*Bestimmtheit*), confronts more clearly the clarified contents of consciousness" (p. 42).

Brief and fragmentary though our discussion has been so far, it does suggest at least the broad framework of ideas within which Beck hopes to deal with value problems. And this much seems clear from what has been said that, as far as Beck is concerned, "when in our naive consciousness we 'feel' objectively given elements of pleasure—such as beautiful and agreeable—and when we feel what are called 'values'—e.g., genteel, good, etc.—then even this does not mean that we experience them simply as states or conditions (*Zuständlichkeitsmomente*) of our own self. Our feeling them is no argument against the fact that, from the very beginning and even before they are felt, they are *in and by themselves* that as which they reveal themselves in our 'feeling'— namely, these particular values" (pp. 43–44).

II

What is true of the relationship of sensations to feelings is true, of course, also of the relationship of the whole external world to our feelings. That world—"its extension in space, its duration in time, its manifold sensory qualities, its static and dynamic relationships"—all this is not simply a "phenomenon of consciousness," "not merely something experienced" or a "projection outwards" on the basis of "impressions," but is "in all its determinateness in and by itself the basic presupposition of our perceptions." It is "not identical with perception, not its product," but its presupposition (pp. 117–118).

But the world which we perceive—a forest, a green meadow, a blue sky—is "not merely extended, large, structured, green, blue, fragrant, quiet, etc." it also has its "moods." We speak of "the wildness, the grandeur, the sublimity of towering mountains," and we call a color "warm or cold," a sound "clear, thin, dull, deep, high," a fragrance "sweet, delicate, mild"; and we mean in all such cases that the "objects" themselves possess these qualities; that because they possess them they elicit in us "corresponding mental and physical responses"; and "that prior to such effects the objects themselves are the way they are and do not attain that character because of my experience of them" (p. 121). Beck thus repudiates all theories which maintain that the "mood" of a landscape, of any object or aspect of the external world is the result of human "empathy"; that we first feel the "mood" and then project it outward and ascribe it to the external objects. He repudiates these theories because, as he puts it, our experience is otherwise. We do not first experience a "mood" of grandeur and then ascribe it to the towering mountains; but seeing the mountains causes in us the "appropriate mood." To call them "pretty" or to call the turbulent ocean "peaceful" would certainly be inappropriate. "I see the gloomy, dismal, sad mood out there in the street without thinking of the objects out there—the weather or the sky, the rain, the street and the houses out there—as alive or as having feelings"; but the "mood" is there—out there (pp. 145–146).

And what is true in the case of "moods" is also true, Beck maintains, in the case of values. We thus return to the opening sentence of the present Chapter.

As we proceed, we must keep in mind that Beck is concerned exclusively with "self-values" (*Selbstwerte*)—with values, that is, which are values intrinsically, and which therefore do not depend upon other values (as "means-values" do) for their character as values; and that he regards "pleasure" as the common characteristic of all "self-values." Pleasure, however, so we already know, is for Beck not simply a psychological datum or mental state. "Even the non-mental can be *lustvoll*" (p. 149),[1] i.e., can be "characterized intrinsically by pleasure." "In its concrete definiteness 'pleasure' is present in every voluptuousness, in every joy or beauty or goodness. . . . In addition to everything that is of the nature of feelings or sensations or things or any other content of experience there is always given also the one identical 'pleasure'" (pp. 150–151). It is the common element in all values. The various species of values are different only insofar as the self-same pleasure "realizes itself" in different objects. If there is confusion on this point, so Beck maintains, it is the result of theoretical discussions of "values" in the abstract. The phenomena of actual experience are clear: "We *hear* the beauty of a melody, *see* the beauty of a painting, of a human form, of a flower. . . . And we also *see* the gentleness of a gesture, . . . the intrinsic goodness of a person, just as we are aware of our own joy, our enthusiasm, and the pleasures of our senses: Always the values belong to the objects in connection with which we perceive them." Such, Beck insists, are "the undeniable facts," the "naked phenomena" of our experience (p. 154).

The situation is somewhat complicated by the fact that we encounter in our experience certain "qualities" which appear to be

---

[1]The term "lustvoll" has no English equivalent that fully expresses its meaning: "characterized intrinsically by pleasure."

values but which may also be disvalues or be at least value-indifferent—e.g., the sublime, the genteel, the decorative, all of which are
undoubtedly experienced as values. Analysis will show, however,
—so Beck points out—that in all such cases value-indifferent elements are involved in the values: magnitude in the "sublime,"
repose in the "genteel," smallness in the "decorative"; and these
elements may in some situations become exaggerated and be then
experienced as disvalues: magnitude as "monstrocity," repose as
"boredom," smallness as "triviality" (pp. 157–158). All values
which for their realization thus depend upon value-indifferent
qualities and which may change as those qualities change are, as
far as Beck is concerned, "not self-values proper" (*uneigentliche
Werte*). And this includes also all values which, though positive
in quality, are opposed to one another in character—e.g., "pride
and humility," "indulgence and abstinence," "ambition and contentment," "faith and scepticism" (p. 162).

When we eliminate from consideration all values which, in the
sense just indicated, are not "self-values proper"—i.e., when we
disregard all values (and disvalues) whose being values (or disvalues) depends upon certain value-indifferent qualities—there remains a very small number of what Beck calls "pure self-values"
and "pure self-disvalues": beauty, goodness, agreeableness, pleasure, and their opposites. And it is "a specific characteristic of the
predicates beautiful, good, pleasurable, that frequently all or most
of them are valid for something which possesses one of these attributes: What is beautiful is frequently also good, agreeable and
pleasing" (p. 165). The opposites of these values, however, are
not also positive values (as is the case with "pride," "ambition,"
"indulgence," and "faith"), but are disvalues: "beautiful—ugly,"
"good—bad," "agreeable—disagreeable," "pleasing—displeasing."
Moreover, as Beck sees it, "beauty, goodness, agreeableness, pleasure are concrete realities—whether taken in substantival or adjec-
tival form." That is to say, the expression "value predicate" has for
Beck the sense, "not of something merely 'posited' in a judgment,
but of a concrete objectivity" (*konkrete Gegenständlichkeit*).
"For us," Beck says pointedly, "not only are the value-indifferent
bearers of values something real, but *the values themselves* (*die
Werte selbst*) are also real" (p. 167).

III

The question now arises, Can the four "pure self-values" just referred to—beauty, goodness, agreeableness, and pleasure—be reduced to but one basic value—to pleasure, for example? Hedonism in all its forms attempts such a reduction. Beck, however, is convinced that only a careful phenomenological analysis can provide an answer.

He begins his analysis with a consideration of "the good," for "the good" seems to be the most comprehensive of the four value terms.

(a) Is there anything valuable that cannot be called "good"? It is significant, Beck points out, that all "objects" in which values are "realized" are called "goods." But we must ask further, Is everything that is called "good" really a *value*? In many cases, what is called "good" is merely "advantageous" or "useful." It is "good for something." And this is what is meant when we speak of "goods"—of objects and conditions which are but means toward the realization of values. "Goods" are not "self-values." Value is attributed to them because of their relation to something else.

The term "good," of course, has also an entirely different meaning—as when we speak of a "good man," a "good deed," or the "goodness" of a person. But deeds also are not "self-values." They are "good" only because they are "means for the realization of values." It is different, however, when we say that someone is "a good man," for it is "preposterous" to say that a person is "good" *only because and in so far as* (*nur weil und sofern*) he performs "good deeds." Even the most formalistic morality, Beck maintains, can ultimately find a basis for the "universal ought" only in the fact that a person finds in the satisfaction of his interest an increase in value (*Wertzuwachs*) and in the violation of that interest a diminution of value (*Wertminderung*). Such interest, however, quite obviously "presupposes a real value that can be increased or diminished." To put it differently, the "self" or "person" is a being that realizes itself only in its development. It is never complete but is always "unfolding itself." "It has the whole law of its development within itself"—its own inner *ought*. What is appropriate to its "nature" that is its *"ought."* "And when the self becomes and is as it *ought* to be, then it is 'good'." Its goodness, in other words, is "faithfulness to itself." The individual "experiences this as moral goodness, as his completion (*Vollendung*), as his innermost pleasure." And this goodness, Beck argues, is in itself a "concretum" even "prior to its realization in a human being, a self, a person" (pp. 169–173).

However, no individual exists in isolation. We experience "objects" and "situations" which themselves have value. We thus speak of "good meals," "good opportunities," "good eyes," "good deeds and dispositions," "good relationships," "good words and thoughts," etc. But in all such cases it is "not the objects themselves in their own existence and separateness from the self" that are said to be "good." The attribution of the value affirms rather a close relationship to our experience. This does not mean, however,—so Beck maintains—that the "objects" in question derive their value from their relation to a self; they already have value "prior to the experience and by themselves" (*schon vor diesem Erleben, aus sich heraus*). The meal, for example, is "good" in and by itself in the sense that it has a "pleasant taste" (*Wohlgeschmack*) which I experience as "agreeable."

What this implies, however, is that "I myself must live in these values [of objects] as if they were actually a specific and characteristic aspect (*Bestimmtheit*) of my self" (p. 175). And indeed, only because, and as long as, I experience those values as my own do I ascribe to them the value of my own self and call them "good." But what is true in the case of "objects" is equally true in the case of "my dispositions, actions, aspirations, etc.", and the more so the more fully I live in and through them—provided only that they in themselves already have a specific value prior to my "living in them." But since all of reality is an object of possible experience, everything in the world can ultimately be related to my own self and can be experienced as "good." As actual and concrete value, "good" is thus the most general value there is (p. 176).

(b) Moral goodness, so Beck has argued, is experienced by us as our own "innermost pleasure." He now points out, however, that not everything that appears to be "self-pleasure" (*Ichlust*) belongs to the field of ethics. "Gaiety, cheerfulness, joy, rejoicing, for example, have very little if anything to do with moral goodness"; for a person who "finds pleasure in vulgarities, for example, is everything else rather than 'morally good'" (p. 177). Still, joy, gaiety, cheerfulness, and rejoicing—i.e., "'pleasure' in the ordinary sense"—are essentially inner values. We must recognize here a basic distinction: "To *have* something, to *do* something, is not identical with *being* something." To be sure, "I must exist when I perceive or feel or aspire; but even as perceiv*ing*, as feel*ing*, as aspir*ing* I am not the perceiving, the feeling, the aspiring" (p. 178). And so it is in the case of gaiety, joy, cheerfulness, and rejoicing. "They are always *acts* of my soul" (p. 179). Even the language we use in speaking of them indicates as much: "I rejoice," "I feel cheerful," "I feel gay."

Also, joy, gaiety, cheerfulness, and rejoicing are always "actual states of consciousness." If I do not feel them, I do not experience them, i.e., I do not live in them, I am not cheerful, I do not rejoice. And what is more, joy, rejoicing, gaiety, and the like have no existence outside my actual consciousness. "It is radically otherwise" in the case of my "being good" (*Gutsein*). "I need neither feel nor experience nor know of it in any way whatsoever, and can yet be good—*be* good in a value-concrete sense (*in wertkonkretem Sinne*). Only in actual self-examination do I come to know *that* I am good or bad, and may then, in addition, be pleased or vexed or indifferent about it. In fact, I can even deceive myself about my moral quality—but never about my joy" (p. 180). In the case of the latter I can deceive myself only as to its cause or its motive.

What all this amounts to is that joy, cheerfulness, and the like are actually *nothing but* "feelings." Their "being" is their "being felt." This is not so when we deal with moral "goodness." To say, for example, that "I feel myself to be good" does not imply that I actually am "good." I may be "bad" or "morally indifferent." But when I say "I feel cheerful," the statement makes no sense unless I do indeed feel cheerful.

It is also important to note that joy, gaiety, cheerfulness, and rejoicing are not "pleasures of the body"—as sensual gratifications are. The difference is clear, for the opposite of "pleasure" in the narrow or bodily sense is "pain," whereas the opposites of "joy," "gaiety," "cheerfulness," and "rejoicing"—of the "pleasures of the soul," that is—are "sorrow," "grief," "distress," and the like. The bodily pleasures, moreover, have physical causes, whereas the "pleasures of the soul" have "motives." They are therefore in a class all by themselves (p. 183).

(c) When next we turn to an analysis of the "agreeable," we must note that this value attains its specific meaning through its realization within the sphere of our body. And we must note also that we never experience the agreeable as being our own state or condition (*Zustand*) in the sense in which we experience joy to be one. "When I experience something agreeable, I am not *for that reason* myself agreeable." On the contrary, when we experience something agreeable, "we project our pleasure into the object that causes it" (p. 189).

The term "agreeable" itself suggests that the value which it designates ultimately involves a relation. One of the relata obviously is the object that is said to be "agreeable." But relative to what other relatum is the object's "agreeableness" asserted? Beck's reply: Relative to me—*"insofar as I am or have a body";* relative, that is, to "the bodily organization of the subject having the experience" (p. 193). To put it differently, "agreeableness" is "the most general, because the purest, value predicate of the sensorially given" and, as such, differs from all other "bodily pleasures"—from "sexual gratification," for example (p. 196).

(d) The value quality "beautiful" also designates a unique sphere of values. As Beck puts it: The term "beauty" does not adequately express "the value-concrete meaning of my self or of my inner experiences." "Neither I myself as a person, nor my feelings, nor my sensations are 'beautiful'" (p. 198). I cannot say "I feel beautiful" as I can say "I feel cheerful." And neither can we say in any strict or meaningful sense that the moral character of a person is "beautiful"—even though his actions, aspirations, and dispositions may rank high in moral value.

This does not preclude the possibility that certain acts, dispositions, or attitudes—joy, love, faith, trust, envy, hate, etc.—"impart to the bodily exterior" of a person certain lines, forms, and rhythms that may strike us as pleasing or as displeasing, as "beautiful" or as "ugly"; and often this "bodily expression" of inner attitudes is taken for "the inner" itself, for "the moral." But this identification Beck rejects. For him, "beauty" and "beautiful" are terms that are employed correctly only with reference to value qualities of "external objects." "According to our thesis," Beck states, "beauty is pleasure realized in external objects"—and is concretely realized. "It is not an abstraction" (p. 202).

What distinguishes "beauty" from other value predicates involving a "concretely given pleasure" is thus the fact that it belongs to "the sphere of the externally objective (*Aussengegenständlichen*) in which it realizes itself."

As Beck sees it, "the externally objective" is not "external" for someone, or "external" to someone, but is "in itself a certain kind of the objective"—"a kind which can best be called 'thingness' (*Dinglichkeit*)." Stated more precisely, "'beautiful' means the realization of pleasure in the impersonal, the unspiritual, and the unfeeling." It is "the realization of pleasure in 'objects' (*Bestimmtheiten*) which, because of their very nature, can be given only in external perception" (p. 205).

IV

We shall return shortly to Beck's interpretation of the "beautiful." At the moment it should be noted merely that, following Beck, we have so far indicated only what distinguishes the four value spheres of the "good," the "inner pleasure," the "agreeable," and the "beautiful" from one another. We have seen that each is a form of pleasure and that they are distinctive only because of the way in which pleasure is "realized." All four are "self-values" (*Selbstwerte*).

We must now consider certain "means-values" which often are, mistakenly, also regarded as "self-values": the "true," the "right," and the "just."

(a) The basic meaning of "true" is of a logical rather than an ontological nature. "Only a judgment is 'true,' not the object referred to in the judgment"; and it is true "when the alleged objective situation exists in and for itself and on its own (*aus sich*)" (p. 206). Is "truth" a value? To this question Beck gives a "radically negative" answer.

As he sees it, the situation is this: "By their very nature human beings have a desire to know"—a desire, that is, "which finds satisfaction in the thinking of true thoughts." They find pleasure in the experience of that satisfaction, and "this pleasure—rather than the true thoughts that satisfy our desire—is a value" (p. 208). Moreover, we experience the type of pleasure here involved (and therefore the value even when we are mistaken about the truth of the thoughts we think—when we believe that they are true though in reality they are false. The value, therefore, is that of an experienced satisfaction, not that of truth. That "true" thoughts are generally regarded as more valuable than "false" ones is justified in the light of their respective "practical significance." That is to say, true thoughts have a "means-value" which false thoughts do not have; they are "good for something." Truth itself, however, is not even a "means-value"; for the truth of a judgment, simply as truth and by itself, produces no effect in the world of real events. It leaves "untouched and unaltered" the objective situation to which the judgment refers. And, of course, "truth is not a self-value."

(b) Earlier in his discussions Beck had rejected the idea that the ultimate presupposition of anything being a value is an *ought,* and had argued that, on the contrary, every *ought* presupposes a value and a "self-value" at that. He now calls our attention to this relationship between value and *ought:* "Every *ought* presupposes as its own content a value-particularity (*Wertbestimmtheit*)." And he continues: "We call something 'right' insofar as it satisfies this value-particularity, i.e., insofar as it actually is *that* and *how* it ought to be; insofar as it *realizes a value*" (p. 213). The question is, Is "right" itself a "self-value"? Is something that "realizes" a value by virtue of this fact itself a value?

Beck's answer is twofold. (1) The question in its second form would have to be answered in the affirmative, he points out, if something were said to be "right" because it is "a means to the realization of a value," "right for something." But in this case "right" designates a "means-value" and is not itself a "self-value."

(2) An act, a deed, may be said to be "right" because it is in itself—i.e., in its very nature—the realization of a value. But the value so realized is not "rightness." It may, for example, be kind-

ness: The deed is "right" because it is in itself an act of kindness, and kindness is a "self-value." This means, however, that in such context "right" is not a "value-specific predicate" but only an expression of the fact *that* such a predicate is involved. "It indicates merely in a completely abstract manner that a value-realization is taking place, not the realized value itself (p. 214).

"Right" is thus either a mere "means-value" or it is a "sequel-value" (*Folgewert*) in the sense of "right because"—in which case it "presupposes a self-value and is not identical with it."

(c) In discussing the problem of "just" and "justice," Beck first points out that the significance of the distinction between "justice as idea" and "justice as fact" or "realized idea"; and he then argues that not the idea of justice is valuable, only its realization "somewhere and at some time." That is to say, as far as Beck is concerned, "only some particular and concrete *something* that is just is valuable; and it is valuable because and insofar as it is just" (p. 215).

The term "justice" obviously is a relational term, the relation being bipolar. More specifically, the relation indicated by the term "justice" is such that "one side is equalized (*findet Ausgleich*) in the other, both sides together forming a kind of equilibrium": "guilt and atonement," "work and compensation," "claim and satisfaction," etc. It must be noted, however, that in all such cases "equalization in the form of justice" is possible only because we deal with "guilt *and* atonement," "work *and* compensation," etc.; i.e., it is possible "only insofar as something belongs to the category of specifically reciprocal pairs." "Not everything, therefore, that is given the attribute 'just' actually is just: neither just decision nor just distribution, neither just share nor just deed, neither just compassion nor just help, neither just luck nor just fate, neither just God nor just man. Fate, God, and man are 'just' only insofar as they permit 'justice' to reign; and this they do only in acts which satisfy just claims, which give just rewards and mete out just punishment" (p. 217). Compassion, hate, help, etc. can be called "just" only insofar as they are acts of a "moral self"; for it is not they that "requite" (*vergelten*); it is I who does that "through them and by means of them." In themselves they (as well as "decision, distribution, share, and the like") are neither just nor unjust." "Justice," Beck stresses again, "is a relation whose relata are neither values nor disvalues as such, but values or disvalues in the categorial form of specifically reciprocal pairs" (p. 218). And the constituents of such "pairs" have a specific relation to "justice." "Punishment," for example, ceases to be "punishment" when it is not just. In fact, so Beck maintains, whenever one relatum of the reciprocal pair is actual, then the absence of the appropriate "equalizing" relatum constitutes "injustice."

"Justice" is realized when both relata of the "reciprocal pair" are realized. In itself "justice is nothing but a 'mere idea'." "Its 'realization' is *not its own* concretization but the concretization of such ideas as 'claim and satisfaction,' 'work and compensation,' whose givenness 'fulfills' the ideal meaning of the term 'justice' " (p. 230). This means, however, that justice is not a relation between the values and disvalues that provide the reasons (*begründen*) for compensation, satisfaction, punishment, etc. It is, instead, the demand that to a given claim there be given also its satisfaction, to a given guilt its punishment. Strictly speaking, therefore, "justice does not mean a relationship at all but the realization, the *that* of the realization . . . of certain states or conditions of the self (punishment, compensation, satisfaction, etc.) that find the ground for an adequate coordination with other states or conditions of the self not in an abstract formula but in a factual condition (*Tatsache*) of the self." "The just equalization (*Ausgleich*) does not take place between that which is the ground for the claim, etc., on the one hand, and the satisfaction, etc., on the other, but within, and in connection with, the self itself" (p. 236).

This means, however, that the terms "justice" and "just" designate a "means-value" only: That which brings about the realization of such concrete "ego-values" (*Ichwerte*) as satisfaction, reward, atonement, etc., is "just"; and " 'justice' is an attribute that belongs to anything insofar as it brings those values into existence." More specifically, "something is 'just' because and insofar as it helps realize, not values in general, but very specific values" —those which constitute "reciprocal pairs" (p. 237).

V

Having thus outlined his general value theory, Beck now presents a series of analyses intended as proof for that theory. These analyses center around the problem of beauty (*Schönheit*). Comparable analyses were projected for related problems in five other areas. To my knowledge, however, these were never published. What is available is thus but a fragment—albeit a very large and detailed fragment.

The specific theme of the analyses here under consideration Beck himself has stated succinctly. "I find," he says, "that so far nobody has dared *as a thinker* to acknowledge what to him was undeniable and self-evident in direct experience: namely, the object-character (*Gegenständlichkeit*) of beauty in the totality of its whole essence as he perceives it, when he perceives it" (p. 243). In other words, it is the "object-character" of beauty that is now under discussion.

In order to clear the ground for his own constructive effort, Beck considers first four "errors" of interpretation. These are: (a) the objectivistic-rationalistic, (b) the subjectivistic-rationalistic, (c) the objectivistic-irrationalistic, and (d) the subjectivistic-irrationalistic.

(a) In the idealistic philosophies prior to Kant the phenomenon of beauty has been analyzed into "a subjective experience of intellectual pleasure" and "an objective value basic to that experience"—a value such as harmony, perfection, and true being. But this dualism, Beck maintains, falsifies the experiential situation. We may *define* beauty as harmony, perfection or true being; but we then deal with empty abstractions. "We *experience* beauty only as grounded in the perception of a particular kind of objective value" (p. 246). That is to say, when beauty is identified with "nothing but perfection," with harmony, consonance, true being, etc., we miss the concrete aspect of pleasure that is characteristic of the actual experience. Moreover, "it can never be made evident" *why* objective perfection, harmony, and the like should "awaken pleasure in me"; why "being an objective value" should be "the sufficient *rational* ground" of the pleasure that is concretely experienced in perception. And neither can the experienced pleasure be the sufficient ground for the object-character of an absolute value such as beauty. But this means that the objectivistic-rationalistic theories fail—and must fail—because of an inherently irrational element.

(b) The subjectivistic-rationalistic theories all attempt a "reductive interpretation" of values, and not of beauty alone. Advocates of such "reductionism" fail to see what is essential to all values: their character as absolute, perfect, ultimate, eternal—the unanalyzable "being there" (*Dasein*) of the values that cannot be dissolved into value-free elements but can only be acknowledged.

(c) Objectivistic-irrationalistic interpretations—and especially the empirically oiented ones—all tend to "divide beauty into an *experience* and an objective *basis* of it." What leads Beck to speak here of an "irrationalism" is the fact that both, the experience and its objective basis, are taken to be in themselves "value-indifferent." That is to say, according to the views now under consideration, "there is nothing in objective reality that in itself produces aesthetic effects." Things produce aesthetic effects only "because and insofar as the sensory-spiritual (*sinnlich-geistige*) organization of a perceptive subject is atuned to them" (p. 262). But why, Beck asks, do certain objects elicit in us pleasure-accentuated perceptions that are aesthetically valuable? This question finds no adequate answer in the objectivistic-irrationalistic theories.

If it be argued that the pleasure is experienced because it is "advantageous to the organism" to be in relation with the objects involved; that "nature uses the pleasurable as bait in order to preserve, enhance, perpetuate, and elevate life"; then, so Beck points out, such argument ignores or distorts what is "evidentially given" in experience and fails to account for the difference between the "aesthetic" and the "useful." More importantly yet, the argument misses the crucial point, for its aim is to show how and in what way certain objects may cause pleasurable experiences when the issue is not one of causal relations at all but of the rational ground for a *value*-response to value-free or value-indifferent facts; and, surely, what in itself is value-free or value-indifferent cannot *cause* a value.

(d) The subjectivistic-irrationalistic thesis states, in effect, that what makes an object aesthetically effective depends entirely upon the "laws of aesthetic experience"—upon the subjective conditions, that is, which determine "the fitness of an object for the actualization of an aesthetic experience." The object provides merely the occasion for the experience. To put it differently, according to the subjectivistic-irrationalistic theories "the beautiful is nothing but experience—not only as to its quality but also (and this is essential) as far as its existence is concerned" (p. 274). The fact that, as a value, "beauty is an elementary absolute" is here brushed aside as an "unimportant illusion."

This interpretation of the aesthetic experience shares with the other three just referred to a crucial deficiency—the failure, namely, of recognizing that aesthetic experience is a form of *cognition*. If the meaning of art is seen merely in the fact that it puts us in a pleasurable mood, that it entertains us or relieves the humdrum of our daily existence, then the creative artist is reduced to the role of an "arranger of festivals"—and this is a reductionism which contradicts the innermost conviction of every painter, sculptor, composer, and poet of some note that he "meant to *say* something" in and through his art (p. 279). And are not we ourselves, in our aesthetic experience, conscious of a "deeper insight into the world"? Do we not feel that the experience has added a new dimension to our understanding? To be sure, we can brush aside such an experience as "subjective delusion"; but "only he can deny its occurrence who has never experienced beauty" (p. 280).

VI

But now another problem arises for Beck. It is this: How can he maintain that "beauty is something objective (*etwas Gegenständliches*)" when one person finds beautiful what another believes to be ugly; when what is accepted as beautiful is different in different cultures and in the same culture (or even by the same individual) at different times? Does not this difference and this variation entail an insurmountable subjectivism?

In reply to this question Beck points out that even in cognitive experience men do not always perceive everything that is intrinsic to the object which confronts them—not everything which, as far as their capacities are concerned, they could perceive. Thus, a person preoccupied with "practical matters" may well fail to see the beauty of an object simply because "he has no use for it." Who, in the hustle and bustle of his every-day activities, actually sees "the richness of the sensory world always spread out before him"? Or who, absorbed in problems of science or philosophy, sees it? The men of practical affairs, as also the men of science, "see everything only so far as this is necessary for their practical or theoretical discernments and purposes." "Beauty, however, lies beyond all this in the fullness of the actually perceivable" (p. 288). Poets and artists, therefore, must open our eyes to what is hidden from us because of our preoccupation with other concerns.

If it now be argued that all this does not explain why some persons see ugliness where others see beauty, Beck replies that this argument is refuted by the fact that "in reality ugliness does not exist." What is called "ugliness" is merely a matter of "undeveloped perception" which, in its narrowness, does not apprehend the objective relationships in and through which beauty is realized but "sees chaos where a more developed sensibility discovers ever new beauties" (p. 289). It is almost incredible, Beck points out, that Mozart's music, for example, "was once heard as dissonance." The explanation is that, in listening to the music, one relates the wrong elements; that "one expects a harmony of elements which has been dissolved in favor of deeper harmonies."—But of this more will be said later. For the moment it is sufficient to note that, although our "perception of beauty depends upon contemplation and an intensive functioning of our senses as well as upon the richness of the world around us," this is no valid argument against the thesis of the objectivity of beauty (*Gegenständlichkeit der Schönheit*).

But there are other points that must be considered.

It cannot be denied, for example, that newness or the unaccustomed enhances the chances of an object of becoming the focal point of our attention and, therefore, of an aesthetic experience. But newness is not beauty. Also, something which we like at first encounter may cease to please us as we become better acquainted with it; and not because we have become accustomed to it, but because we discover upon closer inspection that what made the object appear to be beautiful were only "superficialities"—cheap sensuality, "trashy sweetness," etc.—which covered up the basic emptiness and aesthetic insignificance of the object but which, at their own level, still retain minimal aspects of beauty.

It is also true, of course, that the newness and the unusual character of an object prevent full aesthetic enjoyment, and that repetition and familiarity enhance it. So-called "difficult" music, for example,—a Bach fugue, let us say—really pleases aesthetically only after repeated and intensive listening, for it is only as we become familiar with it that we experience its deepest harmonies and fullest meaning. But all of this simply means that beauty itself has nothing to do with either newness or familiarity; that it is what it is in itself. And while the aesthetically insensitive person depends for his enjoyment of beauty upon the "sensational"—as encountered in the new, the unfamiliar, the rare—it is the artists and the poets (and especially the ablest among them) that open our eyes to the beauty that is all around us.

But beauty often is "beauty of a special kind": sublime or pretty, serious or cheerful, melancholy or gay, stately or playful, and so on (p. 301). And are not such qualities "subjective moods" which we "project into the perceived objects"? The facts are, Beck maintains, that such is not the case. One may, for example, feel depressed and hopeless and yet perceive "the sublime beauty of towering mountains." And it is by no means clear how a projected mood can be transformed into beauty. "Just as we cannot feel ourselves to be 'beautiful,' just so we do not experience pleasure and joy, etc. as beauty but only as pleasure and joy." And, surely, it is true that at times aspects of the world about us convey to us a mood that is diametrically opposed to the mood which we initially experience; that "either gradually or suddenly we accept the mood of the objective situation" (p. 309). Thus, when I am sad and, suddenly, a gay melody strikes my ear, I may at first experience this as an insult. It is repulsive to me. And yet, as I continue to listen, my own mood may be transformed and may take on the character of the mood intrinsic in the music. It is obviously not the subjective mood which is projected onto the object (the music in this case); it is rather "the mood of the object" which replaces our own. "I myself become serene because of my perception of a serene beauty; I experience a sublime feeling when I perceive the sublime" (p. 321). Prior to all experience the "moods" belong to "the beautiful object"; and if they occur in our experience, they do so as the realization of the tendency of all objective contents of consciousness to determine the nature and quality of our experience.

VII

Beck's basic theme is to show that all values—i.e., all "self-values"—are realizations of "pleasure" in something objective (*in einem Gegenständlichen*), and that beauty thus realized is "a category of the externally objective" (*eine Kategorie des Aussenge-genständlichen*).

In order to understand fully what is meant here, a distinction must be made between "inner" and "outer" such that the "outer" expresses or manifests the "inner," and the "inner" reveals itself in the "outer." It is not otherwise accessible. A sentence, for example,—either written or spoken—is the expression of a thought; and the thought is that which finds expression in the sentence. The thought is "materialized" in the sentence. The physical and the intellectual are inseparably intertwined. Analogously, a person is "concretized" in his actions and affections; and he who understands these apprehends in them—and apprehends directly—the "inner" (i.e., the character) of the person (p. 408). Such apprehension is not a matter of inference or guesswork but is an "immediate perception." In general, so Beck maintains, when we encounter living beings, we do not see merely their bodies; we actually see them *as living,* as centers of action. And seeing them so is not a matter of inference or empathy but of direct apprehension. Their "inner" is concretely present in their "outer," is "given" with it, and is "as immediately perceived as is the outer self" (p. 471).

One other aspect of experience must be touched upon before we return to the problem of beauty. It is this: Much in our experience of the world around us apparently does not have its own intrinsic unity but is unified by us as we "see things together"—

a bouquet of flowers, a landscape, and others. Our integrative experience here depends upon the perspective from which the objects are viewed. The "same" landscape, for example, is experienced as quite different as we view it from different points of view —as we view the towering mountains from the valley below, or view the valley from the top of the mountains; and our experience of beauty changes with the change in perspective. This obvious fact appears to contradict any thesis—such as Beck's—that takes beauty to be an objective reality. Beck points out, however, that "even the perspective phenomena are something objective," for the different "views" of the landscape are "objectively given" prior to our experiencing them—"given," namely, relative to the objective points of reference from which the landscape may be viewed. The different "views" are thus objectively present in the situation as relations of actual objects to equally real but specifically designated objects of reference. A subjectivistic interpretation distorts this basic fact (p. 506).

VIII

Beck's thesis is that "beauty is something objective"; that we perceive it as something "out there" in connection with landscapes, flowers, clouds, colors, sounds, houses, pictures, words, movements, and a myriad of other things. But what, precisely, is it that makes these objects beautiful? To this question various answers have been given.

Philosophers have spoken of harmony, perfection, appropriateness and the like; but harmony, perfection, appropriateness of what? "Of the *forms* of objects" that are the concretization of ideas. That is to say, these philosophers have taken beauty to be something ideal within the real. Beck maintains, however, that this view is untenable, for even the ugly forms can appear to be beautiful. And it is not true, so he points out, that we see only the forms of objects when we perceive beauty. What else, then, do we perceive?

Before an answer to this question can be given, we must note that almost all aestheticians have regarded two other aspects as essential to our experience of beauty: the absence of practical concerns and the character of "the apparent or the unreal."

It is true of course that the "beautiful object" is taken out of the realm of the practical; that its beauty is not a matter of "practicality." But this fact can hardly be taken as determining the positive character of beauty. And neither can the element of unreality determine that character. Moreover, it is simply not true that we encounter beautiful objects as unrelated to the practical concerns and as unreal; for "we desire and love them," and desire and love are practical concerns involving real objects. The decisive fact is that the beautiful object reveals itself as something that is not less but more than the object of "sober reality." Beauty stands over against the realities of commonplace experience not as something negative, not as poorer or weaker, but as something positive, as richer and stronger, and as having "the pre-eminence of an absolute."

As Beck sees it, "pleasure is an essential ingredient of beauty"; but it is not the pleasure of the observer. On the contrary: "The pleasurable is perceived as an aspect of the object"; "its objectivity is in the beautiful object" (p. 539). Beck thus asserts the identity of pleasure and reality; and this assertion is the crux of his whole theory. Can it be justified?

The usual interpretation is that pleasure is a subjective state of enhanced and intensified feeling, a "feeling of life-affirmation"; and there is truth in this. However,—so Beck argues—the interpretation is also misleading when it is taken to mean that pleasure is nothing but a subjective state in the experience of the observer. When the phenomenon of pleasure is stripped of all psychological and biological significance, so Beck maintains, there remains "something like affirmation, enhanced existence, intensity, expansiveness, richness" as elements of "objective pleasure." That is to say, the existence (*Dasein*) of the perceived object appears to find in beauty a particular enhancement, an intensification, and an increasing richness. The existence of the perceived object—not that of the subject—"appears to be affirmed" (p. 541).

What is true of some particular object is true also, and especially so, of the whole of reality. Let it be noted, however, that existence itself is already an affirmation. "The perceived world, therefore, in all its particularities possesses the exultation of pure reality." "Existence (*Dasein*) as such—the pure, naked, real existence, and only because it is real, not because it is such and such —is something intensively and exultingly joyful"—as St. Francis of Assisi and Walt Whitman well knew. And in this sense, Beck maintains, "reality and pleasure are one and the same" (p. 627). The world is not a "value-indifferent something" which has value only because we ascribe value to it. The very existence of the world is in itself absolute value. "Pleasure and existence (*Dasein*), both irreducible and inexplicable, are something ultimate and absolute that is neither a *how* nor a *what* but an ultimate *that*" (p. 644); they are an object of perception (*Wahrnehmung*) rather than of reason.

We must note, however, that existence and pleasure are always the existence and the pleasure of something, and that this "something" is never without "form." As Beck puts it: "Without the unity of matter and form there is no reality, no existence," and therefore no pleasure (p. 648); and since he defines beauty as "the pleasure which realizes itself in the determinateness of external objects," it follows that, for Beck, "beauty is synonymous with the existence of external objects"; that "there is nothing in the external world—no color, no form, no material object, etc. —that is real and not also beautiful." "The certainty that existence and value—specifically the existence of external objects and beauty—are identical is the basic intuition (*Grundintuition*)" of Beck's whole theory (p. 653).

If it now be argued that there is also much ugliness in the world, Beck replies that we must carefully distinguish between what is actually *perceived* as beautiful or ugly and what is merely *called* "beautiful" or "ugly."

Let us suppose that we come upon a street where dirty children play in the filth and dirt of the gutter in front of ramshackle houses and where the stench of decaying garbage in the street assaults our nostrils. Would we not shudder and call it ugly? But what, precisely, is our experience here? The scene arouses in us feelings of disgust, of displeasure; and these feelings we project upon, or read into, the external realities. That is to say, "objects are not *perceived* as ugly when they arouse subjective displeasure, they are merely (and mistakenly) *called* ugly" (p. 661). An artist, for example, disregarding his personal feelings, might well perceive beauty where others do not. The crux of the matter is that, as far as Beck is concerned, "ugliness exists nowhere but is a product of our attitude" (p. 741).

IX

When we now consider the role which art plays in human experience, several facts stand out clearly. Thus, as Beck sees it, imitative art has only one purpose: to facilitate our appreciation of the beauty of the very objects of which the work of art is an "imitation." That is to say, in addition to the beauty which such a work of art—a painting, a statue, a literary work—possesses in itself—the beauty of line, of color, of form and composition, the beauty of words, of sounds and of rhythms—it serves the function of presenting the represented object compellingly to our imagination. It makes us see beauty in the bewildering multiplicity of our experiences by isolating, delimitating, and underscoring what beauty there is in the objects. Imitative art thus "educates" our perception of things by bringing into sharp focus what otherwise is easily overlooked. It is a new and creative way of integrating experience.

This thesis Dr. Beck illustrates and supports in detailed discussions of the "visual arts": painting and sculpturing (pp. 776–838), and the "literary arts": epic, lyrical, and dramatic presentations (pp. 838–901).

If it be argued that lyric poetry, for example, is an expression of subjective feelings rather than an "imitation" of some aspect of the world around us, Beck replies that, on the contrary, the poet does not project his own feelings into a landscape (for example)—see Goethe's "Ueber allen Gipfeln ist Ruh' "—but presents what he experiences when he "feels himself into the mood of the landscape"—i.e., he expresses or states the effect which the landscape has upon him. "Before all else, the mood is an objective constituent of the landscape itself and is not projected into it by the poet" (p. 851).

Despite all that happens in a drama, the drama is not simply the telling of a "story." Its real object, Beck holds, are the "persons" that reveal themselves in and through their actions. Whatever is presented "on stage," whatever is said or acted out, is but the occasion and the means for the self-revelation of the innermost being of the persons presented. In fact, it is this innermost being, the essential character, of the persons in the drama that determines the action—the conflicts and resolutions. It is the objective ground of all that happens.

But can we here speak of beauty? It has been Beck's contention that "beauty" is a quality that is objectively real as a constituent of external objects. The "realities" of the dramatic object, however,—the mental states, the personal actions, the feelings and emotions and character qualities revealed on stage—may be pleasure, joy, goodness or evil, but they are not beauty. Still, a well-wrought drama is a new unity of what is presented and the means of presenting it; and in this sense it is an objective "materialization of pleasure" that may be said to be beautiful. In other words, it is the drama that is beautiful in its concretization of particulars, not its "hero." The "hero" is good—good even when he is evil, for the truly artistic drama ultimately frees its "persons" from all guilt (p. 898).

If we now ask, What is the mode of existence of the "objects" in a work of art?—of the "persons" in a novel by Dostoevski, for example, or of a "landscape" in a painting?—Beck replies that it is an existence in the imagination of the writer or painter or in that of the reader or the spectator. And what is true in the case of the "objects" or "persons" in painting and literature is true, of course, also of the "objects" in all other arts. This does not mean, however, that such "objects" are something mental.

To be sure, the act of imagining something is mental—a mental process, a doing or having. But the objects of such a process are no more identical with the process itself as a perceptual object is identical with the act of perceiving. What we see in our imagination—trees, colors, spaces, etc.—is all something non-mental. Even the anger or the sadness "seen" in imagination is not a quality of the act of imagining. Nor is the time of the act of imagining the same as the temporal determinateness of what is being imagined.

Within the realm of the imagined we must distinguish between "configurations" that are arbitrary, vague, monstrous, etc., and "objects" that reveal a strict inner necessity that is determinative of their constituent elements. That is to say, just as it is certain that I do not create geometrical figures simply by imagining them (for they have their own geometrical and, therefore, non-psychological structure which I cannot alter), so it is certain also that there are objects of the imagination which, conforming to their own inner law, are to that extent independent of my imagining them; they, too, have their own inner structures and harmonies. And only when I see in my imagination what thus "belongs together" do I see beautiful and, for me, "real" objects of the imagination (p. 1027). "The objects of the imagination thus disclose themselves (*geben sich*) as being in their very essence objective realities outside the empirical world" (p. 1041). In fact, "every object of the imagination is an absolute world all by itself, occupying its own space (when it is spatial), enduring in its own time (when it is temporal), having its own characteristics (*mit eigenem Drum und Dran*), absolutely without relation to the empirical objects of our experience" (pp. 1048–49). It is completely self-contained—i.e., it is but the integrative complexus of qualities as which it "stands before us" in our imagination, and as such it can be intrinsically beautiful.

Special problems arise in connection with the non-imitative arts, with music, the dance, and with architecture.

Music—i.e, music in the grand manner: fugues, sonatas, symphonies—Beck insists, "exists as independent reality within the sphere of the imaginatively real" (p. 1217). (Performance of the music is merely the occasion for its being presented in experience.) And it is the music itself, the imaginatively real and independent object, that is beautiful. If it should be argued that at least some music is anything but beautiful, Beck replies that, "actually, there are no tones—be they ever so screechy and dissonant—which, in adequate comprehension, are not encountered as beautiful reality" (*ibid.*). "Adequate comprehension" here means (a) that the tones are considered entirely by themselves, i.e., without regard to any psycho-physical side-effects, and (b) that they are taken for what they in themselves are, with their particular timbre and as characteristic of the objects whose tones they are. "We call music unpleasant or terrible when empirically real tones are presented for which there is no corresponding imaginatively real music. Actually, there is only beautiful music, and there are only beautiful tones" (p. 1219). And "music is beauty despite the fact that it is life." It is beauty because in its very essence it is an "outer"—a single level of imaginative reality within which "the tension between the musical totality and all its parts oscillates."

Beck's discussion of music anticipates in all essentials his comments on the dance as an art form. With a discussion of architecture and the "decorative arts" Beck's lengthy analyses come to an end. The work as a whole, however, remains a fragment. It was conceived as a general value theory and as such it is incomplete.

BIBLIOGRAPHY

Beck, Maximilian, *Wesen und Wert,* 2 volumes, Berlin, 1925.

CHAPTER XVI

KRAFT'S PSYCHO-GENETIC APPROACH

Heinrich Rickert, it may be remembered, had stated (echoing in this respect Max Scheler's thesis) that "strictly speaking, value itself cannot be defined, for it is a primitive and underivable concept" (*System der Philosophie,* I, p. 113). Advocates of a value intuitionism have in general taken this position. But if they are right, and if value is indefinable, then it must at least still be possible to delineate the conditions that make possible a meaningful reference to value—just as we can specify the conditions under which we use, for example, "red" or "pain"—words which also designate primitive concepts. The question we face is then no longer simply a matter of definition but of fact. Can appropriate facts be discerned in the broad field of value theory?

When value-theoretical investigations were first initiated, the generally accepted belief was that value problems were problems of empirical fact; that value consists in actual relations of objects to our feelings (Meinong, Kreibig) or to our desires (von Ehrenfels). This approach to value theory was therefore psychological. But even Meinong realized that a psychologistic interpretation could not do justice to the normative aspects inherent in all value problems. (*Über emotionale Präsentation,* pp. 151–52). Max Scheler (*Der Formalismus in der Ethik und die materiale Wertethik,* 1913) completed the break with the earlier tradition. Value was no longer conceived as a relation between subject and object but as itself an object or entity *sui generis* subsisting in an ideal realm of Platonic essences. And Heinrich Rickert argued (in 1904) that values are something "irreal," something which exists neither as real nor as ideal but, nevertheless, is something— namely, "validity" (*op. cit.,* pp. 115, 121, 124). We need not multiply here the references to diverse approaches to and interpretations of value problems. The present book provides the illustrative examples.

Kraft's new approach to the problems of value theory is empirically oriented. Using "red" as his example, he argues that the essence of the concept "red" is a relation of similarity, xRa, between a determinable relatum, a, and a variable, x—between a "standard sample," that is, and instances of color "similar" to it. The extent of what is "similar" is not given *a priori*. Nor is it implied by the definition. It depends on variable factors of interpretation. And "similarity" itself, insofar as it involves a variable, is determinable only in a given concrete situation. So simple a concept as "red," therefore, is already highly complex, and what it designates is by no means a definite, directly intuitable *quale*. (*Grundlagen*, p. 14).

What is true in the case of "red" or any other "simple" concept is true also in the case of values. "Values must be understood as invariant relations involving variable data; and so understood they cease to be something ultimate and irreducible. They, too, consist in relations between objects of a lower order; and it is no longer possible to intuit (*erschauen*) them by themselves alone" (pp. 15–16). "Values as essences," as independent of goods and valuations, are nowhere encountered, and value theory must be empirically grounded.

The weakness of the earlier "psychological value theories" (Meinong, von Ehrenfels, Kreibig) was that they were developed, in part, on intuitive grounds and, in part, through an abstract dialectic. The later psychologists (Haering, Störring) were more scientific, but the meager results of their "experimental" investigations were hardly worth the effort. It is Victor Kraft's contention that only a psycho-genetic approach can lead to dependable and significant conclusions.

I

"The concept 'value' comprises all the characteristics common to beauty, morality, usefulness, etc." (p. 24). This fact, however, is not particularly helpful, for the nature of these more specific values is no more definable than is value as such. In each case, the specific difference lies in factual references, not in their being values. As values they have in common that they add a particular kind of distinction—be it positive or negative—to the material content to which they refer. And it is this fact alone which makes all of them values. The concept "value," in other words, "contains nothing but this value character [of lending distinction] without having itself any factual content" (p. 26). It follows at once, however, that there is an unmistakable difference between a purely descriptive recognition of an object-induced feeling and a valuation of that object. "To know that one loves something or that one is annoyed by something is by no means the same as to value it"—a fact often obscured because many of our descriptive terms are already valuationally loaded (p. 28). Thus, when we find a lecture "boring," the term "boring" quite obviously has valuational overtones.

It is also a fact that objects elicit in us various feeling-responses and, at the same time, distinct attitudes—we either reject or we try to hold on to the object involved; and our attitude is as important as is our feeling. Still, "taking an attitude" (*Stellungnahme*) as such is not yet a valuing. If it were, then "a child of six months," attracted by some sensory impression, would manifest a value response. But this is hardly an acceptable interpretation of the facts. The first explicit valuations on the part of the child—valuations that find linguistic expression—can be observed only when the child is two or three years old (p. 32). At that time, the first value-words used are "good," "bad," and various expressions used as synonyms of these; and all such words are used in a very broad and rather loose sense. But from this time on the acquisition and development of value terms proceeds together with the development of a general conceptual framework.

It has usually been assumed that the growing child uses the value-words to express his own pleasure or displeasure about an object. It is Kraft's contention, however, that what the child means to express is not his subjective feeling but an objective condition; for the distinction between a feeling-state as a purely subjective phenomenon and the object which elicits that state has not yet been made. "The child experiences pleasure and displeasure as something which is co-present with the perceived object" (p. 37). The "subjectifying point of view" (*der subjektivierende Gesichtspunkt*) is as yet foreign to the child of two or three years. His "ego-consciousness" (*Ich-Bewusstsein*) is still only in process of development, and the great separation of external world and inner world is barely beginning to take place. Attention is at this time still focused entirely on the external world. This means that "objectification" is the original and exclusive character of the child's early experience.[1] "The pleasing or displeasing character of objects, their feeling-accentuation, comes into consciousness only as completely fused with the objects themselves as one of their *objective* characteristics" (p. 39. Italics in the original.). A new kind of attribute is thus associated with the objects. This fact, however, is not yet what characterizes value. "The specific character of valuation lies in this that an object is being praised or blamed, that it receives special attention, that it is being treated with distinction" (p. 39). What this amounts to is that we do not comprehend the real nature of valuations if we see it simply in the relation of feelings to the objective situations which elicit them. What is essential is that we consider the pleasure-displeasure accentuations of objects in their relation to the attitudes taken toward them.

To be sure, pleasure and displeasure form a distinctive class of phenomena in our experience. Their perculiarity lies in the fact that they call forth at once an attitude on our part toward whatever causes them. And it is this specific characteristic of pleasure and displeasure that provides the ground for all valuations. But it is the attitude taken toward it, not the pleasure or displeasure as such, which transforms an experience of pleasure or displeasure into a value experience. "The value predicate ascribed to the object is rooted in, and pertains to, the fact that through it the object is being characterized in its relation to our attitude" (p. 51). The value predicate is thus quite distinct from any other predicate that we may ascribe to an object. The various value concepts ("good," "wonderful," "moral," "polite," etc., and their opposites) reflect but the relation of the objects to our various attitudes. That is to say, "the value character reflects a natural, objective accentuation (*Auszeichnung*)—namely, the unique position (*Sonderstellung*) in our consciousness of that which determines our attitude" (p. 55).

---

[1]Kraft's argument here depends upon the researches of Kl. and W. Stern (*Die Kindersprache,* 4th edition, 1928), Karl Bühler (*Die geistige Entwicklung des Kindes,* 1918), and Lohbauer, ("Der Weg zum Ich in der frühen Kindheit," *Zeitschrift für pädagogische Psychologie,* xxxi, 1930).

In time, the child learns to generalize the meaning of value words and thus to transcend his own pleasure-displeasure accentuated experiences. He now forms classes of value objects and his value considerations may now become independent of any actual valuation. Value judgments begin to reflect a value *knowledge* (*Wertwissen*) instead of being direct expressions of an emotion-tinged value experience.

II

Although we have seen already that even the most elementary value experience involves not only the pleasure-displeasure component but an attitude as well, we must now realize that what gives unique distinction to an object is determined by various factors—by specific points of view, by relations to other objects, etc. To illustrate the point, Kraft quotes a boy of fifteen: "I occupy myself with radio: 1. because it is something new and therefore fascinating; 2. because I can show my relatives and friends that I know how to build a radio receiver; 3. when the weather is bad and one cannot indulge in sports, one can listen to the most beautiful concerts, the most informative lectures, sports news, weather reports—in brief, one can listen to whatever one pleases" (p. 61). Each aspect of the complex situation can be regarded as an independent source of valuation. Examination will then show that value experiences involve various strata or levels.

To begin with, there is the large and important field of valuations rooted in the pleasures and displeasures of sensory experience: pleasing tastes (and the culinary arts), fragrance (natural and artificial, and the perfume industry) and the bad odors, noise, pain, cold and warmth (and the industries related to them), sexual pleasures (and what caters to them), and so on. This pleasure-displeasure accentuation of the sensory qualities is, in a way, the prototype for all other valutions: something is distinguished from the rest of our experience because it is agreeable or disagreeable—and it is so in itself, not by virtue of a relation to something else. It must be noted, however, that it is not simply the quality of sensory impressions which elicits pleasure or displeasure; the interrelations of the impressions, their co-occurrence and their succession—i.e., their form and configuration in a broad sense: linear and bodily shapes, proportions, rhythms, melodies, color and tone harmonies—all of these are also sources of pleasure. The disarray and disorderliness of sensory complexities are confusing and therefore disagreeable. They evoke our displeasure. The whole realm of aesthetics, at least in its formal respects, finds here its ground and justification.

Beyond the pleasures and displeasures of sensory experience we find pleasure also in activity—be it bodily or mental—and especially so when the activity leads to a desired goal. The joy that accompanies success and the vexation that follows failure are too well known to require comment. They are, however, so intimately connected with the pleasures and displeasures that stem from our activities as such that they cannot be regarded as a special class of pleasure-displeasure accentuated experiences. But it is necessary to recognize the fact that our own actions must be viewed, not only under the perspective of success (or failure), but under that of our own ability (or lack of it) as well: "I am able to do this!" Under this perspective the difficulty of the achievement becomes determinative of our self-respect. And the enhancement (respectively, the lowering) of our self-respect adds a new component to our feeling-accentuated experience. As a result, the feeling-tone of success or failure becomes too complex to be reducible simply to pleasure and/or displeasure (pp. 69–70).

So far Kraft has shown that sensory qualities, their configurations and relationships, and our own activities are sources of pleasure or displeasure. The question now is, Are there still other sources of pleasure (and displeasure) such that their effects cannot be reduced to the sensory and functional pleasures (displeasures) already referred to?

When flowers give us pleasure, that pleasure is directly related to their fragrance, their color, their form, or to a combination of these. That is to say, the pleasure is directly related to sensory qualities and/or to elementary aesthetic configurations. But if properties of things are to be a new kind of source of pleasure (or displeasure), their effects must be indirect rather than direct. "Poisonous," for example, is such a property. "Poison is valued negatively not because it is sensuously disagreeable or because it causes pain; for poisons can kill painlessly, and poisonous fruits can have a pleasing taste. Poisons are valued negatively because they come into conflict with a basic drive (*Grundtrieb*), the will to live" (p. 71). The feeling-tone is here the result of an interpretative comprehension of what is given in sensory experience as a thing having specific properties, and is, in fact, not simply a feeling of pleasure but "an affective state of mind": "Poisonous things are sinister and call forth aversion" (p. 72). What is significant here is that the affective response is not immediate and directly to the thing as "given" but is mediated by, and depends upon, an interpretation or an understanding of the nature of the thing.

Moreover, purely intellectual phenomena—such as the interrelations of meanings—can likewise elicit an emotional response. One may thus admire the "elegance" of a mathematical proof or the logic of a well-constructed theory. But admiration of this kind is obviously not a sensuously grounded pleasure. This means that "intellectual contents (*geistige Gehalte*) can also call forth original and new feelings" (p. 73). They can call forth affective states of a complex kind.

III

The facts of experience thus reveal that the pleasure-displeasure accentuations—rooted as they are in sensory qualities and their interrelations, and in activities—by no means encompass all that is valued. The more complex affective responses must also be taken into consideration. It is a deficiency of Meinong's and Kreibig's value theories, that the distinction here involved was not clearly drawn, that the term "feeling" was taken to refer to both, pleasure-displeasure and the affections. But it is evident that feelings such as "fear, anger, envy, pride, hope, surprise, reverence, sadness, and so on," are neither qualitatively the same as pleasure and displeasure nor are they derivable from the latter.

The question now is, What characterizes our emotions? What elicits them? And here it is important to note that "they occur most readily when an object is involved which in some sense is already *distinguished* for us" (p. 76)—i.e., which already has value or disvalue for us. We thus experience gratitude when we receive something which we desire or which we value. We feel remorse and shame only when we are dissatisfied with, or value negatively, our own conduct. Even love and hate are experienced only because some person or thing already pleases or displeases us. And, similarly, "hope and worry, disappointment and despair, envy and jealousy pertain always only to objects which already are somehow distinguished, valued, pleasing, or desired" (p. 76). Although this means that they can be aroused more readily, it also means that, for the most part, such emotions are "derivative phenomena" (*Folgeerscheinungen*).

However, emotions may also occur as primary phenomena, not simply as reactions to antecedent valuations. Such emotions are experienced when we respond to a theatrical performance, when we read a novel, a lyrical poem, or when we listen to music. We call the objects that arouse these emotions "wonderful," "delightful," "lovely," "repulsive," "frightful," "wretched," "miserable," etc. (p. 78). The question is, Can such emotions be reduced to pleasure and displeasure? To do so would seem to obliterate the great variety of nuances of our emotional experience and, therefore, the manifold shades and degrees of our valuations. It is Kraft's contention, however, that "the diversity of valuations is determined primarily by the differences in the descriptive content of experience, not by the differences in value character" (p. 79). As far as their "value character" is concerned, our experiences differ only in the "polar dimension positive-negative," and within this dimension in degree only.

Kraft admits that there are undoubtedly occasions of emotional experience when their pleasure-displeasure character does not determine our attitude toward them; when the "affective state" itself determines the attitude. Thus, "the adventurer, the gambler, the 'Hippies,' the Romantic—they all seek the arousal of the emotions as such; they want to experience emotionally, in contrast to the 'calm,' 'sober,' 'bourgeois' existence" (p. 81). Kraft maintains, however, that a large part of man's artistic creations serves no purpose other than to evoke emotional responses—and not pleasure-responses. Melancholy lyric poetry, for example,—

in which the painful emotions of an unhappy love, of parting, of homesickness are ancient themes—falls into this class. Comedy and tragedy, as art forms, are specifically designed to evoke emotions—emotions which, in the case of tragedy at least, are by no means merely a matter of pleasure. "We want to be fascinated, moved, emotionally stirred. . . . And these affective effects (*Gefühlswirkungen*) are being sought not because of the pleasure but because of the excitement, the inner tension (*innere Aufwühlung*)" (p. 81). Tension alone, however, is not sufficient. It must also be resolved. The excitement must ebb away. "Tension and its resolution—that is what we seek and value in fascinating literature" (p. 82) as in music. Although the resolution may be experienced as "pleasure-accentuated" (*lustbetont*), "the fundamental fact is that we do not always seek pleasing (*lustvolle*) emotions. The excitement and inner tension have a stronger attraction for us then have pleasure or displeasure. They determine our attitude in an independent way, not in accordance with the pleasure-displeasure content" (p. 83). And to the extent to which this is true we deal here with an entirely new source of valuation. It remains to be seen how this source can best be characterized.

To begin with, what is valued in literature definitely depends on age-levels, sex, and character types. Analysis reveals, however, that "content" rather than anything else determines such differences in valuation. "It is in each case a different content which provides the readers with what they seek. What they seek, however, is always the same: experience—an experience in imagination because reality does not provide it for them. He who stands in the midst of a full life, he who experiences novels, does not read novels" (p. 86). Children in particular thus enrich their experience through reading; and they desire such enrichment.

But what fairy tales, adventure stories, and novels provide is not only an imaginative experience of "content," it is also an emotional experience. Through identification with him, the reader may experience vicariously the emotional states of the "hero." Still more significant is the fact that, while reading the story, the reader experiences feelings also in his role as *spectator*, as witness (as it were) to the action; and these feelings are quite different from the feelings of the fictional characters themselves. They are the reader's own reactions to the described events. The reader is *moved* by what he "witnesses." The tensions he experiences when, for example, he "witnesses" Hamlet's death-scene, are his own, not those of the characters in the play. But what is it that gives a value-accent to experiences of this kind?

In line with his psycho-genetic approach to value problems, Kraft submits statements made by juveniles as typical of their motives for reading: "It entices me to know what it is like in other countries." "I would very much like to know how our ancestors actually lived." "I would like to know how plants grow and develop." There thus exists a "longing for the new," a desire to know (*Wissbegierde*), which finds satisfaction in reading and study. "This desire does not come into being because the juvenile knows from the very beginning that such studies will give him pleasure. . . . It comes into being all by itself" (p. 93). Indeed, this desire is "developmentally conditioned" (*entwicklungsbedingt*) as our intellectual life unfolds. "And whatever satisfies this need, whatever fulfills this desire, is accentuated by that very fact." "The need itself creates the basis for the accentuation; for it determines directly the attitude toward that which satisfies the need and the desire" (p. 93). For a person who does not have this need, nothing new is significant. Hence, in old age, "fossilized in what is customary," a person will repudiate the new; for the new is now not welcome. It is, in fact, "disagreeable." Far from satisfying a need, it is actually disturbing. What elicits the emotional states brought about by reading a novel or attending a theatrical performance is determined, not by any pleasure involved, but by other factors—by the "anxiety concerning the fate of the hero in critical situations, by the emotion which causes a lump in the throat and makes us weep"—and these are anything but feelings of pleasure (p. 95). And the positive valuation of literary works is not necessarily conditioned by predominantly displeasing (*unlustvolle*) feelings—as it would have to be the case if their value were rooted in pleasure-accentuation (*Lustbetonung*).

The average reader and the juvenile, so Kraft points out, are interested primarily in the material content, not the aesthetic qualities, of what they read. He supports this assertion with a number of quotations (such as the following) in which juveniles state clearly what fascinates them in what they read: "And then the terrible third part. Everything simply tremendous." And now the question is, Why does one voluntarily place oneself in situations of so much suffering and destruction? Back of it all, Kraft assures us, is "a hunger for experience" (*Erlebnishunger*)—a "hunger" which exists at all age-levels and in all forms of human existence. "To satisfy in imagination the needs which actual living leaves unfulfilled—that is the achievement of literature. In this lies the strong biological anchorage for juveniles and adults alike" (pp. 104–105). Although pleasure may be an accompanying circumstance, it is not the heart of the matter: As far as its content is concerned, a literary work is valuationally accentuated only because it satisfies an inner need.

To the extent to which this is true, we have here "a new and different source of accentuation: the satisfaction of an unconscious need, the satisfaction of a desire (*Triebbefriedigung*). We must emancipate ourselves from the idea that pleasure and displeasure are the only sources of a value" (pp. 109–110). The new source gives rise to numerous and significant valuations, and accounts for variations and shifts in valuations. It is a well-known fact, for example, that children and juveniles, and adults as well, live in the same environment of things and other human beings, but what in that environment is significant for each person (and even for the same person at different times) may be something very different. What one person values, another may not value at all. This is so because of the difference in intellectual endowments as well as in the education and development of various individuals. At different stages in a person's development and for different character types the needs that demand satisfaction are also different; and the value-accentuations are determined by these differences.

Kraft finds, however, that accentuation through the satisfaction of an unconscious need is not the only source of valuation besides the pleasure-displeasure accent. A need gives rise to a desire, to a tendency, that is, for action; and the action aims at a goal—a goal that may be consciously projected. The desire itself has thus been transformed in essential respects. It was, to begin with, a drive arising from an unconscious need and was without clearly defined goal; but it is now the conscious pursuit of a determinate goal. Attainment of the goal is accentuated positively, whereas everything that prevents attainment is accentuated negatively (p. 120). Upon this fact depends the large and extremely important area of means-values.

As Kraft sees it, if something is valued as a means, its value is not determined by the pleasure it itself may cause but by its effectiveness as a means. And this presupposes that the effect it produces as a means is actually intended as contributing to the satisfaction of a desire. Further analysis reveals, however, that "functioning as a means" is not in itself sufficient as a basis for valuation, for not everything that functions as a means is actually valued. The most commonly employed means in our daily living, for example,—"windows, water pipes, ovens, soap, locks and keys, etc."—are usually a matter of indifference to us. "Printing, postal service, watches, streetcars, and many more of the technological contrivances which provide important services are praised only in histories of culture; psychologically they are most of the time thoughtlessly used as a matter of course" (p. 122). In order that anything be value-accentuated as a means it is necessary that we are conscious of its function as a means (*Mittelfunktion*). What is not known to be a means can not be valued as such.

If something is valued as a means, its own "intrinsic value character" may well be in competition with its means-value. Painful surgery, for example, may have a positive value as a means to a desired goal: good health; in itself, however, and because of its displeasure accentuation, it may be valued negatively. In some situations the negative value of a particular object may even outweigh the positive value of that object as a means. In any case, however, it is clear that the intrinsic value of an object and its means-value derive from different sources.

Under very special conditions, habit also may determine valuations. But the emphasis lies here upon "under very special conditions." Ordinarily, what has become habitual "sinks below the level of consciousness, into the realm of automatic responses" and is then no longer directly value-accentuated (p. 126). Only when habit is disturbed does that which disturbs it, i.e., "the unaccustomed," receive a negative value accent. This negative accentuation, however, is obviously reducible to the displeasure which results from the interference with what is customary. Only the reestablishment of the habitual accentuates the habitual itself as something of positive value. But even in this case it must be admitted that the valuation can be understood as merely another occasion of a pleasure-accentuated experience and that, therefore, it does not bespeak the presence of a new source of values.

IV

Up to this point we have considered value-accentuations only under the perspective of the individual having a value experience, and have disregarded the influence which other persons may have upon his valuations. We must now augment our discussion in this respect.

As Kraft sees it, a transfer of valuations from A to B may take place (1) when A exerts a "suggestive influence" upon B— be it in a direct or an indirect way; and it may take place (2) when B "imitates" A (p. 129). However, suggestion and imitation both occur only when certain conditions are fulfilled. Not even a child of pre-school age is susceptible to suggestion in all situations. If A is to have a suggestive influence upon B, B must have faith in A. But having faith in A is easier if one has himself no firm basis of knowledge that is relevant to the valuation, or if one has no ground for being critical of A and accepts him as "authority." That suggestion plays an especially prominent role in the life of a child follows directly from these facts. In his eagerness to learn, the child stands ready to believe. His critical faculties have as yet not been developed. But we must not underestimate the role which suggestion plays in the life of adults. Advertising and propaganda depend upon it; and they are proven and effective means of instilling in a naive populace specific value judgments (p. 131).

We may encounter imitation also where there is lack of independent judgment. One believes, for example, that Dr. N. is an exceptionally fine physician because that is the judgment of one's friends. Or one values a historical person or a cultural era in ac-

cordance with the judgment of some historian. Burckhardt's valuations have thus determined for generations the prevailing value
judgments about the Renaissance. Tradition and "authority" play
their part in determining value judgments about art, music, and
literature. To be sure, in all of these cases suggestion and imitation may be intertwined (pp. 132–33), but imitation as a distinctly separate basis for the transfer of valuations is also encountered. It is encountered, for example, in the spreading of changing
fashions. The new style is set in such centers as Paris and London,
or New York and Hollywood, and imitation makes it the fashion
of the time. It is specifically value-accentuated because being
dressed in the latest fashion gives the appearance of social distinction. Not to follow fashion gives the impression of being left behind, of not being up-to-date. "Fashion thus gives social distinction to those who follow it, and brings disesteem to those who dis-
dain it. The enhancement or the lowering of one's ego-feeling
here entailed gives an independent value-accent to 'modern' and
'old-fashioned' " (pp. 133–34). It is important, however, that a
distinction be made between regarding the latest fashion as something valuable because one derives social prestige from it, and regarding it as valuable because one sees in it the prototype of what
is beautiful or right. The latter is an independent valuation that
just happens to coincide with one taken over by imitation.

A transfer of valuations takes place, of course, in the whole
area of traditions, including the trends of the times in art, in literature, in morality, in politics, etc. The transfer itself, however, pertains to the valuation of particular objects or classes of objects. An
object (or class of objects) that is being valued negatively might,
as a result of the transfer, be valued positively, or vice versa. In
most cases, the transfer thus entails a re-valuation; only seldom
does it result in a new valuation. And hardly ever does a transfer
lead to a new value concept; for as soon as the unfamiliar valuation has been made known through value judgments, even the
child must already comprehend the value concepts employed in
those judgments; he must already know what "good," "beautiful," "worthless," etc. mean. Transfer, therefore merely relates a
known value concept to some object or class of objects hitherto not
subsumed under it.

V

So far we have considered only such value-accentuations as pertain directly to individual objects, events, states of affairs, or to classes of them. Very often, however, value-accentuations come about also through some form of "mediation." That is to say, an object or event B is value-accentuated only because of its close association with a value-accentuated object or event A. The association may be purely "factual"—as when historical reliquiae are preserved in a museum because of their association with a national hero (e.g., the bloody shirt of Gustavus Adolphus preserved in a Stockholm museum).

But the transfer of value may also occur on entirely different grounds. A hitherto "indifferent" object, X, for example, may be found to possess a quality which, in itself, is value-accentuated and whose value is extended to all objects possessing it. The value of the quality is now extended to X because X is a member of a certain class of objects, and the transfer is "mediated" logically rather than through factual association (p. 138).

This logical type of transfer of value-accentuation is of immense significance, for the instances of such transfer are legion. The mediation amounts to this: a given object is examined in order to determine whether or not it possesses a specific value-accentuated quality which has been accepted in advance as providing a value standard or a norm of what is valuable. If the object possesses the quality which serves as norm, then it itself is valued; if it does not possess that quality, it is rated negatively. This, obviously, is what we encounter in all art criticism, in economic and moral valuations, and similar situations. We encounter it wherever we attempt to justify a valuation; "for to justify a valuation means nothing other than to demonstrate that it is in harmony with a general principle of valuing, i.e., it means to derive it from more general value judgments" (p. 139). Mediation of the value-accentuation through "valuating classification" (*wertende Klassifikation*) exemplifies this kind of value transfer especially well. It consists in placing the object into an antecedently given (*vorgegebene*) value scale and, thus, in assigning to it a specific "value-height" (*Werthöhe*), a specific rank relative to other value objects.

The behavior pattern, the manner of dress and of speech of various social classes—the aristocratic, the bourgeois, the proletarian, etc.—are thus determinative of how an individual is "ranked" as a member of his society.

VI

That the pleasure-displeasure dichotomy has an important bearing upon all of our valuations—from the low levels of biological existence to the highest cultural levels—seems evident. Kraft has made it clear, however, that pleasure-displeasure accentuations are not in themselves sources of value. They are of special significance only because they, far more than anything else, directly elicit attitudinal responses. But it is the determination of our attitudes as either an approval or a disapproval, not the pleasure or displeasure, that is the source of all values. "Anything immediately determining an attitude can result in value-accentuation" (p. 142).

So far, however, we have considered value-accentuations only as individual phenomena in the experience of some particular person. That is to say, we have considered them only as they are experienced by a person whose attitude is determined by an object which, in some way, is distinctive (*ausgezeichnet*). If we now subsume such experiences under value concepts, or refer to them in value judgments, we transcend this level of personal experience. We abstract from the given context of experience and attain a level of impersonality at which value predicates are "freely available" (*frei verfügbar*). They no longer pertain exclusively to the attitudes taken by some particular person but have reference to comparable experiences of any number of persons and, in principle, to all. This does not mean, however, that an impersonal value judgment asserts that a particular object is actually value-accentuated for any arbitrarily selected person, or that it is actually valued by all. Nor does it mean that all persons actually agree on the value of a given object. Whether or not there is agreement can be ascertained only through a careful analysis of all facets of a given situation, for it may well be the case that an apparent diagreement vanishes when we realize that it was the result of hidden differences in perspective or of subtle shifts in emphasis. The difference in valuations turns out, in that case, to be but a difference in what is valued. "Real contradictions of valuations are encountered only when one compares valuations which pertain not only to the same object but to the same characteristics of that object, or to the same relation, as well" (p. 156).

Does this mean that, ultimately, all conflicts in valuations can be eliminated? Such an ideal assumes that all valuations are reducible to or, at least, converge toward elementary valuations that are beyond dispute. A startling perspective in this respect is found in a field in which one would least expect it—the field of aesthetic valuations. "An extraordinary uniformity apparently prevails in attitudes taken toward elementary aesthetic impressions. That certain proportionalities of surfaces and bodies, of divisions of lines and distances, of distributions of masses are pleasing and others are not, that certain combinations of colors and of sounds are harmonious and others are not, that rhythmic repetition, sequence and order are pleasing—all this seems to be common to the arts of all times and all peoples" (p. 157). Kraft points out, however, that even so it is not certain that this implies a basic law of value-accentuation "which, being independent of the differences of individuals, depends solely upon the nature of the object" (p. 158), for the general agreement is not without exceptions. What pleases may change in the course of a man's cultural development. Attitudes and value judgments change even with respect to one and the same object; and styles, being characteristic of cultural epochs, change with the times. The historical sequence of Greek Classicism, Gothic architecture, Renaissance and Barock art—to identify but a few changes in style—illustrates the point.

However, the purely formal differences in style betray at the same time a contrast that is not purely formal. Renaissance art thus aimed at complete objective clarity while Barock art tried to express what can never be completely grasped: the inexhaustible, the unlimited. Underlying such differences are strong emotional contrasts which really separate Renaissance and Barock: static balance, simplicity, clarity, nobility, grandeur, on the one hand; dynamics, tension, movement, passionate excitement, the pathetic and the colossal, on the other. "It is the difference of emotional needs which, in the arts, leads to a difference in valuation—even when the conception of the purely formal aspects remains identical. For the Italians, Rembrandt and Rubens were but a curiosity of a technical sort to whose emotional life they found no bridge" (p. 160).

But differences in the goals of desire (*Begehrensziele*) no less than emotional differences bring about differences in our valuations of the same objects. Whether or not one can use a particular means depends on whether or not one pursues—at that time or ever—the goal which it serves. The goals change, not only for the individual person but ethnically and historically as well. Instruments of torture (for example) are no longer employed because we no longer try to force a confession of the accused by merely physical means. Formerly such instruments were useful, now they are not. Also, economic goods derive their value from the fact that they are means to an end, to the satisfaction, that is, of our needs; but our needs change as we ourselves change. "How the nature of an object affects an individual is modified by that individual's organization—by its refinement, habituation, association, etc." (p. 161); and differences in valuation arising from such differences are indeed contradictory and irreconcilable.

Still, insofar as the nature of individuals (because of its universal human character) is similar, needs and goals and pleasure-displeasure occasions must also be similar. "Illness, the infirmities of old age, pain and suffering, misery and privation are generally regarded as evils; food and shelter, health and strength are generally regarded as positive values" (p. 162). We must conclude, therefore, that there are generally harmonious valuations, as there are irreconcilable ones, and others that differ but are not irreconcilable. There is no value-accentuation that is universally binding or that is independent of the differences of the valuing subjects. A value judgment, therefore, does not express a universal factual value-accentuation but is "a signal in the sense of a challenge (*Appell*) or invitation to take a specific attitude" toward some specified objects (p. 164).

The specific nature of a value judgment thus consists in the fact that it praises or blames. To attribute a value character to an object means to signalize a directive as to the attitude to be taken toward that object. The value judgment, therefore, expressing an *ought,* can never be translated into a merely factual statement (*Tatsachen-aussage*). This is of utmost importance; for, as a directive—and like commands, demands, and norms—a value judgment is neither true nor false but valid or not.

Still, even a value judgment can be shown to be justified or can be shown not to be justified. If it is shown not to be justified, the argument actually pertains not to the valuation itself but to the factual situation (*Sachverhalt*) that is being valued. That is to say, the repudiation of a value judgment pertains, not to the value character of the object as that object was originally understood, but to some aspect or aspects of the factual situation that gave rise to the original value judgment. Whether a value judgment is to be accepted or is to be repudiated thus depends on the truth or falsity of the factual judgments that are its presuppositions.

VII

As a directive a value judgment is essentially impersonal. It points up the attitude to be taken toward a certain object but does not indicate anyone in particular who ought to take that attitude. Nor is it given in the name of some particular person. It is a general and impersonal directive, augmenting the actualities of a value-accentuation and corresponding attitude as encountered in the experience of a particular individual by generalizing both aspects of experience as a norm that is valid for all. The question is, What precisely does "validity" here mean?

The idea of validity is encountered in areas other than value theory. Every kind of rule or norm may be said to be valid or not to be valid—the laws of society no less then the rules of a game. Thus, when we play chess, we must observe the rules governing the various moves on the chessboard. Playing in accordance with those rules constitutes the game of chess. "Validity" here means that the rules are in force, that they ought to be followed. And this means that the rules determine behavior.

But the effectiveness of the rules is not of a causal nature. We are not unconditionally compelled to do what the rules require us to do. We can violate the rules, for they are merely directives.

But they express an *ought,* nevertheless. If we want to play chess, then we *ought* to observe the rules of the game. The knight, for example, *ought* to be moved only in the specific ways demanded by the rules. The player is enjoined to follow those rules when he is playing the game.

A valid rule or law is one which demands that it be followed. But its validity is one thing, its actual observance is something else. Observance assumes that the rule has been acknowledged as binding. Such an acknowledgement is an individual act, the personal setting of a goal (*persönliche Zielsetzung*); and this is something which validity is not. "Validity is something impersonal, universal, a demand directed toward all" (p. 169). More specifically, the validity of a value judgment means the ascription of a value-character to an object which ought to be universally acknowledged as correct. The justification of the demand for such universal acknowledgement is the crucial problem for all conceptions of "super-individual" (*überindividuelle*) values—such as beauty, usefulness, courage, goodness, and their opposites.

Proofs of the validity of value judgments have often been attempted. They usually consist in showing that a given object possesses qualities which are generally regarded as valuable or are assumed to be so. That is to say, the ascription of a value to an object is "logically justified by subsuming the qualities of the object (or of a class of objects) under a class of characteristics already acknowledged to be valuable. The value character of this latter class is not logically derived but presupposed" (pp. 174–75). And if such subsumption is what is meant by "justifying a value ascription," then the justification can be carried through with logical rigor, and conflicts of value judgments can be decided unequivocally. All that is involved here are judgments of subsumption which disclose logical sequences or dependencies of interlinked valuations.

The crucial problem arises, of course, when we deal with valuations which are no longer derivable in the sense indicated. That is to say, the crucial problem arises when we deal with the basic principles or axioms of valuation (*Wertungsaxiome*). The question is, Does there exist a superindividual agency (*überindividuelle Instanz*) which compels the acknowledgement of a valuation?

Following Brentano, Husserl, and Scheler, some value theorists maintain that there is indeed such an agency, namely our intentional feeling (*intentionales Gefühl*)—the "logic of the heart," as Scheler called it. Through it we presumably obtain a cognition *a priori* of values. Kraft, however, points out that if value is disclosed to a person in intentional feeling, that disclosure remains a strictly personal one. Even if a value should thus disclose itself as objective, there is no evidence of its objectivity except personal illumination; and this can be regarded as trans-subjective only if the validity of the value judgments is as immediately evident as is, for example, the principle of the excluded middle in logic. But such immediate and universally compelling validity is not encountered in the case of value judgments. Proof of this fact is that even so closely allied thinkers as Scheler, Nicolai Hartmann, and D. von Hildebrand have developed essentially different systems and scales of values. "The individual valuations stand equally justified or equally unjustified side by side" (p. 179).

We must admit that a value predicate does not simply give us a directive (*Anweisung*) to take an attitude; it also provides a factual basis—a reason for taking that attitude. It says not simply that one should take such and such an attitude, but that the object is so constituted that one ought to take such and such an attitude toward it. That is to say, the value-character is never ascribed to an object without reference to that object's nature (*Beschaffenheit*); and it is the nature of the object which provides "the factual basis for the ascription of a value-character to it" (p. 180). This fact alone justifies the ascription of a trans-subjetcive valuation to an object.

The requirement here stipulated by Kraft is fulfilled when the object toward which an attitude is to be taken "either constitutes a necessary condition of life or entails the destruction (*Untergang*) of life" (p. 180). The objects which are the indispensable conditions of life are those which are the means for the satisfaction of inescapable needs upon which life depends: air, nourishment, activity, rest, restoration of health, protection against enemies of every kind, and so on. Whatsoever contributes to the satisfaction of these needs everyone must acknowledge as valuable. What prevents these satisfactions must be valued negatively. The key to all these valuations, therefore, is the basic drive for the preservation of life. The value-character of that which satisfies this drive is "objectively determined and universally valid" (p. 181). Equally basic, however, is the drive to avoid unpleasantness (*Unlustvermeidung*).

Now, the nature of man is such that he acts not only instinctively or because of need-fulfilling drives. He can act also in conformity with a plan (*planmässig*). This means that the basic needs are also being satisfied in accordance with conscious intentions (*bewusste Absichten*) which involve a deliberate projection of goals (*Zielsetzung*). But goals thus projected cannot be reached without at least a partial mastery over nature. Such mastery presupposes knowledge of the conditions under which we must act and our ability to modify those conditions in conformity with our intentions.

However, it is also of the nature of man to be a herd animal (*ein Herdentier*); that he lives in a social group. It follows from this that the conditions necessary to the existence and the life of the social group are also conditions for the existence of the individual. Security within the group, for example, is an unconditional presupposition of the existence of the group and of the individual within the group.

"A large number and variety of objects thus have an objectively determined and universally valid (*allgemeingültig*) value because they satisfy universal human needs" (p. 187). More specialized kinds of objects, however, which also satisfy such needs may not be universally valued. This is the case, for example, with all means-values. Although man's basic needs (*vitale Bedürfnisse*) are universal, the means requisite to their satisfaction are not necessarily also universal; for the same goal can often be reached by various means. Technological advances (from stone axe to modern rifle, for example) and a better understanding of the true nature of things (the importance of vitamins, for example) lead to the acceptance of new means and the abandonment of old ones. What is true in the case of tools and the use of raw materials is true also in the case of social institutions. "A large part of what has been developed historically for the regulation of man's social existence need not be universally accepted; for social order can be achieved in a great variety of ways" (p. 188). This means, however, that, although the value-character of a condition or object necessary for the satisfaction of a need or a desire is always objectively determined, it is universally valid only when the condition or object is indispensable to that satisfaction—i.e., when no other condition or object can be substituted for it.

Objects and conditions which are not absolutely necessary for the satisfaction of vital needs and which can be replaced by other objects and conditions may yet have value. And they have value when they function as means for the satisfaction of some specific needs. What objects belong to this group is not univocally determined by their attributes; it depends, in part, also on the conditions under which the objects are encountered. Thus, the value of what may serve as food, of what may serve to preserve good health, and of what is technologically useful depends in each case on the character of some specific situation. And, similarly, the conditions of social existence may also vary in different situations. Despite such differences, however, the objects and conditions here meant constitute the *general classes* of what is "wholesome," "useful," "moral," etc. Their value-character is that of generalized classes. "Food, knowledge, social regulations, and so on must be acknowledged to be valuable because they are necessary conditions for our individual and social existence. The attitude toward them [indicated by their value-character] cannot be repudiated; for, if it were, individual and social existence would be impossible" (p. 191). The presupposition here is, of course, that individual and social existence are to be preserved. Although this is usually agreed to, agreement on this point is by no means absolute; there are exceptions. It is perfectly possible to deny the value of human existence; and "where there is no will to live, one cannot appeal to the necessity of preserving life" (p. 192).

"The normal universal validity of natural values, therefore, rests upon this foundation: if, in conformity with the laws of nature (*naturgesetzlich*), an object is a necessary condition for the satisfaction of a need or a desire inherent in human nature which is universal, then taking an attitude toward that object is objectively determined. If one wants this satisfaction, one can take no other attitude toward the object; and anyone wanting the satisfaction must acknowledge as valid the value judgment which indicates that attitude" (p. 192). This means, however, that "the entire necessity of taking an attitude depends ultimately upon a basic attitude (*ursprüngliche Stellungnahme*): the will, namely, to preserve individual and social existence" (p. 193). This basic attitude, however, is not forced upon us (*uns nicht aufgenötigt*), and our valuations, therefore, have only conditional or hypothetical universality.

When we consider not only universally human needs but also the more specific conditions under which life must go on, then we encounter an ever-increasing variety of valuations—in dress and housing, for example; in the division of labor, in agriculture and industry (depending on natural resources and the means for their exploitation), in matters of defense, in political and judicial arrangements, etc. Such special valuations are valid for all who commit themselves to the respective culture patterns.

The value-character of what constitutes human culture can thus not be uniquely determined—not even for the purely material aspects in their totality—but only for such parts as are indispensable for the satisfaction of universally human needs and for the maintenance of a given culture pattern. Of the spiriutal (*geistigen*) aspects of culture, the value-character of knowledge (insofar as knowledge is needed for action) must be generally acknowledged —as must be the value-character of whatever is necessary for social order and its judicial and moral norms. But much of all this is locally determined and not universally justifiable. It is neither biologically indispensable nor necessary for social existence universally (p. 199).

VIII

Up to this point we have considered the basis of the validity of valuations exclusively from the point of view of the individual; and it is evident that, viewed under this perspective, the most diverse valuations seem equally well justified. Beethoven's late quartettes, for example, have very different value for different people. For some, their richness and originality rank them among compositions of the highest value; for others, however, they are but tonal confusions, formless and ugly, and therefore without value. But the point of view of the individual is not the only perspective under which valuations ought to be judged. There is also an impersonal point of view; and this supercedes the point of view of the individual, disclosing the value proper (*eigentlichen Wert*) of whatever is being judged. Determinative of this point of view is the judgment of the expert. Music is, thus, a cultural good as judged by those who know music. That others may regard it as merely a nuisance does not alter this fact. This means, however, that individual value judgments are not of equal value. "There are valuations of music and of the arts in general which supercede individual valuations. These are the valuations that are generally represented and acknowledged" (p. 200). As with the arts, so it is with the valuation of science and research for their own sake. It takes the expert to value them. This means that, above individual valuations, there is a collective valuation which dominates the scene and determines "the" value. The individual does not simply live his own individual life, but also a communal one within the social whole in which he exists as a dependent (*unselbständig*) member. Because of this fact the valuations occur under conditions other than merely those of his own personal life. Through the interactions of individuals in their social existence points of view other than the purely personal become valid for valuation, namely, those of the social whole, of the communal generality; and through personal interactions in conformity with, or in opposition to, individual valuations a social control over them, and thus a higher court of appeal for their validity, becomes effective. Individual valuations are subsumed under a super-individual point of view (pp. 201–202). And in this manner an order of rank (*Rangordnung*) of values is established. Its basis may be seen in the fact that the overwhelming majority of the members of a social group is agreed on numerous, and especially on basic, valuations. Such agreement follows directly from the conditions under which the social group finds existence at all possible.

Strictly speaking, it is not even true that the valuation of an object is ever a matter of individual choice; for each valuation is conditioned by two factors: by the characteristics of the valued object, and by the characteristics of the valuing subject. The characteristics of the subject are determined by heredity and environment, and by the individual's biographical history that is the result of both. If these conditions are, in general, similar for a number of persons, then the individuals concerned will, in general, agree in their valuations. That cultural conditions—tradition, law, religion, art, science, economy, social stratification, in brief, the whole culture pattern of a people and the trends of the times—play their part in conditioning those valuations requires no further argument. Individual variations occur only within general uniformity; and valuations that are predominant in a social group are usually regarded as correct. Deviations from them are not accepted as equally valid. He who adheres to valuations not generally accepted is looked upon as "an ignoramus, as one who is in error, as a heretic, and is condemned (*geächtet*)" (p. 212). Differences in valuations thus have their social repercussions.

It is evident, however, that even the super-individual valuations derive ultimately from individual valuations—albeit from the valuations of a great many individuals who, because they live under similar conditions and influence one another, value similar objects similarly.

Still, there is also a difference. The content of the collective valuations differs from that of valuations made from the point of view of an individual. It pertains to what is of common interest or at least, as in the case of the arts and of science, it involves the interests of a large number of people who arouse no enmity within the collective whole.

Collective valuations, furthermore, have greater stability and, as tradition, are usually passed on from one generation to another. Habituation re-enforces their super-individual validity. "*What are generally regarded as the eternal, the true, the self-evident valuations are nothing other than the socially dominant and traditional valuations.* Because the individual always encounters them as given and as super-individual, they are again and again regarded as *absolute* values." (p. 215. Italics in the original). To put it differently, absolute values are those valuations that are accepted as a matter of course (*selbstverständlich*) by a nation or an Age

—such as the Age of Enlightenment or the Age of Romanticism. But "personalities come forward—philosophers, writers and artists—who emancipate themselves from the traditional valuations and form their valuations independently" (p. 216). The authority of the dominant valuations is thus challenged. The individual denies their validity because he believes himself to be in the right. The result is a contradictory manifoldness of valuations—a non-uniformity that has become ever more prominent during the last two hundred years. The more we restrict our investigation to specific valuations within a social whole, the greater is the diversity and the more restricted the unifying tradition. Nevertheless, the more we concentrate on the universal and humanly necessary valuations, the more far-reaching is the uniformity of socially valid valuations that transcend generations, peoples, and cultural epochs. But an unconditional universality of valuations simply does not exist; and neither is there an absolute rightness or wrongness of valuations (p. 221).

This does not mean, however, that all valuations dissolve into purely individual and irreconcilable attitudes. The difference of the valuations is actually much smaller than it appears to be. For one thing, many of the apparently contradictory valuations do not pertain to the same object or to the same characteristics of an object, and thus are not really contradictory at all. And secondly, the attitudes of people living under essentially the same conditions largely adjust to the same pattern. Far-reaching uniformity thus prevails especially with respect to the most important, the basic valuations—not only as far as the material conditions of human existence are concerned, but, more importantly, as far as cultural values are involved also. Only absolute values are ruled out on principle. A theory which keys value to human attitudes can find no basis justifying the idea of absolute values.

BIBLIOGRAPHY

Kraft, Viktor, *Die Grundlagen einer Wissenschaftlichen Wertlehre,* Wien, 1937.